How to Do *Everything* with

with

Micro... FrontPage 2003

David Plotkin

Collectibles Online

File   Edit   View   Favorites   Tools   Help

Back

http://www.collectibles~online.net

Collectibles Online

Home

Showroom

Appraisal

Forum

Contact

...tions

Clothes

Welcome to our online directory of quality collectible furnishings and antique accoutrement for the home or office. We have the largest selections organized and approved by experts in their field. Join our mailing list to stay current on the latest fresh arrivals.

The McGraw·Hill Companies

McGraw-Hill/Osborne
2100 Powell Street, 10th Floor
Emeryville, California 94608
U.S.A.

To arrange bulk purchase discounts for sales promotions, premiums, or fund-raisers, please contact **McGraw-Hill**/Osborne at the above address. For information on translations or book distributors outside the U.S.A., please see the International Contact Information page immediately following the index of this book.

How to Do Everything with Microsoft® Office FrontPage® 2003

1234567890 FGR FGR 019876543

ISBN 0-07-222973-X

Publisher	Brandon A. Nordin
Vice President	
& Associate Publisher	Scott Rogers
Acquisitions Editor	Katie Conley
Project Editor	Monika Faltiss
Acquisitions Coordinator	Tana Allen
Technical Editor	Bill Bruns
Copy Editor	Dennis Weaver
Proofreader	Claire Splan
Indexer	Irv Hershman
Composition	Tara Davis, Lucie Ericksen
Illustrators	Kathleen Edwards, Melinda Moore Lytle, Lyssa Wald
Series Design	Mickey Galicia
Cover Series Design	Dodie Shoemaker
Cover Illustration	Tom Willis

This book was composed with Corel VENTURA™ Publisher.

This book is for Marisa, my wife. Making a book is a team effort, because someone has to pick up the load for the extra work while I do my writing. Marisa did that, and provided constant encouragement when the beta version of FrontPage kept crashing! Thanks, hon!

About the Author

David Plotkin is a private consultant specializing in Data Administration. He designs computer systems and databases for a living, and is a self-taught web-tool user. He maintains web sites for various nonprofit and charitable organizations, and has written several other computer books on database topics and graphics.

About the Technical Editor

Bill Bruns is a veteran of finance and data retrieval in the Information Age. Bill is the Chief Financial Officer for Jacob Marlie Financial, Inc. (http://www.jacobmarlie.com/), a web-based invoicing and collections agency for fraternal organizations. Currently, he is the Coordinator of Technology and Media at the College of Education and Human Services at Southern Illinois University. He teaches "An Adventure of the American Mind," which instructs K-12 teachers on how to use the Library of Congress American Memory database to create a multimedia curriculum for their children.

For six years, he has been a technical editor working on at least 125 books relating to the Internet, web servers, HTML, operating systems, and office applications.

Originally planning to work in television production, his interest turned to computers and finance while working on an undergraduate internship at Square One TV, a children's mathematics show produced by the Childrens Television Workshop in New York City.

Bill holds bachelor's degrees in Telecommunications and English Literature from Indiana University, a master's in Public Administration from New York University, and is a Certified Netware Engineer.

Bill, his wife Debbie, his daughter Marlie, his son Will, and his three bearded dragons currently reside in Carbondale, Illinois.

Contents

V

Acknowledgments

Five people deserve special mention. My agent, Carole McClendon, found the contract and negotiated some great terms. Acquisitions Editor Katie Conley helped me through the process of revising the book and following the rules for McGraw-Hill/Osborne. I think the results speak for themselves, and I am grateful for their help! Katie also was most sympathetic and supportive, when, right in the middle of everything, I lost my "main" job and had to find other employment.

Acquisitions Coordinator Tana Allen did a great job of pulling everything together for the book and keeping everything running smoothly.

Copy Editor Dennis Weaver not only had the "eagle eyes" required of a copy editor (spotting stuff even missed by the tech editor), but punched up my prose to make it read better. Thanks, Dennis!

Project Editor Monika Faltiss really made a difference, keeping everything straight, resolving any issues, and in general, just keeping everything on track. An experienced project editor like Monika can make all the difference between having a good experience as you go through final proofreading or suffering the horror of realizing that everything is mixed up. Believe me, I know.

Introduction

Introduction to FrontPage 2003

- What a web site is
- How the World Wide Web works
- What you need to build your own web site
- Who should read this book
- How this book is organized

The fact that you bought this book—or are considering buying it—means you are ready to join the ranks of the huge number of people who are building and maintaining web sites using Microsoft FrontPage 2003. Whether you bought FrontPage 2003 as a stand-alone package or as part of Office XP, you have one of the premier packages available for putting yourself, your family, or your business on the World Wide Web.

What Is a Web Site?

But just what is a web site? This may seem like a strange question to ask—after all, you see web sites every day, so you probably think you know what a web site is, and maybe you do. But it is helpful to understand what a web site *really* is, because it will be much easier for you to build a web site if you understand (at least a little bit) what is happening behind the scenes.

What Is a Web Page?

First, let's answer the question, what is a web page? Believe it or not, a web page is a text file. It doesn't have pictures, buttons, or any of the other "fancies" you see on your screen. Instead, the text file contains a description of the web page in a special programming language called Hypertext Markup Language (HTML). HTML uses programming commands, called *tags*, to describe the page layout, and includes other information, such as onscreen text and paths to the locations of graphics. A page's HTML also includes the destinations for links to other locations (called hyperlinks). Of course, the programming can become very complex when special features such as frames, tables, scripts written in other languages, and dynamic effects are included on the page. Nevertheless, if you are competent in HTML, you can code your own web pages—and that is exactly how all web pages were created in the early days of the Internet.

As with any other programming language, writing code in HTML is a trial-and-error process. First, you design the page, gather up the elements you will need (such as graphics), and write the code. Then you have to try and load that code in a browser (a tool for viewing web pages), find the coding errors, fix them, and try again. Once you find all your coding errors, you still aren't done. Perhaps your page doesn't look the way you intended—the table cells are too narrow, or the text doesn't have the right effects. Back to the code/debug cycle.

Fortunately for you (and me too), there is an easier way. FrontPage 2003 implements a WYSIWYG (what you see is what you get) environment for building web pages. With FrontPage 2003, you can type in your text, add graphics, format the text, align the paragraphs, build hyperlinks, and construct the rest of your web page in an interactive environment where you can see what your web page will look like as you build it and even test most features. When you are done, FrontPage 2003 writes the HTML code (and sometimes Dynamic HTML and even JavaScript) that describes the web page for you. It never makes a syntax error, and you never even have to see the code (although you can if you want to). Further, if you make changes to the web page, FrontPage 2003 automatically regenerates the HTML—you never have to worry about it.

Constructing a Web Site

A web site is a set of related web pages. Starting with a *home* page—the page that opens when you navigate to a web site—you can build a set of pages related to each other through hyperlinks. Hyperlinks are points on the page you can click to navigate to another page. The home page is just a regular web page with a special name, so the hosting web server knows to display that page first. (The special name, by the way, is either Default.htm or Index.htm.)

FrontPage 2003 contains a set of tools for relating web pages together into a web site. It also includes templates for building special-purpose web sites, such as a web site for customer service or for hosting a discussion group. These templates actually build sets of related web pages for you, making your job much easier.

Special Features of FrontPage 2003

If all FrontPage 2003 did was provide a great environment for building web pages and web sites, it would still be a pretty good tool. But wait, there's more. One of the main problems with building web sites is that the most sophisticated features, such as forms, site searches, guest books, common page templates, and hit counters (a feature that counts how many times someone has viewed your page), require a sophisticated interaction with the server hosting the site (more on this topic shortly). Prior to FrontPage 2003, you had to know how to write programs in a scripting language that could communicate with the Common Gateway Interface (CGI). This wasn't too much of a problem for professional web developers, but for the average builder of a web site, this requirement basically put these advanced features out of reach.

FrontPage solved this problem by introducing the *FrontPage server extensions*. This is a package of programs the service hosting your web site installs on their server. Once these extensions have been installed, implementing forms and other sophisticated features is simply a matter of stepping through a wizard: following specific instructions and answering a few questions. Of course, the hosting company has to install these extensions on their server or your forms won't work. But, perhaps because FrontPage became popular very quickly and carries the weight of the Microsoft marketing machine behind it, many hosting companies have installed the extensions. They also advertise this fact. If you see "FrontPage enabled" or "Supports FrontPage" or something to that effect, you can be sure all your special features will work.

Another package of extensions is made up by the *SharePoint Team Services*. These services enable collaboration among people creating a web site, and some sophisticated features—like Data View (which can display XML documents)—require that SharePoint Team Services be installed on the web server.

Getting Your Site onto the Web

Normally, you build your web site and its pages on your local machine. However, this does not make your site available to people using the Internet. To make your site available on the Internet, it must be present on a host computer that is connected to the Internet on a more-or-less continuous basis. Your web site must have a fixed *address* (formally known as an *IP address*) so that people can consistently find it. While it is just barely possible to host your web site on your own local machine, there are some really good reasons not to, especially if you are limited to a dial-up modem and would like to turn your computer off once in a while. The better option is to contract with a *web presence provider* (WPP). These companies own computers (servers) on which they can host your site. These servers are online all of the time, have very fast Internet connections, and can usually provide you with statistics, such as how many times your site was viewed and which pages are the most popular. Of course, hosting your site on someone else's computer is usually going to cost you some money, typically in the neighborhood of $10 to $30 a month for a personal site. There are a number of free WPPs, but most do not support the FrontPage server extensions.

FrontPage makes it easy to move your web site to a host computer, a process known as *publishing*. In fact, another advance that FrontPage has made popular is to make publishing easy. Using FrontPage's publishing function, you can upload your web site to the host over an Internet connection, refresh individual pages as necessary, and remove pages that are no longer included in your web site.

Once your web site is present on the host computer, the hosting company will give you a way to find the web site on the World Wide Web. While technically this amounts to the IP address of your site (a rather odd-looking number you can't possibly remember), the hosting company will provide you with an easier address, usually beginning with *www*. For example, www.osborne.com takes you to the home page for McGraw-Hill/Osborne. Hosting companies will often provide you with an address that appends your username to the hosting company's own address, such as www.hostingcompany.com/dplotkin. At any rate, this address, provided by the hosting company, is what you can give to your friends, family, and coworkers so they can find your site in their browsers. The actual IP address of your site is resolved to this more-friendly text string by computers known as *domain name servers*. If you don't care for this method of identification, you can register for your own *domain name*. Your WPP will usually help you with this, as a special form has to be forwarded to the organization that monitors and assigns domain names. And you have to pay a fee to register and keep your own domain name. But provided that the domain you want is not in use (and you can afford it), this is the easiest way for people to find your site. For example, my domain name is www.dplotkin.com. This is exactly how the big boys do it.

Who Should Read This Book

Every author would like to believe that everyone who wants to use the software about which the book is written is the target audience, but most of the time that is not true. This book is targeted at people who want to build moderately sophisticated sites using FrontPage 2003, and it assumes you know nothing about the program other than how to install it on your computer. It will explain all the features you need to create and maintain complex sites, including publishing the site to a WPP. This book will teach you how to build pages, maintain your site, and check for all kinds of errors. It does, however, assume you've used some sort of word processor so that you know how to type text, select the text, and edit it.

If you just want a "quick and dirty" web site that you can create in a day or two, you can skim Parts I and II and read enough of Chapter 18 to learn how to publish your site. When you need more details, you can refer to the other parts of the book as appropriate. This book does not really cover advanced development topics, as it does not cover the intricacies of using Java and JavaScript (although it does cover the basics). Nor does it cover the collaborative features of FrontPage 2003, which are more appropriate to businesses running an Intranet.

How This Book Is Organized

This book is broken into four parts. Part 1 introduces you to the general features of FrontPage 2003. This part also tells you how to build web pages, using all the tools provided. These tools include adding and formatting text, adding graphics, working with lists, using themes to achieve a unified look, and adding and formatting tables.

Part 2 tells you how to connect pages together into a web site, using such features as hyperlinks, shared borders, and image maps. This part also tells you how to use link bars to set up a structure for your site and create reusable sets of hyperlinks, and how to include forms to gather user feedback. You also learn how to implement frames to display multiple pages at once.

Part 3 covers advanced topics, such as FrontPage's components, XML, and page options. You will learn how to incorporate Java applets and ActiveX controls (many of which can be found on the Internet). You will also learn the fine points of managing your web site using reports and tasks you can assign to members of your team or use to keep track of items that need to be completed. Finally, you'll learn the ins and outs of publishing your web site to a host server.

Part 4 covers how to route information from your web site to a database, how to search the contents of a database on the web, and the details of building a complete database interface—including a logon page.

Part I

Build Web Pages

Chapter 1

Navigate in FrontPage 2003

How to...

- Understand menus and toolbars
- Use the FrontPage views
- Configure the editors
- Get an overall view of your web site

FrontPage 2003 is a powerful tool for creating and maintaining intranet web sites as well as sites on the Web. Using FrontPage 2003, you can create web pages, complete with formatted text and graphics, tables, buttons, animations, and sound. You can add frames, borders, and hyperlinks to connect the pages into a web site—or connect the pages to other web sites. But probably the most seductive feature of FrontPage (if your web site is running on a specially enabled server) is its ability to provide sophisticated web functionality—such as forms, a guestbook, dynamic effects, and even special-purpose web sites (such as a corporate presence web site)—without writing any code. If you are familiar with HTML, JavaScript, Java, or other supported scripting languages and you enjoy creating such special touches manually, you can add your own programs to a FrontPage web project. Once you have built your site, FrontPage provides management tools such as reports and tasks to help you maintain the site. Finally, FrontPage automates the process of publishing your web site to a web presence provider (WPP) so it will be accessible to Internet browsers.

As you can probably imagine, FrontPage needs a capable and flexible interface to enable you to perform all these functions without being overwhelmed. This chapter introduces you to all the aspects of this interface and demonstrates how to customize it to your own way of working.

Understand the Interface

The main FrontPage window (shown in Figure 1-1) displays all the standard features of a Windows program as well as most of the main FrontPage elements. Not all the elements are visible in every view, and you can configure the window to turn certain elements on and off. For example, if you don't want to see the Folder List, you can turn it off.

The Menu Bar

As with virtually every other Windows program, the top of the active window is occupied by the *menu bar*. To choose a command, click the menu heading (such as File), and then select the menu command you want (such as Save). In this book, we will refer to this action like this: "Choose File | Save."

FrontPage 2003 does implement one nonstandard menu feature: the *tear-off menu*. The submenu Insert | Form displays a title bar:

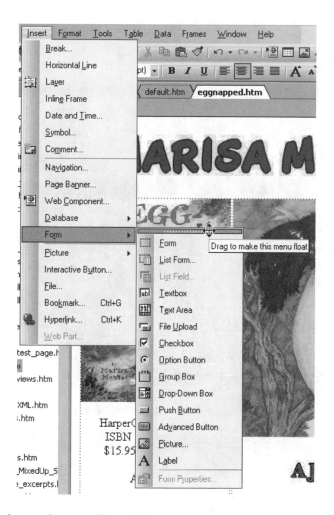

To convert a submenu into a toolbar, click on its title bar (the dotted line at the top of the submenu) and "tear off" (drag) the submenu from the menu. Using the submenu as a toolbar has the advantage of making the commands instantly available with a single mouse click. On the other hand, the toolbar takes up valuable screen space.

NOTE *When you are through working with the elements in a tear-off toolbar, you can click the Close button in the upper-right corner to close the toolbar and remove it from the screen. The submenu remains available from the main menu at all times, even when the toolbar equivalent is visible.*

One of the more controversial menu features of all Office XP programs is the Recent Commands option. When this option is enabled, the menu commands you frequently use migrate to the top of the menu, and menu commands you don't frequently use disappear from the menu.

Folder List   Quick Tag Selector   Select an open page or the web site view   Menu   Toolbar   Task Pane

Select the page view   Main view area   Choose a page size for viewing

FIGURE 1-1   The FrontPage main window is your "home base" for navigating in FrontPage.

Many people find these changes disconcerting (I am one of those people!). Fortunately, you can disable this feature. To do so, choose Tools | Customize to open the Customize dialog box. Click the Options tab and select the Always Show Full Menus check box.

The Toolbars

Just below the menu bar are the toolbars. Toolbars contain buttons for the most-often-used functions in FrontPage 2003. It is easier to click a toolbar button than to hunt down a command in the menu bar. A small down arrow appears next to some of the buttons in the toolbar. Clicking the button performs the default task associated with it, while clicking the down arrow displays a submenu of additional buttons. If you can't remember the function of a button in a toolbar, simply hover your mouse pointer over the button to see a *ScreenTip* that tells you the purpose of the button.

> **NOTE**   *If you find the ScreenTips annoying, you can turn them off. From the Options tab of the Customize dialog box, clear the Show ScreenTips On Toolbars check box.*

The Standard and Formatting Toolbars

By default, FrontPage 2003 displays only two of its many toolbars: the Standard toolbar and the Formatting toolbar. The Standard toolbar contains common functions you use throughout FrontPage 2003.

The Formatting toolbar is similar to the Formatting toolbars in other Microsoft Office programs. Its primary purpose is to help you format text and paragraphs. The main difference between the Formatting toolbar in FrontPage and the same toolbar in other applications is that the available text styles conform to HTML standards. The Formatting toolbar is discussed more in Chapter 3.

The Other Toolbars

FrontPage provides other toolbars that perform specialized tasks, such as allowing DHTML Effect, modifying drawings and pictures, creating and modifying tables, and positioning items on the page. You can see a list of these toolbars by right-clicking a blank space at the end of any FrontPage toolbar or choosing View | Toolbars. Many of these toolbars are covered later in the book.

The Quick Tag Selector

The Quick Tag Selector isn't strictly a toolbar. Instead, it resides (when activated) at the top of any page you are viewing in the main window area. When you select an item on the page, the Quick Tag Selector displays the list of HTML open tags that appear in the HTML code previous to that item. Moving the mouse over one of the tags displays a rectangle around the portion of the page defined by that tag and its closing tag. Clicking the tag selects the area of the page. When you hover the mouse pointer over a tag, a small down arrow becomes visible. Clicking on the down arrow displays a drop-down menu with choices for selecting just the tag, selecting the tag contents, editing the tag, removing it, inserting HTML, and other HTML coding options.

> **NOTE**   *To turn the Quick Tag Selector on and off, choose View | Quick Tag Selector.*

The Main Window Area

The bulk of the FrontPage screen is taken up by the main window area. This is where you do your actual work, and the contents change depending on which view you are in. For example, if you are in Page view, the main window area is where you view and build your pages. If you are in Web Site view, this is where you perform the web site maintenance tasks described in the section "Make Use of the Web Site Views," later in this chapter.

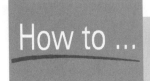 **Change the Page Size**

When you are viewing a page in FrontPage, you can change the size of the page by clicking the current page size in the lower-right corner of the status bar:

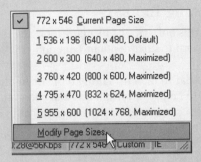

Pick one of the predefined sizes, or create a new page size by choosing Modify Page Sizes. This opens the Modify Page Sizes dialog box:

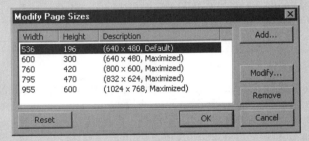

From here, you can modify an existing page size (click the Modify button) or create a new page size by clicking the Add button. Then just fill in the width and height (in pixels), a description, and click OK to add your new page size to the list.

You can also choose a page size or modify the page sizes by choosing View | Page Size.

The Folder List

The Folder List is a navigation tool that displays the folders and files that make up your web site. You can expand a folder that has files or subfolders by clicking on the "+" sign next to the folder name, much like Windows Explorer. To open any file and begin working with it, select the file in the Folder List and choose Open from the shortcut menu. Alternatively, you can just double-click the file. The file will open in whatever application is associated with the file type.

You can tell which files are currently open in the Page view by the icon displayed for the page in the Folder List. If the page is open, the Page icon is displayed with a small pencil overlaying the icon.

You can change the width of the Folder List by moving the mouse over its right border, holding down the left mouse button, and dragging the border left or right. You can also hide the Folder List. To do so, deselect Folder List in the View menu or click the small x in the upper-right corner. If the Folder List is hidden, select View | Folder List to redisplay it.

NOTE *You can quickly create a new page or folder by clicking on the appropriate icon in the in the upper-right corner of the Folder List.*

The Navigation Pane

As will be discussed shortly, FrontPage provides the Navigation view to show you the structure of your web site. However, as we'll see in Chapter 10, choosing the Navigation view from the Web Site view displays the Navigation view in the main window area. As a result, you can't use the Navigation view when you want to see both a page and the structure of the web site at the same time. FrontPage provides another view of the web site structure: the Navigation Pane (see Figure 1-2). Unlike the Navigation view, the Navigation Pane displays the structure as a tree. Other than that, though, the Navigation Pane functions pretty much the same way the Navigation view does. To access the Navigation Pane, choose View | Navigation Pane. Alternatively, if you are viewing the Folder List, click the Navigation tab at the bottom of the Folder List.

NOTE *To switch back to the Folder List from the Navigation Pane, click the Folder List tab.*

The Task Pane

The Task Pane provides easy access to options related to a whole variety of common tasks. These tasks include creating a new page or web site, getting Help, performing searches, using the clipboard, creating layout tables, performing DHTML scripting, cell formatting, working with

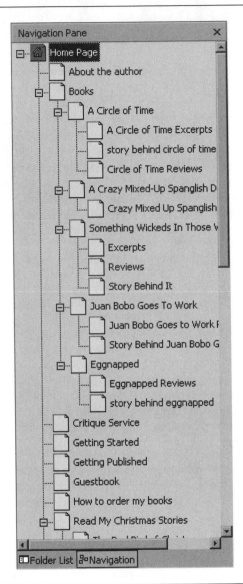

FIGURE 1-2   The Navigation Pane enables you to see both your web pages and the structure of your web site at the same time.

themes, and many other tasks. You can switch tasks by clicking the small down arrow to the right of the Task Pane title and choosing the task from the drop-down list:

To show or hide the task pane, choose View | Task Pane, or View | Toolbars | Task Pane. The Task Pane is docked to the right edge of the screen by default. However, you can move the Task Pane by clicking and holding down the left mouse button on the title bar, and dragging the Task Pane away from the right edge. Once you have undocked the Task Pane, it turns into a free-floating window. You can drag this window and dock it to any edge of the screen.

Use Page View

The view where you'll probably spend most of your time in FrontPage is the Page view. Page view is your document editor—it's where you build your web pages, create and format text, add graphics, set up hyperlinks, and create forms and tables. In short, you add all the content to your web site using the Page view.

Page view gives you four ways of looking at your web page: Design, Code, Split, and Preview. If you have multiple pages open, you can switch between the pages in any of these views either by selecting the page you want from the Window menu or by clicking on the page tab for the page you want.

If you open enough pages, the tabs won't all fit in the Page view. In that case, FrontPage displays a set of arrows in the upper-left corner of the Page view so that you can scroll left and right through the tabs.

To quickly close all the open pages, select Windows | Close All Pages.

Design Page View

Figure 1-1 shows the Design Page view. To switch to this view from any other view, click on the Design button at the bottom-left corner of the working area. Design Page view is where you actually build your web pages, using all the tools we'll discuss in this book. While this view gives you a pretty good idea of what your page will look like, the layout is not exact—nor are elements such as DHTML and hyperlinks functional. Design Page view is a *working* environment, not a testing environment.

Actually, you can follow hyperlinks in the Design Page view. To do so, CTRL-click on the hyperlink.

Code Page View

As discussed in the Introduction, web pages are largely made up of HTML code. When you use FrontPage as most people do—by adding and modifying text and graphics in the Design Page view—FrontPage automatically generates the HTML code that makes up your page. The nice thing about FrontPage is that you don't have to know HTML. You don't even have to look at this programming code if you don't want to. Still, there are times when it can be helpful to work with a page's HTML source code, as well as other code such as JavaScript. This is especially true if you know how to program, and you want to add your own code to the page. The Code Page view (see Figure 1-3) enables you to view and even modify the defining code for a web page. To switch to this view from another view, click on the Code button at the bottom-left corner of the working area.

Although it makes the most sense to add your own HTML code in the Code Page view, you can add HTML directly in the Design Page view. To do so, choose Insert | Web Component to display the Insert Web Component dialog box, click the Advanced Controls, and choose HTML from the list of available controls. Click Finish to display the HTML Markup dialog box:

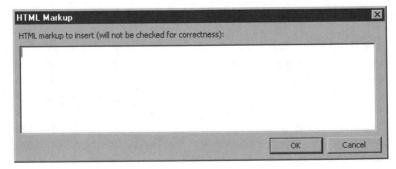

```
 / Web Site \ default.htm \ eggnapped.htm \                                          ×
 1 <html>
 2
 3 <head>
 4 <meta http-equiv="Content-Language" content="en-us">
 5 <meta name="GENERATOR" content="Microsoft FrontPage 5.0">
 6 <meta name="ProgId" content="FrontPage.Editor.Document">
 7 <meta http-equiv="Content-Type" content="text/html; charset=windows-1252">
 8 <title>Eggnapped</title>
 9 <meta name="Microsoft Border" content="none, default">
10 </head>
11
12 <body>
13
14 <p align="center">
15 <img border="0" src="images/MarisaCACMoose.jpg" align="middle" width="487" height="75"></p>
16 <table border="0">
17   <tr>
18     <td rowspan="4" valign="top">
19       <p align="center">
20       <a href="images/Egg-Napped%20Cover.JPG">
21       <img border="0" src="images/eggnappedcoversmall.jpg" width="207" height="280"></a></p>
22       <p align="center">HarperCollins <i>Publishers</i><br>
23       ISBN 0-06-028950-3<br>
24       $15.95/Canada $23.95<br>
25       32 pages<br>
26       Ages 3 to 7
27       <p align="center">
28       <a target="_self" href="how_to_order_my_books.htm">
29       <img border="0" src="images/ClickHereToBuyMyBookAnim.gif" width="105" height="78"></a><p align="
30       <a href="eggnapped_reviews.htm">Reviews</a><br>
31       <br>
32       <a href="story_behind_eggnapped.htm">Story Behind<br>
33       the Story</a></font><p align="center"><font face="Arial"><a href="#Top">Back to
34       Top</a></font><p align="center"><font face="Arial">
35       <a href="somethingwicked.htm">To Next Book</a></font><p align="center"><font face="Arial">
36       <a href="juanbobogoestowork.htm">To
37       Previous Book</a></font><p align="center"><font face="Arial"><a href="books.htm">To Main Book
38       Page</a></font><p align="center">
 ⌐Design ⊟Split ⊞Code ⌐Preview ◄                                                    ►
```

FIGURE 1-3   The Code Page view is where you can see—and change—the code that defines the web page you are working on.

Enter your HTML in the dialog box and click OK. The code you enter by means of this dialog box is *not* checked for correctness, however, so be careful.

Split Page View

The Split Page view (see Figure 1-4) shows you both the code and the design views of the page. Selecting an item in either view also highlights the item in the other view. For example, if you select an image in the Design view, FrontPage selects the section of code that defines the image properties on the page. If you make changes to the Design view, those changes are reflected instantly in the Code view. However, if you make changes in the Code view, those changes are *not* reflected in the Design view until you click in the Design view.

FIGURE 1-4 Modify the code (top) or the design (bottom) of the page you are working on.

Make Use of the Web Site Views

Although the Page view is where you'll spend most of your time, there are other views that are very important for managing your web site. These views provide you with a way to see important aspects of the site, as well as run reports to identify potential problems. In addition, one of the views helps you plan the tasks involved in building and maintaining the site. To get to the Web Site view, click the Web Site tab at the top of the main window area. To switch between the Web Site views, click one of the buttons along the bottom of the main window area.

Examine Files with the Folders View

The Folders view (Figure 1-5) exists for the benefit of those who wish to work with their web site simply as a set of folders and files. To access the Folders view, click on the Folders button

Did you know?

You can sort the Remote Web Site view and the Folders view on the content of any of the columns by clicking on the column heading. Clicking the same column again reverses the sort order (that is, from ascending to descending). In Remote Web Site view, you can also right-click a file, choose Arrange from the shortcut menu, and select one of the items in the submenu (which are the same as the column headings).

at the bottom of the Web Site view or choose View | Folders. You can view the contents of a folder by double-clicking the folder, just as in Windows Explorer.

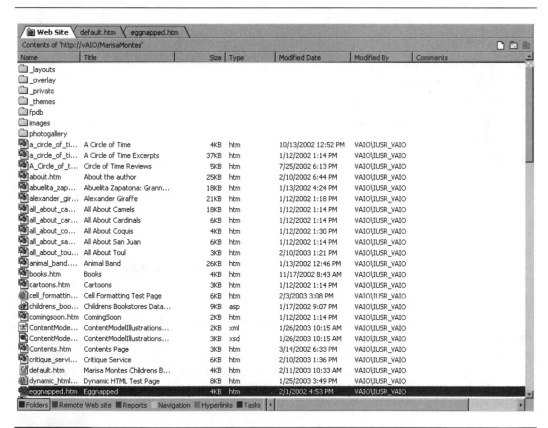

Name	Title	Size	Type	Modified Date	Modified By	Comments
_layouts						
_overlay						
_private						
_themes						
fpdb						
images						
photogallery						
a_circle_of_ti...	A Circle of Time	4KB	htm	10/13/2002 12:52 PM	VAIO\IUSR_VAIO	
a_circle_of_ti...	A Circle of Time Excerpts	37KB	htm	1/12/2002 1:14 PM	VAIO\IUSR_VAIO	
A_Circle_of_t...	Circle of Time Reviews	5KB	htm	7/25/2002 6:13 PM	VAIO\IUSR_VAIO	
about.htm	About the author	25KB	htm	2/10/2002 6:44 PM	VAIO\IUSR_VAIO	
abuelita_zap...	Abuelita Zapatona: Grann...	18KB	htm	1/13/2002 4:24 PM	VAIO\IUSR_VAIO	
alexander_gir...	Alexander Giraffe	21KB	htm	1/12/2002 1:18 PM	VAIO\IUSR_VAIO	
all_about_ca...	All About Camels	18KB	htm	1/12/2002 1:14 PM	VAIO\IUSR_VAIO	
all_about_car...	All About Cardinals	6KB	htm	1/12/2002 1:14 PM	VAIO\IUSR_VAIO	
all_about_co...	All About Coquis	4KB	htm	1/12/2002 1:30 PM	VAIO\IUSR_VAIO	
all_about_sa...	All About San Juan	6KB	htm	1/12/2002 1:14 PM	VAIO\IUSR_VAIO	
all_about_tou...	All About Toul	3KB	htm	2/10/2003 1:21 PM	VAIO\IUSR_VAIO	
animal_band....	Animal Band	26KB	htm	1/13/2002 12:46 PM	VAIO\IUSR_VAIO	
books.htm	Books	4KB	htm	11/17/2002 8:43 AM	VAIO\IUSR_VAIO	
cartoons.htm	Cartoons	3KB	htm	1/12/2002 1:14 PM	VAIO\IUSR_VAIO	
cell_formattin...	Cell Formatting Test Page	6KB	htm	2/3/2003 3:08 PM	VAIO\IUSR_VAIO	
childrens_boo...	Childrens Bookstores Data...	9KB	asp	1/17/2002 9:07 PM	VAIO\IUSR_VAIO	
comingsoon.htm	ComingSoon	2KB	htm	1/12/2002 1:14 PM	VAIO\IUSR_VAIO	
ContentMode...	ContentModelIllustrations...	2KB	xml	1/26/2003 10:15 AM	VAIO\IUSR_VAIO	
ContentMode...	ContentModelIllustrations...	3KB	xsd	1/26/2003 10:15 AM	VAIO\IUSR_VAIO	
Contents.htm	Contents Page	3KB	htm	3/14/2002 6:33 PM	VAIO\IUSR_VAIO	
critique_servi...	Critique Service	6KB	htm	2/10/2002 1:36 PM	VAIO\IUSR_VAIO	
default.htm	Marisa Montes Childrens B...	4KB	htm	2/11/2003 10:33 AM	VAIO\IUSR_VAIO	
dynamic_html...	Dynamic HTML Test Page	8KB	htm	1/25/2003 3:49 PM	VAIO\IUSR_VAIO	
eggnapped.htm	Eggnapped	4KB	htm	2/1/2002 4:53 PM	VAIO\IUSR_VAIO	

FIGURE 1-5   These files and folders are all contained in the currently open web site.

NOTE

Some of the folders visible in the Folders view may be subwebs—*web sites that are nested inside the current web site. These are designated by a folder symbol with a globe superimposed on it.*

TIP

By default, Folders view does not display hidden files or folders. To show them, choose Tools | Web Settings and click on the Advanced tab in the Web Settings dialog box. Then check the Show Hidden Files And Folders check box.

The Folders view provides quite a number of ways of working with your files. The simplest way to make changes is to use the shortcut menu. Two different types of shortcut menu are available, depending on whether you right-click on a folder or right-click on a file.

If you right-click a file in the Folders view, the shortcut menu has the following options:

- **Open**   Loads the page either into the page editor or into another editor you have already defined for the file type. See the "Configure the Editors" section later in this chapter for more information on how to configure FrontPage to work with a different editor.

- **Open With**   Loads the page into an editor that you select from a submenu that appears.

- **Open In New Window**   Opens the page in a new window that you can size independently of the main window area.

- **New From Existing Page**   Creates a copy of the selected page, which you can then modify, rename, and save.

- **Preview In Browser**   Loads the page into your browser.

- **Preview In Multiple Browsers**   Loads the page into all the browsers you have set up (see Chapter 2 for information on how to configure the browser preview).

- **Cut**   Removes the file from the display and places it on the clipboard, making it available to be pasted elsewhere. (This command is also available in the Edit menu.)

- **Copy**   Copies the file to the clipboard and makes it available to be pasted elsewhere. (This command is also available in the Edit menu.)

- **Paste**   Pastes the file that is currently residing in the clipboard (as a result of using Cut or Copy) into the selected folder or web site. If the folder or web site already contains a file with the same name as the file you are pasting, FrontPage automatically renames the pasted file. (This command is also available in the Edit menu.)

- **Set As Home Page**   Sets the selected page to be the home page for the web site. This is the page that someone sees when they type in the web address of the web site.

- **Rename**   Enables you to change the name of the file by typing a new name into the Folders view. Choosing Rename selects the existing name; you can then type in the new name. FrontPage recalculates any hyperlinks to a renamed file so that the hyperlinks are not broken. (As an alternative to using this shortcut menu option, you can also rename a file by clicking it, pausing, then clicking again.)

- **Delete**   Deletes the file from the web site. However, hyperlinks that point to the deleted page from other pages remain in those other pages, and must be removed manually (the best way is by using the Broken Hyperlinks report, as detailed in Chapter 17). You can also delete a file by selecting it and pressing DELETE.

- **Publish Selected Files**   Publishes the selected files to your web site, as discussed in Chapter 18.

- **Don't Publish**   This option is a toggle—select it once to turn it on and select it again to turn it off. When this option is on, the file will *not* be included when you publish your web site (as discussed in Chapter 18). This condition is indicated by a red "x" through the file's icon in the Content Pane.

NOTE   *Selecting Don't Publish has the same effect as opening the file's Properties dialog box, clicking on the Workgroup tab, and checking the Exclude This File When Publishing The Rest Of The Web check box.*

- **Properties**   Opens the Properties dialog box for the selected file.

NOTE   *You can create either a new page or a new folder by clicking the New Page icon or the New Folder icon in the upper-left corner of the Folders view. The Up One Level option is also available if the current view is not the topmost level of the web site. Choosing the Up One Level icon takes you up a level in the web hierarchy, to the parent folder or web site.*

If you right-click a folder in the Folders view, the shortcut menu has the following options (as well as some of the options described above):

- **Convert To Web**   Available for folders only. This converts a folder to its own web site, removing it from the web site it was in before. This folder is no longer considered part of the original web site. Therefore, it won't be published along with the original web site unless you specifically include subwebs (see Chapter 18).

- **Convert To Folder**   Available for subwebs only. Converts a subweb to a folder of the parent web site. There are some things to keep in mind when converting a subweb to a folder. First, pages in the subweb will take on the "theme" of the parent web site (see Chapter 6 for more on themes). Second, only people with access to the parent web site will be able to see the pages in the new folder. Finally, any tasks connected to pages in the subweb (see Chapter 17) are removed.

View Reports

The Reports view (see Figure 1-6) provides a series of reports that provide useful information about your Web site. This view is accessible by clicking on the Reports button at the bottom of the Web Site view, or by choosing View | Reports | Site Summary. The reports, which are discussed in considerable detail in Chapter 17, provide you with such information as internal and external hyperlinks, pages that load slowly, pages that contain broken or unverified hyperlinks, a list of

Name	Count	Size	Description
Usage data	4	0KB	Hits and download bytes for the period from 11/30/2002 to 1/15/2003
All files	713	10,412KB	All files in the current Web
Pictures	547	8,107KB	Picture files in the current Web (GIF, JPG, BMP, etc.)
Unlinked files	92	1,139KB	Files in the current Web that cannot be reached by starting from your home page
Linked files	621	9,273KB	Files in the current Web that can be reached by starting from your home page
Slow pages	57	10,792KB	Pages in the current Web exceeding an estimated download time of 30 seconds at 56Kbps
Older files	487	9,195KB	Files in the current Web that have not been modified in over 72 days
Recently added files	211	1,081KB	Files in the current Web that have been created in the last 30 days
Hyperlinks	1987		All hyperlinks in the current Web
Unverified hyperlinks	141		Hyperlinks pointing to unconfirmed target files
Broken hyperlinks	2		Hyperlinks pointing to unavailable target files
External hyperlinks	141		Hyperlinks pointing to files outside of the current Web
Internal hyperlinks	1846		Hyperlinks pointing to other files within the current Web
Component errors	0		Files in the current Web with components reporting an error
Uncompleted tasks	3		Tasks in the current Web that are not yet marked completed
Unused themes	0		Themes in the current Web that are not applied to any file
Style Sheet Links	28		All Style Sheet Links in the current web site.
Attached Pages	0		All files that are associated with a Dynamic Web Template.

FIGURE 1-6   Let FrontPage's reports tell you where you have problems with your web site.

uncompleted tasks, and old pages in the web site. You can run reports by choosing the report you want from the View | Reports menu, or by clicking a line in the Site Summary report (to run the detailed report).

Navigate the Structure of Your Web Site

You can create a navigation structure for your web site by organizing your web pages in Navigation view. The Navigation view (see Figure 1-7) provides a visual display of the organization of your web site that makes it easy to make additions or reorganize it. To access the Navigation view, click on the Navigation button at the bottom of the Web Site view or choose View | Navigation. The purpose of the Navigation view is to show you the structure of your web site—that is, to establish a hierarchy of pages and illustrate how the pages are connected. The connections are shown on pages in the web site by means of *link bars* based on the Navigation view (see Chapter 10 for more on link bars and how to use the Navigation view). The lines in the main window of the Navigation view show which pages are connected by hyperlinks in the link bars.

In the Navigation view main window, you can expand or collapse the page hierarchy as well as zoom in and out. You can also swap the view between portrait and landscape.

Use Hyperlinks View

Figure 1-8 shows the Hyperlinks view. This view shows the hyperlinks that connect the individual pages in the web site. In other words, the Hyperlinks view shows you the web site as a web site, with the relationships between the pages clearly visible. To access the Hyperlinks view, click on

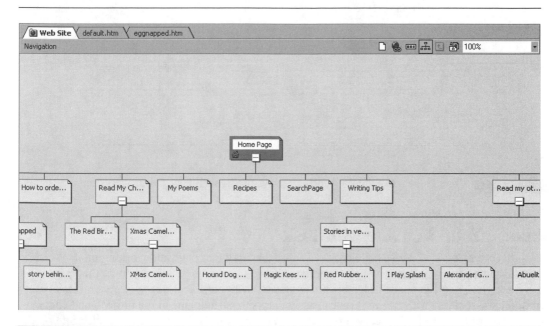

FIGURE 1-7   See the navigation structure of your web site with the Navigation Web
Site View.

the Hyperlink button in the Web Site view or choose View | Hyperlinks. You can center the view
on any page. To do so, right-click on a page in the main Hyperlinks view and choose Move To
Center. Note that the Move To Center option is not available when you right-click on the page
that is *already* in the center.

The shortcut menu displayed when you right-click in a blank area of the main window in
Hyperlinks view offers the following commands for configuring how the Hyperlinks view works:

- **Show Page Titles**   By default, the pages in the Hyperlinks view are labeled with their
  filenames. If you want them labeled with their titles instead, choose this option. When
  the check mark appears alongside the menu command, the command is active; selecting
  it again turns the command off and redisplays the filenames.

- **Hyperlinks To Pictures**   Normally, FrontPage does not show hyperlinks to pictures,
  which can clutter up the Hyperlinks view. However, if you would rather see these hyperlinks,
  toggle this command on. The linked images are shown with the Graphic icon.

- **Repeated Hyperlinks**   Pages often contain multiple links to another page. By default,
  FrontPage only shows one of these links to avoid cluttering up the Hyperlinks view.
  However, if you would like to see all instances of links between two pages, toggle this
  command on.

- **Web Settings**   This command displays the Web Settings dialog box.

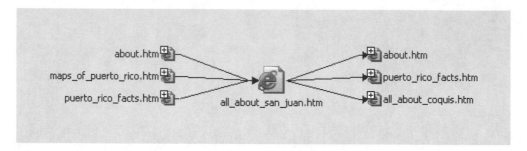

FIGURE 1-8   The Hyperlinks view visually displays the hyperlinks of your web site.

Manage Your Web Site with Task View

Tasks that are associated with a page are useful for launching that page and working on it. When you work on a page, you can even have FrontPage mark it as complete when you exit the page. With Task view, you can create tasks that are associated with particular pages or general tasks that are not associated with a page. You can assign tasks to participants in the project, and check the progress of those tasks. To access the Task view, choose the Tasks button in the Web Site view or choose View | Tasks. The Task view is shown in Figure 1-9.

Compare the Local and Remote Web Sites

Of course, in the end the whole idea of building a web site is to publish it where others can see it. The Remote Web Site view shows your local web site on the left and the contents of your published web site on the right (see Figure 1-10).

Clicking on the Remote Web Site Properties button in the upper-right corner of the Remote Web Site view enables you to specify where (what URL) you want your web site published and other properties of the remote web site.

You can publish an entire web site either from your local web site to a remote web site, or the other way around. You can also publish individual files via the buttons between the two web site listings or by drag and drop. Finally, you can also filter the listed files from the View drop-down list in the upper-left corner of the view.

Status	Task	Assigned To	Priority	Associated With	Modified Date	Description
● Not Started	Check for accuracy	David	Medium	Abuelita Zapatona: Grann…	1/29/2003 10:4…	Check with Grandma t
● Not Started	Add new library review	David	Medium	Circle of Time Reviews	1/30/2003 5:51…	A new library review f
● In Progress	Add new photos from 2002 cruise	David	Medium	Photo Gallery	1/30/2003 5:53…	

Web Site \ default.htm \ eggnapped.htm
Tasks

FIGURE 1-9   Task view is probably the most powerful of your web management tools.

Filter the files you can see

Publish selected files from the local to remote web site

Click to specify the publishing destination for your web site

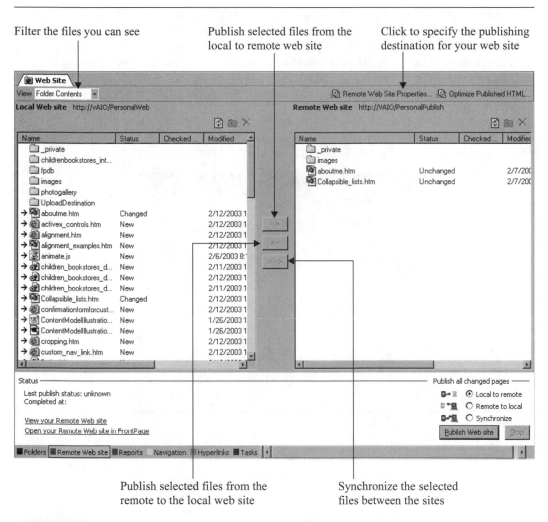

Publish selected files from the remote to the local web site

Synchronize the selected files between the sites

FIGURE 1-10   Compare the local and remote web sites to figure out what you need to publish.

For more details on how to publish your web site, see Chapter 18.

Configure the Editors

When you first install FrontPage, it makes sure that "normal" web file types are *associated* with an appropriate editor. For example, if you open a file in the Folders view whose filename ends with .htm, the file opens automatically in FrontPage. If you open a .doc file, the file opens automatically in Microsoft Word. However, quite a few common file types you'll need to use to create a web site do not have an editor associated with them in FrontPage. An example is a GIF or JPG graphical file type. By default, if you double-click a graphic in a web page, FrontPage will display a dialog box that tells you no editor is associated with this file type. This can be quite inconvenient, because you'll have to close the page, open your graphics editor, load the image, modify it, save it, and reopen the page!

There is an easier way: Configure FrontPage to open the appropriate editor automatically when you double-click the file to open it. Here's how:

1. Choose Tools | Options to open the Options dialog box. Choose the Configure Editors tab to set up editors for additional file types.

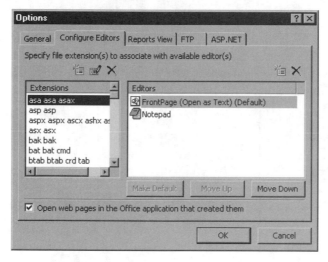

2. Choose the New Extension button to open the Open With dialog box. This is the leftmost icon (with the yellow star) just above the list of extensions.

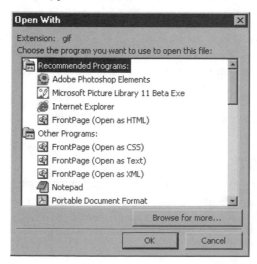

3. Type the filename ending that identifies the type of file you want to open in this editor. For example, enter **gif** for a GIF graphic file type.

4. Either pick an application from the list of programs in the Open With dialog box, or click the Browse For More button and navigate to the application on your hard drive.

5. Click OK to close the Open With dialog box and add the new extension and its associated editor.

You can add more than one editor to a file type. To do so, choose the extension, click the New Editor button (the left button above the list of Editors) and repeat steps 4 and 5 to add another editor. Once you have multiple editors in the list, you can rearrange the list order using the Move Up and Move Down buttons. You can also set an editor as the default editor by selecting it and clicking the Make Default button. The default editor is used to open the file type if you double-click on a file in the Folder List. All the editors in the list are available from the submenu that appears when you click Open With in the shortcut menu.

NOTE   *You can remove the association between an extension and an editor by selecting the editor and clicking the Delete Editor button (the right-hand button above the list of editors).*

You can create web pages in other Office applications. For example, you can create a word processing document in Word or a spreadsheet in Excel. If you then save the file as a web page, you can incorporate the web pages into your FrontPage web site. However, by default, if you open a web page in FrontPage that you created in another Office document, the page opens in the original Office application rather than in the FrontPage editor. If you don't like this behavior and would rather have all your web page files open in the FrontPage editor, clear the Open Web Pages In The Office Application That Created Them check box.

TIP   *If you have a web page editor you prefer over FrontPage's editor, associate the .htm file type with this alternate editor.*

Work with Toolbars

As mentioned earlier in this chapter, toolbars are handy for getting at often-used commands. The toolbars work just like every other toolbar in Microsoft Office.

By default, FrontPage displays only two toolbars: the Standard toolbar and the Formatting toolbar. However, you can configure the FrontPage toolbars to make them more useful for you. You can modify toolbars as follows:

■ **Turn toolbars on and off**   Right-click any toolbar to display the list of toolbars. To display a hidden toolbar, click the toolbar in the list to add a check mark next to its name. Click it again to hide the toolbar and remove the check mark.

■ **Dock and undock toolbars**   You can click on the line at the left end of the toolbar (docked to the top or bottom) or at the top of the toolbar (docked to the left or right edge) and drag the toolbar onto the desktop, converting it into a *floating window*. Dragging the title bar of the floating window and dragging it to the edge of a screen redocks the toolbar. Floating toolbars can be resized like any other window.

■ **Add or remove buttons**   If you click on the arrow at the right end of the toolbar (docked to the top or bottom) or the bottom of the toolbar (docked to the right or left edge), and then choose Add Or Remove Buttons from the menu, you'll see a short menu that includes the name of the toolbar. Click on the name to display a complete list of buttons in the toolbar. Click a button to add a check mark (make the button visible) or remove a check mark (hide the button).

Chapter 2

Build a New Web Page

How to...

- Create a new web page
- Import files from outside your web site
- Use the rulers and grid
- Preview your page in a browser
- Save your web page
- Create a template for later use

Now that you have FrontPage configured the way you want and you understand the basics of navigating through the many available views, it's time to learn how to build web pages. FrontPage provides many tools for creating web pages. You can build a new web page from scratch or use one of the many templates provided. You can also open existing files and import pages from another web site.

When you are working on a web page, you should periodically save your work. You can create a web page template so that it is easy to create new pages based on a common look and feel.

Create a New Web Page

A web site consists of many pages, so the first thing you need to learn how to do is create a web page. Since you will normally be creating web pages as part of ongoing web site development, you should create a web site to experiment with as we proceed. To create a new web site, follow these steps:

1. Choose File | New. The Task Pane opens, displaying your choices for creating a new web page or a new web site.

NOTE   *If you have the Startup Task Pane option checked (choose Tools | Options and it is the first check box in the Startup section of the General tab), the Task Pane will appear automatically when you start a new web site.*

2. Choose More Web Site Templates to open the Web Site Templates dialog box.

3. Specify the location on your hard drive where you want the new web site located by typing the location into the Specify The Location Of The New Web field on the right side of the dialog box.

4. Double-click the Personal Web Site icon in the Web Site Templates dialog box.

5. FrontPage proceeds to create the new web site, which takes a moment or two.

6. If you are presented with a new empty page, click the Close box in the upper-right corner of new_page_1.htm to close this page, as you won't be using it. You should then be looking at the default view of the screen, as shown in Figure 2-1.

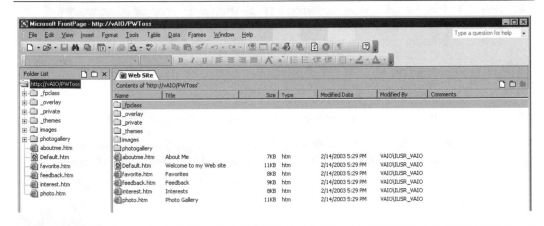

FIGURE 2-1   The default view of the FrontPage screen, ready to add pages.

Use General Templates to Create a Web Page

You can create a new page from the File menu. This technique is the most flexible: You can select the page template (how the page looks) from a list of available templates, and name the page prior to creating it.

To create a new web page from File menu, use the following steps:

1. Choose File | New. FrontPage displays the New Task Pane.

2. In the New Page section of the Task Pane, select More Page Templates.

3. FrontPage opens the Page Templates dialog box and presents a set of common web page templates, as shown here.

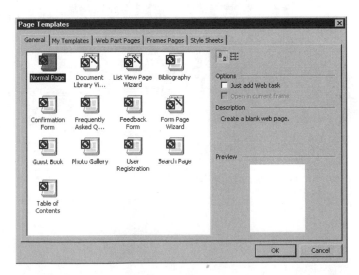

4. Select the template you want. As you select each template, a preview of the template appears in the Preview area in the lower-right corner and a textual description is displayed in the Description section on the right side of the dialog box.

SHORTCUT *To quickly create a web page from a template, double-click on the template.*

5. If you want to add a style to your web page, click the Style Sheets tab and pick a style.

NOTE *If you check the Just Add Web Task check box, FrontPage gives you a chance to name the page and select a title, then creates the page as well as a task to finish the page later. Creating a task to build a web page is covered in Chapter 17.*

6. Click OK to create the new page (see Figure 2-2).

7. Right-click anywhere on the page and choose Page Properties from the shortcut menu, or choose File | Properties. The Page Properties dialog box opens.

8. Enter a descriptive title for the page. Click OK to close the Page Properties dialog box.

NOTE *The page title appears in the title bar of web browsers when displaying the page. It also appears in the Favorites or Bookmark list if viewers add the page to their list of favorites or bookmarks—so picking a good title is very important.*

9. Choose File | Save. The Save As dialog box opens (see Figure 2-3). This box enables you to give your file a name as well as decide where it will be stored.

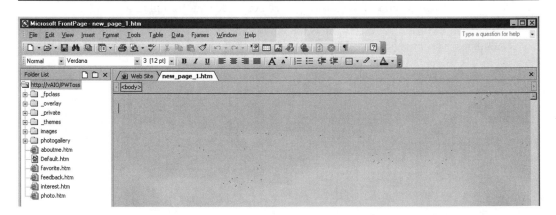

FIGURE 2-2   A newly created page in the Personal Web Site, ready to have a meaningful title assigned to it.

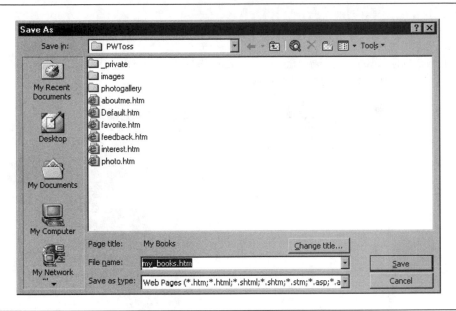

FIGURE 2-3   Use the Save As dialog box to save your web page.

10. Enter the name of the file in the File Name field. If you wish to change the page title, click the Change Title button and enter the title in the Set Page Title dialog box that appears.

11. Click Save to save the page.

The default filename is the page title you gave the page, with spaces replaced by underscores. Choose a location to store your new file. The default location is in the web site in which you are working, and that is usually a good choice. However, as with any other file dialog box in FrontPage, you can navigate to any location on your hard drive, network, or the Internet and place the file wherever you wish.

 See "Save Your Web Page" later in this chapter more information on saving a page.

Import Files and Folders

You can create web pages by importing files and folders from other directories on your hard drive or network. Importing files and folders copies them and makes them part of your current web site. You can also import Internet web sites.

Import Files and Folders From a Drive

To import files or folders from your hard drive or network, use the following steps:

1. Choose File | Import to open the Import dialog box. Use this dialog box to import files and folders from your hard drive, your network, or the Internet.

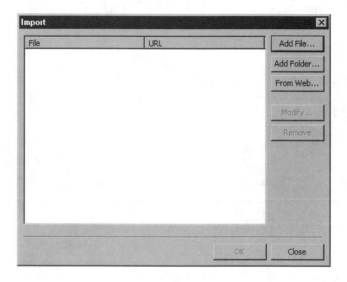

2. To add a file, click the Add File button. This opens a standard File Open dialog box, labeled Add File To Import List.

3. Choose a file from the list of files on your hard drive or network. The name of the file is displayed in the File Name field at the bottom of the dialog box.

> **SHORTCUT**   *Want to import multiple files from one folder? Hold down the* CTRL *key and click each of the files you want to import from that folder. This multiple-selection technique saves a lot of time. If you change your mind about one of the files, just click it again (with the* CTRL *key still held down).*

4. Choose Open to return to the Import dialog box. The file you chose is now listed, ready to be imported.

5. Continue adding files by repeating steps 2–4.

> **NOTE**   *You can change the location within your web site into which your file will be imported. Click the Modify button in the Import dialog box and use the resulting Edit URL dialog box to change the filename or path. For example, if you are importing a graphic file (such as a .jpg file), you can import the file into the images folder within your web site by adding* **images/** *in front of the filename.*

6. To add a folder, click the Add Folder button to open the File Open dialog box.

7. Navigate to the folder you want to import and choose it in the dialog box. Then click OK to add the folder and all its contents to the list in the Import dialog box.

8. Continue adding folders by repeating steps 6 and 7. When you are through, you'll have a list of files and folders to import. If you change your mind about a file or folder, simply select it in the Import dialog box and click the Remove button.

9. Click OK to begin the process of importing. When the importing process is complete, you can view the new list of files in the Folder List.

Import an Internet Web Site

To import a site from the Web, make sure the Import dialog box is open (choose File | Import if it is not open) and proceed as follows:

1. Click the From Web button. FrontPage opens the Import Web Wizard.

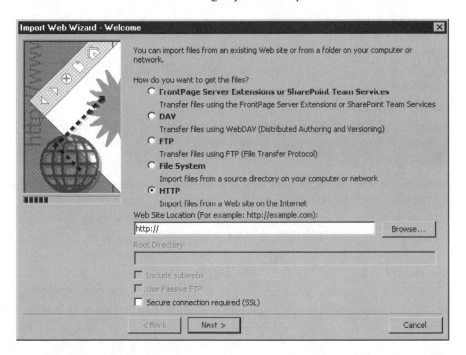

2. Choose the type of web site from the radio buttons. The most common choice is the default, HTTP, which enables you to import files from a regular web site.

NOTE *Although the HTTP option is selected by default, you can choose the File System radio button. If you do, the default value in the Location field changes to C:\. You can either type in a filename or click the Browse button to open the New Publish Location dialog box. Then choose the desired folder, just as in the previous set of steps. You can also check the new Include Subwebs check box to import a folder and all its subfolders.*

3. Type in the URL for the remote web site into the Web Site Location field. If the remote web site requires a secure connection (SSL), check the Secure Connection Required (SSL) check box. Then click Next.

4. If you don't want to add the imported files to the currently open local web site (the default), clear the Add To Current Web Site check box, and specify a different web site as the destination of the imported files. Then click Next.

5. Decide whether to limit the number of imported "levels" (hyperlinks) away from the home page for the site. For example, if you choose to limit to two levels, the page you chose and all the pages linked to that page, and all the pages linked to those pages, will be imported. So be careful what you choose!

TIP   *To import just the home page and any files (such as graphics) used on the home page, set the limit to zero.*

6. Decide whether to place a limit on the amount of data to import. This is a good safeguard, especially if you don't really know how much data is in the pages linked to the page you are importing. By establishing a data limit, you can make sure you don't import too much.

7. Decide whether to limit your import to just text and graphics. If you *don't* limit the import to just text and graphics, you can import, Java, JavaScript, ActiveX controls, and who knows what else!

8. Click Next to proceed, then click Finish to exit the Import Web Wizard and begin the import process. Unlike importing files and folders, you can't queue web locations in the Import dialog box and import them all at once.

NOTE   *During the import process, FrontPage tries to protect your existing site from having files overwritten. Thus, if it encounters a file that has the same name as a file in the destination web site, it will ask whether you want to overwrite the existing file. If you answer "no," FrontPage will automatically rename the imported file for you.*

Create a New Page from an Existing Page

If you already have a web page that you want to use as the starting point for a new web page, FrontPage makes this task easy. To create a new web page based on an existing web page, use the following steps:

1. Choose File | New to display the Task Pane.

2. In the Task Pane, select From Existing Page. This displays a standard File Open dialog box, labeled New From Existing Page.

3. If the page you want to use is not in the current web site, choose the web site or folder that contains the page from the Look In drop-down list.

Import Files Using FTP

If the Internet site containing the files you need uses File Transfer Protocol (FTP), you can import files from that site using the Import Web Wizard. To do so, choose File | Import to open the Import dialog box, click the From Web button, and choose FTP from the list of radio buttons in the Import Web Wizard dialog box.

Fill in the address of the FTP site (beginning with ftp://) and click the Next button. As with importing a web site, you have the opportunity to change the destination of the imported files. Then click Next and click Finish. If this is the first time you have connected to this FTP site and it requires a username and password, FrontPage will prompt you for that information. Type in the required information and click OK. FrontPage displays the Remote Web Site view, with your destination web site on the left and the FTP site on the right. You can then use the techniques discussed in Chapter 18 to copy the files from the FTP site to your local web site. Notice that FrontPage sets the default for Publish All Changed Pages to "Remote to Local," just as you would expect.

4. Pick the page you want to use as the basis for the new page, and click the Create New button. A new page is created within your web site based on the page you selected.

NOTE *The new page uses the theme (see Chapter 6 for more information on themes) from your current web site.*

 *To quickly create a new web page that is a copy of an existing page, right-click on the page you want to copy in the Folder List and choose New From Existing Page in the shortcut menu.*

Use the Rulers and Grid to Lay Out a Page

FrontPage 2003 provides both rulers and a grid to help you lay out a page. The rulers run across the top of the screen and down the left side, as shown in Figure 2-4 .You can turn the rulers and grid on and off, snap page elements to the grid, modify the origin of the rulers (the 0,0 point), and configure the rulers and grid to your liking.

View the Rulers and Grid

You can choose to view the Rulers, the Grid, or both. To toggle the ruler on and off, choose View | Ruler and Grid | Show Ruler. To toggle the grid on and off, choose View | Ruler and Grid | Show Grid.

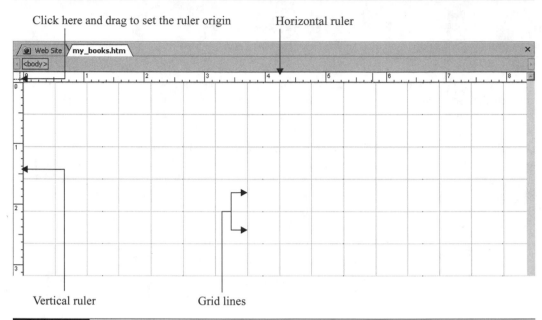

Click here and drag to set the ruler origin   Horizontal ruler

Vertical ruler   Grid lines

FIGURE 2-4   The rulers and grid make it easy to see how page elements align to each other and their position on the page.

The Snap To Grid selection (View | Ruler and Grid | Snap to Grid) allows you to snap the position of an item to a grid point. However, this only works when you can freely drag an item to a position on the page, as described in Chapter 14.

Modify the Ruler Origin Point

To modify the origin point for the rulers, click in the square in the upper-left corner (where the rulers meet) and drag to set the new origin point. The ruler markings adjust to show the new 0,0 point. You can set the origin to the upper-left corner of a selection by selecting an item (graphics or text) and choosing View | Ruler and Grid | Set Origin From Selection.

If you choose View | Ruler and Grid | Set Origin From Selection without making a selection, the origin is set back to the default location at the upper-left corner of the page.

You can reset the origin back to the default position by choosing View | Ruler and Grid | Reset Origin or by double-clicking the square at the upper-left corner (where the rulers meet).

Configure the Ruler and Grids

You can configure the ruler and grid by choosing View | Ruler and Grid | Configure to open the Page Options dialog box with the Ruler and Grid tab displayed:

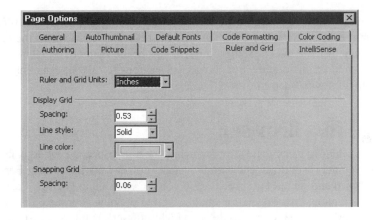

From here, you can make the following adjustments:

■ **Adjust the Ruler and Grid Units**   Use the Ruler and Grid Units drop-down list to choose the units you want to use when viewing and setting the ruler and grid. Choices include Inches, Pixels, Centimeters, and Points.

TIP   *Points is a measure that comes from the publishing world. There are 72 points to the inch.*

■ **Set the Display Grid Spacing**   Choose the spacing between the grid lines (in the units you set in the previous bullet) by specifying a value into the Spacing field of the Display Grid section.

■ **Set the Display Grid Line Style**   Set the style of the line that FrontPage uses to display the grid by choosing it from the Line Style drop-down list. Choices include Solid, Dashes, and Dots.

■ **Set the Display Grid Line Color**   Set the color of the line that FrontPage uses to display the grid by choosing it from the Line Color drop-down list. Clicking the down arrow displays a standard color selection box from which you can pick a color:

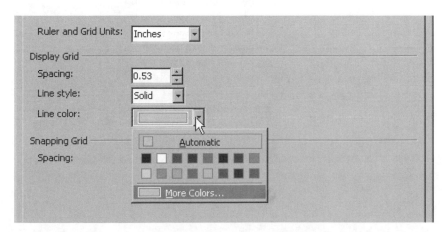

■ **Set the Spacing for Snapping to the Grid**   The *snapping grid* and the *display grid* are two different grids. Adjusting the display grid (as described earlier) sets the properties of the visible lines on the screen. Setting the spacing for the snapping grid (by specifying a value in the Spacing field of the Snapping Grid section) sets the dimensions of the grid to which an item will "snap-to."

Preview a Page in a Browser

The Preview Page view does a pretty good job of showing you how your page will look in a browser. However, the view you get is not exact, and certain features do not work in Preview. For example, you can't fill out a form and submit the results when you are working in Preview Page view.

To remedy this situation, FrontPage 2003 enables you to preview your page in a browser. When you install FrontPage 2003, it tries to detect which browser(s) you have installed, and automatically sets up options for previewing in that browser in various resolutions under the File | Preview in Browser menu item:

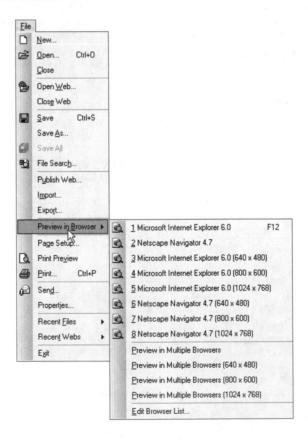

Use Preview In Browser

To preview an open page in a browser, select the combination of browser and resolution from the File | Preview in Browser submenu.

NOTE   *The options in the submenu that do not include a resolution enable you to preview the page in the current screen resolution. Thus, if you are running your computer at 1280 × 1024 and choose Microsoft Internet Explorer 6.0 from the submenu, the page is previewed at 1280 × 1024.*

SHORTCUT   *To quickly preview a page from the Folder List in the default browser (the top one in the File | Preview From Browser submenu), right-click on the file and choose Preview in Browser from the shortcut menu.*

If you have multiple browsers installed on your machine, you can preview the page in multiple browser/resolution combinations at the same time. This can be handy because Internet Explorer and Netscape Navigator do *not* display pages in exactly the same way, especially when the page uses Cascading Style Sheets. To preview an open page in multiple browsers at the current screen resolution, choose File | Preview in Browser | Preview in Multiple Browsers. To preview an open page in multiple browsers at a particular screen resolution, choose File | Preview in Browser and choose the resolution you want from the Preview in Multiple Browsers section of the submenu. You can also preview a page in the Folder List in multiple browsers by choosing Preview in Multiple Browsers from the shortcut menu for the page.

Configure Preview In Browser

You can configure the browsers and screen resolutions available in the File | Preview in Browser submenu by selecting Edit Browser List from the submenu. This opens the Edit Browser List dialog box:

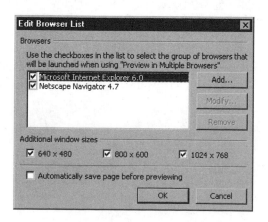

To make an installed browser available for previewing, check the check box for that browser. Clear the check box if you don't want to be able to preview with that browser. To make a window's size available for previewing, check the check box for that window size. Clear the check box if you don't need to preview in that window size.

Some pages don't work properly in a browser unless you have saved any changes. To have FrontPage do that for you automatically before previewing in the browser, check the Automatically Save Page Before Previewing check box.

You can add your own browsers to the list. You'll need to do this for nonstandard browsers or for browsers you install after you installed FrontPage. To add your own browsers, click the Add button to display the Add Browser dialog box:

Fill in the name you want displayed for the browser in the Name field, and type in (or use the Browse button) to specify the full path to the program that runs the new browser. Click OK to finish, and the new browser will appear in the Edit Browser List dialog box.

 *You can modify (click the Modify button) or remove (click the Remove button) any browsers you have added yourself. You cannot modify or remove browsers that were automatically detected by FrontPage.*

Save Your Web Page

Before you go very far in building a web page, you'll need to know how to save the page so it is not lost if your machine locks up or a similar misfortune strikes. Saving a web page isn't very different from saving any other type of file. To save a web page for the first time, choose File | Save. This opens the Save As dialog box (see Figure 2-3, earlier in this chapter). From here, you can choose to save the file in the current web site on your hard drive (the most usual choice), in a different location on your hard drive, or a network drive—or even on the Internet.

 After the first time you save a web page, choosing File | Save again simply saves the page under the same filename, so you won't see the Save As dialog box again. However, you can also save the page under a different filename (perhaps to clone the page and then change it). To do that, choose File | Save As.

Create Your Own Templates

If you find that you use a page that has a particular "look" to it over and over again, you may wish to create your own template that includes the main properties of the page. For example, you might have a page in which you have customized the colors, the background, and the font you use for the heading. Your page might also always have certain elements present, such as navigation bars, a list that uses a special graphic for a bullet, and a timestamp. Rather than having to create this page from scratch each time (or customizing an existing FrontPage template), you can create and use your own template.

To create a new template, first build the page you want to use as a template. Include as many of the common elements as possible so you won't have to do too much customizing later. Then use the following steps:

1. Choose File | Save As to open the Save As dialog box.

2. Click the small arrow at the right side of the Save As Type field and choose FrontPage Template (*.tem) from the drop-down list.

3. Enter the filename in the File Name field. Then click Save.

4. FrontPage displays the Save As Template dialog box. Here you can enter the descriptive parameters of your new template.

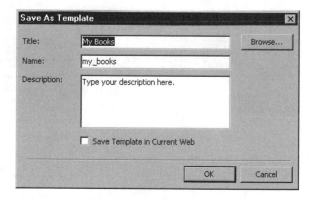

5. Enter the title of the template, the name, and a description. If you want the template saved only as part of the current web site, check the Save Template In Current Web check box.

6. Click OK. If there are any graphics on the page, FrontPage displays the Save Embedded Files dialog box. This is because graphics associated with a template are saved in a different place than the graphics associated with a regular page in a web site.

7. Click OK to save the embedded files to the destination suggested by FrontPage and create the template.

Once you have saved your new template, the template will be available in the My Templates tab of the Page Templates dialog box (which appears when you create a new web page). As you can see here, you can now choose your new template by its title, see a preview of it, and read the description.

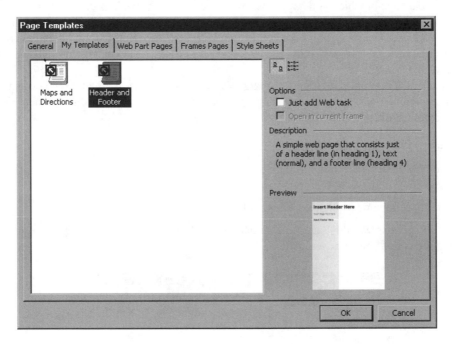

Chapter 3

Place Text on a Web Page

How to…

- Add and format text and paragraphs
- Build lists of items

Once you have a page created, you can add text to it, setting the font, style, effects, color, and other properties.

It's easy to add lists of text to your page and set the alignment and indent properties of paragraphs. Of course, FrontPage supports the normal Windows cut, copy, and paste operations.

Add Text to a Web Page

Despite all the advances in web page technology, a great deal of the information on a web page is still text. FrontPage makes it easy to add text to a page in Page view. To start adding text, position the blinking text cursor where you want the text to appear and begin typing. From there, you can move the cursor and select text just as you would in virtually any word processor.

Format Text

Of course, you are probably going to want to use a variety of text effects to make your web page more exciting (but don't overdo it). After all, a page full of just plain text isn't very interesting. FrontPage lets you change the font, font style, effects (such as bold, italics, and underline), font size, and color. You can either use the Formatting toolbar or bring up a special dialog box for modifying text.

Adjust the Text Style with the Formatting Toolbar

The Formatting toolbar is the quickest way to make changes to the style of your text. Not all of the tools on the Formatting toolbar apply to text; some of the tools apply to paragraphs, which will be covered in "Apply Paragraph Styles," later in this chapter. If you haven't moved the Formatting toolbar from its default location, it is the second toolbar at the top of the FrontPage screen (see Figure 3-1).

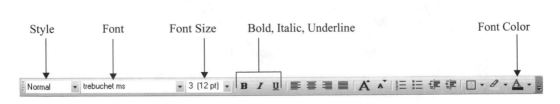

| Style | Font | Font Size | Bold, Italic, Underline | Font Color |

FIGURE 3-1 The Formatting toolbar provides a set of tools for formatting text and paragraphs.

As with all other Office applications, you can choose the font, font size, and font color from the toolbar drop-down lists, and select an effect (Bold, Italic, Underline) by clicking the appropriate button in the toolbar.

Format Text with the Font Dialog Box

You can format your text from a single dialog box. To do so, select the text you want to format and choose Format | Font, or choose Font from the shortcut menu. FrontPage displays the Font dialog box.

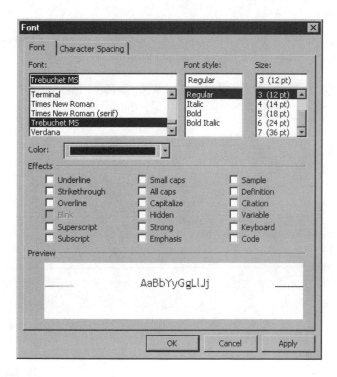

The Font dialog box consists of two tabs. The Font tab lets you make the same formatting choices as the Formatting toolbar. The Character Spacing tab enables you to control how letters are spaced and positioned in a line of text.

To apply text format using the Font tab, make your choices from the dialog box. As you make your choices, a preview of the changes to your text is shown in the Preview area of the dialog box. You can adjust the Font, Font Style, and Size from the scrolling windows at the top of the dialog box.

TIP   *To remove all the selected styles, choose Regular from the Font Style list.*

Choose the effects by checking or clearing the check boxes in the Effects section of the dialog box. Some of the effects are holdovers from the early days of HTML. For example, Strong is the same as Bold, and Emphasis is the same as Italics.

To change the color, choose the color you want from the Color drop-down menu. This menu works identically to the Font Color button in the toolbar.

The Automatic selection enables FrontPage to set the color based on its own rules for color. For example, choosing Automatic ensures that you do not end up with black text on a black background. Essentially, if you want to return a color to its normal default value, choose Automatic.

The Character Spacing tab contains two types of adjustments—Spacing and Position—which enable you to set the spacing between letters and their position on the line.

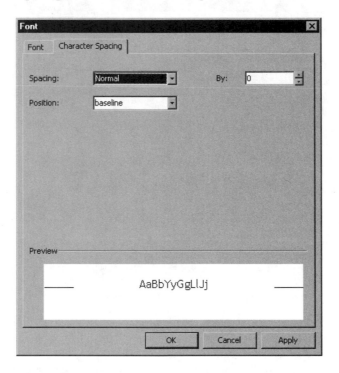

Spacing controls how far apart the letters are placed. To adjust the spacing, choose the type of spacing you want to perform: Expanded (letters farther apart) or Condensed (letters closer together). Then, use the By spinner to set the amount. To remove all special spacing, select Normal from the Spacing drop-down list.

The Position drop-down list sets where the text appears relative to an imaginary line called the text baseline. If you chose a Position value of Raised, the text will appear above the text baseline. If you choose a Position value of Lowered, the text will appear below the text baseline. Set the amount by using the By spinner. To remove all special positioning, select Baseline from the Position drop-down list.

Work with Lists

When you need to present information in a structured way, lists are extremely useful. Lists help you communicate information in a concise and memorable way. You can use bulleted lists or numbered lists. Bulleted lists are better when there is no particular order to the list. Numbered lists help you represent the order of the information, such as performing a sequence of steps. They can also be used to rank things in order of importance. You can use graphics for the bullets in a bulleted list, and even create sublists when you need to break down one list item into smaller parts. Figure 3-2 shows examples of both a bulleted list and a numbered list, as well as the use of small pictures as bullets.

NOTE   *When a web page includes a theme, the default picture bullets are controlled by the theme, although you can pick another picture to use as the bullet (see Chapter 6 for more information on themes). In addition, you can't use plain bullets on a page with a theme. If you want to use plain bullets on that page, you'll have to remove the theme from the current page by choosing Format | Theme to open the Theme Task Pane. Select the top item (No Theme) from the All Available Themes list in the Task Pane.*

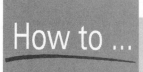 **Remove Character Formatting**

Once you have applied complex character formatting to text, it can be tedious to remove that formatting—turning off all the special effects, resetting the font, and so forth. The easiest way to remove the character formatting is to choose Format | Remove Formatting. For pages that do not use a theme, this returns the text to plain text with the default settings (Times New Roman, size 3, regular typeface, color black). However, if the page does use a theme, removing the formatting returns the text to the default font for that theme.

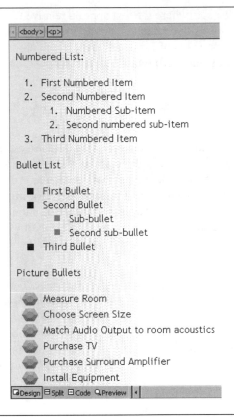

FIGURE 3-2 Both bulleted lists and numbered lists are useful in adding structure to the information on your web page.

Create a Bulleted List

To create a plain bulleted list on a page without a theme, use the following steps:

1. Place the text cursor where you want to start the list and choose Format | Bullets and Numbering. FrontPage opens the Bullets and Numbering dialog box. Click the Plain Bullets tab.

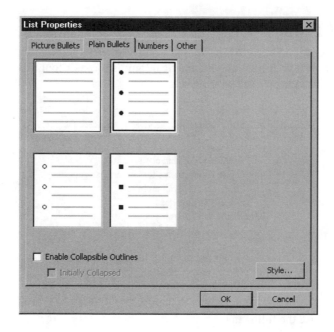

2. Choose the page icon that contains the bullet style you want.

3. Choose OK. The dialog box disappears and a bullet appears on the page.

4. Start typing your list, pressing ENTER at the end of each list item to move to the next line and create a bullet.

5. When you are done with the list, press ENTER twice to stop inserting bulleted items.

To insert a new item in the list, position the text cursor at the end of a line and press ENTER to add a new line and bullet.

The quickest way to start a bulleted list is to choose Bulleted List from the Style drop-down list in the Formatting toolbar, or click the Bullets button in the same toolbar.

Create Nested Lists

You can create a sublist within a list to break down a bullet into more detail. There are no limits to how deeply you can nest your lists, but the practical limit is three or four. After that, it gets pretty hard for the reader to keep track of the levels.

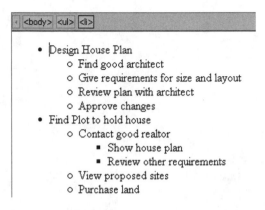

To create a sublist, use the following steps:

1. Place the text cursor at the end of a bulleted item in a list. Press the ENTER key to make a new bullet, but don't type anything.

2. Click the Increase Indent button twice. The first bullet of the nested list appears, indented under the parent list. By default, the nested list has a different style bullet than the parent, but you can change that if you wish, using the information in the last section.

3. Type the items in the nested list. Press the ENTER button at the end of each item to move to the next line and create the next bullet.

4. To end the nested list, press ENTER to get a bullet without any text. Press the Decrease Indent button twice. This creates a bullet in the parent list, no matter how deeply nested the sublist is.

You can promote a bullet to the parent list by placing the text cursor in the bulleted item and clicking the Decrease Indent button twice. To demote an item to the list nested below it, place the text cursor in the item and click the Increase Indent button twice.

Create a Numbered List

To create a numbered list, use the following steps:

1. Place the text cursor where you want to start the list and choose Format | Bullets and Numbering. FrontPage opens the Bullets and Numbering dialog box. Click the Numbers tab. Choose the numbering format for your numbered list.

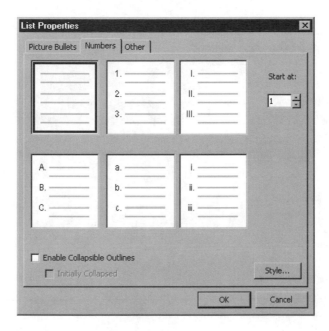

2. Click the page icon that contains the numbering format you want to use.

3. Choose the number with which to start the list from the Start At spinner.

4. Choose OK. The dialog box disappears and a number appears on the page.

5. Start typing your list, pressing ENTER at the end of each list item to move to the next line and create the next number in the list.

6. When you are done with the list, press ENTER twice to stop inserting numbered items.

SHORTCUT *The quickest way to start a numbered list is to choose Numbered List from the Style drop-down list in the Formatting toolbar, or click the Numbering button in the same toolbar.*

Specify a Picture Bullet

You can use pictures as the bullets in the bulleted list. Don't overdo it—it is best to use simple graphics to avoid cluttering up the scenery.

To create a bulleted list using pictures, use the following steps:

1. Choose Format | Bullets and Numbering, and click the Picture Bullets tab.

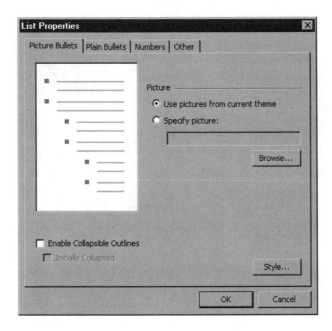

2. If you want to use the default picture bullet for the page's theme, choose the Use Pictures From Current Theme option. Otherwise, click the Specify Picture option.

3. You can type a path to a picture to use as a bullet, but you'll be better off clicking the Browse button to open the Select Picture dialog box.

4. Select a picture from the dialog box and view the preview of the picture in the dialog box. Click Open to select the picture.

5. Choose OK in the Bullets and Numbering dialog box to use the picture. The dialog box closes and the first bullet appears.

6. Start typing your list, pressing ENTER at the end of each list item to move to the next line and create a bullet.

7. When you are done with the list, press ENTER twice to stop inserting bulleted items.

If the graphic you choose is not already saved within your web site, FrontPage displays the Save Embedded Files dialog box when you save the web page. Rename the image file to something intelligible and save it to your web site.

Change the List Format

You can quickly change the list format—converting a numbered list to a bulleted list, changing the bullet or numbering style, or changing the picture bullet. To do so, make sure the text cursor is somewhere in the list and choose Format | Bullets and Numbering (to display the Bullets and Numbering dialog box), or choose List Properties from the list's shortcut menu (to display the List Properties dialog box). Select the tab for the type of bullets you want—for example, if you are converting a numbered list to a bulleted list, click on the Plain Bullets tab. Then pick the page icon for the type of bulleted list or numbered list you want. When you click OK, the entire list is converted to the new format.

You can remove the list format altogether using this technique as well. Simply choose the page icon that contains no bullets or numbers.

 *To quickly remove a bullet from a single line in a list, click anywhere in that line and then click the Bullets button in the Formatting toolbar (which deselects the button). This technique also works for numbered list—just click the Numbers button in the Formatting toolbar instead.*

You can also change the list style for just a single item in the list. To do so, click on the item and choose List Item Properties from the shortcut menu. In the List Item Properties dialog box, pick the page icon for the list format you want to use.

TIP *If you want to convert the list to one of the standard HTML list styles (these appear in the Style drop-down list of the Formatting toolbar), click on the Other tab and pick the list format from the List Style list box.*

Set Up a Collapsible Outline

If you've ever used Word or another word processor that supports outlining, you'll know how useful it is to be able to expand and collapse the outline to view it at different levels of detail.

You can achieve the same effect with FrontPage—clicking a bullet or numbered list item that has a sublist opens that sublist, and clicking it again collapses the sublist.

Bulleted List

- Purchase a copy of FrontPage
- Buy this excellent book on how to use FrontPage
- Read the book
- Build your web site
- Find a WPP that supports FrontPage extensions

Bulleted List

- Purchase a copy of FrontPage
- Buy this excellent book on how to use FrontPage
  - Go to the store
  - Find the book
  - Pick it up and carry it to the cash register
  - Pay
  - Walk out
- Read the book
- Build your web site
- Find a WPP that supports FrontPage extensions

To create a collapsible outline, select a bulleted or numbered outline that contains one or more sublists. Right-click anywhere in the list and choose List Properties from the shortcut menu. Check the Enable Collapsible Outlines check box. If you want the outline to be collapsed when you first view it, check the Initially Collapsed check box.

Since the finished web page gives no indication that there is a collapsed sublist within a list, you should give your reader some clue. Two common methods include adding an ellipsis (...) to the end of the list item on which you can click to open a sublist, and changing the style of the bullet for that line.

Apply Paragraph Styles

FrontPage supports styles of text you can apply to a paragraph. The style you have seen the most of up to this point is Normal. However, if you click the Style drop-down list at the left end of the Formatting toolbar, you'll see quite a few other styles available. To see how they work, place the text cursor in a paragraph and choose a style from the Style drop-down list. Table 3-1 summarizes

Style	Description
Normal	Default text: 12 pt., left-aligned, one line of space before and after the paragraph.
Heading 1	Used for largest headings: 24-pt. bold, left-aligned, one line of space before and after the paragraph.
Heading 2	Used for medium-sized headings: 18-pt. bold, left-aligned, one line of space before and after the paragraph.
Heading 3	Next size smaller headings: 14-pt. bold, left-aligned, one line of space before and after the paragraph.
Heading 4	An excellent choice for subheadings: 12-pt. bold, left-aligned, one line of space before and after the paragraph.
Heading 5	A good bold style, slightly smaller than Normal text: 10-pt. bold, left-aligned, one line of space before and after the paragraph.
Heading 6	A really tiny font, good for legalese, disclaimers, and other stuff you don't want people to read: 8-pt. bold, one line of space before and after the paragraph.
Address	A style designated for putting the web page author's address on the page. This style is normally displayed in italics.
Formatted	A style designed to allow you to insert tabs and spaces and have them show up in the text. In Normal style, inserted tabs and spaces do not display either in the web page or the browser. With Formatted style, however, these elements do display, making this style ideal for formatting that requires extra spaces or multiple levels of indent. However, Formatted style does *not* wrap—it appears as one long line. You have to force the wrap by inserting line breaks (press SHIFT-ENTER to add a line break). By default, the formatted style uses a fixed (non-proportional) font, such as courier.
Bulleted List	A format that places a bullet in front of each paragraph and the proper indenting for creating bulleted lists. You can replace the bullets with small pictures. Bulleted lists are discussed in much more detail earlier in this chapter.
Numbered List	A format that places a number in front of each paragraph and the proper indenting for created numbered lists. Numbered lists are discussed in much more detail earlier in this chapter.
Directory List	Visually, this style looks exactly like a bulleted list. This style is usually used for (what else?) directories of files.
Menu List	This style looks exactly like a bulleted list.
Defined Term/ Definition	These two styles are actually meant to be used together. The term being defined is entered first in Defined Term style. When you press ENTER, FrontPage automatically switches to the Definition style, which you use to provide the definition. After entering the definition, press ENTER again to switch back to the Defined Term style. Of course, you can use this pair of styles for any formatting that requires a heading/explanation style. Figure 3-3 shows an example of using these styles.

TABLE 3-1   The Styles in the Style List, Used to Format Paragraphs

the styles available for your use, and Figure 3-3 shows a screen with all the headings on it, along with Normal style text. It also shows a sample of a Definition list.

 "Pt." refers to "points." Points are a way of measuring the height of text—there are 72 points in an inch. For example, 10 pt. and 12 pt. are common text sizes.

Format Paragraphs with the Paragraph Dialog Box

You can format the layout for a paragraph by choosing Format | Paragraph or selecting Paragraph from the shortcut menu. Either way, the Paragraph dialog box opens. In the Paragraph dialog box, you can set the alignment, indentation, and spacing. As you make changes to these settings, the sample text in the Preview area gives you an idea of what your text will look like.

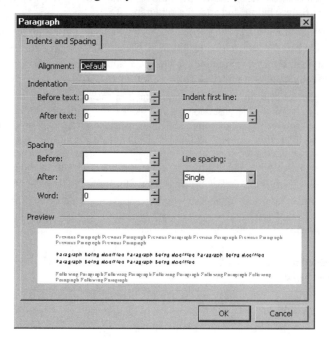

To set the layout of a paragraph, you can adjust the following settings:

■ **Alignment** Use the Alignment drop-down list to set the alignment of the paragraph to left, right, center, or justify (stretches across the screen from margin to margin unless the line ends with a return).

 You can also set the alignment (left, right, center, or justify) from the alignment buttons in the Formatting toolbar.

■ **Indentation** You can set three types of indentation. The Before Text spinner controls the left margin. The After Text spinner controls the right margin—that is, the distance from the right edge of the text to the right margin increases as you increase the After

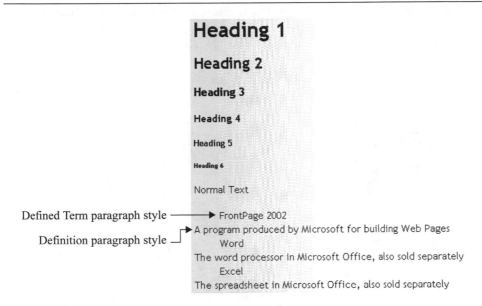

Defined Term paragraph style ⟶

Definition paragraph style ⟶

FIGURE 3-3   The heading styles and lists provide flexibility in how you format your text.

Text indent amount. The Indent First Line spinner increases the left indent for the first line of the paragraph only. This is handy if the style you use requires that the first line of a paragraph be indented. Placing a negative number causes the first line of the paragraph to be indented less than the balance of the paragraph—known as a "hanging indent."

NOTE   *You can't indent the first line of a paragraph the way you would with a word processor, by pressing the* TAB *key. This is because both FrontPage and browsers ignore such extraneous tabs except in the Formatted Text style.*

■ **Spacing**   You can set four kinds of spacing. Before sets the amount of white space between this paragraph and the preceding paragraph. After sets the amount of white space between the paragraph and the following paragraph. Word increases the space between individual words. Finally, Line Spacing sets the spacing between lines of text in the paragraph to single, 1.5, or double-spaced.

Set Up Borders and Shading

FrontPage provides options for you to set the background color of a paragraph, or you can use a picture as a background for a paragraph. Additionally, you can place borders around one or more sides of a paragraph, choose a color for each border, and apply special effects to the borders. To set the borders and shading, place the text cursor in the paragraph you want to change and choose

Format | Borders And Shading to display the Borders and Shading dialog box. Here you can establish the size, type, and color of borders and background for a paragraph. Any changes you make are visible in the Preview section on the right side of the dialog box.

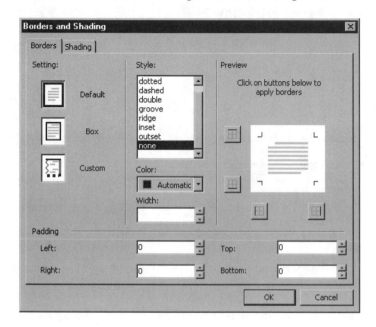

Configure the Borders

The first selection you will want to make is to establish the general type of border. In the Settings section, choose Default (for no border), Box (for a solid border all the way around), or Custom (for customized borders). Nothing actually changes when you choose Custom, but you can then proceed to click individual border buttons in the Preview section to turn specific borders on and off.

NOTE　*If you choose the Box option and then turn off one of the borders, the Settings selection automatically changes to Custom. Also, you can choose Default at any point to remove the borders, and choose Box at any time to place a solid border all the way around the paragraph.*

If you are using the Box setting, configuring the rest of the border parameters is fairly simple:

1. Choose the style you want from the Style list. Each style (such as dotted, dashed, groove, and so on) provides a different effect, and this effect is visible in the Preview area.

2. Choose a color from the Color drop-down list. This list looks similar to the Font Color tool. You can pick from the color palette, a theme color, or your custom colors (if you've defined any), or you can choose More Colors to choose or set up a custom color.

3

3. Select the width for the border from the Width spinner. Notice that if you had not chosen the Box selection in the Settings section, changing the Width to a number higher than zero automatically chooses the Box selection.

4. In the Padding section, choose the amount of padding (blank space) between the border and the text. You can set the padding independently for the top, bottom, left, and right. A higher number provides more white space around the paragraph's text.

The Custom setting gets somewhat more complicated, because you can set the style, color, and width for *each* border. Here is how it works:

1. Turn on each border you want to use by clicking the buttons in the Preview section. When the button is shown as pressed, the border is present.

2. Set the style, color, and width as discussed above. Notice that the borders do *not* change their appearance in the Preview section.

3. Click a border button to apply the formatting you set in step 2 to that particular border. You'll see the change appear in the Preview area. If you want to turn the border off, you'll need to click the border button again, which removes the border.

Once you have created the border you want, there is a quick and easy way to adjust the size of the border—as well as the paragraph within the border. Simply click in the paragraph, and the border displays a set of sizing handles. Click on a handle and drag the border to adjust the size. If you try to drag either the left or right border past the edge of the paragraph's text, FrontPage adjusts the paragraph's width and height so that the text does not extend past the border. You cannot drag the top or bottom borders past the edge of the text.

You can also turn borders on and off using the Border tool in the Formatting toolbar. Click the small down arrow alongside the Border tool to display a list of border choices.

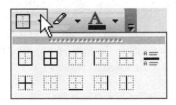

Click on the border option you want. For example, to establish a border around a paragraph, click on the Outside Borders tool in the list of border choices. These options are toggles: click on the option again to turn the border off.

Configure Shading

To configure the shading for a paragraph, click the Shading tab of the Borders and Shading dialog box.

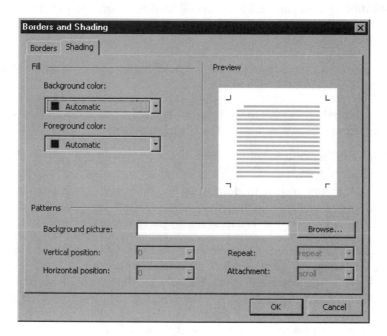

To set the background color for the paragraph, click the Background Color drop-down list. This action displays the standard Color Selection tool.

Choose a foreground color by clicking the Foreground Color drop-down list. The foreground color sets the color for the text in the paragraph, and overrides any text color you may have set.

If just having a background color isn't good enough for you, you can use a graphic image as the background for the paragraph. Be careful, though—many graphics are so busy that it is very difficult to read text against them. To assign a graphic as a background, use the following steps:

1. Type the name of the graphic into the Background Picture field. Alternatively, click the Browse button to open the Select Background Picture dialog box so you can choose a graphic.

2. Choose the vertical position for the graphic from the Vertical Position drop-down list. This is the vertical position (top, center, or bottom) of the graphic, relative to the paragraph. Note that if you choose a repeating graphic (see step 4), this is the vertical position where the repeating group starts.

3. Choose the horizontal position for the graphic from the Horizontal Position drop-down list. This is the horizontal position (left, center, or right) of the graphic, relative to the

3

paragraph. Note that if you choose a repeating graphic (see step 4), this is the horizontal position where the repeating group starts.

4. Choose how you want the graphic to repeat by making a selection from the Repeat drop-down list. When you repeat a graphic, multiple copies of the graphic are placed edge to edge (called "tiling") to provide a background for the paragraph (see Figure 3-4). The choices are Repeat (repeats both horizontally and vertically), Repeat-x (repeats horizontally only), Repeat-y (repeats vertically only), and No Repeat.

Use the Attachment drop-down list to choose whether you want the background picture to scroll relative to the browser (choose Scroll) or to remain fixed while the browser scrolls (choose Fixed).

NOTE *As mentioned in steps 2 and 3, the tiling starts at the specified horizontal and vertical positions. Thus, for example, if you set both the Horizontal Position and Vertical Position to center and choose Repeat in the Repeat drop-down list, the tiled graphic will begin in the very middle of the paragraph and repeat to the right edge and the bottom edge. Additionally, the Attachment setting has no effect unless the graphic is large enough to fill the browser window or is tiled.*

Choose More Colors

Any time you choose a color in FrontPage, you have the option of using any color your computer can display. However, the default Color Selection tool does not display all those colors. To access additional colors, click the More Colors button at the bottom of the color tool. This opens the More Colors dialog box. Using this dialog box, you pick any color you want and save it to your collection of custom colors, making it easy to pick the same color again.

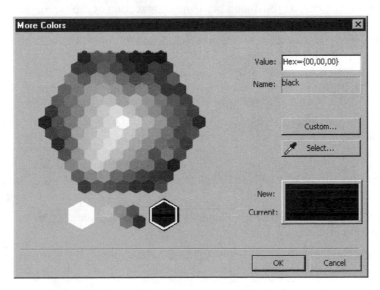

FIGURE 3-4   A tiled background for a paragraph can make your text very hard to read.

In the More Colors dialog box, you can pick one of the colors in the color wheel by clicking it. When you choose a new color, that color is shown in the New section of the rectangle in the lower-right corner of the dialog box. The hexadecimal (base 16) value for the color is shown in the Value field in the upper-right corner. If you know the hexadecimal value for a desired color, you can type it into this field.

NOTE   *The hexadecimal values vary from 00,00,00 (white) to FF,FF,FF (black).*

Another way to choose a color is to click the Select button (the one with the eyedropper on it). When you do, your mouse pointer turns into an eyedropper. As you move the mouse pointer over the screen (including outside the dialog box), the New section of the rectangle shows the color under the pointer. When you see a color you want to use, simply click it. Thus, by using the Select button, you can choose any color you see. To help you remember what the eyedropper does, think about it "sucking up" a color.

If you still don't see a color you want to use, you can click the Custom button, which opens the Color dialog box. The Color dialog box enables you to pick any color your computer can display.

There are five ways to choose a color from the Color dialog box. When you have the color you want, click OK in the Color dialog box and OK in the More Colors dialog box to return to the web page. The ways to pick a color from the Color dialog box are

- ■ **Choose a Basic Color**   Choose one of the colored rectangles in the Basic Colors section of the dialog box. The color's numeric values are displayed using both the HSL and RGB systems.

- ■ **Pick an Existing Custom Color**   Choose one of the colored rectangles in the Custom Colors section of the dialog box.

- ■ **Pick a New Custom Color**   On the right side of the Color dialog box is a large square that displays every color your computer can display. To choose a color, click it in the square. Then select the brightness you want from the color slider at the far-right edge of the dialog box.

- **Specify Hue, Saturation, and Luminance**   If you know the values that define the color in the HSL system, you can type the values into the Hue, Sat, and Lum fields.

- **Specify Red, Green, and Blue**   If you know the values that define the color in the RGB system, you can type the values in the Red, Green, and Blue fields.

3

If you know you are going to want to add the selected color to your set of custom colors, click the square in the Custom Colors section of the dialog box *before* defining your color. After defining your color, click the Add To Custom Colors button. This changes the color of the square in the Custom Colors section to the defined color.

It is important to click the square in the Custom Colors section before defining your color. If you define the color and then click the square, the color you defined will be replaced by the square's existing color.

Paste the Way You Want

Normally, when you copy and paste an item, it retains all its formatting, including its style, size, paragraph alignment, and other characteristics. However, there are times when all you want is the plain text, so that you can format it yourself without having to remove all the original formatting. "Paste the way you want" makes it quick and easy to choose either to keep all the original source formatting or to remove all formatting. To use this feature, paste an item just the way you would normally. The pasted item displays a small Paste Options icon.

Click on this icon and choose either Keep Source Formatting or Keep Text Only from the shortcut menu. You can go back and change your mind later if you wish.

If you don't want to see the Paste Options icon, select Tools | Page Options, switch to the General tab, and clear the Show Paste Options Buttons check box.

Chapter 4

Add Graphics and Sound to Your Web Page

How to...

- Add graphics to a web page
- Customize your collection of clip art
- Change the properties of a picture
- Modify graphics using FrontPage's tools

You can communicate a lot of information with plain text, but pages that contain only unbroken text are boring! Adding graphics (within reason) adds interest to the page, as well as communicating graphic-based information. You can use prepackaged graphics, such as commercial clip art, or add pictures and other graphics from files on your hard drive or the Internet. Once you have added graphics to your web pages, you can change their size, how text wraps around them, and many other properties. You can even use tools built right into FrontPage to modify the graphics themselves.

Add Graphics to a Web Page

You can only go so far with text, even when you add fancy formatting to it. Sooner or later, you'll want to add graphics to your web pages. You might want to emphasize a point with a graphic or animation, or publish photographs of your last family function. Whatever the reason, it's really not very hard to dress up your web site with graphics.

Comprehend Graphic Formats

If you have been working with computers for a while, you probably know that there are a number of graphic formats. For a while, it seemed as if each new graphic application pioneered its own format. However, for the Internet, you'll want to use just two graphic formats: GIF (Graphics Interchange Format) and JPEG (Joint Photographic Experts Group). All graphics-capable browsers support these two formats and can display them without any help. Other graphics formats, such as PCX, BMP, and TIFF, can often be displayed by browsers using plug-in applications. However, since you can't guarantee that people who come to your site will have these additional applications, it is safest to stick with GIF and JPEG.

NOTE *There is another web graphics format, PNG. However, this format is not widely supported, so it is best not to use it for now.*

The two graphic formats each have strengths and weaknesses, which make them useful for different purposes. GIF is quite compact and can handle up to 256 colors. It is great for line art and graphics that do not require continuous shading (such as you see in photographs). Further, most competent graphic editors allow you to reduce the number of colors in a GIF file, making the file smaller. JPEG files are slower to decompress (open onscreen) than GIF, but can support continuous shading and 16.7 million colors—making them a better choice for photographs. You can also adjust the amount of compression to reduce the size of a graphic at the expense of the quality. That is, the more a file is compressed, the more the image quality is degraded.

Store Graphics on Your Web Site

In general, it is best to include all graphics you use on your web site within your current web site file structure. While it is certainly possible to display graphics located elsewhere on your computer or network—or even located remotely on the Internet—you can't guarantee that the graphic will always be visible, especially since graphics outside your current web site are not published to the hosting server when you publish the site.

FrontPage maintains a special folder called *images* within the file structure of your web site. It is highly recommended that you store all your graphics in this folder. You can copy or import graphics files to the images folder before placing the graphics on a page, or (as discussed shortly) save copies of graphics located elsewhere into the *images* folder when you save the page.

Add Graphics from a File

You can add graphics to your web page from two general locations: your hard drive/network drive or from the Internet.

Add an Image from Your Hard Drive

To add a graphic from your hard drive (or a network drive) to a web page, use the following steps:

1. Choose Insert | Picture | From File. This displays the Picture dialog box:

2. If the graphic you want is already present in the *images* folder, double-click the folder to open it and select the file you want. Otherwise, type the filename (complete with the path) in the File Name field, or use the Look In list to navigate to the file location and choose the file.

3. Click Insert to place the graphic on the page, or choose Select from the graphic's shortcut menu.

Add an Image from the Internet

To add a graphic from the Internet to a web page, use the following steps:

1. Choose Insert | Picture | From File. This displays the Picture dialog box.

2. Click the Search The Web button (the third button to the right of the Look In field).

3. Your browser opens to the Web Search portion of MSN. From here you can search for a picture on the Internet, or specify a web address that contains the picture you want to use.

4. Once you have navigated to the site that contains the picture you want, right-click on the picture and choose Save Picture As from the shortcut menu.

5. In the Save Picture dialog box, specify where you want to store the picture. Then click Save to save the picture to your hard drive.

NOTE   *Once you are done saving the picture to your hard drive, you can close the browser.*

6. Once you have the picture safely stored on your hard drive, use the instructions in the previous section to place the picture in a web page.

Save Embedded Images

As mentioned earlier, it is best to keep images you are going to use in your web site within the file structure of the web site. If you placed image files from outside your current web site file structure on a web page, you are given the opportunity to copy those files into your web site when you save the page. To do so, use the following steps:

1. Choose File | Save to save the web page. This opens the Save Embedded Files dialog box. All files located outside your web site file structure are listed in the dialog box.

4

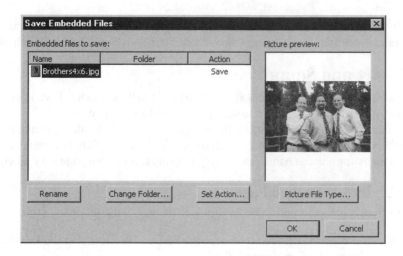

2. Choose a file by clicking it, and then choose Change Folder.

3. In the resulting Change Folder dialog box, navigate to the folder in which you want to save a copy of the graphic (the *images* folder is recommended). Open the folder by double-clicking it. The folder name appears in the Look In field at the top of the dialog box.

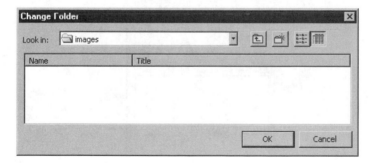

4. Choose OK. In the Save Embedded Files dialog box, the selected folder (*images*) appears in the Folder column. Click OK to save copies of the graphic files as well as the web page.

NOTE   *You can select multiple files and change the folder for all selected files at one time. To select multiple files, CTRL-click each file you want.*

   If you decide you don't want the image to be saved into the current web site, you can prevent it. From the Save Embedded Files dialog box, select the file and click the Set Action button, then select the Don't Save option.

You can also specify some special options about the picture file by clicking on the Picture Options button. These options are discussed in "Insert Clip Art into Your Web Page," later in this chapter.

Insert Clip Art and Sound

When you installed FrontPage 2003, you had the option of installing clip art. If you purchased FrontPage as part of the Microsoft Office suite, you get the Office clip art as well. These galleries include traditional clip art, icons, and buttons for web pages, as well as videos, sound, and photographic images. You'll probably add clip art to your web pages often, because the buttons and web-related icons supplied as part of the gallery help dress up a web page very nicely.

Insert Clip Art into Your Web Page

To add a picture from the clip art collection to your web page, use the following steps:

1. Choose Insert | Picture | Clip Art or choose the Insert Clip Art tool in the Drawing toolbar. This opens the Clip Art Task Pane.

4

2. Use the Search In drop-down list to pick which of your clip art collections you want to search through. Choices include My Collections, Office Collections (if you installed FrontPage along with the rest of Microsoft Office) and Web Collections. Select the check boxes for the collections in which you want to search.

3. Use the Results Should Be drop-down list to specify which types of media files you want to look for. The media files are grouped into Clip Art, Photographs, Movies, and Sound. Click the small plus (+) next to each type of group to expand the list and display the types of files included. You can select or clear the check boxes for the individual file types if you wish.

4. Enter any keywords you want to search for in the Search For field. You can search for multiple keywords by typing them into this field, separated with commas.

5. Click the Go button to locate any matching graphics. The graphics appear in the Task Pane.

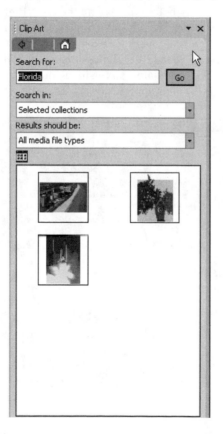

6. Move the mouse over the piece of clip art you want to insert into your web page and click the small down arrow that appears at the right side of the clip art's image.

7. Select Insert (the top selection in the shortcut menu) to add the clip art to your page. Or, you can click and drag the clip art onto the web page.

Another quick way to insert a piece of clip art is to double-click on it in the Clip Art Task Pane. This automatically inserts the clip art at the location of the text cursor.

When you save a page to which you've added clip art, you automatically see the Save Embedded Files dialog box so you can save a copy of the clip art to your web site. The name of the clip art is generally something unintelligible (such as pe03254_.gif), so you'll want to use the Rename button in the Save Embedded Files dialog box to rename the clip art to something you'll recognize. Just click the Rename button, type the new name, and press ENTER. Then click OK to save the copy of the clip art to its new location with its new name.

Additionally, if the clip art is not in GIF or JPEG format, FrontPage will convert the clip to one of these formats automatically before displaying the Save Embedded Files dialog box. By default, FrontPage will convert the file to a GIF if it has 256 colors or fewer; otherwise, it converts it to a JPEG. However, you can override this choice by clicking the Picture File Type button that appears in the Save Embedded Files dialog box when a file conversion is necessary. Doing so displays the Picture File Type dialog box, where you can pick whether you want to use JPEG or GIF, and specify the options appropriate for each file type.

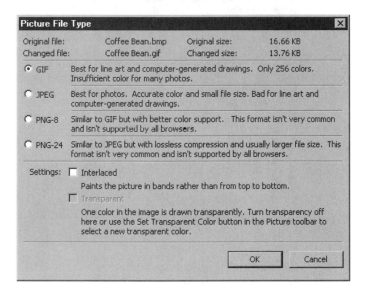

For a GIF file, these options are

- **Interlaced** This option is a special way of saving GIF files. If you choose this option, the GIF is loaded into a browser in increments. The first increment is in low resolution, and each succeeding increment adds progressively higher resolution. Thus, the person

4

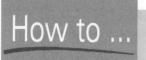 **Insert Sound into Your Web Page**

You can add sound to a web page from the Clip Organizer. If you do, the sound leaves no visible indicator on the page; it is added as the *background sound* for the page. Configuring the background sound is discussed in Chapter 6. To add a sound, use the same steps discussed earlier for inserting a piece of clip art, but make sure to include sound files in the search (check the Sounds check box in the Results Should Be drop-down list). You add a sound clip exactly the same way you add clip art.

viewing the web page can get an idea what the image looks like before it has fully loaded, and perhaps choose not to wait for the full image to load. For large GIFs, it is considered good manners to create them as interlaced.

■ **Transparent**   One of the ways to give your web pages a more integrated appearance is to use transparent GIFs. A transparent GIF image lets the page background appear through one of the colors in the image (you can only set one color as transparent). Note that this option is available only if you have modified the GIF to actually *have* a transparent color, as discussed later in "Make Transparent Images."

For JPEG files, you can set the following options:

■ **Quality**   JPEG stores files in a compressed format and is a "lossy" format—as the compression level increases (making the file smaller), more and more information is left out of the file, leading to the degradation of the image. Specify a value in the Quality spinner between 100 (high quality) and 0 (low quality).

■ **Progressive Passes**   This option loads the image into the browser in increments and works much like the Interlaced option for a GIF (described previously). The first increment is in low resolution, and each succeeding increment adds information until the graphic is fully built.

 Once you set the quality and save the image, you can't change the Quality setting again. Keep a backup copy so you can delete the current image, and reinsert it from the original file.

Add Horizontal Lines

You can use horizontal lines to break up sections on a web page. To do so, choose Insert | Horizontal Line. This adds the line to the page.

Break up your page with horizontal lines, like this one:

_____

Provided you haven't assigned a theme to the page, you can adjust the properties of the horizontal line by right-clicking the line and choosing Horizontal Line Properties from the shortcut menu. This displays the Horizontal Line Properties dialog box. Here you can change the height, width, color, and alignment of the horizontal line.

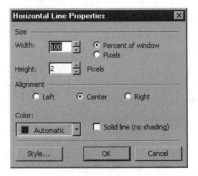

From this dialog box, you can change the width of the line by typing a number in the Width field or by using the spinner. You can choose to set the width as either a percent of the window width (recommended) or in absolute pixels. You can also set the height of the line using the Height spinner, although this quantity can only be set in pixels. Choose the alignment by selecting an option from the Alignment section of the dialog box, and choose the line color from the Color drop-down list. You can check the Solid Line (No Shading) check box, which removes the shading effect on a thick line and (as you would expect) displays it as a solid line.

Set the Picture Properties

Once you've placed an image on a web page, you can modify many of the image properties. To do so, choose Picture Properties from the shortcut menu to open the Picture Properties dialog box. Most of the interesting properties are on the General tab.

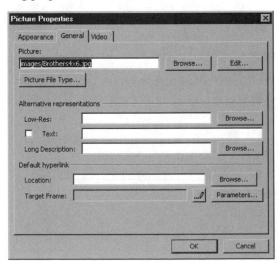

Set the General Properties

The General tab enables you to set the picture source, type, alternative representations, and default hyperlinks. The default hyperlinks portion of this dialog box will be discussed in Chapter 9.

Specify the Picture Source

The Picture field lets you change the image file that serves as the source for the picture. This field displays the full pathname to the file if the web site is disk-based, or just the folder within the Web if the Web is server-based. To change the picture source, type a new path, or click the Browse button to select a picture file from the Picture dialog box. You can also edit the picture (provided you have associated an editor with this type of file) by clicking the Edit button.

Adjust the File Type

You can change the type of file and adjust how the file is saved. To change the type of the file, click the Picture File Type button to open the Picture File Type dialog box, discussed previously in this chapter. If you choose to convert the file, FrontPage displays the Save Embedded Files dialog box so you can name the new graphic file and choose where to save it.

Alternative Representations

The Alternative Representations section of the dialog box enables you to specify (you guessed it) alternative representations for a graphic image. In the Text field, type a short phrase that describes the image. This text string is displayed when the page first loads, prior to loading the images. In addition, if you hover the mouse over the graphic while viewing the page in a browser, the contents of the Text field appear in a small window near the mouse pointer. In a browser configured to not display graphics, the text alternative representation is the *only* thing related to the graphic that is displayed.

In computer terms, a "string" is a sequence of typed characters.

The Low-Res (low resolution) option is another way to give the viewer something to see while the full graphic loads. If you have specified the Low-Res option, the page initially loads into the browser just displaying the text and a low-resolution version of the graphic. Only after that does the browser go back and load the full graphic. To set up the Low-Res option, open the full graphic and use a graphic editor to create a version that loads faster (has a smaller file size). Common techniques for reducing file size include reducing the number of colors, cropping unimportant portions of the graphic, and reducing the physical dimensions of the graphic. Once you've created the low-resolution version, specify the filename in the Low-Res field.

Set the Appearance Properties

From the Appearance tab, you can set the layout and size of the graphic image.

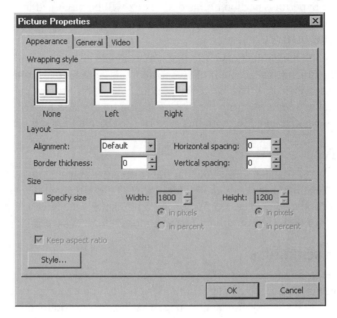

Set the Wrapping Style

If you place a graphic inside a block of text (by positioning the text cursor within the text block before inserting the graphic), the wrapping style is set to None. This means that the text does *not* wrap around the graphic. Instead, the text before the graphic is located above the picture, and the text after the graphic is located below the picture, as shown here:

Tiger, Tiger, Burning Bright|

The tiger is a fierce beast--the second-largest of the felines (smaller only than the lion).

But it has been hunted almost to extinction. Yes, there are few that are man-eaters, but these are rare, and are mostly the old or sick tigers that can't catch anything better tasting than a human being. The tigers roam Asia and the Indian sub-continent, and appear almost nowhere else in the world, except for zoos. They are exclusively meat-eaters -- just like any other cat. The powerful front paws are awesomely efficient at scooping food into their jaws.

To change the wrapping style, select either the Left icon or the Right icon in the Wrapping Style section of the dialog box. If you choose Left, the graphic is located at the left margin, and the text flows to the right side of the image.

4

Tiger, Tiger, Burning Bright

 The tiger is a fierce beast--the second-largest of the felines (smaller only than the lion). But it has been hunted almost to extinction. Yes, there are few that are man-eaters, but these are rare, and are mostly the old or sick tigers that can't catch anything better tasting than a human being. The tigers roam Asia and the Indian sub-continent, and appear almost nowhere else in the world, except for zoos. They are exclusively meat-eaters -- just like any other cat. The powerful front paws are awesomely efficient at scooping food into their jaws.

If you choose Right, the graphic is located at the right margin, and the text flows to the left side of the image.

Tiger, Tiger, Burning Bright

The tiger is a fierce beast--the second-largest of the felines (smaller only than the lion). But it has been hunted almost to extinction. Yes, there are few that are man-eaters, but these are rare, and are mostly the old or sick tigers that can't catch anything better tasting than a human being. The tigers roam Asia and the Indian sub-continent, and appear almost nowhere else in the world, except for zoos. They are exclusively meat-eaters -- just like any other cat. The powerful front paws are awesomely efficient at scooping food into their jaws.

> **NOTE**   *Choosing Left or Right in the Wrapping Style section automatically sets the value of the Alignment drop-down list to Left or Right. Changing the value in the Alignment drop-down list to something other than Left or Right (for example, Top), automatically changes the wrapping style back to None.*

Set the Spacing and Border Thickness

Using the settings in the Layout section of the dialog box, you can set the following:

- **Horizontal Spacing**   To set the amount of white space to the left and right between a graphic and any surrounding text or another graphic, use the Horizontal Spacing spinner. Higher numbers provide more white space.

- **Vertical Spacing**   To set the amount of white space above and below between a graphic and any surrounding text or another graphic, use the Vertical Spacing spinner. Higher numbers provide more white space.

- **Border Thickness**   If you want a black border around your graphic, set the thickness of that border with the Border Thickness spinner.

Align Graphics and Text

The Alignment drop-down list controls how adjacent text lines up with a graphic. From the Appearance tab, choose the value you want from the Alignment drop-down list. If you choose

Top, Middle, or Bottom, a single line of text aligns with the top, middle, or bottom of the graphic, as shown in Figure 4-1.

You can also use the Alignment drop-down list to make text adjacent to a graphic wrap around the graphic, with the same effect as discussed in "Set the Wrapping Style," earlier in this chapter. To do so, choose Left or Right from the Alignment drop-down list. If you choose Left, the graphic is located at the left margin and the text flows to the right side of the image. If you choose Right, the graphic is located at the right margin and the text flows to the left side of the image. If you want to return the alignment to the default value (text does not wrap around the graphic), choose Default from the Alignment drop-down list.

NOTE   *If you simply want to center or right-align a graphic on the page, select the graphic and choose Format | Paragraph (or choose Paragraph from the shortcut menu). Then choose Center or Right from the Alignment drop-down list in the Paragraph dialog box. Alternatively, you can choose the Center or Align Right buttons in the Formatting toolbar.*

The rest of the choices in the Alignment list are less useful, as they don't seem to make any discernable difference to the text that wraps around the graphic when used. However, they are described in Table 4-1.

A line of text aligned at the top of the graphic

A line of text aligned at the middle of the graphic

A line of text aligned at the bottom of the graphic

FIGURE 4-1   FrontPage enables you to align text with the top, middle, or bottom of an image.

Option	Effect
Texttop	Aligns tallest text with the image top
Absmiddle	Aligns image with middle of current line
Absbottom	Aligns image with bottom of current line
Baseline	Aligns image with text baseline of current line

TABLE 4-1   Additional Alignments for Graphics and Text

Set the Size of the Graphic

In the Size section of the Appearance tab, you can specify the size of the graphic as well as choose to maintain the aspect ratio. To specify the size, check the Specify Size check box, and enter the size of the graphic by typing a quantity in the Width and Height fields, or by using the Width and Height spinners. You can specify the size of the graphic either in pixels (choose the In Pixels option) or as a percent of the browser window size (choose the In Percent option). If you choose to maintain the aspect ratio (the original ratio of the width to the height) by checking the Keep Aspect Ratio check box, changing either the Width or the Height automatically changes the other quantity.

 You should maintain the aspect ratio of a graphic wherever possible. If you don't, the graphic can become so distorted that it is unrecognizable. This is especially true of thumbnails (small representations of images designed to give you an idea of what the larger image looks like).

If you clear the Specify Size check box, the graphic returns to its original size.

You can also adjust the size of a graphic by clicking the graphic, and then clicking and dragging one of the square dots around the perimeter of the graphic (sizing handles). If you click and drag a sizing handle in a corner of the graphic, the aspect ratio is automatically maintained; otherwise, you can stretch or shrink either the width or height of the graphic independently by using the top, bottom, or side sizing handles.

NOTE   *As we said earlier, reducing the size of a graphic is one way to make your images download faster. Unfortunately, merely resizing the* appearance *of the graphic does not enable the graphic to load faster, because the original graphic file is still just as large—it just looks smaller on the page. To make a graphic load faster, you must reduce the size of the file itself. Two ways to do this are cropping the graphic (removing unnecessary edges) or reducing the number of colors. Another way is to load the graphic into a graphic editor, and then use the editor's resampling capabilities to reduce the image to the size you need and resave the file at that size.*

Incorporate Special Breaks to Coordinate Graphics and Text

Thus far, you've learned how to align a single line of text with the top, middle, or bottom of an image, as well as how to make text flow around an image that sits against the left or right margin. However, you may want to use multiple lines of text as a caption alongside an image and continue the balance of the text below the image. For example, look at Figure 4-2. There is a multiline caption, and the rest of the text should continue along the bottom border. However, since the text caption at the right of the graphic is aligned to the bottom of the image, it falls below the image, looking awkward.

To fix this problem, use the following steps:

1. Change the picture alignment to Left. To do so, select Picture Properties from the image's shortcut menu, switch to the Appearance tab, and choose Left from the Alignment drop-down list.

2. Now both lines of the caption are positioned on the right edge of the graphic. However, any other lines you type also are positioned to the right of the image.

The Menorah is the symbol of Hanukah, a Jewish holiday that falls around the same time as Christmas. It has eight candles, plus the center candle, from which all the other candles are lit.

Hanukah celebrates a military victory and the subsequent miracle, in which the oil for the holy lamp -- of which there was only a one-day supply -- burned for a full eight days until more oil could be obtained.

FIGURE 4-2   The image is positioned against the left margin, and the caption "spills off" the bottom of the image with its current default alignment.

The Menorah is the symbol of Hanukah, a Jewish holiday that falls around the same time as Christmas. It has eight candles, plus the center candle, from which all the other candles are lit.

Hanukah celebrates a military victory and the subsequent miracle, in which the oil for the holy lamp -- of which there was only a one-day supply -- burned for a full eight days until more oil could be obtained.

4

3. Position the cursor at the point where you want the balance of the text to be below the image, and choose Insert | Break to display the Break dialog box. Special line breaks give you control over the relationship between text and graphics.

4. Choose the Clear Left Margin option and click OK. The balance of the text is moved below the graphic.

The Menorah is the symbol of Hanukah, a Jewish holiday that falls around the same time as Christmas. It has eight candles, plus the center candle, from which all the other candles are lit.

Hanukah celebrates a military victory and the subsequent miracle, in which the oil for the holy lamp -- of which there was only a one-day supply -- burned for a full eight days until more oil could be obtained.

NOTE *If the graphic is aligned right, use Clear Right Margin in the Break dialog box instead. If you have two images of dissimilar size, one aligned left and the other aligned right, choose Clear Both Margins from the Break dialog box.*

Modify an Image Using FrontPage's Graphics Tools

FrontPage includes a whole host of tools for modifying an image once you place it on a page. These tools are accessible from the Pictures toolbar (see Figure 4-3), which appears

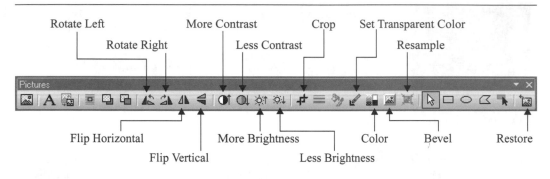

FIGURE 4-3   The Pictures toolbar provides tools that manipulate a graphic image.

automatically when you select a graphic. The Pictures toolbar has 14 buttons to help you modify the graphic.

If you make a change to a graphic image and save the page, you will see the Save Embedded Files dialog box so you can (if you wish) provide a filename for the changed version of the graphic and save the changed version without affecting the original. However, *every* graphic in your web site that referred to the original image will now automatically refer to the new, changed image file. If that is not what you want, you'll have to select each graphic and redirect it to the original unchanged version using the Picture field in the General tab of the Picture Properties dialog box.

TIP   *To avoid having to do all this redirection, you can create a copy of the image and place the copy on the web page before changing it. The easiest way to do this is to select the image file in the Folder List, choose Copy from the shortcut menu, then paste the copy back into the images folder (if that is where you keep your images). Rename the copy (choose Rename from the shortcut menu), and place the copied image you want to change on the web page. Now, when you change the image and give it a new name, the references to the original image are unaffected.*

Flip and Rotate a Graphic

You can rotate an image 90 degrees clockwise or counterclockwise by using the Rotate Right and Rotate Left buttons in the Picture toolbar. You can also reverse the image left to right using the Flip Vertical button, and reverse the image top to bottom by using the Flip Horizontal button.

Adjust the Brightness and Contrast

There are four buttons on the Picture toolbar that adjust contrast and brightness. To increase the contrast, click the More Contrast button; to decrease the contrast, click the Less Contrast button. To add brightness to the image, click the More Brightness button; to decrease the brightness, click the Less Brightness button. Each time you click a button, it applies the intended effect again to incrementally add or decrease contrast or brightness.

Crop an Image

You can crop an image—cut out a rectangular area of the image to use. This is handy if the image (usually a photograph) has unneeded areas around the borders and you haven't removed those areas using an image editing tool.

To crop an image, select the Crop tool. A dashed cropping rectangle appears on the image (see Figure 4-4). Click the sizing handles to adjust the size of the cropping rectangle until only the desired portion of the graphic is included in the rectangle. Click the Crop button again, and the image is cropped.

Make Transparent Images

When you add an image to a page that has a background color other than the background color of the image, the effect is somewhat jarring. To achieve an integrated effect when you add an image to a page, you may wish to use a transparent image. A transparent image allows the page to show through parts of the image. So, for example, you could change the predominant background color of the image to be transparent so it will look much more like it belongs on the page. You can see the difference in Figure 4-5. You can only choose one color to be transparent, and this effect only works on GIFs.

To make a color transparent, select the graphic and click the Set Transparent Color button. Move the mouse cursor (which now looks like the eraser end of a pencil) to the color you want to make transparent, and click. All places in the graphic that are drawn in the color become transparent (invisible).

If you change your mind about using a transparent color, click the Set Transparent Color button again, and click on the color you previously chose to be transparent in the image.

Cropping rectangle

FIGURE 4-4   Use the cropping rectangle to show where the new edges of a graphic will be.

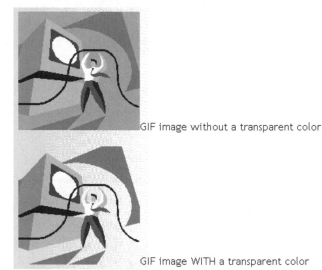

GIF image without a transparent color

GIF image WITH a transparent color

FIGURE 4-5   A transparent GIF (the lower image) harmonizes with the page much better than the one above it, which contains all opaque colors.

Alternatively, you can choose a different color to be the transparent color by clicking on a different color in the image. The previously transparent color is restored to its original color, and all places in the graphic that are drawn in the newly selected color become transparent.

Adjust the Color Options

The Color button in the Pictures toolbar displays a shortcut menu when you click on it. Although there are four options in this menu (Automatic, Grayscale, Black & White, and Wash Out), only two of them (Grayscale and Wash Out) are active when you are working with clip art or photographs.

Convert an Image to Grayscale

The Grayscale option converts the image to shades of gray. Selecting the Grayscale option again returns the image to its original colors.

Use the Wash Out Option

The Wash Out option washes out the image by 50 percent. This has the effect of reducing the color intensity. Unlike the Grayscale option, selecting Wash Out again does not reverse the effect, nor does it wash the image out further. The only way to return to the original image is to use Edit | Undo.

Bevel the Image Borders

Bevel creates a beveled outline around the image. This beveling is done using white and gray, so it shows up best on a background color other than white or gray.

Make an Image Larger or Smaller with Resample

If you need to make an image larger or smaller, the Resample tool is very useful. To use it, select the image and use the sizing handles to adjust the size. Then click the Resample button.

4

Restore the Image with the Restore Button

If you change an image and decide you don't like the way it looks, you can simply reinsert the original image from its file—provided you haven't saved the image yet. To restore the image, simply click the image and then click the Restore button. In addition to removing any other changes you have made, the image is returned to its original size, overriding any resizing.

Chapter 5

Add Photos To Your Web Site

How to...

- Create a Photo Gallery and adjust the layout
- Add pictures and captions to your Photo Gallery
- Customize the pictures in the Photo Gallery
- Add a Shockwave Flash file to your web page

With the advent of digital cameras and inexpensive flat-plate scanners, it has become fast and easy to create digital photographs or convert photographs into digital form. One interesting use for digital photos is to post them on your web site, where friends and family can view and download them. Unfortunately, displaying a set of full-size photos on a web page can make the page take a long time to display in a browser. And, it can be a lot of effort to add and format textual descriptions for the photos. One solution to displaying full-size photos is to display "thumbnails"—reduced-size versions of the photos that give the reader some idea of what the photo looks like. Ideally, you would link the thumbnail to the full-size photo so that the reader could click on the thumbnail to view the photo.

The FrontPage Photo Gallery tool provides a tool to automate most of the process of creating a photo gallery (see Figure 5-1 for a sample). Using the Photo Gallery, you can create a custom layout of photographs, generate the thumbnails, link them to the full-size images, and add textual descriptions that are visible in the gallery. You can also easily modify individual thumbnails and text.

David and Marisa's Formal Cruise Pictures

A tux makes anyone look good -- even Marisa's husband David (Nov. 2001)

White dinner jacket and a formal dress...awesome! (Nov. 2001)

A formal portrait aboard the Norwegian Sea, September 2000.

FIGURE 5-1   Display your digital photos in FrontPage's Photo Gallery.

Create a Photo Gallery

To create a photo gallery, choose Insert | Picture | New Photo Gallery. This displays the Photo Gallery Properties dialog box.

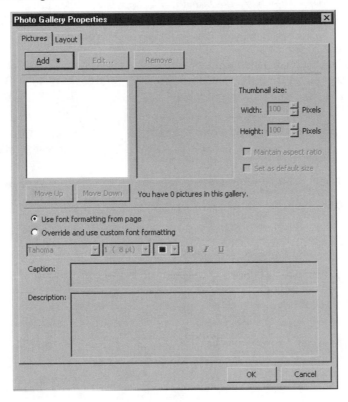

5

NOTE *You can also add a Photo Gallery by creating a new page based on the Photo Gallery page template (in the General tab of the Page Templates dialog box). However, you have to change everything about the page to customize it for your use, so it is actually less work to start with a new photo gallery.*

The first step is to add pictures to the gallery. To do so, click the Add button and pick one of the two options:

■ **Pictures From Files**   Displays the File Open dialog box, from which you can pick one or more files on your hard drive or network.

■ **Pictures From Scanner Or Camera**   Retrieve pictures using your scanner or camera. The device must be connected to your computer when you choose this option, at which point FrontPage walks you through the process of moving the digitized picture from the scanner or camera to your computer.

Once you have created a list of pictures for the photo gallery (see Figure 5-2), you can customize how each picture and caption is displayed in the gallery.

You can also create a Photo Gallery by choosing Insert | Web Components and picking the Photo Gallery option from the Insert Web Component dialog box. Pick one of the available layouts from the dialog box (these are the same as the layout options discussed below), and click Finish to display the Photo Gallery Properties dialog box.

FrontPage displays the photos in the gallery in the same order as the list. To change the order of the pictures, select a picture in the list and click Move Up (moves the picture higher in the list) or Move Down (moves the picture lower in the list).

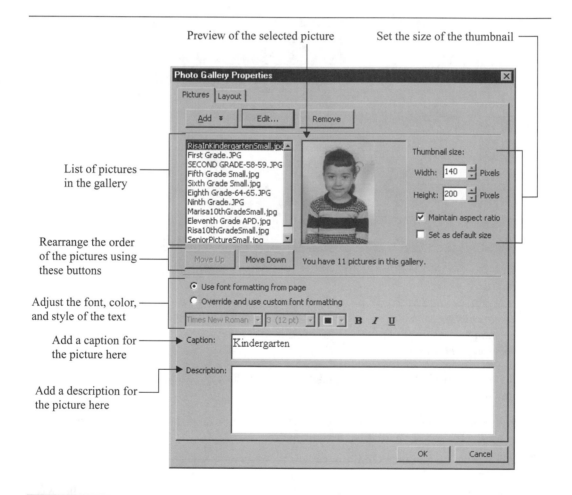

FIGURE 5-2   Work with the pictures in the gallery using the Photo Gallery Properties dialog box.

You can see a thumbnail preview of the currently selected picture in the square to the right of the picture list. You can also set the thumbnail size (in pixels) using the Width and Height spinners. If you check the Maintain Aspect Ratio check box, adjusting either dimension automatically adjusts the other dimension to maintain the original ratio of height to width and display the thumbnail without distortion. If you have a set of pictures that are all the same size, you may want to set up a thumbnail size you like and check the Set As Default Size check box so that each picture will have that thumbnail size as the default.

Each picture has two text fields: the caption and the description. Where the caption and description are displayed depends on the layout you pick for the photo gallery (more on this shortly). For example, in the Horizontal layout, the caption (normally fairly brief) is displayed immediately below the thumbnail in the photo gallery and the description is displayed underneath the caption. In the Montage layout, however, the caption appears only when you hover the pointer over a picture, and the description is not displayed at all. To create a caption and description, just type the text you want into the Caption and Description fields. You can change the font, size, color, and effects (Bold, Italic, or Underline) using the text tools immediately above the Caption field.

The last step in setting up a photo gallery is to choose a layout for your thumbnails. To do so, click on the Layout tab in the Photo Gallery Properties dialog box.

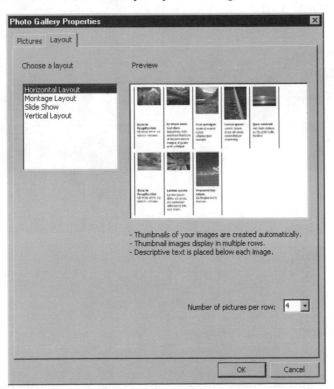

Choose a layout from the list in the left window, and view the preview in the Preview window. A textual description of the layout is provided below the Preview window. For some layouts, you can also pick the number of pictures per row from the Number Of Pictures Per Row drop-down list.

The most useful part of the textual description is the explanation of how the caption and description are displayed in that layout. This explanation keeps you from having to go back and change the layout later to get the caption and description to your liking.

Once you are done setting up the photo gallery, click OK to create the gallery. If the pictures you chose are stored outside your web site, FrontPage will offer to copy them to your web site. As always, this is highly recommended.

Edit Pictures in the Photo Gallery

The Photo Gallery Properties dialog box enables you to do a limited amount of editing on individual pictures. To edit a picture, select the picture in the list and click the Edit button to open the Edit Picture dialog box.

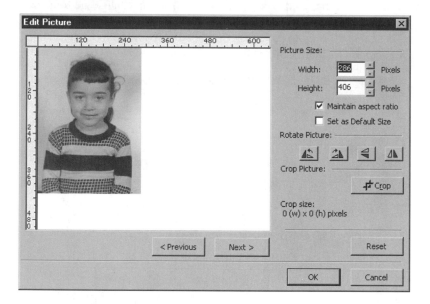

This dialog box shows a larger version of the picture than the thumbnail in the Photo Gallery Properties dialog box. You can cycle through the other pictures in the gallery using the Next and Previous buttons.

You can return the picture to the condition it was in when you opened the Edit Picture dialog box by clicking the Reset button.

Here are the editing operations you can carry out:

■ **Change the Width and Height** If you want to change the size of the picture, you can do so using the Width and Height spinners. It is advisable to leave the Maintain Aspect

Ratio check box checked so that the picture is not distorted as you adjust the dimensions. You can also check the Set As Default Size check box to set this size as the default for the other pictures in the gallery. Realize, however, that FrontPage resizes the rest of the pictures the moment you click OK to close the Edit Picture dialog box.

CAUTION   *It is not a good idea to increase the size of a small picture. When you do this, the pixels in the picture all get larger, and you can see the blockiness (called "pixelation").*

■   **Rotate or Flip the Picture**   You can rotate a picture left (counterclockwise) or right (clockwise), and flip it vertically or horizontally using the buttons in the Rotate Picture section of the dialog box.

5

 **Crop a Picture**

Pictures often contain extraneous material that detracts from the main subject, or just increases the file size of the picture (and thus the download time) without adding anything interesting to it. The Edit Picture dialog box enables you to "crop out" the unnecessary parts of the picture. To do so, use the following steps:

1.   Click the Crop button. This places a cropping rectangle in the large preview of the picture.

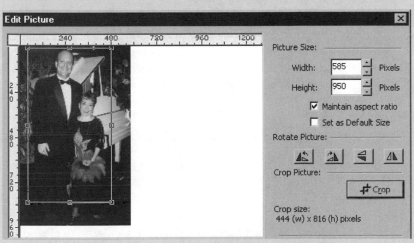

2. Use the mouse pointer to adjust the cropping rectangle. You can either click and drag a new rectangle, or click on a sizing handle and drag to resize the rectangle. The cropped size is indicated just below the Crop button.

3. Click the Crop button again. The Edit Picture dialog box crops the picture to the desired dimensions. Click OK to save the results. FrontPage saves the cropped picture and regenerates the thumbnail preview for the photo gallery.

 *FrontPage saves the cropped picture by the same name as the original, overwriting the original picture file. If you don't want to lose the uncropped picture, make sure to make a copy of it before cropping it.*

Add Shockwave Flash Movies To a Web Site

Macromedia Flash is an application that enables you to build complex animations and even simple programs. You often find Flash animations on professional web sites, and you can add a Shockwave Flash movie to your FrontPage web site.

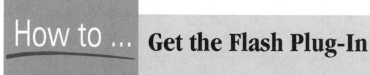

How to ...   Get the Flash Plug-In

To play a Shockwave Flash file you need a special "plug-in" from Macromedia. If you already have the plug-in on your computer, you can view the Flash file in the Preview Page view or when you preview the page in a browser. If you don't have the plug-in, the Flash file will not be visible in Preview Page view, or in a browser. To easily obtain the plug-in, add a Shockwave Flash file to a web page as described below, then use the following steps:

1. Connect to the Internet.

2. Open the page containing the Shockwave Flash file and preview the page in a browser.

3. After a few moments, a dialog box will appear asking if you want to download and install the Macromedia Flash player. The dialog box varies, depending on which browser you are running:

    ■ For Internet Explorer, click OK and wait while the Flash player downloads and installs. When it is done, the Shockwave Flash file will begin to play.

    ■ For Netscape Navigator, click the Get the Plug-in button and follow the instructions on the web page to download and install the plug-in.

Place a Flash File on a Web Page

To add a Flash file to a web page, choose Insert | Picture | Flash and choose the Flash file from the Select Flash File dialog box (which is a standard File Open dialog box). Click Insert to place the file on the page.

5

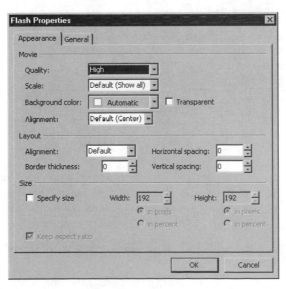

Unlike images and clip art, FrontPage does not give you a chance to save the Flash file into the web site (with the Save Embedded Images dialog box) when you save the web page. Thus, it is best to import the Flash files into your web site before placing them on the page.

Configure the Flash File

You can configure the Flash file by choosing Flash Properties from the shortcut menu for the Flash file.

The options in the Layout and Size sections of the Appearance tab work just like the Picture Properties dialog box, covered in Chapter 4. The rest of the options allow you to do the following:

- ■ **Choose the Quality of Playback**   Use the Quality drop-down list to choose the quality of playback. Low-quality playback loads and plays faster, but looks blocky. High-quality playback takes longer to load, but looks better and is more smoothly animated.

- **Scale** Some Flash files have a border, and you can choose to turn the border off (choose No Border) or minimize the border to a small area around the file (choose Exact Fit) using the Scale drop-down list. To return to the default scale, choose Default (Show All).

- **Background Color** Many Flash files have a color designated as the Background Color. You can choose the background color from the Background Color drop-down list, or allow the page to show through the areas of the Flash file that use the background color. To do so, click the Transparent check box.

- **Alignment** Use the Alignment drop-down list to align the Flash file *within* the area allotted for display of the file. This effect is most noticeable when you set the Scale to Default (Show All).

In the General tab of the Flash Properties dialog box, only a few of the fields are of interest.

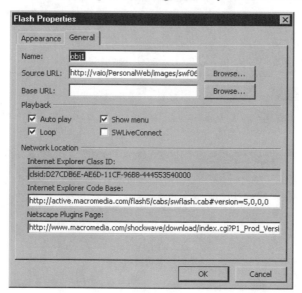

- **Adjust the Source** As mentioned earlier, FrontPage does not automatically prompt you to save the Flash file to your web site. If you set up the Flash file and then realize that you need to import it into your web site, you can do so, then use the Source URL field in the General tab to redirect the source of the file to its new location in your web site.

- **Auto Play** Check the Auto Play check box to have the Flash file start playing as soon as the web page loads.

- **Loop** Check the Loop check box to have the Flash File loop continuously. If you don't check the Loop check box, the animation will play only once.

- **Show menu** If you check the Show menu check box, a shortcut menu is available when someone right-clicks the Flash file in a browser. This menu includes the ability to zoom in and out, change the quality, stop and start playing the animation, turn looping on and off, and rewind or fast forward the animation.

Chapter 6

Format the Page

How to...

■ Set page background and colors

■ Set page margins

■ Set up workgroup properties

■ Apply themes to pages and sites

■ Modify theme characteristics

■ Add banners, comments, dates, and times to a page

Now that you've learned how to create a page and add text, graphics, and some fancy effects, you need to learn how to apply formatting that applies to the page as a whole. This formatting includes specifying the page background, applying "themes" (coordinated sets of colors and bullets), setting margins, and managing pages with the workgroup tools.

Set Page Properties

You can set many properties for your web pages using the Page Properties dialog box.

To open the Page Properties dialog box, right-click anywhere on the page and choose Page Properties from the shortcut menu. Alternatively, you can choose File | Properties.

The Page Properties dialog box has several tabs, and we'll cover most of them in this chapter. Some page properties (such as the Default Target Frame) will be deferred for discussion in later chapters.

Set the General Properties

From the General tab, you can change the title of the page by typing it in the Title field, and a description by typing it into the Page Description field. You can also add a background sound to play when the reader first enters the page. To add a background sound, type the path to the sound file in the Location field of the Background Sound section, or click the Browse button to open the Background Sound dialog box and pick the sound file. Then click OK to pick the sound and return to the Page Properties dialog box. Choose the number of times you want to repeat the sound from the Loop spinner. You can choose to loop forever by checking the Forever check box, but this can become very annoying!

Specify the Formatting

The Formatting tab of the Page Properties dialog box is only available if the page does not have a theme assigned to it.

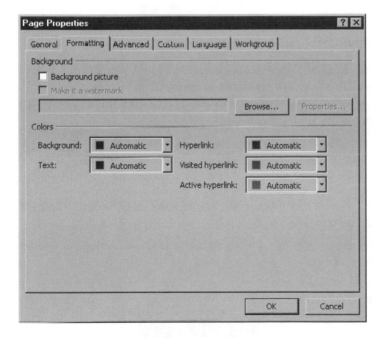

When a page does have a theme, the Formatting tab is missing.

Assign Background and Text Colors

To use a single color for the page background, click the Background drop-down list in the Colors section of the Formatting tab. This displays the standard Color tool, covered in Chapter 3. Choose the color you want to use from the Color tool. You can also pick a default color for all the text on the page from the Text drop-down list. This text color can be overridden by assigning colors to specific text on the page.

Assign Hyperlink Colors

You can assign colors to the three types of hyperlinks: Hyperlink (a hyperlink you have not visited), Visited Hyperlink (hyperlinks that you have visited), and Active Hyperlink (the currently selected hyperlink). Be sure to choose distinct colors for these different types of hyperlinks, as most people (including me) use the color cues to remember whether they have been to the hyperlink's destination. Clicking any of these drop-down lists displays the standard Color tool.

Assign a Background Picture

If you wish, you can use a picture as the background for the page. Remember that a busy picture will make the page exceedingly hard to read, so you should pick a simple picture, such as a subdued texture.

To add a background picture, use the following steps:

1. Check the Background Picture check box.

2. If you want to use the Watermark feature, check the Watermark check box. Normally, when you scroll a page that contains a background picture, the picture scrolls too. However, when you use the Watermark feature, the background picture remains stationary—that is, the page scrolls over the background picture.

NOTE   *You can only see the effect of the watermark in Preview mode. The Design Page mode always scrolls the background picture.*

3. Type the path to the background picture, or click the Browse button to open the Select Background Picture dialog box. Choose a background picture and click OK to return to the Page Properties dialog box.

4. Choose OK to close the Page Properties dialog box and display the web page with the background picture (see Figure 6-1).

5. When you save the web page, you'll see the Save Embedded Files dialog box if the background picture is not part of the current web site. Save the images into your web site, as discussed in Chapter 4.

Set Up Page Margins

You can set the top, left, bottom, and right margins of the page from the Advanced tab of the Page Properties dialog box. The margins are all specified in pixels.

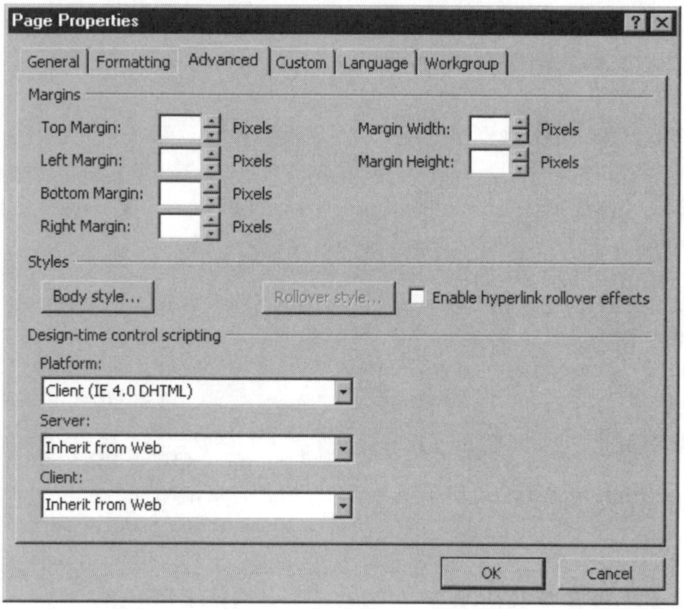
Page Properties
General
Formatting
Advanced
Custom
Language
Workgroup
Margins
Top Margin: Pixels
Left Margin: Pixels
Bottom Margin: Pixels
Right Margin: Pixels
Margin Width: Pixels
Margin Height: Pixels
Styles
Body style...
Rollover style...
Enable hyperlink rollover effects
Design-time control scripting
Platform:
Client (IE 4.0 DHTML)
Server:
Inherit from Web
Client:
Inherit from Web
OK
Cancel

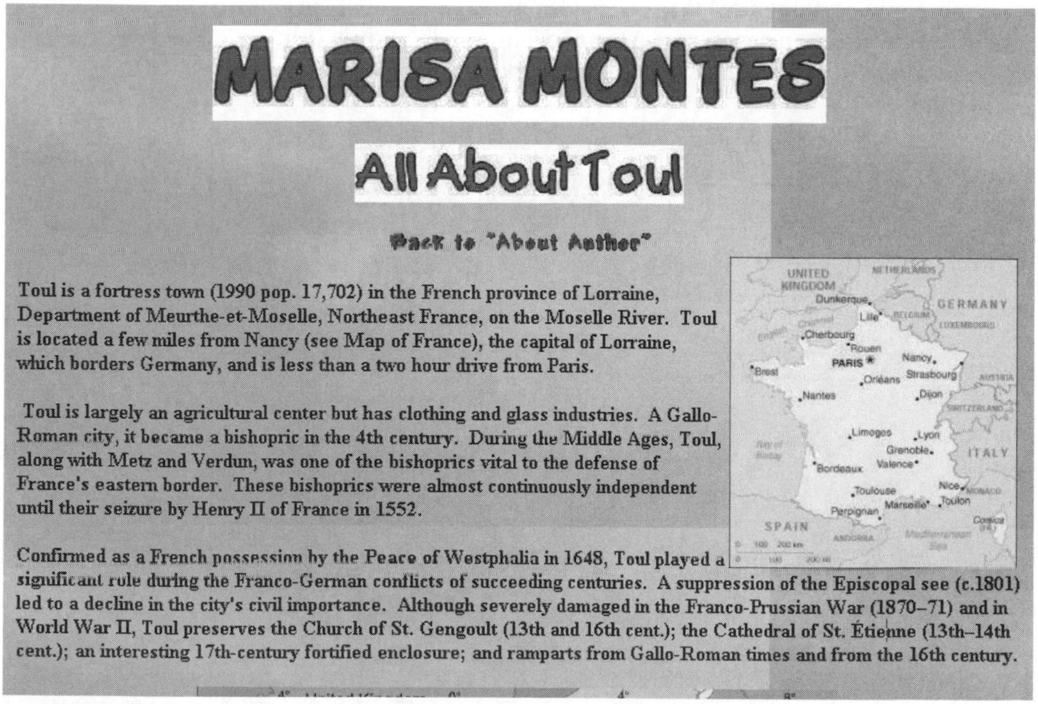
MARISA MONTES
All About Toul
Back to "About Author"
Toul is a fortress town (1990 pop. 17,702) in the French province of Lorraine, Department of Meurthe-et-Moselle, Northeast France, on the Moselle River. Toul is located a few miles from Nancy (see Map of France), the capital of Lorraine, which borders Germany, and is less than a two hour drive from Paris.
Toul is largely an agricultural center but has clothing and glass industries. A Gallo-Roman city, it became a bishopric in the 4th century. During the Middle Ages, Toul, along with Metz and Verdun, was one of the bishoprics vital to the defense of France's eastern border. These bishoprics were almost continuously independent until their seizure by Henry II of France in 1552.
Confirmed as a French possession by the Peace of Westphalia in 1648, Toul played a significant role during the Franco-German conflicts of succeeding centuries. A suppression of the Episcopal see (c.1801) led to a decline in the city's civil importance. Although severely damaged in the Franco-Prussian War (1870–71) and in World War II, Toul preserves the Church of St. Gengoult (13th and 16th cent.); the Cathedral of St. Étienne (13th–14th cent.); an interesting 17th-century fortified enclosure; and ramparts from Gallo-Roman times and from the 16th century.
UNITED KINGDOM
GERMANY
Dunkerque
Lille
Cherbourg
Rouen
PARIS
Nancy
Strasbourg
Brest
Orléans
Nantes
Dijon
Limoges
Lyon
Grenoble
ITALY
Bordeaux
Valence
Toulouse
Nice
Toulon
Perpignan
Marseille
SPAIN

FIGURE 6-1 A page with a background picture can add pizzazz—as long as you don't overdo it!

You can also provide values for the Margin Width and Margin Height, but there is no apparent effect from setting these quantities.

Enable Hyperlink Rollover Effects

A rather neat effect is hyperlink rollovers (see Figure 6-2). If you have these enabled and you move your mouse pointer over a hyperlink, the properties of the hyperlink change to call attention to the hyperlink. You have quite a bit of control over these effects.

To activate hyperlink rollover effects, check the Enable Hyperlink Rollover Effects check box in the Advanced tab of the Page Properties dialog box. Then click the Rollover Style button to open the Font dialog box.

All the text options discussed in Chapter 3 are available, including changing the font, color, size, style, and effects. You can also switch to the Character Spacing tab to adjust the spacing (Normal, Expanded, or Condensed) and Position (Subscript, Superscript, and so forth).

When you have the effect set up just the way you want, click OK in the Font dialog box. Click OK in the Page Properties dialog box and switch to Preview to see the hyperlink rollover effect in action.

Manage Your Pages with Workgroup Properties

FrontPage provides some powerful tools for managing the construction of your web site. These tools are especially useful if more than one person is participating in the construction, because you can categorize the web pages, assign them to individuals, and set their review and publishing status. All these tasks can be completed from the Workgroup tab of the Page Properties dialog box.

Regular Hyperlink:

Jump to Home Page

Rollover Hyperlink:

Jump to Home Page

FIGURE 6-2   With hyperlink rollover effects, a hyperlink can really call attention to itself.

NOTE   *Many of the properties you set here can be adjusted using FrontPage's reports (see Chapter 16).*

6

Work with Categories

When creating a web site with a workgroup, you can use categories to classify web pages. Sample categories include Business, Competition, Goals/Objectives, In Process, and Waiting. Using such categories, you can assign not only what part of your business or project the web page belongs in, but also the current state of the page. You can assign multiple categories to a page, and create new categories if the categories supplied with FrontPage don't meet your needs. The current categories assigned to a page are visible in the Item(s) Belong To These Categories field (this field can't be edited—it is for display only).

To assign a page to a category, check the category's check box in the Available Categories list box. To remove a category from a page, clear the check box.

You can adjust the list of categories by clicking the Categories button to display the Master Category List dialog box.

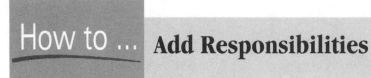

How to ... Add Responsibilities

You can assign web pages to someone, making it his or her responsibility to create or enhance the web page. Realize, however, that you can type anyone's name (or anything else, for that matter) as the responsible party, and FrontPage does not validate the entry.

To assign a page to someone, you can choose a name from the Assigned To drop-down list or type a name into the field. New names you type into the list are not automatically added to the list of available names. You won't be able to choose this new name from the drop-down list for another web page unless you add the name to the list of names. To add names to the drop-down list (making them available on any page), click the Names button to open the Usernames Master List dialog box.

To add a name, type the name into the New Username field and click the Add button. To remove a name, select the name in the list box and click the Remove button. To reset the list to the default, click the Reset button.

From this dialog box, you can do the following:

■ **Remove a Category** If you are not going to use a category, you can select it in the list box and click the Remove button. The category disappears from the Master Category List and is also removed from the list for any pages that were assigned to it.

- **Add a Category**   To add a new category, type the new category in the New Category field. Then click the Add button to add the category to the list. This category will now be available in the Available Categories list box for all pages.

- **Reset the Category List**   If you add or remove any categories, the Reset button becomes available. Clicking it returns the list to the default, removing any added categories and adding back any deleted categories.

Set the Review Status

If you have developed a methodology for creating web pages, a page may go through several stages of review, including management approval, legal, and marketing review. To keep track of the current status of a web page, you can use the Review Status drop-down list. To record the current status, either choose the status from the drop-down list or type in a status. Like the Assigned To list (see the previous section), a new status you type into the list is not automatically added to the list of available statuses. You won't be able to choose this new status from the drop-down list for another web page unless you add the status to the list of statuses.

To add a new status to the list of statuses available in the Review Status drop-down list, click the Statuses button. This opens the Review Status Master List dialog box. This dialog box looks like the Master Category List and the Usernames Master List dialog boxes. To add a status, type the status into the New Review Status field and click the Add button. To remove a status, select the status in the list box and click the Remove button. To reset the list to the default, click the Reset button.

Set the Publish Status

A page has one of two publishing statuses: Publish or Don't Publish. If you set the status to Publish, the page will be published to your site's web host server the next time you use FrontPage to publish your web site. Conversely, if you set the status to Don't Publish, the page will not be published to the host server. This feature can be handy when you have added pages to your site that you don't want viewed by the outside world.

To change the publishing status to Don't Publish, check the Exclude This File When Publishing The Rest Of The Web check box. Clear this check box to return the page publishing status to Publish. When the status is set to Don't Publish, the page appears in the Folder List with a small red x on its icon.

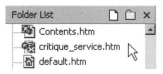

NOTE   *You can also adjust the publishing status directly in the Folder List. To do so, right-click on a page and select Don't Publish from the shortcut menu. This menu item is a toggle: if it is already checked, selecting it again will return to the page to Publish status.*

Work with Themes

A theme is a collection of properties you can apply to selected pages or to your whole web site. These properties include a coordinated palette of colors, button styles, bullet styles, page background properties (graphic, color, rollover effect), and text styles. The purpose of a theme is to give a consistent look to your site. To pick a theme for your page or site, use the Themes Task Pane, shown in Figure 6-3.

Apply Themes to Pages or a Site

To apply a theme to a page or a site, open the Themes Task Pane by choosing Format | Theme. The Themes Task Pane displays the following information:

- **Current Theme** At the top of the Task Pane is the current theme—that is, the theme (if any) attached to the currently selected page. This page may be selected in the Folder List, Web Site Folders view, Navigation view, or Hyperlinks view. Or, it may be the open page in the main window area. If you select multiple pages in either the Folder List or the Web Site Folders view, the current theme reflects the last-selected page.

- **Web Site Default Theme** If you assigned a default theme for the entire web site (which can be overridden on a page-by-page basis), the web site default theme identifies which theme that is.

- **Recently Used Themes** Any themes you've applied to a page appear in the Recently Used Themes portion of the Task Pane.

- **All Available Themes** All available themes are displayed in this section of the Task Pane, including the web site default theme and recently used themes.

To apply a theme, move the mouse over the theme you want to use. A down arrow appears on the theme thumbnail. Click the down arrow to display the shortcut menu.

To apply the theme to the whole web site, choose Apply As Default Theme from the shortcut menu. The theme is applied to all pages to which you did not apply an individual theme. To apply a theme to a set of pages, select the pages you want and choose Apply To Selected Page(s) from the shortcut menu.

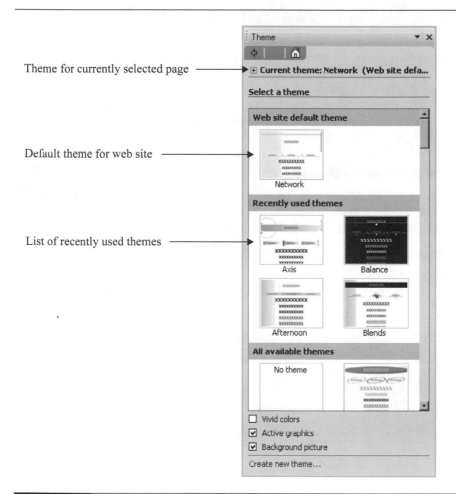

Theme for currently selected page

Default theme for web site

List of recently used themes

FIGURE 6-3   The Themes Task Pane shows you a preview of what a theme looks like, as well as providing the tools for customizing a theme.

TIP   *The easiest way to select a set of pages to apply a theme to is from the Folder List or the Web Site Folders view. All other views that display pages (such as the Web Site Navigation view or Hyperlinks view) enable you to select only a single page at a time.*

Set Theme Options

You can modify some of the options associated with a theme using the three check boxes at the bottom of the Themes Task Pane. The available options are

■ **Vivid Colors**   Provides a brighter set of theme colors.

■ **Active Graphics** Converts the buttons and bullets into Dynamic HTML elements that support DHTML formatting (discussed in Chapter 14).

■ **Background Picture** Some themes include both a background color and a background graphic. Themes only use one of these options at a time, and those themes that include both either use the background graphic or the color as the default. By checking the Background Picture check box, you can override the color default and use the background picture instead. By clearing the check box, you can override the background picture default and use the color instead.

Modify the Properties of a Theme

FrontPage provides many themes, and one may be perfect for you to use just the way it is. If you want to modify a theme to make it more to your liking, however, FrontPage provides all the tools you need. To modify a theme, open the Themes Task Pane and either choose Customize from a theme shortcut menu or click the Create New Theme hyperlink near the bottom of the Task Pane. Choosing Customize from the shortcut menu enables you to use the selected theme as a starting point, whereas clicking Create New Theme enables you to start building a theme from a generic starting point. Either way, FrontPage displays the Customize Theme dialog box, which displays the current properties of the theme as well as three buttons: Colors, Graphics, and Text.

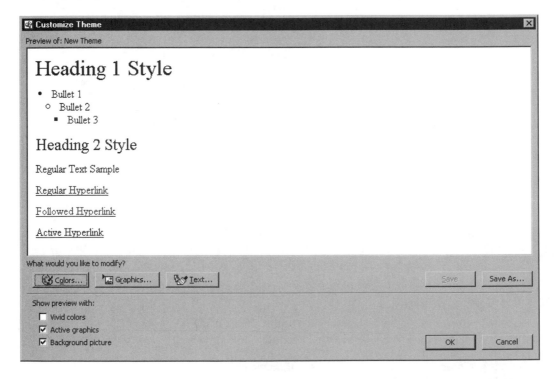

Modify Theme Colors

To modify the theme's colors, click the Colors button to open the Customize Theme dialog box. This dialog box contains three different methods for modifying a theme's colors. Each method has its own tab. The first tab is Color Schemes, shown here:

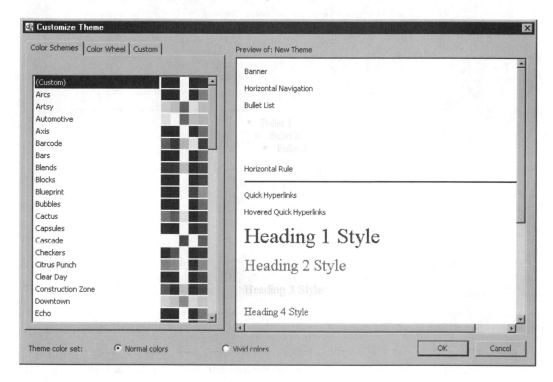

The Color Schemes tab enables you to choose a color scheme from another theme. To do so, choose the name of the theme whose color scheme you want to use from the list of themes on the left side of the dialog box. Click the Vivid Colors option to use a richer color set. The Preview Of area on the right side of the dialog box shows you how your choice will look. Choosing an already defined color scheme is useful in giving you a starting point for making further color modifications. You can also create a theme that combines a color scheme from one theme with custom graphics and text specifications.

The Color Wheel tab (see Figure 6-4) contains a color wheel from which you can choose a specific color. However, note that selecting a color in the color wheel actually changes all the colors in the scheme, not just one color. To make a color selection, either click anywhere in the

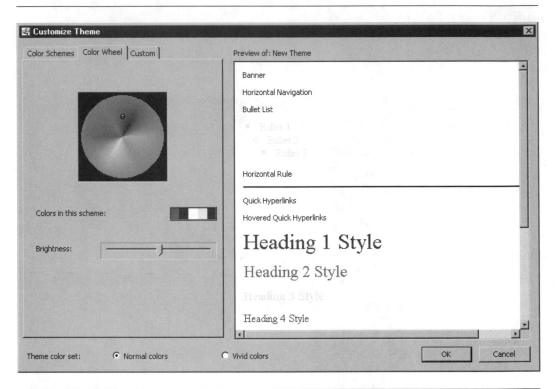

FIGURE 6-4 Use the Color Wheel tab to choose a set of colors and their brightness.

color wheel or click the tiny round cursor in the color wheel and drag it to the color you want to use. Adjust the brightness of the color set using the Brightness slider. As you make changes, the Preview Of area shows what your selection of colors will look like.

The last tab, Custom (see Figure 6-5), enables you to select individual colors for each element in the theme. To do so, choose the item whose color you want to modify from the Item drop-down list. Then click the Color drop-down list to display the standard Color tool. Pick the color you want from the available colors or click More Colors to open the More Colors dialog box and pick any color your computer can display. Continue choosing items and assigning colors until you have a set of colors you are happy with.

Modify Theme Graphics

You can change the graphics assigned to any element of a theme. You can change the background graphic and the graphics assigned to bullets, hyperlinks, buttons, and so on. If the element also includes text (as banners and many navigation buttons do), you can also change the text

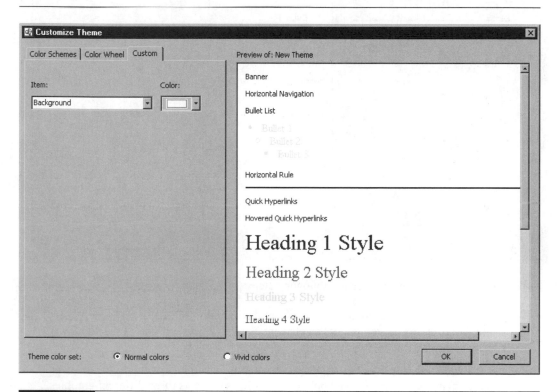

FIGURE 6-5   Use the Custom tab to define individual colors for each element in a theme.

6

characteristics. Clicking the Graphics button in the Customize Theme dialog box displays the following version of the dialog box:

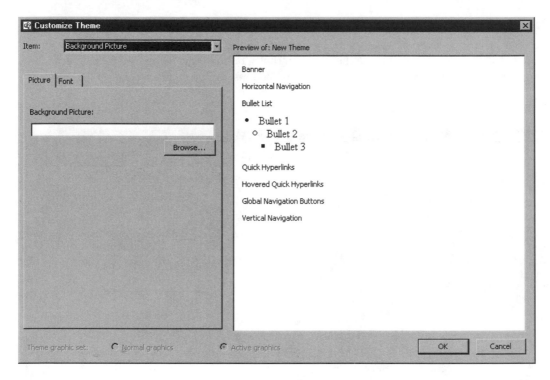

To change a graphic element, use the following steps:

1. Choose the element you want to change from the Item drop-down list at the top of the dialog box. As soon as you choose an element, the Preview Of portion of the window adjusts to display that element.

2. In the Picture tab, specify the graphic you want to use for the element. Some elements (such as many of the buttons and bullets) may use as many as three different graphics: the graphic used for the "normal" picture, the graphic used for the "selected" picture, and the graphic used for the "hovered" picture (used when you move the mouse pointer over the button). If the element does use multiple graphics, you can specify all the graphics in the Picture tab. Use the Browse button alongside each Picture field to open the Open File dialog box and choose an image to use.

3. If the selected element includes a text component, switch to the Font tab.

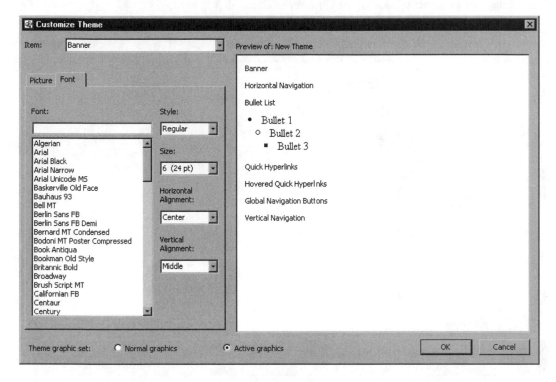

4. Choose a font from the list of fonts on the left side of the Font tab. If the selected element uses multiple fonts (for example, one for each of the button states discussed in step 2), the list of fonts is displayed in the Font field, separated by commas. You can customize your list by selecting your own desired fonts. Be sure to use the same number of fonts as were initially displayed in the Font field.

5. Choose a style, size, horizontal alignment, and vertical alignment from the appropriate drop-down lists.

Modify Theme Text

The last modification you can make is to change the text characteristics of theme elements that do not have a graphic associated with them. These include the body text and all the headings. To make changes to these text-only elements, click the Text button in the main Themes dialog box. This displays still another version of the Customize Theme dialog box.

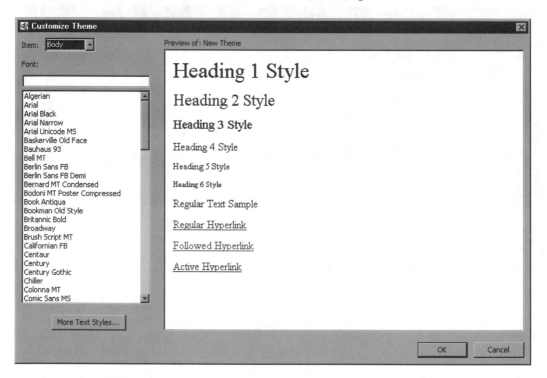

Choose the element you want to change from the Item drop-down list. Then choose the font you want to use from the list of fonts located just below the Font field.

Save Your Theme Changes

Two other buttons also appear in the Customize Themes dialog box: Save and Save As. Use the Save button to save your changes to the currently selected theme, overwriting the theme. The Save As button saves your changes to a new theme (this is much safer). When you select the Save As button, you must enter a new name for the theme in the Save Theme dialog box that appears. Clicking OK in the Save Theme dialog box saves your theme under its new name, and the new theme is then available in the list of themes.

Add Page-Based Elements

You can customize your web page further by adding a page banner, comments, and a timestamp. You can also set up the transition used to make the page appear when the reader opens the page in a browser (called a page transition).

Title Your Page with a Page Banner

A page banner is a special header for a page. It always appears at the top of the page, and can consist of either just text or text and a graphic. However, if you do choose to include a graphic in the page banner, you can't pick the graphic yourself—you can only use the banner graphic for the page's theme. If the page does not include a theme, you can't use a graphic in the page banner.

> **TIP**   *If you want to include a graphic banner on a page that does not have a theme, and the banner is the only thing on the page you want to have associated with a graphic image, create a small empty graphic using any graphics tool, and call it empty.jpg. Create a theme that associates every graphic element except the banner with empty.jpg. Create the graphic you want to use for the banner, and associate the banner with that graphic.*

To create a page banner, choose Insert | Page Banner. FrontPage opens the Page Banner Properties dialog box:

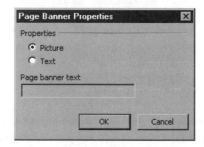

Choose either the Picture or Text option, and fill in the text of the page banner in the Page Banner Text field. This text appears regardless of which option you picked. Click OK to create the page banner.

> **NOTE**   *The text field is only available if you have added the page to the Navigation view. Also, the default text that appears in the Page Banner Properties dialog box is the page's title in the Navigation view. If you change the text, you are also changing the page title in the Navigation view.*

Once you create the page banner, you can change its properties by right-clicking it and choosing Page Banner Properties from the shortcut menu. More importantly, you can also choose Font or Paragraph from either the shortcut menu or the Format menu to change the font, size, style, effects, and alignment of the page banner. You can also use the tools in the Formatting toolbar.

> **NOTE**   *Unlike normal text, you can't select and change the font or paragraph properties of only a portion of the page banner—your changes apply to all the text in the banner.*

Add Comments

If you have ever taken any programming classes, one of the first things you learned was to add comments to your code so someone else could figure out what you have done. Comments are also helpful in reminding you what *you* did and why you did it. The same is true of web pages.

FrontPage enables you to add comments to your web pages, as shown in Figure 6-6. Comments are a special kind of text. You can see them in the normal Page view in FrontPage, but they don't display in a web browser or in the preview Page view.

CAUTION *Your comments are visible if a reader views the HTML source for your page. So word your comments carefully to avoid embarrassing yourself!*

To add comments to your web page, choose Insert | Comment. This opens the simple Comment dialog box, where you can enter the text of the comment. When you close the Comment dialog box, the comment is inserted into the web page at the text cursor location.

To change the text of a comment after you have added it to the web page, right-click the comment and choose Comment Properties from the shortcut menu. The Comment dialog box appears again, with the existing text of the comment already present. Make any changes to the text and click OK. You can change the font and paragraph properties by selecting the text of the Comment and choosing Font or Paragraph from either the comment's shortcut menu or the Format menu, or by using the tools in the Formatting toolbar. Your changes apply to all the text in the comment—as with the page banner, you can't change just a portion of the text in the comment.

TIP *Although you can set the font color of a comment, FrontPage overrides any changes you make to this one property and always displays comments in the default purple. However, if you are really determined to change the comment color, you can. Select the comment and switch to the Code Page view. At the beginning of the highlighted line of HTML that defines the comment, you'll see something like "webbot bot = PurpleText". Change PurpleText to some other color, such as "RedText", and the color of the comment will change!*

A line of text aligned at the bottom of the graphic

Comment: This page displays the various graphic alignments, and how they relate to text. Set the graphic alignment from the Picture Properties dialog box.

FIGURE 6-6   Add comments to your web pages to help you remember what you did.

Add a Date and Time

When you are building many web pages, it is very handy to be able to keep track of the last time a page was modified. It can also be helpful to people viewing your web page to have this information. You have the option of inserting just a date, just a time, or a date and time. You can also decide whether the date/time should reflect when the page was last edited or when the page was last automatically updated.

To add a date and time to a page, choose Insert | Date and Time to display the Date and Time Properties dialog box.

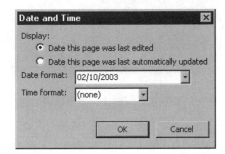

Make the following selections from the Date and Time Properties dialog box:

- **Date Format**   Select (None) from the Date Format drop-down list to suppress the date. Otherwise, choose the format of the date you want to display from this drop-down list. Formats available include a variety of orders for the month, day, and year, both two- and four-place years, and formats that include spelling out the day of the week and month name.

- **Time Format**   Select (None) from the Time Format drop-down list to suppress the time. Otherwise, choose the format of the time you want to display from this drop-down list. Formats available include both A.M./P.M. and 24-hour formats, varying degrees of precision, and the ability to show the difference between local time and Greenwich mean time (the formats that include TZ, for time zone).

You can change the font and paragraph properties by selecting the date/time and choosing Font or Paragraph from either the Date/Time's shortcut menu or the Format menu, or by using the tools in the Formatting toolbar. Your changes apply to all the text in the date/time—as with the page banner, you can't change just a portion of the text in the date/time.

Transition Between Pages

If you've worked with Microsoft PowerPoint, you are probably familiar with page transitions—special effects that take place as a PowerPoint slide is displayed or exited. Such effects go by names such as wipes, fade ins, blinds, and so on. You can use page transition effects with FrontPage web pages as well. In addition, you can apply a transition effect when the user enters or leaves the site.

To attach a page transition, open the web page to which you want to attach page transitions. Choose Format | Page Transition to display the Page Transitions dialog box.

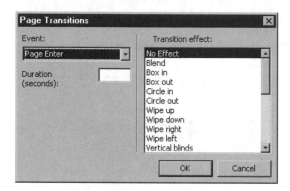

From the Page Transitions dialog box, make the following selections:

■ **Event**   From the Event drop-down list, choose when the selected transition will occur. Your choices are to have the transition occur when the page is entered, when the page is exited, when the site is entered, and when the site is exited. There can, of course, be only one type of transition for the Site Entered and Site Exited choices.

■ **Duration (seconds)**   You can vary how long the transition effect goes on. It's a good idea to keep the transitions short (if you use them at all—I don't) because they can quickly become annoying when the person just wants to see the page. Enter the duration in seconds. You can include a decimal point (for example, 4.5 seconds).

■ **Transition Effect**   Select the transition effect you want from the Transition Effect list box.

You can set page transitions for multiple events on a page. Simply go back and select a different event from the Event drop-down list and specify the other quantities.

NOTE   *To preview the transition, switch to the Preview page mode.*

Chapter 7 Work with Tables

How to...

- Insert or draw a table
- Add, delete, and modify rows and columns
- Split a table
- Modify cells
- Set table properties
- Fill a table with data
- Convert text to tables and tables to text
- Build tables using Word and Excel
- Layout text and graphics using Layout Tables
- Apply visual elements to cells in a Layout Table

Tables are exceedingly useful tools when building a web page. With tables, it is easy to line up items on the page in rows and columns, giving the page the layout you want. Many two-column and three-column lists on web pages are actually contained in a table. You may not realize this because the outlines of the table can be made invisible. Tables are also very useful for aligning images on a page.

Although tables have been used for a long time to align objects, FrontPage also includes a special type of table specifically designed for just this purpose—the *layout table*. These tables allow much finer control over the size of cells, and thus of the objects on a page.

Understand Basic Table Concepts

FrontPage tables are similar to tables in other Microsoft Office applications. For example, if you have ever worked with tables in Microsoft Word, you are already familiar with many of the features of FrontPage tables, although FrontPage tables give you many more configuration options. In fact, as you'll see later in this chapter, it is easy to convert a Word table into a FrontPage table.

The basic premise of tables is that they arrange information into rows and columns (see Figure 7-1). The intersection of each row and column is referred to as a *cell*, much like the cells in a spreadsheet. You can place any information you want into a cell—text, graphics, hyperlinks, and even another table.

Insert a Table

The simplest way to add a table to a web page is to insert it (you can also draw a table, covered in the next section). There are two ways to insert a table: from the Standard toolbar and from the Table menu.

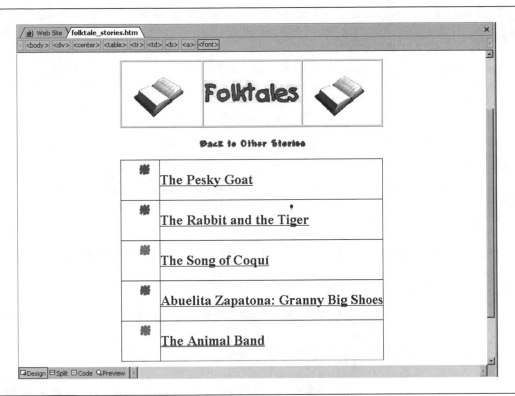

FIGURE 7-1   A table makes it easy to arrange information into rows and columns.

Insert a Table from the Standard Toolbar

To insert a table from the Standard toolbar, click the Insert Table button. FrontPage displays a small worksheet from which you can choose the number of rows and columns you want in your table. Drag the mouse pointer over the worksheet. As you do, the status line at the bottom of the worksheet tells you how many rows and columns will be present when you release the left mouse button to create the table.

You aren't limited to choosing a table that is the initial size of the worksheet. If you drag the mouse pointer past the initial boundaries of the worksheet, the worksheet will grow to add more rows or columns.

Once you release the left mouse button, the table appears.

After you create a table—or anytime the text cursor is located within the boundaries of a table—FrontPage displays the Tables toolbar (see Figure 7-2). This toolbar contains a set of tools for modifying table properties, which will be discussed throughout this section.

If the Tables toolbar does not appear when the cursor is within a table, choose View | Toolbars | Tables to turn the Tables toolbar on.

The Draw Layout Table, Draw Layout Cell, Insert Vertical Layout Cell and Insert Horizontal Layout Cell tools are used only with Layout tables. These will be covered in "Work with Page Layout Tables," later in this chapter.

Insert a Table from the Table Menu and Set the Properties

To insert a table into a web page using the Table menu, choose Table | Insert | Table. This displays the Insert Table dialog box.

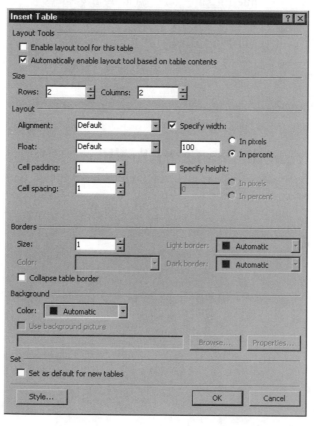

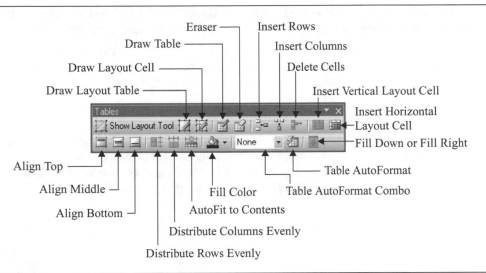

FIGURE 7-2   Use the tools in the Tables toolbar to quickly modify the properties and contents of a table.

Use the fields in the Insert Table dialog box to configure the table as follows:

- **Enable layout tool for this table**   If you wish to use the table layout tools (see "Work With Page Layout Tables," later in this chapter) right away, check the Enable Layout Tool For This Table check box. This check box is checked automatically if at any point you use any of the table layout tools to modify the table. You can clear the check box to hide the table layout tools.

- **Automatically enable layout tool based on table contents**   Certain types of table content—especially content from the various web templates—will automatically turn on the table layout tools if you check this check box. If you don't want the table layout tools turned on automatically, clear this check box.

- **Specify the number of rows**   Use the Rows spinner to set the number of rows in the table. You can also type the number of rows into this field.

- **Specify the number of columns**   Use the Columns spinner to set the number of columns in the table. You can also type the number of columns into this field.

- **Set the table alignment**   Use the Alignment drop-down list to specify whether you want the table against the left margin, the right margin, or centered on the page. Note that if you specify the width of the table to be 100 percent of the page width, the table alignment setting doesn't really change anything. Also note that if you leave the Table Float set to Default (see the next bullet point), you cannot type text alongside the table—any text you type will appear below the bottom of the table.

- **Set the table float**   If you set the float (using the Float drop-down list) to anything other than Default, it overrides the value of the alignment. That is, if you set the alignment to Center but set the float to Left, the table will be aligned with the left side of the page. Unlike Alignment, however, Float does allow text alongside the table.

■ **Set the cell padding**   Use the Cell Padding spinner to specify the amount of white space (in pixels) you want between the cell's contents and the inside edge of the cell boundary. You can override this quantity on a cell-by-cell basis.

■ **Set the cell spacing**   Use the Cell Spacing spinner to specify the amount of white space (in pixels) you want between cells.

■ **Set the width of the table**   If you want to specify the width of the table, check the Specify Width check box. You can set the width in either pixels or in percent by choosing the appropriate option. Type the width into the Specify Width text field. When you add contents into the cells, the table height will expand to maintain the specified width.

TIP   *Be careful about specifying the width of the table in pixels. If the reader has a browser set to a lower resolution than yours—which renders objects larger than a high-resolution display—the table could spill off the side of the screen, forcing the reader to scroll back and forth to see the table contents. It is much better to set the table width in percent, as the browser will then scale the table so that no horizontal scrolling is necessary (assuming you don't set the table width to a value greater than 100 percent).*

■ **Set the height of the table**   If you want to specify the height of the table, check the Specify Height check box. You can set the height in either pixels or percent by choosing the appropriate option. Type the height into the Specify Height text field. Note that if you specify a height that is too small to contain the contents of the table, FrontPage will ignore the specified height.

■ **Set the border size**   Use the Size spinner in the Borders section to set the thickness of the table border in pixels. A value of 0 specifies no border.

NOTE   *If you choose a border size of 0, the table and cells are outlined in dotted lines in the normal Page view so you can tell where the table is. However, these outlines are not visible in the Preview mode or when viewed with a browser.*

■ **Set the border color**   This option is only available if the page containing the table does not use a theme. To set a single color for the table border, click the Color drop-down list and choose a color from the standard color tool. This color is used both for the table border and as the default for the cell border (but you can override the cell border color if you wish). If you want a two-color border scheme, pick one color from the Light Border drop-down list and another from the Dark Border drop-down list. With a two-color scheme, FrontPage uses the light border color for the left and top borders, and the dark border color for the right and bottom borders. These colors are also used as the default cell border colors, but the color is scheme is reversed—that is, the light border color is used for the right and bottom borders, and the dark border color is used for the left and top borders.

■ **Collapse table border**   When the Collapse Table border check box is cleared, each cell in the table has its own complete set of borders (as shown in the top table in Figure 7-3). However, if you clear this check box, each cell shares borders with its neighbors. If you set the color of the cell borders to different values for adjacent cells (as discussed later in this chapter), you get a conflict. Basically, when this happens, a cell controls the color of its right and bottom border (as shown in the bottom table in Figure 7-3). Since, for example, the cell to the left controls *its* right (and bottom) borders, the left border of the selected cell is actually controlled by the border color for the cell to its left.

■ **Set the background color**   You can set the background color for the table by selecting the color from the Color drop-down list in the Background section. This background color also serves as the default background color for all the cells, although you can override the background color on a cell-by-cell basis. To add a background picture to the table, check the Use Background Picture check box and specify the picture to use. If the image is smaller than the table, it is tiled to fill the entire table. As with other backgrounds, it is best not to use a very detailed graphic as a background image.

■ **Set as default for new tables**   If you want the table properties to be used for any new tables you create, check the Set As Default For New Tables check box. You can, of course, then customize any new tables by using the Table Properties dialog box.

When you are done setting the table's initial properties, click the OK button to create the table. At any time, you can go back and adjust the table properties by right-clicking in the table and choosing Table Properties from the shortcut menu.

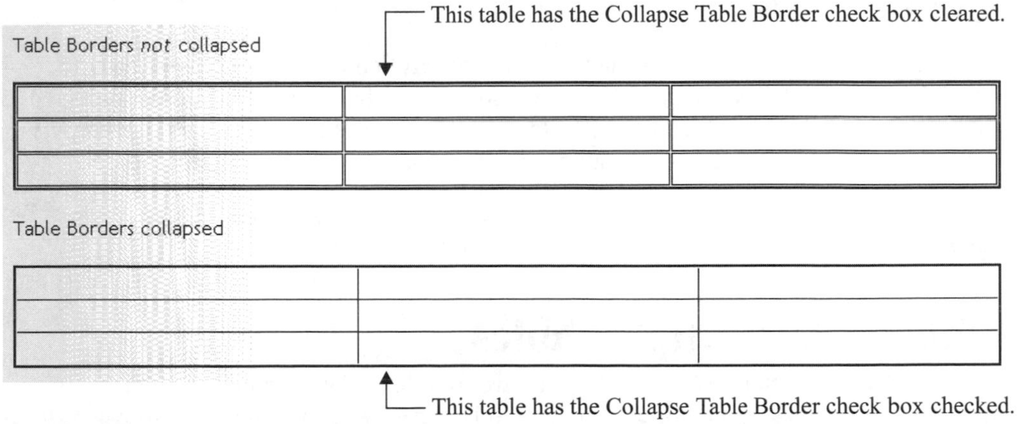

FIGURE 7-3   The top table shows cells with all their borders; in the bottom table, the table borders are collapsed.

Draw a Table

You can also draw a table, first drawing in the outlines and then subdividing the table into rows, columns, and cells. To draw a table, choose Table | Draw Table, or select the Draw Table tool from the Tables toolbar. The mouse cursor turns into a pencil, and you are ready to draw the table.

To draw a table, use the following steps:

1. Hold down the left mouse button and drag the drawing tool diagonally across the page to create a rectangle that is about the size of the table you want. When you release the mouse button, FrontPage creates the table border with a default thickness of 1 pixel. The table consists of one large cell.

2. Drag the drawing tool horizontally or vertically within the table border to create new cells, columns, and rows. As you draw, a dotted line indicates where the new cell border is going to be.

3. You can adjust the size of a cell by moving the pointer on top of the cell border until it becomes a double-headed arrow. Drag the border to adjust the size of the cell. This technique works for table borders as well.

If you need to erase a border (to delete the boundary between cells), choose the Eraser tool from the Tables toolbar. Click and drag the Eraser tool across a border until the border turns red to indicate it is selected. Release the mouse button and the border disappears. The table borders cannot be erased this way—you won't be able to select these borders with the Eraser tool.

 You can use the Draw Table tool to add cells to any table, regardless of how it was originally created. You can erase cells in any table as well.

Split a Table into Multiple Tables

You may find that you need to split one table into two (or more). For example, someone may provide a table of calendar events for the whole year. However, when you publish this calendar table on your web site, you might wish to insert the month as a text line for the events for that month. FrontPage makes it easy to split a table. To do so, click in any cell of the table just below where you want the split to be. Choose Table | Split Table. The table splits into two parts: All rows above the cell containing the text cursor become one table, and all rows from the cell containing the text cursor on down become another table. FrontPage even inserts a text line between the two newly formed tables, as shown in Figure 7-4.

These rows were above the cell containing the text cursor.

Name	Address	City	State	Zip
David Smith	1224 Ygnacio Road	Walnut Creek	Ca	94596
Margaret Johnson	151 Larkey Lane	Walnut Creek	Ca	94597
Joe Guericke	2200 Rudgear Road	Walnut Creek	Ca	94598
Sarah Greenlee	1144 Concord Ave	Concord	Ca	94592
George Course	4468 1st Ave	Concord	Ca	94592

Marsha Piejon	50887 2nd Ave	Concord	Ca	94592
Mike Karlon	402 Clayton Valley Rd.	Clayton	Ca	94567
Robert Carruthers	903 Fort Street	Clayton	Ca	94567
Stuart White	12 Bollinger Canyon Way	San Ramon	Ca	94568
Matthew Perry	2310 Crow Canyon	San Ramon	Ca	94568
Norman Mathewson	3344 4th St.	Concord	Ca	94593

The text cursor is in this cell.

FIGURE 7-4   The results of splitting a table: two tables and a text line between them

Add Content to Cells

As mentioned earlier, you can populate the cells of a table with almost anything you can put on a page. As you insert content, the cell will resize to hold the content.

To add text to a cell, place the text cursor in the cell and begin typing. The text wraps around when it reaches the cell margin, and it will push the bottom of the row down to make room if necessary. You can add text and paragraph formatting just as you would with any other block of text: creating bulleted and numbered lists; adjusting font, size, style, effects, and color; and setting the alignment of the paragraph. To move quickly from one cell to another, press the TAB key.

To insert images or any other page element, click in the cell and use the appropriate menu to insert the item. For example, to insert a clip art image, choose Insert | Picture | Clip Art and follow the normal procedures to insert a piece of clip art.

You can embed another table in a cell as well. To do so, click in the cell and choose Table | Insert | Table. You can't draw a table within a cell—you must insert it. If you specify the table width in percent, the percentage refers to the width of the containing cell. For example, if you specify the table width to be 100 percent, the new table will fill the entire width of the cell that the new table is contained in. If you specify the embedded table width in pixels, the containing cell width will expand (if necessary) to hold the table, overriding any cell width you might have set. If necessary, the outside table width will also expand to hold the contained table.

You can fill the cells in a table with specified content by using the Fill Right and Fill Down functions. To use the Fill Right function, use the following steps:

1. Add content (text, graphics, and so forth) into one or more cells in a column.

2. Select the cells containing the contents you want to duplicate and all the cells to the right of these cells you want to fill with this content.

3. Select Table | Fill | Right or click the Fill Right tool in the Tables toolbar. The selected cells are filled with the content, as shown in Figure 7-5.

Fill Down works similarly, except that you add your content to one or more cells in a row, then duplicate that content to cells below them in columns by selecting Table | Fill | Down or by selecting the Fill Down tool in the Tables toolbar.

Select Parts of a Table

FrontPage provides quite a few tools for modifying the layout of a table. However, before you can use most of these layout tools, you need to know how to select individual cells, entire rows and columns, and the table as a whole. Here is how you select portions of a table:

- To select a single cell, click in the cell and choose Table | Select | Cell. The selected cell turns black to show that it is selected.

- To select multiple adjacent cells, click in a cell and drag the mouse pointer over the adjacent cells. As you do, all the selected cells turn black to show that they are selected.

- To select a column, move the mouse pointer over the top of the column until it becomes a down arrow and click to select the column. Alternatively, click any cell in the column and choose Table | Select | Column.

- To select a row, move the mouse pointer to the left end of the row until it becomes a right-facing arrow and click to select the row. Alternatively, click any cell in the row and choose Table | Select | Row.

- To select the entire table, click any cell in the table and choose Table | Select | Table.

Participant		Race	Time 1	Time2	Time 3
			0.0	0.0	0.0
			1.0	1.0	1.0
			2.0	2.0	2.0

These cells contain the content to be duplicated (filled) in the cells to their right.

These cells now contain the duplicated contents.

FIGURE 7-5   Fill cells with content automatically using Fill Right.

NOTE   *To delete a table, select the entire table and press the* DELETE *key.*

Work with Rows and Columns

You aren't limited to the number of rows and columns you specified when you first created the table. FrontPage makes it easy to add or remove both rows and columns from your table.

SHORTCUT   *You can add rows to a table as you are typing text into the table. To do so, simply press the* TAB *key (the same key you use to move from one cell to the next) when the text cursor is in the cell at the lower-right corner of the table. FrontPage adds another row, and you can keep entering your text.*

Add Rows and Columns

If you don't get the table exactly the right size, you can add rows and columns to the table:

- ■ To insert a single row above the currently selected cell or row, click the cell (or select the row) and choose Insert Row from the cell's shortcut menu, or click the Insert Row button in the Tables toolbar.

- ■ To insert a single column to the left of the currently selected cell or column, click the cell (or select the column) and choose Insert Column from the cell's shortcut menu or click the Insert Column button in the Tables toolbar.

- ■ To control the position and number of added rows and columns, choose Table | Insert | Rows Or Columns. This displays the Insert Rows Or Columns dialog box.

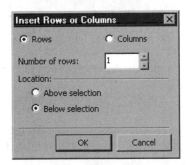

Choose the option you want (Rows or Columns) and then use the spinner to select the number of rows or columns you want inserted. Use the options in the Location section to determine whether you want the insertion done Above Selection or Below Selection (for Rows) or Left of Selection or Right of Selection (for Columns).

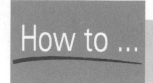 **Delete Cells, Rows, and Columns**

To delete one or more cells, select the cells you want to delete and select Table | Delete Cells, or choose Delete Cells from the cell's shortcut menu. Alternatively, you can click the Delete Cells button in the Tables toolbar.

To delete a row or column, select the row or column and select Table | Delete Cells, or choose Delete Cells from the cell's shortcut menu. Alternatively, you can click the Delete Cells button in the Tables toolbar.

SHORTCUT   *Need a quick way to insert multiple rows or columns into the table? Select multiple rows or columns by clicking and dragging to highlight them. Then choose the Insert Column or Insert Row command from the shortcut menu. For example, if you select three columns and then choose Insert Column, three new columns will be inserted to the left of the leftmost selected column.*

Size Rows and Columns

You can change the size of a row or column easily. To change the size of a column, move the mouse pointer over the left or right edge of the column until it becomes a double-headed arrow. Click and drag the border. As you do, a dashed line appears to show you where the border will be when you release the mouse button.

Participant		Race	Time 1	Time2	Time 3
			0.0	0.0	0.0
			1.0	1.0	1.0
			2.0	2.0	2.0

Changing the size of a row works just the same way. Move your mouse pointer over the top or bottom of the row until it becomes a double-headed arrow. Click and drag the border. As you do, a dashed line appears to show you where the border will be when you release the mouse button.

Distribute Rows and Columns Evenly

You can select multiple adjacent columns or rows and quickly give them an even distribution—that is, make all the selected columns or rows the same size. To provide an even distribution of columns, select the columns and choose either the Distribute Columns Evenly button in the Tables toolbar, or the Distribute Columns Evenly menu option in the shortcut menu or the Table menu. For rows, the Tables toolbar button is called Distribute Rows Evenly, as is the menu option in the shortcut menu and the Table menu.

 One of the side effects of distributing rows evenly is that all cells and *the table have their width set in pixels. This has the disadvantages discussed earlier—the table may expand past the width of the page on another computer.*

Work with Cells

You can modify a table structure by working directly with the cells. Unlike a spreadsheet, tables do not have to be even sets of rows and columns. You can remove cells, merge multiple cells into a single cell, and even stretch a cell across multiple columns and rows. In short, you are free to arrange your table pretty much any way you please.

Split and Merge Cells

If you find that a regular rectangular grid of cells doesn't meet your needs, you can split and merge cells to get the exact table layout you want. To split a cell, click in the cell and choose Split Cells from either the shortcut menu or the Table menu. Alternatively, you can choose the Split Cells button in the Tables toolbar. FrontPage will then display the Split Cells dialog box.

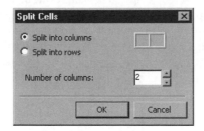

In the Split Cells dialog box, choose whether to split the cells into columns or into rows by picking the appropriate option. Use the Number Of Columns spinner (which becomes the Number Of Rows spinner if you picked the Split Into Rows option) to set the number of rows or columns to split the cell into. Data in the original cell is preserved. If you split a cell into columns, the original data is placed in the leftmost cell. If you split a cell into rows, the original data is placed in the uppermost cell. Figure 7-6 shows a table that contains split cells. The cell in the lower-left corner has been split into columns, and the cell in the upper-right corner has been split into rows.

You can merge multiple adjacent cells into a single cell. To do so, select the cells you want to merge by clicking and dragging to highlight the cells. Choose Merge Cells from the shortcut menu or the Table menu. Alternatively, you can use the Merge Cells button in the Tables toolbar.

Cobol	Pascal	Basic
Fortran	Algol	Java
Assembler	C++	Forte

FIGURE 7-6   The lower-left cell has been split into columns; the upper-right cell has been split into rows.

Data in all the cells is preserved and moved into the merged cell. The contents of each of the original cells is placed on its own line in the merged cell.

Add Cells to the Table

You can easily insert more cells into an existing table. To do so, select Table | Insert | Cell. The new cell is added to the left of the current cell and the current cell (and all cells to its right) is pushed to the right.

Adjust Cell Size with AutoFit

Once you have placed the content into your table, you may find that some cells are too large for their content and some cells may even be empty. This can result in a table that is too large and takes up more space on the web page than it needs to. To rectify this situation, click in any cell in the table and choose Table | AutoFit To Contents, or click the AutoFit To Contents button in the Tables toolbar. The table shrinks to the minimum size necessary to contain the contents (see Figure 7-7).

Full-size table

David	Fred	Larry
Norman	Nathalie	Joseph

AutoFit to contents table

David	Fred	Larry
Norman	Nathalie	Joseph

FIGURE 7-7   Using the AutoFit function shrinks the table to the minimum size necessary to hold its contents (the bottom table was shrunk, the top was not).

Set Cell Properties

You can customize the way a cell looks and acts from Cell Properties dialog box.

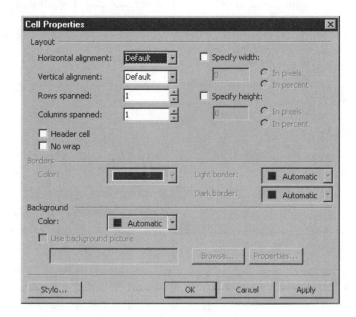

With the Cell Properties dialog box, you can align the contents of the cell, customize the border and background, and set the size of the cell. To display the Cell Properties dialog box, select one or more cells and choose Cell Properties from the shortcut menu or choose Table | Table Properties | Cell.

Align the Cell Contents

Depending on what you put into a cell, you may wish to change the alignment of the contents. For example, images usually look best when they are centered, whereas text (except for column headings) usually looks best when it is left-aligned. You can set the alignment of cell contents using the Horizontal Alignment and Vertical Alignment drop-down lists in the Cell Properties dialog box. You can change the vertical alignment using the Align Top, Center Vertically, or Align Bottom buttons in the Tables toolbar.

NOTE

You can also set the horizontal alignment of a cell's contents using the Formatting toolbar or the Paragraph dialog box. To open the Paragraph dialog box, select the cell's contents and choose Format | Paragraph. The value you choose from the Alignment drop-down list in the Paragraph dialog box overrides any alignment selections you make in the Cell Properties dialog box or the Formatting toolbar.

Span Rows and Columns

You can force a cell to stretch across more than one column or row. This is called *spanning*. The effect is similar to merging cells into a larger cell. The difference is that when you span a cell, the cells it spans across are pushed down or sideways, as if you had inserted cells. You can then delete these cells if you wish. In Figure 7-8, the large cell in the center of the table was created by spanning a cell across two columns and two rows. The cells that were pushed out of the way are clearly visible at the right edge of the table.

To set the cell span, use the Rows Spanned and Columns Spanned spinners in the Cell Properties dialog box.

Add Header Cells

Many tables have column headers that tell you what kind of data is in each column. Some tables also have row headers. A quick way to emphasize these header cells is to select them and check the Header Cell check box. This adds bold formatting and centers the contents of the cell.

NOTE   *If you set the horizontal alignment for a cell using the Paragraph Properties dialog box, the alignment settings you specified override the center alignment that usually results from checking the Header Cell check box.*

Specify the Minimum Cell Width

You can set the minimum cell width in the Cell Properties dialog box by checking the Specify Width check box and entering a value in the field. Specify whether the entered value is in pixels or percent—as mentioned earlier, percent is usually the better choice to allow for different browser resolutions.

Adjusting the minimum cell width is a tricky business. For example, say you had a four-column table and you set the minimum width of each cell to 25 percent so that all the columns had the same width. If you then adjust the minimum width of a single cell in a column of cells, you may not see any change. For example, if you reduced the minimum width in our four-column example to 15 percent, the column width would not change because the other cells in the column are still

Spanned Cells

Regular	Regular	Regular		
Regular	Spanned		Regular	
Regular			Regular	Regular
Regular	Regular	Regular		

FIGURE 7-8   Cell spanning enables you to create large cells that cross multiple rows and columns.

"holding" the column width at 25 percent. Only after changing the minimum width of all the cells in the column would you see the column shrink.

There is another bit of strangeness associated with minimum column widths as well. You can set the sum of the minimum widths of columns to be more than 100 percent, and FrontPage is perfectly happy with this situation. For example, you could set all the columns in our four-column example to be 75 percent of the total width. If you do this, FrontPage scales the first cell to be as close as possible to the specified width, shrinking the other cells (if necessary) for this to occur. However, FrontPage won't shrink the cells past the point where they can't display their contents.

Suppress Word Wrap

Word wrap is a feature used in word processors and other text-based programs. It automatically breaks a line of text when it reaches the margin or border of a text area, and "wraps" it around to the next line. Checking the No Wrap check box turns off word wrap in the cell. Be careful when you turn off word wrap, as it is hard to predict what a nonwrapped cell will do to the table layout in a browser, especially if the browser is running at a lower resolution than you used when you designed the table.

Modify the Border Colors and Background

You can specify the border colors of a cell using the Borders section of the Cell Properties dialog box. The border color controls work just like the borders for a table, discussed earlier in this chapter. However, the border color settings you specify in the Cell Properties dialog box override the border colors you set in the Table Properties dialog box.

You can also set a background color or a background picture for the cell by using the Background section of the Cell Properties dialog. As with the borders, the color or graphic overrides any settings you specified for the table.

If the background graphic is too large to fit into the cell, only as much of the graphic as will fit in the cell is displayed. However, the visitor to your web site will have to wait for the graphic to load even if he or she can only see a small part of the graphic. Therefore, it is better to pick a small graphic that fits inside the cell.

AutoFormat a Table

It can be a lot of work to set up an attractively designed table. You may have to specify the colors for borders and backgrounds, as well as fonts and colors for headings and other cells. FrontPage offers a potential solution to doing all this work manually, however: AutoFormat. FrontPage includes a set of predefined formats that you can apply to tables. The AutoFormats include specifications for borders, shading, font, color, and even whether to autofit the cells to their contents. Once you have applied an AutoFormat, you can use it "as is" or as the starting point for further customization.

There are two ways to apply AutoFormat to a table. The quickest (and simplest) way is to pick the format you want from the Table AutoFormat Combo tool in the Tables toolbar.

Of course, there are drawbacks to using the Table AutoFormat Combo tool—you don't get to see a preview of the format you are applying, and you don't get to customize which parts of the format you want to apply (you do get to specify this using the other Table AutoFormat options). Still, once you know the formats (they are the same ones that are available using the other Table AutoFormat options), the Table AutoFormat tool is quick and easy to use.

To preview and customize a Table AutoFormat before applying it to a table, choose Table | Table AutoFormat or select the Table AutoFormat tool from the Tables toolbar. This displays the Table AutoFormat dialog box.

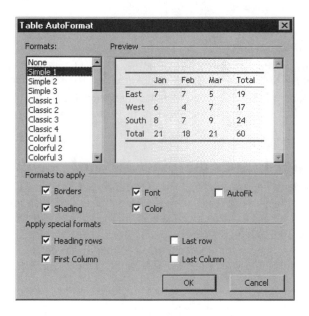

Pick the format you want from the Formats list, and view the preview of that format in the Preview area on the right side of the dialog box. Check or clear the check boxes to specify which portions of the format to apply to the table in the Formats To Apply section and the Apply Special Formats section of the dialog box. For example, if don't want the table to have a border, clear the Borders check box. As you make these selections, you can preview the effect of the change in the Preview area.

Add a Table Caption

A table caption is essentially a title for the table. To add a table caption, click anywhere in the table and choose Table | Insert | Caption. A blank line is inserted at the top of the table, with a blinking text cursor. You can then type the text of the caption. If you wish, you can use all the text and paragraph formatting tools discussed previously to customize the caption text. You can also insert graphics into the caption by choosing Insert | Picture and selecting the picture the usual way.

To change the position of the caption, right-click the caption and choose Caption Properties from the shortcut menu, or choose Table | Table Properties | Caption. This opens the Caption Properties dialog box. In this dialog box, choose the option you want for the position of the caption: Top Of Table or Bottom Of Table.

Convert Text to Tables

FrontPage provides a feature to convert plain text into a table. This can be very handy if you want to display data as a table that is already on a web page. For example, you could export the contents of a company address book in a comma-delimited (separated) format, insert the file into a web page, and then convert the text into a table of company contacts.

To convert text into a table, select the text you want to convert, and choose Table | Convert | Text To Table. This displays the Convert Text To Table dialog box.

Choose the option that corresponds to how you want to separate the text:

■ **Paragraphs**   This option creates a single-column table, with each paragraph in its own row (and in its own cell).

■ **Tabs, Commas, Or Other**   If your text is delimited by tabs, commas, or some other character, choose one of these options. If you choose the Other option, enter the delimiter character into the text field. Each piece of delimited text is placed in its own cell (column). FrontPage creates a new row in the table each time it encounters a new paragraph. Figure 7-9 shows both the original comma-delimited text (each line is a paragraph) and the table it would become. Notice that the original text does not include spaces after the commas. Normally, of course, the table replaces the text; you are not left with both when you are done.

■ **None (Text In Single Cell)**   Choosing this option places all the selected text into a single-cell table.

Text

David,Plotkin,1069 Christina Ln,Walnut Creek,Ca,94597
Fred,Plotkin,4455 Braeton Way,Fort North,NY,00217
Brenda,Plotkin,1314 Cape St.,Melbourne,Fl,45609
Larry,Plotkin,909 13th St.,Corvallis,Or,92557
Norman,Plotkin,20 Triple Oak Dr.,Monterey,Ca,93940
Ruben,Montes,22910 Cordoba Dr.,Salinas,Ca,93908

Converted to table:

David	Plotkin	1069 Christina Ln	Walnut Creek	Ca	94597
Fred	Plotkin	4455 Braeton Way	Fort North	NY	00217
Brenda	Plotkin	1314 Cape St.	Melbourne	Fl	45609
Larry	Plotkin	909 13th St.	Corvallis	Or	92557
Norman	Plotkin	20 Triple Oak Dr.	Monterey	Ca	93940
Ruben	Montes	22910 Cordoba Dr.	Salinas	Ca	93908

FIGURE 7-9   The comma-delimited text converts cleanly into a table.

Convert Tables to Text

If the data you have is already in a table, you can convert it back to regular text. To do so, click anywhere in the table and choose Table | Convert | Table To Text. Each cell in the table is converted into a separate line of text on the page.

Create a Table from a Word Table

If you are more comfortable working in a word processor such as Microsoft Word, you may wish to create the table in Word and then add it to a FrontPage web page. To do so, simply select the entire table in Word and copy it to the clipboard (choose Edit | Copy, or press CTRL-C). Switch to FrontPage and paste the table into the web page (choose Edit | Paste, or press CTRL-V).

Create a Table from an Excel Spreadsheet

If you are familiar with entering content into a spreadsheet such as Microsoft Excel, you may wish to enter your data into a grid of cells in Excel, and then convert the cells into a FrontPage table. Realize that you can only create a regular rectangular grid of cells this way. To create a table from a grid of Excel cells, select the cells in Excel and copy them to the clipboard (choose Edit | Copy, or press CTRL-C). Switch to FrontPage and paste the table into the web page (choose Edit | Paste, or press CTRL-V). Most of the formatting you can apply to a cell in Excel is transferred to FrontPage. However, some effects—such as a background fill pattern—are not preserved, so view the results in FrontPage carefully and reapply any lost formatting you want.

Work with Page Layout Tables

Layout tables (see Figure 7-10 for a sample) are a special type of table that FrontPage provides so that you can create complex layouts of text and graphics on a web page. Once you have built a layout table, you can fill the cells with content, just as you did with regular tables, discussed earlier in this chapter.

NOTE   *Interestingly enough, layout tables are not really a special kind of table at all. Instead, they are just regular tables (with cells) nested together in very complex ways. You could build any of these layouts manually. The advantage of using the layout tables is that you don't have to worry about the mechanics of building the tables—you just draw what you need, and FrontPage does the rest.*

7

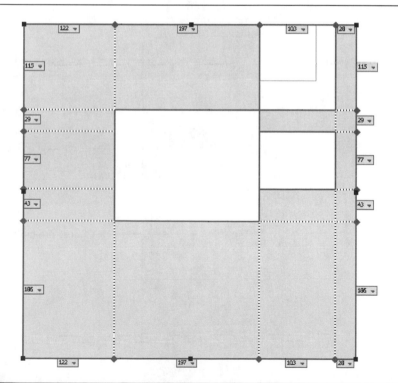

FIGURE 7-10   Create custom layouts by building a layout table.

Create a Page Layout Table

The first step is to create the boundaries of the layout table. To do so, choose Table | Layout
Tables and Cells to open the Layout Tables and Cells Task Pane (see Figure 7-11).

You can create a layout table three different ways:

- **Use the Insert Layout Table Hyperlink**   Click the Insert Layout Table hyperlink near
  the top of the Task Pane to create a single-cell layout table of a default size.

- **Use the Draw Layout Table Button**   Click the Draw Layout Table button to draw a
  single-cell layout table. The mouse cursor turns into a pencil. Click and drag on the
  page to define the boundaries of the layout table. This tool is also available in the
  Tables toolbar.

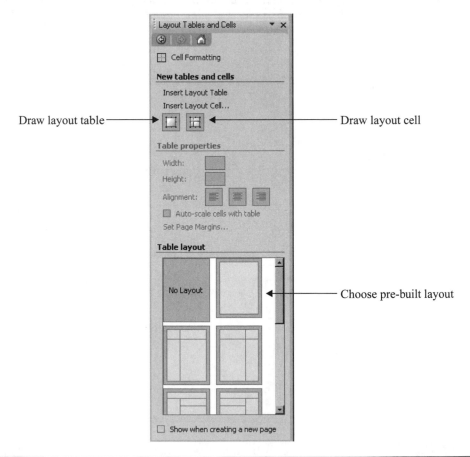

FIGURE 7-11   The Layout Tables and Cells Task Pane provides all the tools you need to build
these useful structures.

■ **Use a Predefined Layout** The Choose Layout section of the Task Pane contains set of predefined layouts. If one of these layouts meets your needs, click it to create the layout table.

When you first create a layout table, FrontPage displays it showing a green border with a *flag* on each border showing the length of that border.

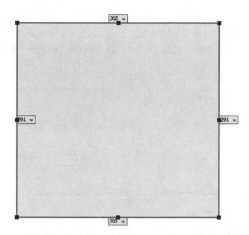

If you click anywhere else on the page (including inside the layout table), the highlighted border disappears, leaving just a dotted line to indicate the presence of the table. To reselect the table, move the mouse pointer over the dotted line until it turns green, then click.

Clicking inside the table provides a text cursor so that you can type content into the table.

Add Layout Cells to a Layout Table

There are three tools you can use to add layout cells to a layout table, and they all work differently. The three tools (discussed next) are the Draw Layout Cell tool, the Insert Layout Cell Hyperlink tool, and the tools in the Tables toolbar.

Once you've added a layout cell to a layout table, the cell is displayed with a blue border (if it was created with the Draw Layout Cell tool or one of the toolbar tools) or a green border (if it was created with the Insert Layout Cell Hyperlink tool) and a flag that shows the dimensions of the cell:

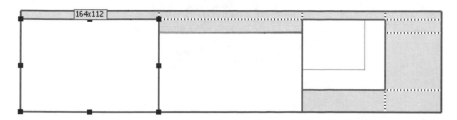

As with a layout table, if you click anywhere else on the page, the blue or green border disappears. To redisplay it, move the mouse pointer over the border of the layout cell and click. This actually shows the borders of *all* the layout cells, but only the selected layout cell displays the dimension flags.

Use the Draw Layout Cell Tool

The first tool for adding layout cells is the Draw Layout Cell tool, located just to the right of the Draw Layout Table tool. To add a layout cell using this tool, click the tool to turn the mouse cursor into a pen. Then simply click and drag inside the layout table to create a layout cell:

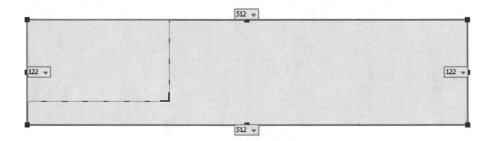

There are some limitations to using this tool. First of all, you cannot add a layout cell in any rectangle of the layout table where you have typed text—even if you later erase the text. You also cannot draw a layout cell inside another layout cell. Attempting either of these operations with the Draw Layout Cell tool changes the mouse cursor into a text cursor.

Use the Insert Layout Cell Hyperlink

The second tool you can use to add layout cells to a layout table is the Insert Layout Cell Hyperlink tool, located just below the Insert Layout Table hyperlink. Clicking this hyperlink displays the Insert Layout Cell dialog box:

Exactly what you can do at this point depends on several factors:

- What did you select before trying to create the layout cell? Options include selecting the layout table border, selecting a layout cell border, clicking inside a layout cell, or clicking inside the layout table but *not* inside a layout cell.

- Was there text content in the layout table or layout cell, and did you select any of that content before continuing?

Depending on the choices above, various options are available in the Insert Layout Cell dialog box. The first set of options are in the Layout section of the dialog box:

- **Horizontal**   Inserts a horizontal layout cell. You can set the height of the layout cell.

- **Vertical**   Inserts a vertical layout cell. You can set the width of the layout cell.

- **Inline**   Inserts an inline layout cell. Depending on whether you selected a border or clicked inside a layout cell, the inline layout cell is placed either alongside the layout cell (if you selected the layout cell border) or inside the layout cell (if you clicked inside the layout cell). Either way, you can set both the height and width of the layout cell.

NOTE   *If there is an obstruction that would prevent placing a horizontal or vertical layout cell, the OK button will be grayed out and unavailable. Also, if you choose a height or width dimension that would cause the new layout cell to conflict with another layout cell, you will get an error message, requiring you to shrink the specified dimension.*

The Location section of the Insert Layout Cell dialog box provides three options as well. These options govern the placement of the new layout cell:

- **Before Selection**   Places the new layout cell before the selected content. For example, if you select text content and then choose Before Selection, the layout cell is inserted into the text and positioned just before the first character of the selected text.

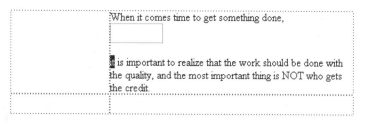

- **After Selection**   Places the new layout cell after the selected content. For example, if you select text content and then choose After Selection, the layout cell is inserted into the text and positioned just after the last character of the selected text.

■ **Wrap Selection**   This option is only available if a layout cell (or layout table) contains text content and you have made a selection in that text. All the text (not just what you selected) is wrapped inside the new layout cell.

The available options are summarized in Table 7-1. Many combinations are not shown because they are not available. For example, if you click inside a layout table, only the *Inline* option is available in the Layout portion of the Insert Layout Cell dialog box, so that is all that is shown in Table 7-1.

Before Insert	Content Selected?	Layout	Location	Result
Click inside layout table	No	Inline	Before Selection or After Selection	Layout cell in upper-left corner of table or rectangular area where cursor was located.
Click inside layout table	Yes	Inline	Before Selection	New layout cell inserted between prior text and beginning of selected text.
Click inside layout table	Yes	Inline	After Selection	New layout cell inserted between end of selected text and following text.
Click inside layout table	Yes	Inline	Wrap text	Entire contents of layout table text are inserted and wrapped in new layout cell.
Select boundaries of layout table. Either with or without content.		Inline	Before Selection	New layout cell above existing layout table.
Select boundaries of layout table. Either with or without content.		Inline	After Selection	New layout table below existing layout table.
Click in a layout cell	No	Inline	Before Selection or After Selection	Adds a new layout cell in the upper-left corner of the existing layout cell.
Click in a layout cell	Yes	Inline	Before Selection	New layout cell inserted between prior text and beginning of selected text. The minimum width you can set is the width of the selected text.

TABLE 7-1   Summary of Options for Insert Layout Cell Hyperlink

Before Insert	Content Selected?	Layout	Location	Result
Click in a layout cell	Yes	Inline	After Selection	New layout cell inserted between end of selected text and following text.
Click in a layout cell	Yes	Inline	Wrap Selection	Entire contents of layout table text are inserted and wrapped in new layout cell.
Select a layout cell	N/A	Horizontal	Before Selection	Adds horizontal layout cell above existing cell.
Select a layout cell	N/A	Horizontal	After Selection	Adds horizontal layout cell below existing cell.
Select a layout cell	N/A	Vertical	Before Selection	Adds vertical layout cell to the left of existing cell.
Select a layout cell	N/A	Vertical	After Selection	Adds vertical layout cell to the right of existing cell.
Select an empty layout cell	N/A	Inline	Before Selection or After Selection	Adds a new layout cell in the upper-left corner of the existing cell.
Select a layout cell with text	No	Inline	Before Selection	Adds a layout cell inside the selected cell but positioned ahead of the text.
Select a layout cell with text	No	Inline	After Selection	Adds a layout cell outside the selected layout cell on the right (aligned with the top).

TABLE 7-1   Summary of Options for Insert Layout Cell Hyperlink *(continued)*

Insert a Layout Cell With the Tables Toolbar

The Tables toolbar contains two tools used for inserting Layout tools: Insert Vertical Layout Cell and Insert Horizontal Layout Cell (see Figure 7-2, earlier). To use these tools, make your starting selection, then choose the tool from the toolbar. If another layout cell would obstruct the creation of a vertical layout cell or a horizontal layout cell, that tool is unavailable in the toolbar. As with the Insert Layout Cell hyperlink, the starting selection can include selecting the layout table border, selecting a layout cell border, clicking inside a layout cell, and clicking inside a layout table but not within a layout cell.

Adjust the Dimensions of Layout Tables

Once you create a layout table, you can adjust the size of the table in one of two ways. The first way to adjust the dimensions is to move the mouse over one of the sizing handles. These are the small squares visible in the corners and in the middle of each side of the table.

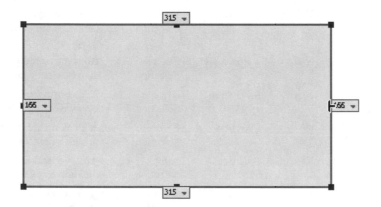

The mouse turns into a T-shaped move tool, and you can click and drag the sizing handles to resize the table. Note that if a layout table contains many layout cells (see Figure 7-12), the sizing handles of the table may be hard to see, but they are still there—you just have to look for them.

The other way to resize a layout table is to type the new width and height into the Table Properties section of the Layout Tables and Cells Task Pane.

> **NOTE**   *Normally, if you attempt to resize a layout table that contains layout cells, the size of the table is constrained by the layout cells. That is, you can't shrink the table to the point where it is not large enough to contain the layout cells. To remedy this situation, check the Scale Layout Cells With Layout Table check box in the Layout Tables and Cells Task Pane. This enables the layout cells to shrink (and grow) in proportion to the layout table.*

Modify Layout Table Rows and Columns

As you add layout cells to a layout table, FrontPage builds a grid of rows and columns to hold the layout cells.

You can change the width of columns or the height of rows by clicking and dragging one of the dotted grid lines. This automatically resizes any layout cells contained in that row or column. You can't drag the grid line past the boundaries of the adjacent column or row, and the adjacent column or row can only shrink to its minimum dimension (2 pixels for columns and 19 pixels for rows on my machine).

If you select the main layout table, each row or column displays a size flag located around the perimeter of the main layout table (visible in Figure 7-12). Using the flag shortcut menu, you can adjust the row height or column width.

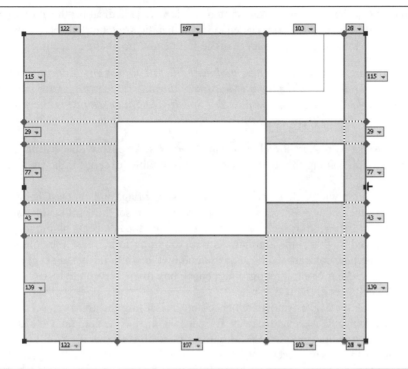

FIGURE 7-12   A layout table containing many layout cells can get pretty busy!

To change the row height, click one of the row sizing flags and choose Change Row Height. This displays the Row Properties dialog box.

Set the height using the Row Height spinner. The row height is increased to this height, and the height of the table is increased by the same amount.

Normally, each cell in a layout table is sized independently of all other cells. That means that you can't enlarge one cell if another cell gets in the way. To get around this problem, check the Clear Contradicting Height check box. If you do, the conflicting cell shrinks as you increase the height (or enlarges as you shrink the height) of the cell you are working with.

You can also check the Make Row Autostretch check box. This disables the ability to set the row height. Instead, the layout table is expanded to its full height, stretching the height of all rows proportionally. If the table is already taller than the full height, no changes occur.

> NOTE   *Make Row Autostretch sets the height of the table to 100 percent. You can see this by clicking on the border of the layout table and choosing Table | Properties | Table to open the Table Properties dialog box. The Specify Height check box is checked, and the height is set to 100 (in percent).*

If you choose Make Row Autostretch, you can also choose Use Row Spacer Image. This places a reference graphic along the right edge of the layout table, except for the right edge of the autostretched row.

To change the column width, click one of the column sizing flags and choose Change Column Width. This displays the Column Properties dialog box. You can set the width using the Column Width spinner. The column width is increased to this width, and the adjacent column immediately to the right is narrowed by this same amount. As with dragging to increase the column width (discussed above), the new column width is constrained by the width of the adjacent column.

You can check the Clear Contradicting Width check box to enable you to resize a layout cell even when another cell gets in the way.

You can also check the Make Autostretch check box, disabling the ability to set the column width. Instead, the layout table is expanded to the full page width, and the column width is expanded to fill the extra space. As with rows, Make Column Autostretch sets Specify Width in the Table Properties dialog box to 100 (in percent).

If you choose Make Column Autostretch, you can also choose Use Column Spacer Image. This places a reference graphic along the bottom edge of the layout table except for the bottom border of the autostretched column.

> NOTE   *Choose Use Column Spacer Image from the column shortcut menu to display the spacer image at the bottom of the column.*

Adjust the Properties of Layout Tables

As mentioned earlier in this chapter, a layout table is actually just a regular table, albeit one that can have a complex set of cells and other tables embedded in it. As a result, you can set all the same properties for a layout table as you can a regular table, as discussed previously in this chapter. For example, you can select the layout table and choose Table Properties from the shortcut menu or choose Table | Properties | Table to open the Table Properties dialog box. You can set the table alignment from this dialog box, or by clicking one of the Alignment buttons in the Table Layout Properties of the Layout Tables and Cells Task Pane. You can also add content to a layout table, including text and graphics, just as you would with a regular table.

Adjust the Dimensions of Layout Cells

To adjust the size of a layout cell, select the cell (by moving the mouse pointer over the edge until it turns blue or green, and click). As with the layout table, you'll see sizing handles at the corners and in the center of each side. Simply click and drag one of the sizing handles to change the size of the layout cell.

NOTE *You cannot change the size of a layout cell so that it overlaps another layout cell.*

You can move a layout cell by clicking and dragging the flag at the top of the cell. You cannot drag the layout cell to a position where it will overlap another layout cell, nor can you drag it outside the layout table. In addition, you cannot drag some of the layout cells created with the Insert Layout Cell hyperlink (those showing a green border) to a new location.

TIP *To move a layout cell one pixel at a time, select the layout cell and press an arrow key. To change the size of a layout cell one pixel at a time, hold down the CTRL key and press an arrow key.*

Adjust the Properties of Layout Cells

7

There are two ways to adjust the properties of a layout cell. For cells created with either the Draw Layout Cell tool or the toolbar tools (which have a blue border), you can choose Cell Properties from the shortcut menu or select Table | Table Properties | Cell to display the Cell Properties dialog box, discussed earlier in this chapter.

For all layout cells, including those created with the Insert Layout Cell hyperlink, you can apply formatting by using the Cell Formatting Task Pane.

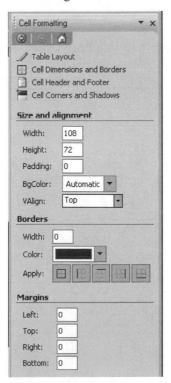

Adjust the Size and Alignment

The Size and Alignment section of the Cell Formatting Task Pane enables you to set some of the same properties as the Cell Properties dialog box, including Width, Height, Background Color, and Vertical Alignment. In addition, you can set the padding (distance between the content and the edge of the cell) on a cell-by-cell basis.

Create Borders

The Borders section of the Cell Formatting Task Pane enables you to set the individual borders for a layout cell. To create a border, select the layout cell and use the following steps:

1. Type the border thickness into the Width field.

2. Choose the thickness from the Thickness drop-down list.

3. Click one of the buttons at the bottom of the Borders section to apply the color and thickness to that border. In order from left to right, the buttons apply the border to All Borders, Left Border, Right Border, Top Border, and Bottom Border. You can click multiple buttons (such as the right border and the left border buttons) to apply the settings to multiple borders.

To remove (turn off) a border, click on the button for that border a second time without adjusting either the color or width.

Adjust the Margins

The Margins section of the Cell Formatting Task Pane enables you to add margins to the left, top, right, and bottom of a layout cell. When you add a margin, the edge of the cell moves the appropriate amount to increase the active area of the cell. For example, if you add a 5-pixel left margin, the left border of the layout cell moves 5 pixels to the left, increasing the overall width of the layout cell.

Add a Header and Footer

You can add a header and a footer to a layout cell. To do so, click the Cell Header And Footer hyperlink at the top of the Cell Formatting Task Pane to display the Header and Footer section of the Cell Formatting Task Pane.

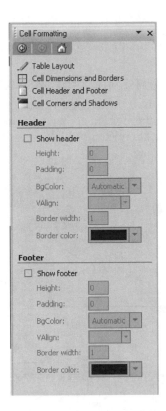

To add a header, check the Show Header check box and fill in the Height, Padding, Background Color (BgColor), Alignment (Valign), Border Width, and Border Color. To add a footer, check the Show Footer check box and fill in these same quantities for the footer. The result might look like this (with some text typed in the header and footer):

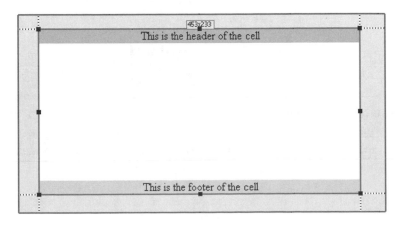

 *You can format any text in the header or footer using the standard text formatting tools. You can even insert graphics into the header and footer.*

Create Visual Elements with the Cell Formatting Task Pane

The last two sections of the Cell Formatting Task Pane give you the ability to add graphical corners and shadows to a layout cell. To open this portion of the Task Pane, click the Cell Corners and Shadows hyperlink at the top of the Cell Formatting Task Pane to display the Corners and Shadows sections of the Cell Formatting Task Pane.

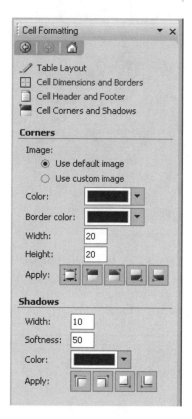

Create and Customize Corners

Using the Corners section of the Cell Formatting Task Pane, you can add colored, rounded corners to any (or all) of the corners in a layout cell. Here is a sample of what you can do with this tool:

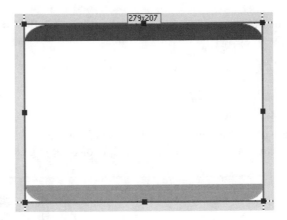

To add one or more corners to a layout cell, select the cell and use the following steps:

1. Choose the corner color from the Color drop-down list. This is the color used in the corners themselves.

2. Choose the border color from the Border color drop-down. This is the color of a thin corner border.

3. Set the curvature of the corners by typing a number into the Width and Height fields.

4. Apply the corner design to the layout cell by clicking one or more of the Apply Corner buttons at the bottom of the Corners section. These are buttons are, from left to right, All Corners, Top Left Corner, Top Right Corner, Bottom Left Corner, and Bottom Right Corner. You can click more than one button to apply the corner design to multiple corners.

To remove (turn off) a corner, click on the button for that corner a second time without adjusting either the colors or curvature (Width or Height).

If you don't like the corner graphics provided by FrontPage, you can substitute your own graphics. To do so, click the Use Custom Image option to display a new version of the Task Pane.

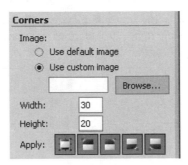

Either type in the name of the image to use, or click the Browse button to pick the image from a dialog box.

You can type and format text into the colored corner sections at the top and bottom of the layout cell.

Create and Customize Shadows

Using the Shadows section of the Cell Formatting Task Pane, you can add a drop shadow in one of four different directions to a layout cell. Here is a sample of what you can do with this tool:

To add a shadow to a layout cell, select the cell and use the following steps:

1. Choose the shadow color from the Color drop-down list.

2. Set the size of the shadow by typing a value into the Width field.

3. Set the softness of the shadow by typing a number between 0 and 100 into the Softness field. A value of 0 is a sharp shadow, while higher numbers create a softer, shaded effect.

4. Click one of the four Apply Shadows buttons to apply the shadow to the top left, top right, bottom left, or bottom right corner shadows.

To remove (turn off) the shadow, click on the button for that shadow a second time without adjusting any of the shadow parameters.

Applying a shadow increases the size of the layout cell unless an adjacent layout cell prevents this. In that case, the active area of the layout cell is decreased to make room for the shadow—and removing the shadow leaves you with a smaller layout cell.

Part II

Build Web Sites

Chapter 8

Build an Initial Web Site

How to...

- Create a new web site
- Import an existing web site
- Open an existing web site
- Delete a web site

Up to now, you've only built individual web pages. However, to post your pages on the Internet, you need to know how to create a complete web site—the entire collection of pages, images, documents, and any other files needed. Fortunately, FrontPage provides you with tools to help you build web sites. Using FrontPage's predefined web site styles, you can easily create the framework for a personal web site, corporate web site, or even a complex, special-purpose site such as a discussion group web. You can import existing web sites from a hard drive or the Internet, which is very convenient if someone else created a web site you now want to maintain in FrontPage. You can also decide how and where you want to store your new web site.

Once you have created the framework of your web site, you can use the tools you've already learned to create the web pages.

Understand Disk-Based and Server-Based Web Sites

This version of FrontPage does not require, and does not include, a personal web server such as Microsoft's Internet Information Server (IIS). When you use FrontPage to create a new web site, you can simply specify a physical directory on your hard drive to store all the files needed to later publish your web site to the Internet (see Chapter 18 for more information on publishing a web site). A web site set up this way is called a disk-based web site. Overall, this technique is simple and works fairly well.

However, there is a drawback to creating a disk-based web site. Certain features of FrontPage web sites cannot be tested using a disk-based web site, including forms (see Chapter 11), many components (see Chapter 13), Dynamic HTML effects (see Chapter 14), and databases (see Chapter 21). These features need the FrontPage extensions and *SharePoint Team Services*, a special package of services that run with a web server such as IIS. In order to test these features on a disk-based web site, you must publish your web site (see Chapter 18) to an appropriately configured web server, and test them on the remote web server. Of course, if you find errors, you'll have to fix them and then republish your site to the remote server to test them again. If you have a sizable web site, this cycle can take a long time.

The alternative is to set up a web server on your local machine by installing IIS with the FrontPage Server extensions and SharePoint Team Services 1.0 (which comes with Office XP and FrontPage). When you create a new web site, you can choose to "locate" it on the server provided on your computer by IIS (you can also choose to locate it in a directory on your hard drive, as before). Doing so creates a server-based web site. The IIS URL is usually called http://default, although you can rename it if you wish. Thus, if you create a web site called myweb, its full address on your computer is http://default/myweb if you use a server-based web site. To test all the web site's features, access your server-based web site with a browser by using the web site's URL (for example, http://default/myweb). You can use a browser to navigate through the entire web site on your local machine. However, realize that your response time will be much better on your local machine than what you'll get once you are accessing the web site on the Internet!

Most features of FrontPage 2003 will work just fine on a server running IIS, FrontPage Server Extensions, and SharePoint Team Services 1.0. However, to use all the capabilities of FrontPage 2003, you have to host the site on a server running *Windows Server 2003*, the latest operating system from Microsoft. When properly installed with IIS and SharePoint Team Services version 2, you can host your FrontPage site and use all its capabilities. Just to confuse matters further, the database features of FrontPage (discussed in Chapters 19-21) do NOT work on a server equipped with Windows Server 2003 and SharePoint Team Services 2.0.

NOTE   *The examples in the screen shots in this book mostly use IIS server-based web sites, because testing a server-based web site is so much easier.*

Create a Web Site

8

To create a new web site, choose File | New. This opens the New Task Pane.

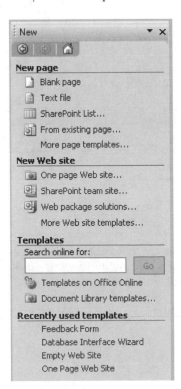

From the New Task Pane, you have several options: create a new empty web site, create a web site based on templates you have used recently, or create a new web site based on the FrontPage built-in templates.

To create a new web site using one of the built-in FrontPage web site templates, use the following steps:

1. In the New Web Site section of the Task Pane, choose More Web Site Templates. The Web Site Templates dialog box opens to show you a variety of templates you can use to create your new web site.

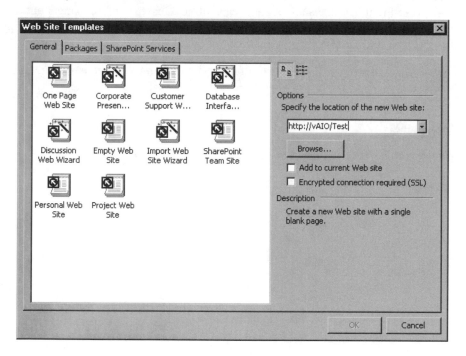

2. Pick one of the templates. Each template you click displays a description of the template's purpose in the Description area at the lower-right corner of the New dialog box.

NOTE   *If the web site already exists and you just need to import it into FrontPage, pick the Import Web Wizard. For more on using this useful wizard, see "Import an Existing Web Site," later in this chapter.*

3. Specify where you want the web site to be located by using the Specify The Location Of The New Web field. For a disk-based web site, the default location is *C:\My Documents\My Webs*. You will probably want to create a subdirectory for each new disk-based web site you create. If you installed a web server, you will also have the option of picking http://default (or whatever the server URL is called on your machine). To specify the location of the new web site, you'll need to add to this path, because you can't create a web site directly in http://default. For example, you can locate the web site at http://default/myweb.

> **NOTE**   *You can actually specify a URL on the Internet as the location to create your web site, if you wish. However, I don't recommend this approach because you will need to be connected to the Internet at all times when you want to work on the web site, and you won't have a copy of the web site on your local machine. In addition, you'll most likely need to log in to the remote server every time you want to make changes to the site, and any mistakes you make will be visible to the whole world the moment you make them.*

4. Click OK. FrontPage creates the structure of your new web site, including the folders it needs to work properly. It also creates the new home page and any other pages that are part of the chosen template (unless you chose the Empty Web template).

> **NOTE**   *The "home page" is the title of the page that someone first sees when navigating to your site. The filename chosen by FrontPage varies depending on whether you chose to create a disk-based site or a server-based site. The file is called index.htm for a disk-based site, and default.htm for a server-based site.*

Import an Existing Web Site

Occasionally, you will need to bring a web site that has already been created into FrontPage. You might run into this situation if you take over the maintenance of an existing site, for example. The site might be disk-based or residing on a network hard drive, or it might be an operating web site on the Internet. FrontPage makes it easy to import a site using the Import Web Wizard.

To import a web site into FrontPage from a hard drive or network drive, use the following steps:

1. Choose File | New to open the New Task Pane. Choose More Web Site Templates to open the Web Site Templates dialog box.

2. Specify the location of the new web site on your hard drive (disk-based web site) or on your local web server (server-based web site).

3. Double-click the Import Web Site Wizard icon.

4. Click OK. FrontPage creates the initial web site structure and then starts the Import Web Wizard.

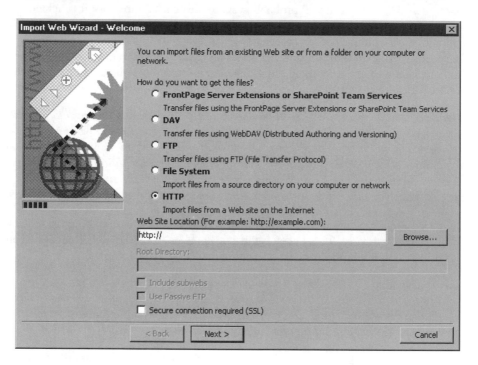

5. Choose the File System option.

6. In the Web Site Location field, enter the path to the files that comprise the web site. You can use the Browse button to open a dialog box in which you can pick the folder. If the folder contains subfolders you need to include, check the Include Subfolders check box.

7. Click the Next button twice to read and enjoy Microsoft's heartfelt congratulations on completing this oh-so-difficult set of tasks. Then click the Finish button.

8. FrontPage imports the web site, updates the hyperlinks, and presents you with the finished web site. This process can take a few minutes for a complex web site, so be patient.

To import an existing web site from an Internet site, you must be connected to the Internet. Use the following steps:

1. Choose File | New to open the New Task Pane. Choose More Web Site Templates to open the Web Site Templates dialog box.

2. Specify the location of the new web site, either on your hard drive (disk-based web site) or in terms of your local web server (server-based web site).

3. Double-click the Import Web Wizard icon.

4. Click OK. FrontPage creates the initial web site structure and then starts the Import Web Wizard.

5. Choose the HTTP option.

6. In the Location field, enter the Internet URL from which you want to import the site. If the site requires a Secure Sockets connection, check the Secure Connection Required (SSL) check box.

7. Click Next twice. In the Set Import Limits panel of the Import Web Wizard (see Figure 8-1) you can limit what you download. Your options are

- **Import the Home Page Plus Linked Pages**   Set how many levels of pages that are linked to the web site home page you want to import by checking this check box and using the spinner to set the number of levels. For example, if you choose to download two levels, the following pages will be downloaded: the home page, all the pages hyperlinked to the home page, and all pages hyperlinked to those pages.

- **Import a Maximum Of**   If you want to limit the total amount you download (measured in kilobytes), check this check box and enter the number of kilobytes (KB) in the text field.

- **Import Only HTML and Image Files**   Finally, if you just want to download only text and image files (leaving out JavaScript, Java, and other components), check this check box.

8. Click Next, and then click Finish. The import begins and proceeds until either the entire web site has been imported or the limits you set in step 7 (if any) are reached.

NOTE

If the web site you are importing was created with FrontPage, you may get a warning that the theme of the imported web site will be replaced by the theme of your new web site. Just click Yes to continue with the import process. If you click No, the import process stops.

When the import process has completed, FrontPage presents you with the imported web site. If you limited the amount of information (either in kilobytes or the number of page levels) included in the import, the resulting web site is likely to be incomplete, missing graphics, pages, and components. If you want to retrieve the missing information, you'll need to reimport the web site, allowing either more data or more page levels—or not putting any limits on the download.

A partially imported web site may have problems with the following elements:

- **Graphics**   If a graphic was not downloaded, it cannot be displayed on a page. Missing graphics are displayed as a small, red "x".

- **Components**   Special effects and features may be nonfunctional because the component is missing from the web site. If the component is called by the web page's HTML, you will get an error when you open the page or try to trigger the effect.

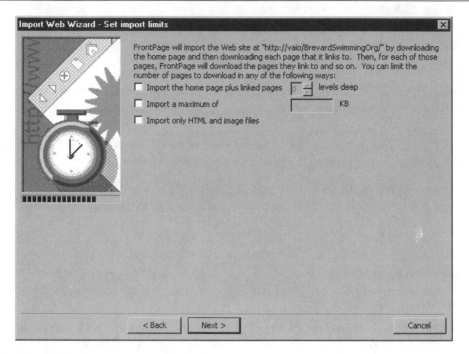

FIGURE 8-1   Limit the amount you want to download from an Internet web site during the import.

- **Hyperlinked Web pages**   If you click on a hyperlink that links to a missing page, you will get an error because the page is not available to display.
- **JavaScripts**   Features implemented via missing JavaScripts will not function.
- **Themes**   Themes will not display properly if the images that make up the theme have not been imported.
- **Databases**   If you either send the results of a form to a database (see Chapter 19) or retrieve database contents from a form (see Chapter 20), the forms will not function. You will get an error if you try to open a database results form or send form results to a missing database.
- **Forms**   If a form uses either a missing confirmation or error form, you will get an error when you submit the results of the form.

Open an Existing Web Site

There are quite a few ways to open a web site once you have created it. First of all, you can choose File | Recent Webs to see a list of recently opened web sites. Click one of these web sites or simply type the number of the web site as it appears on the list.

Another way to open a web site is to choose File | Open Web. This opens the Open Web dialog box, from which you can pick the web site you want to open.

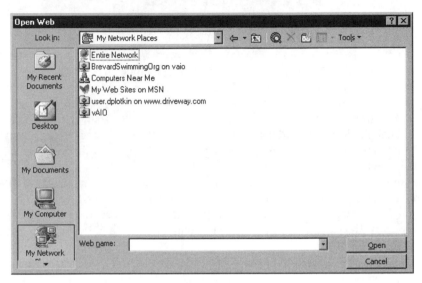

To open a disk-based web site, enter the name of the folder containing the web site in the Web Name field.

To open a server-based web, choose either Web Folders from the left column (Windows 98 and ME) or My Network Places (Windows 2000 and XP). You should see a web folder corresponding to the "root" web site for your server-based web sites (http://default or whatever you named your root web site). Double-click on this web folder to open it, and inside you'll find a set of web folders for each server-based web site you built with FrontPage.

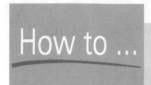

Pick a Location from the Look In Field

The Look In field at the top of the Open Web dialog box enables you to specify where you want to look for the web site. Choices in the Look In field include all your hard drives and network drives, My Network Places (or Web Folders, depending on your version of Windows), and FTP sites you define to store your web site files on another computer. (See Chapter 18 for more information on setting up and accessing FTP sites with FrontPage.) You can also click the Search the Web button (the small globe with a magnifying glass) to open your browser and look for a web page on the Internet. This URL of the web page may come in handy later.

The column on the left side of the Open Web dialog box also lets you navigate easily to often-used destinations. Exactly what appears in this list depends on which version of Windows you are running. For example, in Windows 2000 and XP, the list includes My Recent Documents, Desktop, My Documents, My Computer, and My Network Places.

This is because FrontPage creates a web folder automatically for each new server-based web site you create. Click one of the web folders to place the folder name in the Web Name field. Then click Open to open the web site.

You can enter a full URL for an Internet site in the Web Name field. If you do, FrontPage will try to open the site directly from the Internet. However, in order for this work, you'll need the username and password to access the site.

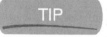

You can have FrontPage automatically open the last web site you worked with. This is handy if you frequently work on one web site. To set this option, choose Tools | Options and check the Open Last Web Automatically When FrontPage Starts check box.

Delete an Existing Web Site

If you no longer want to use a web site, you can delete it and recover the space. To delete a web site, open the site and make sure the Folder List is visible. Click the top line of the Folder List—the line that contains either the full pathname to the folder that contains the web site (disk-based) or the full URL of the web site (server-based). Press the DELETE key, or choose Edit | Delete. FrontPage confirms the deletion with the Confirm Delete dialog box.

If you want to preserve the files and folders that make up the web site, but you no longer want FrontPage to recognize this folder or URL as a FrontPage web site, choose the first option. You may wish to keep the files on your hard drive for a while in case you find you need to reuse a web page file or image from the deleted site. However, this web site won't clutter up your list of active web sites. If you want to delete the web site completely (including all the files and folders), choose the second option (Delete This Web Entirely). This frees up the space on your hard drive.

8

Chapter 9

Build Hyperlinks

How to...

- Add text hyperlinks to pages in your web site
- Add text hyperlinks to Internet pages
- Create graphic hyperlinks
- Define bookmarks and create hyperlinks to bookmarks
- Build image map hyperlinks
- Verify and recalculate hyperlinks

Virtually every web site has more than one page in it. If it didn't, it wouldn't be very interesting! In order to navigate from one page to another—and to various points within pages—you must use hyperlinks. In essence, hyperlinks are the glue that holds a web site together.

Understand and Use Hyperlinks

Hyperlinks let you navigate the Internet easily. Unless special permission is needed, you can access almost any page on the Internet by specifying its full URL in your browser. However, how could you possibly know the location of every page you want to visit? You can't, and with hyperlinks you don't have to. Once you reach the main page of a site, it can provide hyperlinks to other pages of interest. Simply by clicking one of these links, you can view the page without knowing its URL. Thus, hyperlinks are one of the most important elements of web pages (besides content, of course).

What Are Hyperlinks?

There are three main kinds of hyperlinks. They are

- **Internal Hyperlinks**   Hyperlinks that point to destinations contained within your own web site.
- **External Hyperlinks**   Hyperlinks that point to destinations on another web site.
- **Bookmarks**   Hyperlinks that point to a specific place on a page on your web site. If you are familiar with Microsoft Word, you have seen bookmarks in action.

A hyperlink always has two points of interest: the hyperlink itself and the destination of the link. The destination is where you end up when you click the hyperlink. The most common destination of a hyperlink is another web page—either inside or outside your web site. However, the destination of a hyperlink can be almost anything, including images, audio or video clips, programs, and so forth.

The hyperlink itself is attached to either a piece of text (sometimes referred to as *hypertext*) or a graphic (such as a button). In fact, you can attach multiple hyperlinks to a single image by creating an *image map*. We'll explore how to do that later in this chapter.

Someone browsing your site needs to have a clue where the hyperlinks are on a page, so they know where to click to trigger a hyperlink. Text-based hyperlinks are displayed in a browser underlined in blue unless the reader has already navigated to the destination of the hyperlink, in which case the hyperlink text is shown in purple. In addition, moving the mouse pointer over hypertext or a graphic that contains hyperlinks changes the mouse pointer into a pointing hand:

Click here to search my web site for information

NOTE   *The hyperlink colors displayed on your page may be different if you change the default hyperlink colors in the Background tab of the Page Properties dialog box.*

TIP   *When building a web page,* don't *use blue underlined text in your normal (nonhyperlink) content. Since most people are used to associating blue underlined text with hyperlinks, this will cause confusion.*

In addition to the automatic ways of clueing people in to the presence of a hyperlink, you can add your own effects. For example, in Chapter 6, you saw how you can add rollover effects to "flag" a hyperlink's presence. You can also add Dynamic HTML effects (discussed in Chapter 14) or use an "interactive button" component to call attention to a hyperlink (discussed in Chapter 13).

Add Text Hyperlinks to Pages in Your Web Site

The most common hyperlink you'll build while constructing your web site is a link to another page on your web site. You can either create a link to a page that already exists or create the hyperlink and the page it links to at the same time.

Create Text Links to Existing Pages in Your Web Site

To create a link to an existing page in your web site, use the following steps:

1. In Page view, select the text that will be used as the hyperlink. If the text doesn't already exist, type it into the page and then select it.

TIP   *You should make the hyperlink text descriptive of the destination. For example, a hyperlink that returns to your home page could say "Return to Home Page."*

2. Right-click the selected text and choose Hyperlink from the shortcut menu. Alternatively, click the Hyperlink button in the Standard toolbar or choose Insert | Hyperlink. The Insert Hyperlink dialog box opens (as shown in Figure 9-1).

Pick an existing
file or web page

Display different lists of files to
pick a hyperlink destination from

Text of the hyperlink

Move up one folder

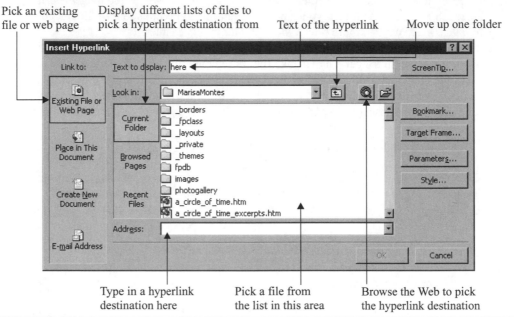

Type in a hyperlink
destination here

Pick a file from
the list in this area

Browse the Web to pick
the hyperlink destination

FIGURE 9-1   Specify the destination of your new hyperlink with the Insert Hyperlink
dialog box.

NOTE   *The Text To Display field at the top of the Insert Hyperlink dialog box shows the text
you selected in step 1 (above). You can change the hyperlink text by making changes
in this field.*

3. Create the hyperlink in one of the following ways:

■ Click the Existing File Or Web Page button and select a page in your current web
site from the list of files in the Insert Hyperlink dialog box.

■ Click the Folders button (labeled Browse For File) to open the Link To File dialog
box and navigate to a page that is stored on your hard drive or network drive. Click
the file to which you want to link.

■ Use the Address field to type the exact path to the file to which you want to link.

■ Click the Browsed Pages button to choose a hyperlink destination from web pages
you have viewed recently.

■ Click the Recent Files button to choose a hyperlink destination from files you have
recently created or edited.

4. If you want to change the ScreenTip (which appears when you hover the mouse over the hyperlink), click the ScreenTip button, fill in the text of the ScreenTip, and click OK.

5. Click OK in the Insert Hyperlink dialog box to create the link.

You'll know the link was created because the text is now blue and underlined—unless you have changed the hyperlink default colors, or the theme you are using overrides the color and effect for hyperlinked text.

You can also create a hyperlink using the Folder List or the Navigation Pane. To do so, open the page that you want to add a hyperlink to in the Page view. From either the Folder List or the Navigation Pane, drag the page to which you want to link into the open page.

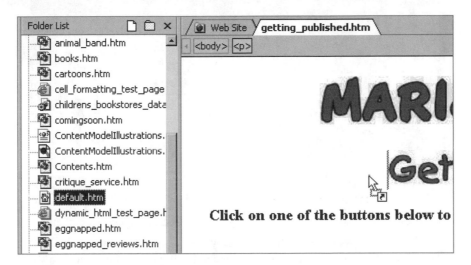

The hyperlinked page title is used as the text of the new hyperlink, but you can change that if you wish by modifying the Text To Display field in the Edit Hyperlink dialog box.

You can test your hyperlink in Design Page view or Preview Page view. In Design Page view, hold down the CTRL key and click the hyperlink to switch to the destination page. In Preview Page view, simply click the hyperlink to navigate to the destination page.

Create Text Links to New Pages in Your Web Site

If you want to create hyperlinks as you build your web site—and perhaps determine the need for new pages as you create hyperlinks—you can create the link and the page at the same time.

To create hyperlinks in this way, use the following steps:

1. In Page view, select the text that will be used as the hyperlink. If the text doesn't already exist, type it into the page and then select it.

2. Right-click the selected text and choose Hyperlink from the shortcut menu. Alternatively, click the Hyperlink button in the Standard toolbar, or choose Insert | Hyperlink. The Insert Hyperlink dialog box opens.

3. Click the Create New Document button in the list of buttons at the left edge of the dialog box. FrontPage displays a new version of the Insert Hyperlink dialog box.

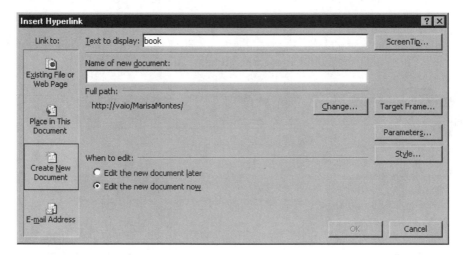

4. Enter the name of the new document in the (can you guess!) Name Of New Document field.

5. In the When To Edit section, choose when you want to edit the new document:

■ **Edit The New Document Later** When you click OK to complete the Insert Hyperlink, the new page is created but you are still viewing the page into which you inserted the hyperlink.

■ **Edit The New Document Now** When you click OK to complete the Insert Hyperlink, the new page is displayed, ready for editing.

6. Click OK to create the new page and hyperlink. The new page is a blank web page— you do not have the opportunity to pick from the web page templates if you create a page in this manner.

When you customize, name, and save the new page, the hyperlink automatically adjusts to point to the new page with the name you gave it.

Create Links to Other Files

Although the most "normal" destination for a hyperlink is a web page either within or outside your web site, you are not limited to hyperlinking to web pages. You can link to any file, including graphic files (JPG or GIF), documents (such as a Word or Excel document), and even program files. The Link To File dialog box (which appears when you click the Browse For File button) includes a Files Of Type drop-down list near the bottom.

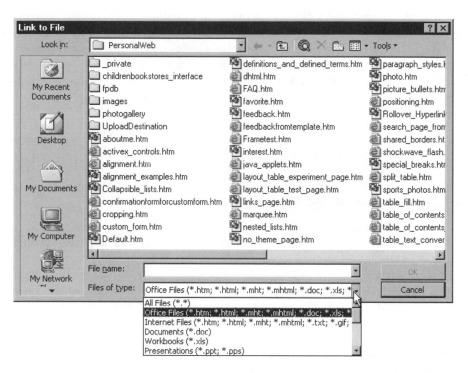

These files include all the different Microsoft Office applications' documents and templates, and all the common Internet files (HTM, HTML, and so forth), as well as the recognized web graphics formats (JPG and GIF).

If you build a link to one of these file types and then preview the page in a browser to test the link, the result will depend on how you have your computer configured. For example, if you have the Office application (such as Word or Excel) installed on your computer, you are given the choice to either download (Save) or open the linked item:

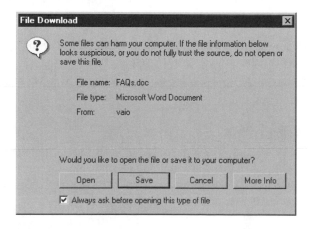

If you choose to open the file, it will open in FrontPage (or within your browser if you preview it in the browser). You can even edit the document if you are using Internet Explorer. However, if you choose a file type that is *not* a recognized document file for an application installed on your computer, clicking on the link opens a dialog box that enables you to pick a destination on your hard drive or network and download the file to your computer.

If the file type is an executable file (ending in .exe), the resulting dialog box enables you to either download the files or open it directly from the web. Opening an application directly from the Internet is not a good idea for large applications such as Word (winword.exe).

Create Links to External Web Sites

It is only a little more involved to create a hyperlink to another web site on the Internet. This can be quite handy. Instead of duplicating someone else's content on your web site (which wastes space and could get you in big trouble for copyright violation), you can simply provide a link to the information on another web site. An advantage to this approach is that if the information is updated on the destination page, you'll be pointing to the most up-to-date information. However, if the destination site changes its structure and the linked page disappears (or the filename changes), your link will be broken—and your viewers will get the dreaded HTTP 404 (file not found) error. Thus, if you link to external web sites you'll want to test these links periodically. An easy way to verify all your hyperlinks is to use the report designed exactly for this purpose. This report (and many other useful reports) is discussed in Chapter 17.

To create a link to an external web site, you must be connected to the Internet. After selecting the hyperlink text and opening the Insert Hyperlink dialog box, use the following steps:

1. Click the middle button in the row of buttons adjacent to the Look In field. It is labeled Browse The Web. This action opens your browser.

If you know the exact URL of the page or file you want to link to, you can skip the rest of the steps and just enter it in the Address field. Make sure that the entire URL is entered, including the http:// portion.

2. Use the standard browser techniques to navigate to the page to which you want to link. Once you have reached the page, return to FrontPage.

3. The Insert Hyperlink dialog box now shows the site in the Address field. Click OK to create a hyperlink to this site.

Reformatting Hyperlinks

Under normal circumstances, hyperlinks are displayed in a blue, underlined font. However, you can modify the font properties of a hyperlink, applying virtually any font, color, size, and effect you want. To do so, simply select the hyperlink text and make your modifications as described in Chapter 3 in the "Format Text" section.

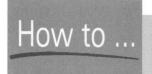 **Build a Graphic Hyperlink**

When building hyperlinks, you aren't limited to just using text—you can use a graphic as a hyperlink as well. The technique is identical to setting up a text hyperlink, except that you select the graphic (instead of text) prior to defining the hyperlink. However, unlike a text hyperlink, a graphic gives no indication that it represents a hyperlink unless you move the mouse pointer over the graphic.

When you define a graphic hyperlink, you have an alternate method of defining the destination of the hyperlink. To use this alternate method, right-click the graphic and choose Picture Properties from the shortcut menu, then switch to the General tab.

```
Picture Properties                                            [X]

 Appearance  General  Video

 Picture:
 images/ToOrderMyBooksAnimCrop.gif       Browse...      Edit...
  Picture File Type...

 Alternative representations

   Low-Res:        [                    ]    Browse...

   ☐  Text:        [                         ]

   Long Description: [                    ]    Browse...

 Default hyperlink

   Location:       [                    ]    Browse...

   Target Frame:   [                ]  ...✏   Parameters...


                                    OK          Cancel
```

To specify the hyperlink destination, type it into the Location field, or click the Browse button to open the Edit Hyperlink dialog box and select the hyperlink as discussed earlier. Click OK to close the Picture Properties dialog box and add the hyperlink to the picture.

Create and Link to Bookmarks

Standard hyperlinks take you from page to page or from web site to web site. Bookmarks allow you to jump to a specific location within a web page.

What Are Bookmarks?

As with hyperlinks, linking with bookmarks requires two things: the hyperlink itself and the destination of the link. A *bookmark* is the destination. It is a special placeholder you can place on a web page. Bookmarks are most useful when you create a long scrolling page that contains a lot of information arranged in a structured fashion. Thus, typical uses for bookmarks include a table of contents or alphabetical toolbar at the top of a long page. You might also create links throughout a long page that instantly return you to the top of the page.

To link using bookmarks, you must set up both the link and the bookmark.

Create Bookmarks

Before you can link to a bookmark, you must create the bookmark, using the following steps:

1. In Page view, select the text or graphic you want to link to. As with hyperlinks, you can select any text (including a single letter, word, or line) or a graphic. Headings or subheadings on the page are prime candidates for bookmarks because you often want to jump straight to a heading.

2. Select Insert | Bookmark. The Bookmark dialog box opens.

TIP   *If you highlighted text before opening the Bookmark dialog box, the default name of the bookmark is the text you highlighted.*

3. Give the bookmark a name in the Bookmark Name field. The name should be short but meaningful, since you'll need to recognize the bookmark name when you build the hyperlink that links to it.

4. Click OK to close the Bookmark dialog box and create the bookmark.

In Design Page view, the bookmark appears with a dashed underline. However, the bookmark is invisible in Preview Page view or in a browser.

> ### Mami's Banana Omelet (Tortilla de Guineo)

NOTE *You can create a bookmark without first designating text or a graphic as the bookmark. If you do, the bookmark is created at the cursor position. The location of the bookmark is designated on the page by a small flag that shows the dashed underline. This flag is not visible in Preview Page view or in a browser.*

You can jump directly to a bookmark on a page within FrontPage. This can be handy to navigate quickly to a particular section on a page so you can modify that section. To jump to a bookmark, choose Insert | Bookmark to open the Bookmark dialog box. In the Other Bookmarks On This Page text box, pick the bookmark to which you want to jump. Click the Goto button to jump to the bookmark.

Edit and Delete Bookmarks

If you want to change the name of a bookmark, right-click the bookmark and choose Bookmark Properties from the shortcut menu to open the Bookmark dialog box. To change the name of the bookmark, simply type the new name into the Bookmark Name field and click OK. FrontPage reconfigures any hyperlinks that use this bookmark as a destination to reflect the new bookmark name.

To delete a bookmark, choose the bookmark from the Other Bookmarks On This Page text box and click the Clear button. The bookmark is deleted and the dashed underline disappears from the page. However, note that any hyperlinks that used this bookmark as a destination are *not* automatically modified, and will now be nonfunctional because they point to a nonexistent bookmark. You will need to locate and repair these broken hyperlinks.

Link to Bookmarks

Once you've built a bookmark, you can create a link to it. Although the normal use of bookmarks is to link to them from the same page on which the bookmark is located, you can actually link to a bookmark from any page—it is just another hyperlink destination. Thus, creating a link to a bookmark is very similar to creating any other hyperlink. Use the following steps:

1. In Design Page view, select the text that will be used as the hyperlink. If the text doesn't already exist, type it into the page and then select it.

2. Right-click the selected text and choose Hyperlink from the shortcut menu. Alternatively, click the Hyperlink button in the Standard toolbar or choose Insert | Hyperlink. The Insert Hyperlink dialog box opens.

3. To link to a bookmark in the current page, click the Place In This Document button to display a list of bookmarks for the document:

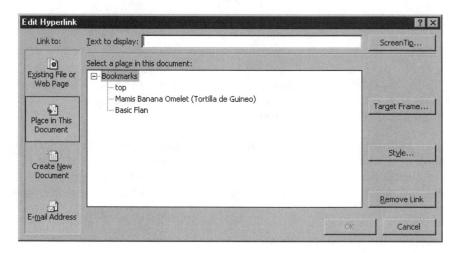

4. Choose the bookmark and click OK. This creates the hyperlink to the bookmark on the web page.

If you want to create a hyperlink to a bookmark on a *different* web page, first create the hyperlink to the page as detailed in "Create Text Links to Existing Pages in Your Web Site," earlier in this chapter. With the Insert Hyperlink dialog box still open, click the Bookmark button to open the Select Place In Document dialog box:

Pick the bookmark from the list of bookmarks in the dialog box and click OK to create the hyperlink to the bookmark on the web page.

HTML provides an automatic bookmark called "top." This bookmark takes you back to the top of the current page, even if you didn't define a bookmark there. This is handy when you have a long page. You can provide one or more hyperlinks that take the reader back to the top of the page. You might want to word this hyperlink "Back to Top." To use this automatic bookmark, create a hyperlink that points to the current page. Then, click at the end of the current page name in the Address field (such as Default.htm), and type #top.

E-mail from a Hyperlink

Have you ever seen a hyperlink in a web page that says something like "Click here to send an e-mail"? When you clicked such a link, your e-mail program opened, ready for you to compose your e-mail. The e-mail address was probably already filled in, and the subject might have been filled in as well!

You can easily create this sort of hyperlink in your web site. This type of link is called a "mailto" link because the HTML keyword that appears in the hyperlink is "mailto," rather than the http:// keyword that indicates the target of the hyperlink is a location (either a Web page or a bookmark).

To create a mailto link, use the following steps:

1. In Page view, select the text that will be used as the hyperlink. If the text doesn't already exist, type it into the page and then select it.

2. Right-click the selected text and choose Hyperlink from the shortcut menu. Alternatively, click the Hyperlink button in the Standard toolbar, or choose Insert | Hyperlink. The Insert Hyperlink dialog box opens.

3. Click the E-mail Address button to open a new version of the Insert Hyperlink dialog box:

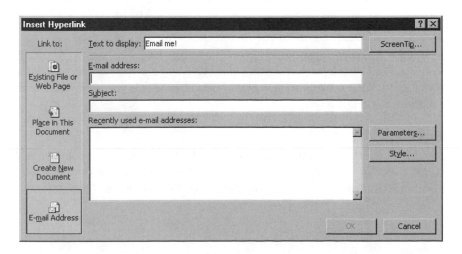

4. Enter the e-mail address in the E-mail Address field of the dialog box. As you begin to type the e-mail address, FrontPage automatically fills in the necessary "mailto" keyword.

5. If you wish, you can specify the subject of the e-mail as well by typing it into the Subject field.

6. Click OK to close the Insert Hyperlink dialog box and create the e-mail hyperlink.

When viewers click on the hyperlink in a browser, their e-mail application will open automatically. The e-mail address you specified (and the subject, if you defined one) will be automatically filled in.

Modify and Delete Hyperlinks

As you modify your site, you may find that you need to revise a hyperlink. For example, you may decide that you no longer need a hyperlink, but you want to keep the text or graphic that the hyperlink is attached to. Or you may want to redefine the destination page of a hyperlink. To make this sort of change, use one of the methods discussed previously to open the Edit Hyperlink dialog box (the simplest way is to right-click the hyperlink and choose Hyperlink Properties from the shortcut menu). From this dialog box, you can do the following:

- **Modify the Hyperlink Destination**   To change the destination page of a hyperlink, reselect the page using the previously discussed techniques. You can link to any of the destinations mentioned earlier, including web pages within your site and external web pages.

- **Delete the Hyperlink**   To delete the hyperlink, click the Remove Hyperlink button to clear the contents of the Address field and then click OK. The hyperlink is deleted, and the blue text and underline (if it was a text-based hyperlink) disappear.

- **Modify the Bookmark Destination**   To modify the bookmark that a hyperlink links to, or add a bookmark to a link, pick a bookmark from the list of bookmarks you can display by clicking on the Place In This Document button.

Build Image Maps

Up to this point, you've created hyperlinks attached to a block of text or a single graphic. It is also possible to attach multiple hyperlinks to an image. Clicking a particular part of the graphic links to one destination, while clicking another part of the graphic sends you somewhere different. Welcome to the world of *image maps*.

What Is an Image Map?

An image map is a graphic that contains one or more hyperlinks within its boundaries. To define an image map, you specify the graphic as well as one or more *hotspots*. A hotspot is a bounded area within the graphic to which you can attach a hyperlink. Since an image map graphic can contain multiple hotspots, and each hotspot can be attached to a hyperlink, the overall image map can contain multiple hyperlinks.

Image maps can be very handy in any situation where a particular area of an image needs to have meaning. For example, if you were running a travel site, you could place a graphic of the state of Florida on your web page. Clicking different areas of the state (such as cities, national parks, and so on) could provide information about that area.

Add a Graphic to the Page

The first step in building an image map is to add the graphic to the page. There is really nothing special about the graphic at this point, so you can add the graphic just as detailed in Chapter 4, in the section "Add Graphics from a File." To insert a picture from a file, choose Insert | Picture | From File. To insert clip art, choose Insert | Picture | Clip Art.

Once you add the graphic to the page and select it, FrontPage makes the Pictures toolbar available. If you don't see it, you may have turned it off. To reenable the Pictures toolbar, right-click on any toolbar to display a list of toolbars and click on Pictures in the list. By default, the Pictures toolbar appears at the bottom of the screen, but as with any other toolbar, you can drag it off the bottom and position it as a window or dock it against a different edge of the screen. Some of the tools in the Pictures toolbar (see Figure 9-2) are designed especially for creating hotspots for image maps, and we'll cover those tools in the next few sections.

Create Hotspots Using Text in a GIF

If you just need a rectangular hotspot (either with or without a text label), the easiest way to create it is to use the Text tool in the Pictures toolbar. This technique only works for GIF graphics. If you try to use the Text tool for a JPEG, FrontPage will automatically convert it to a GIF, warning you beforehand that this conversion may cause the number of colors to decrease. To create a hotspot using the Text tool, use the following steps:

1. Click the Text tool in the Pictures toolbar. A small, rectangular hotspot appears in the selected GIF.

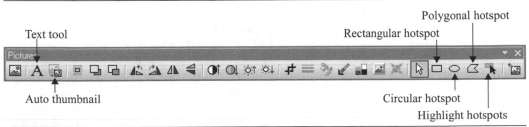

FIGURE 9-2   Use the special tools in the Pictures toolbar to define hotspots.

2. Type any text you want in the hotspot.

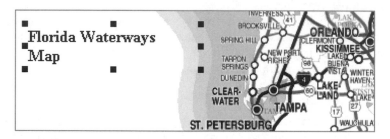

3. Select the hotspot by clicking in the graphic outside the hotspot, then clicking in the hotspot again. When the hotspot is selected, you'll be able to see the sizing handles.

4. Click inside the hotspot and drag it to the location where you want it. This location must be within the bounds of the graphic. If you want to resize the hotspot, click one of the sizing handles and drag the rectangle to the size you want. To edit the text, click within the text to provide the text cursor and edit the text using standard techniques.

Once you have created the hotspot with the Text tool, you can attach a hyperlink to it. To do so, right-click the hotspot and choose either Picture Hotspot Properties or Hyperlink from the shortcut menu (or choose Insert | Hyperlink). This opens the Insert Hyperlink dialog box. Create a hyperlink for the hotspot just as you would any other hyperlink.

Create Hotspots Using the Pictures Toolbar Tools

The rest of the hotspot tools in the Pictures toolbar work somewhat differently from the Text tool. For one thing, you can add a hotspot to a JPEG without converting it to a GIF. In addition, the moment you draw the hotspot on the graphic, the Insert Hyperlink dialog box appears. Therefore, you must have the hyperlink's destination created—and the address at hand—prior to creating the hotspot, because if you click Cancel in the Insert Hyperlink dialog box, the hotspot is not created.

NOTE   *You can, of course, choose the Create New Document option in the Insert Hyperlink dialog box, and create the hyperlink destination "on the fly."*

To create a hotspot using one of the Pictures toolbar tools, click the tool shape you want to use. If you choose the Circular or Rectangular tool, click and drag inside the outline of the graphic to create the shape (Figure 9-3 shows using the Circular Hotspot tool).

The moment you release the mouse button, the Insert Hyperlink dialog box appears. Select the hyperlink as usual, and click OK to close the dialog box and create the hyperlink. Once the hotspot is created, you can click in it to select it (the sizing handles appear), and drag it to a new location or resize it by dragging one of the sizing handles. You can also right-click a hotspot and choose Picture Hotspot Properties or Hyperlink from the shortcut menu to open the Edit Hyperlink dialog box and change the hyperlink.

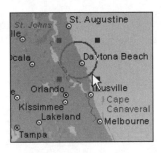

| FIGURE 9-3 | Click and drag with the Circular Hotspot tool to create a hotspot in an image. |

The Polygonal Hotspot tool is often used to outline a particular area of a graphic. For instance, you could use it if you wanted to outline a Florida county on the graphic in Figure 9-3. To create the hotspot with Polygonal Hotspot tool, click where you want the hotspot to start. Continue clicking around the outline of the area you want highlighted. To complete the hotspot, click the start of the outline again. At this point, the Insert Hyperlink dialog box opens and you can proceed to define the hyperlink as described above.

NOTE *When editing the shape of the polygonal hotspot, you can adjust the shape by dragging any of the sizing handles. The sizing handles appear at each of the spots you clicked to originally create the shape.*

Sometimes it is helpful to see just the hotspots in a graphic. To hide the graphic in which the hotspots are embedded, click the Highlight Hotspots button in the Pictures toolbar. This shows the outline of all the hotspots (see Figure 9-4). You can select a hotspot (it turns black), or double-click the hotspot to open the Edit Hyperlink dialog box. However, you can't resize or move the hotspots in this view.

Create an Auto Thumbnail for an Image

If you've ever waited for a page full of images (especially photographs) to load in your browser, you know it can take a while! Many people may give up and go elsewhere if your page takes too long to load. One common trick to shorten the download time for a web page is to use thumbnails. A thumbnail is a reduced version of an image. This reduced version (which loads much faster than the full image) gives the reader an idea of what the full image will look like. If you attach a hyperlink to the thumbnail and attach the hyperlink destination to the full image, the reader can click the thumbnail to view the full image.

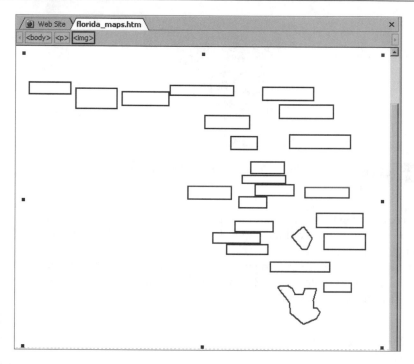

FIGURE 9-4   Click the Highlight Hotspot button to see just the hotspots in an image map.

TIP   *If you have a lot of photos to display, you are better off using the Photo Gallery, described in Chapter 5.*

You can configure how FrontPage creates the auto thumbnail by choosing Tools | Page Options and clicking the Auto Thumbnail tab.

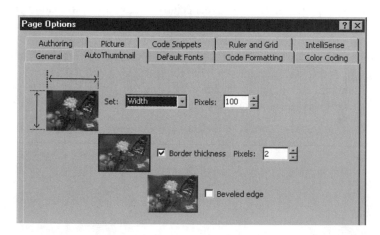

From this dialog box, you can configure the following properties of an auto thumbnail:

- **Size**   Bigger thumbnails give a better idea of what the image is, but also lead to bigger files. To set the size of the thumbnail, choose the dimensions from the Set drop-down list. Choices include Width, Height, Longest Side, and Shortest Side. Set the value for the selected dimension by using the adjacent Pixels spinner. You can specify the size for more than one of these dimensions, but only one of the dimensions—the last dimension you set—has any effect on the thumbnail size.

- **Border Thickness**   If you want the thumbnail to have a border, check the Border Thickness checkbox. Set the thickness of the border in the adjacent Pixels spinner.

- **Beveled Edge**   If you want the thumbnail to have a beveled edge, check the Beveled Edge check box.

NOTE *The changes you make to the Auto Thumbnail properties apply to subsequently created thumbnails. Existing thumbnails don't change.*

FrontPage makes it very easy to use hyperlinked thumbnails. To do so, use the following steps:

1. Create a web page that contains the photos you want to display, in the order you want to display them. Save the page, and allow FrontPage to copy any images into the Image directory of the current web site.

2. Click an image, and choose the Auto Thumbnail button in the Pictures toolbar.

3. FrontPage automatically creates a reduced version (thumbnail) of the graphic, and replaces the full version with the thumbnail (see Figure 9-5). The thumbnail is actually a hyperlink to the full version of the graphic.

4. Switch to Preview and click one of the thumbnails. The page is replaced by a page containing the full version of the graphic.

FIGURE 9-5   With Auto Thumbnail, FrontPage created a thumbnail version of all the graphics on this page and added a hyperlink to the full version.

5. Switch back to Design Page view, and save the page (File | Save). FrontPage provides the Save Embedded Files dialog box so you can save the automatically created thumbnail images.

6. Click OK to save the thumbnail images and finish saving the page.

Recalculate Hyperlinks

Hyperlinks are very important to a web site because they let you navigate the site easily. However, FrontPage also uses hyperlinks in some of the special-purpose web pages and components it can create for you. These include the table of contents component (see Chapter 13) and shared borders (see Chapter 10). Because of this, it is important to keep FrontPage's internal "map" of hyperlinks complete and up to date. Thus, you should periodically recalculate the hyperlinks. To do so, choose Tools | Recalculate Hyperlinks. Click OK in the dialog box that warns you that the process can take a few minutes, and wait for the process to finish. Once it is done, your table of contents, shared borders, and other automatically maintained hyperlinks will be complete and accurate.

Chapter 10

Build Shared Borders, Link Bars, and Dynamic Web Templates

How to...

- ■ Add and customize shared borders
- ■ Work with the Navigation view
- ■ Create custom link bars to link to any web page
- ■ Create link bars based on the Navigation view
- ■ Create Dynamic Web Templates to place common content on pages

Another way to add common content to web pages is to use Dynamic Web Templates. You can define multiple templates, and attach any defined template to one or more web pages. Not only does this provide common content on each page, but it also limits where custom content can be added to an attached web page. FrontPage includes a special tool called shared borders. As you will see, shared borders enable you to give a web site a consistent look and feel, as well as making it easy to place the same content (like a copyright notice or "Back to Home Page" button) on each page. Another good use of shared borders is to have FrontPage place an automatically maintained set of hyperlinks between pages (called link bars) that makes navigating your web site easy.

You can also create custom link bars—reusable sets of hyperlinks that can include links to any web page.

Understand and Use Shared Borders

When you create a web site, it is important that your pages look like they were well planned and designed to work together. We've already discussed one tool that can help you achieve this effect: themes. Shared borders is another tool that can help your site have a consistent look and feel.

What Are Shared Borders?

A shared border is an area of the page that is the same on each web page on which it appears (see Figure 10-1). Thus, you can add text and graphics to a shared border, and that text and graphics will appear on each page. A shared border can be turned on or off for a page, but cannot be customized to look different on one or more pages of the web site. As you can probably guess from the name, the shared borders are located around the borders of the page, and you can activate the top, left, right, or bottom shared borders.

Shared borders are most powerful when used with link bars based on the navigation structure (covered in more detail later in this chapter). In essence, these link bars are automatically maintained hyperlinks that make it easy to find your way around the web site. You can create a structure of your web site (like an organization chart) using the Navigation view (also covered later in this chapter), and FrontPage will automatically construct the appropriate hyperlinks in the link bar based on the navigation structure.

Add Shared Borders to a Site

To add shared borders to a site, choose Format | Shared Borders to open the Shared Borders dialog box (shown in Figure 10-2).

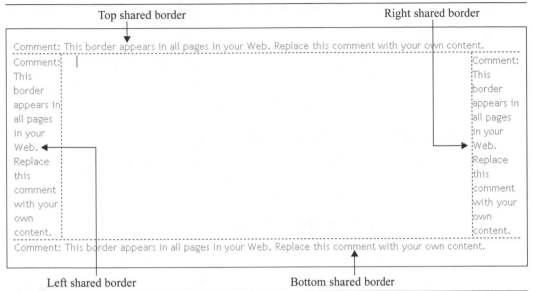

FIGURE 10-1   Shared borders allow you to place the same content on each page of your web site.

NOTE   *If Format | Shared Borders is unavailable, choose Tools | Page Options and click the Authoring tab. Then check the Shared Borders check box.*

10

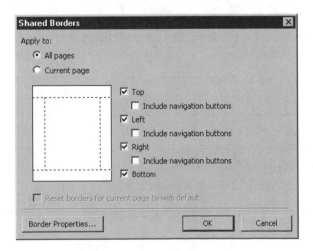

FIGURE 10-2   Use the Shared Borders dialog box to specify which borders to display.

To add any of the shared borders to the page, click in the Top, Left, Right, or Bottom check boxes. To determine how much of the web site to apply the shared borders to, pick one of the options at the top of the dialog box. The All Pages option applies this set of shared borders to all the pages in the web site. The Current Page option applies this set of shared borders only to the current page. Thus, you can set up the entire site to use top and left shared borders by picking the All Pages option. You can then open individual pages and turn on additional shared borders or turn off existing shared borders and pick the Current Page option to change only that page.

Add Color and Images to Shared Borders

FrontPage enables you to set the background color or use a picture for the background of a shared border. To do so, right-click in any shared border and pick Border Properties from the shortcut menu. This displays the Border Properties dialog box.

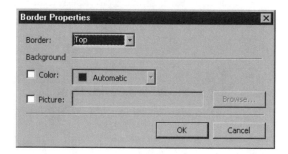

If you have more than one shared border active, pick the shared border you want to customize from the Border drop-down list. To add a background color, check the Color check box, and pick the color from the Color drop-down list.

To add a picture to the background, check the Picture check box and either type in the filename (including the full path) for the picture or click the Browse button and choose the picture from the file dialog box that appears.

You can only pick a background picture from the current web site. The file dialog box used for picking the picture file does not allow you to navigate to another location on your hard drive. Therefore, you'll need to copy the background picture into your current web site before you can add it to the shared border as a background.

Customize Shared Borders Content

You can place virtually any page element in a shared border—graphics, text, components (where appropriate), and even hyperlinks. Anything you place in the shared border shows up on every page that includes the shared border. In general, you add items to a shared border just as you would to any other portion of the page. You can format text using all the same font and paragraph formatting tools.

> **TIP**   *One very handy use of the bottom shared border is to put copyright and revision information there.*

Page banners work a little differently, however. When you add a page banner to the top shared border, it automatically takes the name of the page as it is displayed in Navigation view (covered later in this chapter). Thus, page banners are *not* the same on every page.

Enable Navigation Buttons

Navigation buttons (see Figure 10-3) give readers hyperlinks they can click to navigate their way through your web site. Depending on the theme, these hyperlinks can show up as text links or buttons. The set of navigation buttons are actually a special form of link bar, discussed later in this chapter. This *navigation bar* provides buttons on each page that reflect the structure of your web site, and can give readers easy ways to navigate "down" to subordinate pages or "up" to the parent page—and even make a quick jump back to the home page. The really nice thing about the navigation bar is that FrontPage keeps track of it, and as the reader browses from one page to the next, FrontPage makes sure that the navigation buttons on the current page reflect the structure of the web site. And, if you change the structure of your web site, FrontPage will make sure the navigation bar reflects the structure change as well. You'll see how to create the structure of your web site in the next section.

Navigation "buttons"

Comment: This border appears in all pages in your Web. Replace this comment with your own content.

About Me
Interests
Favorites
shared borders
Photo Gallery
Feedback

Comment: This border appears in all pages in your Web. Replace this comment with your own content.

Comment: This border appears in all pages in your Web. Replace this comment with your own content.

FIGURE 10-3   Navigation buttons give your readers an easy way to navigate through the structure of your web site.

You can add a navigation bar containing the navigation buttons to the top, left, and right shared borders. Use the Shared Borders dialog box (see Figure 10-2) to turn on the navigation buttons. To place a set of navigation buttons in a shared border, check the Include Navigation Buttons check box right below the check box for the shared border. The Include Navigation Buttons check box is only available if the All Pages option is selected in the Shared Borders dialog box.

If you enable navigation buttons on a page that is not included in the Navigation view (structure of the web site), the buttons will not be visible in the shared border. Instead, a note will prompt you to add the page to the Navigation view.

Work with the Navigation View

To build meaningful navigation bars and make sense of their properties (which we will discuss shortly), you need to tell FrontPage the structure of your web site. You can think of the structure of your web site as being similar to an organization chart. At the top of the chart is the home page (CEO), and successive levels of pages (departments) fall below that. Once you specify this organization structure, FrontPage will be able to create and maintain your navigation bars.

You set up the structure of your web site using the Navigation view (see Figure 10-4). To open the Navigation view, choose the Web Site view, then click the Navigation button at the bottom. The Folder List (if turned on) displays all the pages in your web site, and the large area to the right is where you'll build your web site's "organization chart." Initially, this area contains only the home page, which is normally the top layer of your web structure.

Build the Web Structure

To begin building the structure of your web site, use the following steps:

1. To create the second level of the web site, drag a page from the Folder List into the main window. As you do, a connector appears between the home page and the dragged page. Position the page below the home page and release the mouse button.

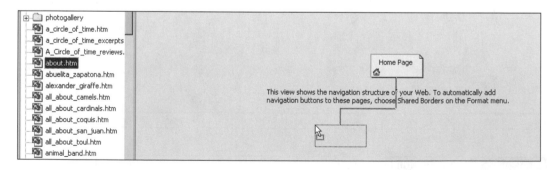

2. Continue dragging pages into the main window. As you move a page close to a page already in the window, the connector will connect to that page. By maneuvering the pages in the main window, you can build your web site structure's second level, third level, and so forth. When it is done, you might have something like that shown in Figure 10-5.

You can rearrange the structure easily. For example, if you want to change the order of pages connected to a common parent page, just drag one of the pages horizontally and release it where you want it. The other pages will move out of the way to make room for the relocated page. You can also change the parent of a page. To do so, start dragging the page until the connector disconnects from the current parent. Continue to move the page close to the intended parent until the connector connects to the new parent page.

Add Existing Pages in Navigation View

To add an existing web page to the web site structure in Navigation view, right-click on a page in the Navigation view and choose Add Existing Page from the shortcut menu. This opens the Insert Hyperlink dialog box. From this dialog box, you can choose an existing page in the web site. You can also choose an address on the Internet, create a new document and hyperlink to it, and insert an e-mail address link. In fact, about the only type of hyperlink you *can't* insert is a bookmark.

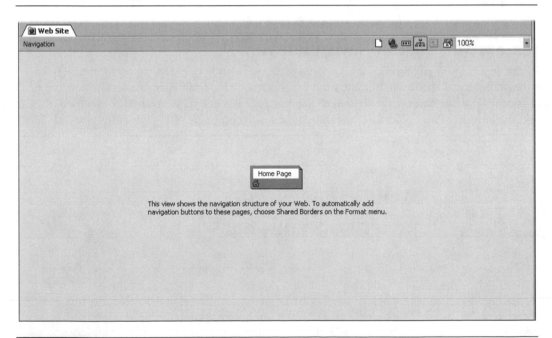

FIGURE 10-4   Use Navigation view to build the structure of your web site.

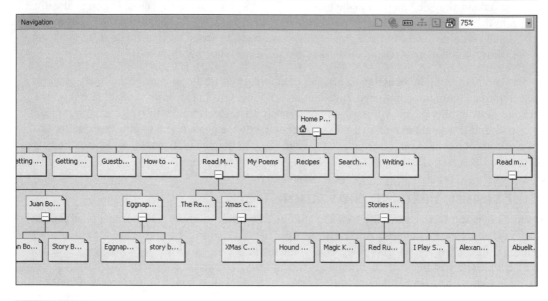

FIGURE 10-5   A complete web site structure might look something like this.

Create a New Page in Navigation View

You can create a new page and connect it to its parent page all in one step. To do so, right-click the parent page and choose New | Page from the shortcut menu. FrontPage creates the new page and attaches it to the parent page. However, the new page has not yet been created as a file—it does not show up in the Folder List, nor can you access its properties (the Properties entry in the

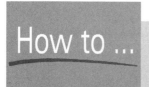

Exclude Pages from Navigation Link Bars

At times, it may be appropriate to place a page in the navigation structure, but *not* include it as a hyperlink in the navigation link bar. A good example might be the confirmation page for a form—since the reader should only reach the confirmation page after submitting the form. To exclude a page from the navigation link bar, right-click the page and deselect the Included In Navigation Bars option. There is also a button for this purpose in the Navigation toolbar. FrontPage excludes the selected page and any subordinate pages, and changes their icons to gray to indicate their state.

shortcut menu is grayed out and unavailable). To complete the creation of the page, double-click it in Navigation view to open it in Page view.

TIP   *It is best to give the new page a meaningful name before double-clicking it to open it. The name of the page is used as the default title and filename when the page is created, so a meaningful name is better than "new_page_1". To give the page a name, click its icon, then click its name. The name becomes selected, and you can type a new name. Alternatively, you can choose Rename from the page's shortcut menu and enter the new name.*

Delete a Page in Navigation View

You can delete a page from the Navigation view. To do so, right-click the page and choose Delete from the shortcut menu, or select the page and press the DELETE key. This opens the Delete Page dialog box.

The Delete Page dialog box gives you two options: to remove the page from all the navigation bars (and thus from the main window of the Navigation view), or to delete the page from the web site altogether. Choose the option you want and click OK.

Customize the Navigation View

You can customize how the Navigation view looks. Here are the available options:

■ **Zoom In and Out**   You can change the zoom level to zoom in and see more details, or zoom out and see more of the overall diagram. To change the zoom level, use the Zoom drop-down list in the Navigation title bar to set the zoom you want. Alternatively, you can right-click a blank area of the Navigation view main window and pick Zoom from the shortcut menu.

■ **Expand and Collapse Subtrees**   You can collapse the view of subordinate pages by clicking the minus sign (–) on a page. To reexpand the subtree, click the plus sign (+) that replaced the minus sign when you collapsed the subtree. You can also choose to view just a page and its subtree (see Figure 10-6) by right-clicking the page and choosing View Subtree Only in the shortcut menu, or by clicking the View Subtree Only button in the Navigation title bar. To return to viewing the whole tree, click on the View Subtree Only button once again—either in the Navigation title bar or in the shortcut menu for the parent page. Or, you can just click the button that appears above the page at the top of the subtree.

10

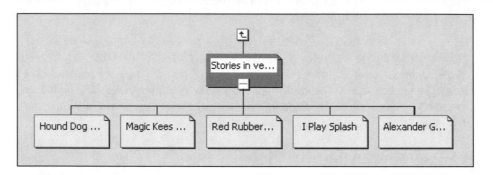

FIGURE 10-6
Focus on one page and its subtree by viewing only that part of the structure.

■ **Switch Between Portrait and Landscape**   Sometimes, you can see more of your web structure by viewing it laid out from left to right, rather than top to bottom. To switch between portrait and landscape modes, click the Portrait/Landscape button in the Navigation title bar. You can also right-click in an empty area of the main window and choose Portrait/Landscape from the shortcut menu.

Rename Pages in Navigation View

The icon names you see in Navigation view are very important and just a little confusing. These names are *not* the same thing as either the filename or the title of the page, although the icon name is initially set to the same value as the page's title. The icon's title is important not only because it is the only visible label in Navigation view, but also because this title is what FrontPage uses for the page banner of a page. In addition, it is used as the hypertext or button label for any references to this page in a navigation bar. For example, let's say you create a page with a filename of MyPage.htm and title (in Page Properties) of MyPage. You then change the icon name to Silly Page. The page banner or any hypertext or button in a navigation bar whose hyperlinked destination is this page will use Silly Page as the hypertext or button label.

There are two ways to rename the icon in Navigation view. First of all, you can click the icon, pause, and then click again. This selects the icon name and makes it editable. Just type the new name. The second way is to right-click the icon and choose Rename from the shortcut menu. This action makes the name editable.

Link with Link Bars

Link bars are aids to navigating both your web site and the Internet. There are two types of link bars. The first has already been mentioned: navigation bars are based on the structure of your web site. Once you specify how you want the link bar configured, FrontPage will automatically maintain navigation bars for you, modifying them as necessary when you change the structure of the web site. In addition, the navigation bar on a particular page reflects where that page is in the structure of the web site. Navigation bars are discussed in the next section.

The other type of link bar is a "custom link bar." Essentially, a custom link bar is a reusable set of hyperlinks. You construct a custom link bar by specifying the set of hyperlinks to be included in it. Once built, you can place the custom link bar in any web page—and even embed it in a shared border so that it appears on every page. Custom link bars are discussed later in this chapter.

Navigate with Navigation Bars

Navigation bars are easy to create and configure, and are one of FrontPage's best ease-of-use features. Before navigation bars, it was up to you to rebuild sets of hyperlinks if you restructured your web site. With navigation bars, you can concentrate on content and let FrontPage worry about the "housekeeping" of navigating the structure of your web site.

Add a Navigation Bar to a Page

You can add a navigation bar to a page in several different ways. One of those ways was covered earlier in this chapter: checking the Include Navigation Buttons check box in the Shared Border dialog box. The other way you can add a navigation bar to a page is to use the following steps:

1. Position the text cursor where you want the navigation bar.

2. Choose Insert | Navigation to open the Insert Web Component dialog box with the Link Bars option already selected in the Component Type list.

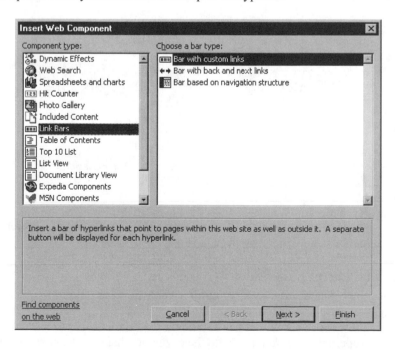

3. In the Choose A Bar Type list, click on Bar Based On Navigation Structure. Then click the Next button to proceed.

You can also choose Insert | Web Component, pick Link Bars from the Component Type list, and then click on Bar Based On Navigation Structure in the Choose A Bar Type list.

4. The next dialog box displays a list of styles for the navigation buttons. Choose one of the styles in the Choose A Bar Style list and click Next to proceed. If you choose the Use Page's Theme option (the first one in the list), the button styles will change if you change the page theme.

5. From the next dialog box, pick either a horizontal or vertical orientation for the navigation buttons.

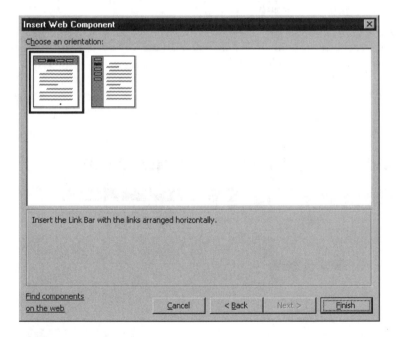

6. Click Finish to proceed. FrontPage opens the Link Bar Properties dialog box so you can configure the navigation bar's hyperlinks (see Figure 10-7). The next section details how to set exactly which hyperlinks are displayed in a navigation bar.

Configure a Navigation Link Bar

You can configure a navigation bar to specify exactly what hyperlinks it is to display, as well as set how the navigation bar displays those links.

To set up which levels of your web structure a navigation bar is going to link to, you can adjust the link bar properties when you first build the navigation bar (see the previous section)

Home page

Page from which relationships
will be drawn

These pages will be shown
in the navigation bar

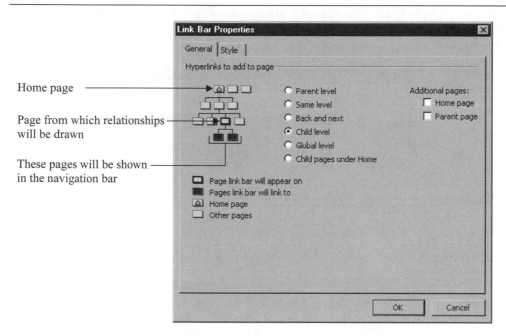

FIGURE 10-7   Use the Link Bar Properties dialog box to set which hyperlinks to display and
how to display them.

or by modifying the properties later. To modify the properties of an existing navigation bar,
switch to Design Page view, right-click in a navigation bar, and choose Link Bar Properties
from the shortcut menu. The Link Bar Properties dialog box appears (see Figure 10-7, above).
You can independently configure each of the navigation bars on your page. For example, if you
choose to place a navigation bar in both the top and left shared borders, you can set up each one
separately. However, the top navigation bar has the same configuration on every page in which it
appears. This is also true of the left or right navigation bars.

The Link Bar Properties dialog box shows you a representation of the general structure of a
web site. The purpose of this structure is to show you which related pages will have hyperlinks
in the navigation bar. As you make selections from the options in the Hyperlinks To Add To Page
section, pages that will be hyperlinked are represented by a blue rectangle. The page from which
the relationships are drawn is represented by the rectangle with the blue border.

You have many options about what pages you want hyperlinked in the navigation bar. You
can link to the Parent Level (up one level), pages on the Same Level, the Child Level (down one
level), only to the Global Level (pages at the same level as the home page) of the web, and only
the pages just beneath the home page (Child Pages Under Home). You can also just use buttons
that navigate back to the previous page you visited and (once you have used the Back button)
forward to the page you just stepped back from (Back And Next). In addition, you can add links
to both the home page and the parent page.

 *Use the three available shared border navigation bars for different purposes. For example, use the left navigation bar for child pages, and the top navigation bar for the same level or parent level (whichever makes more sense in your web site).*

You can adjust the style of the navigation bar at any time by clicking on the Style tab in the Link Bar Properties dialog box.

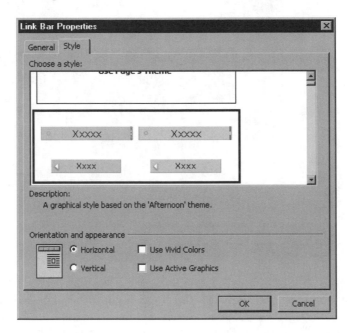

Choose a style of button and pick either the Horizontal or Vertical option to change the orientation of the navigation buttons. You can also choose Use Vivid Colors or Use Active Graphics to brighten and animate the navigation buttons—just as you could with themes (see Chapter 6).

Insert a Navigation Bar Without Shared Borders

You can use navigation bars even when you don't have shared borders on a page. To do so, place the text cursor where you want to add the navigation bar and choose Insert | Navigation, then pick the Bar Based On Navigation Structure, just as you did before. This opens the Link Bar Properties dialog box. Pick the options you want and click OK to create the new navigation bar. You can move the navigation bar around just like a block of text. However, since this navigation bar is not in a shared border, it does not automatically appear on the other pages of the web site. Unlike navigation bars placed in shared borders, you can uniquely configure the navigation bar on each page. For example, the navigation bar on one page could show child pages, while the navigation bar on another page could show parent pages.

Insert a Navigation Bar with Existing Shared Borders

Although it doesn't happen very often, you may wish to insert navigation bars when you already have shared borders on the page—even when some of those shared borders already include a navigation bar. One reason would be to add a navigation bar to the bottom shared borders, which you cannot otherwise configure to include a navigation bar with the Shared Borders dialog box. Another reason would be if you want to include two navigation bars in a shared border. For example, the "normal" navigation bar in the top shared border might be configured to display pages at the same level in the web site. You could add a second navigation bar that displays child pages. The Corporate Presence Wizard (a wizard for building a corporate web site) uses this trick.

NOTE *Remember, since the navigation bar is in a shared border, it will appear on every page of the web site that displays the shared border.*

To add a navigation bar to a shared border, click in the shared border and create a navigation bar as previously discussed.

Build a Link Bar with Custom Links

A custom link bar enables you to create a set of hyperlinks that you can use over and over. Thus, if you have a standard set of hyperlinks to web sites that you want available on many pages, create a custom link bar and just include it on those pages. In fact, if you place the custom link bar in a shared border, the link bar will be available on every page that includes the shared border. Custom link bars don't *look* much different from navigation link bars—but they are very useful because you can include hyperlinks to pages outside of your web site as well as pages in your web site.

Create and Insert a Custom Link Bar

To create a custom link bar, use the following steps:

1. Position the cursor and choose Insert | Navigation to open the Insert Web Component dialog box with the Link Bars option selected in the Component Type list.

2. Choose Bar With Custom Links from the options in the Choose A Bar Type list on the right side of the dialog box. Click Next to proceed.

3. Pick a style for the buttons in the custom link bar from the list of available styles. Click Next to proceed.

4. Choose either Horizontal or Vertical as the orientation for the buttons in the custom link bar. Click Finish.

5. FrontPage opens the Link Bar Properties dialog box. If you have not yet created any custom link bars, the first thing you'll see is the Create New Link Bar dialog box.

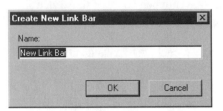

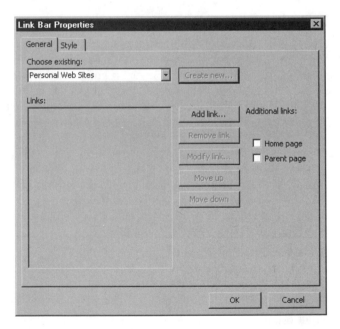

NOTE   *The Link Bar Properties dialog box associated with custom link bars is very different from the navigation link bar Link Bar Properties dialog box.*

6. Type in a name for the custom link bar and click OK. This action closes the Create New Link Bar dialog box and makes the Link Bar Properties dialog box available.

7. Click the Add Link button to open the Add To Link Bar dialog box where you can define the link. This dialog box is identical to the Insert Hyperlink dialog box, except that it doesn't allow you to choose bookmarks.

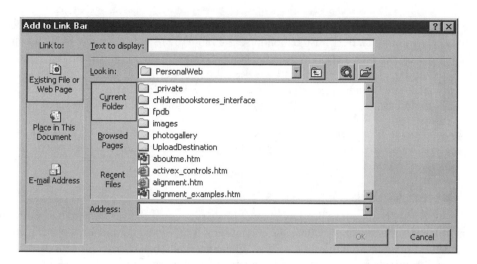

8. Use any of the techniques for specifying a hyperlink discussed in Chapter 9 to specify a link.

9. Type the text to display on the button in the Text To Display field.

10. Click OK to return to the Link Bar Properties dialog box.

11. Repeat steps 8–10 to continue adding links to the custom link bar.

12. If you want to include the home page or the parent page (for the page on which the custom link bar is shown), check the Home Page check box or the Parent Page check box.

13. Click OK to create the custom link bar and add it to the page.

In addition to adding a link, you can perform the following operations from the Link Bar Properties dialog box:

■ **Remove Link**   Click the Remove Link button to delete the selected hyperlink.

■ **Modify Link**   To change the address for the link or the text to display, click the Modify Link button to open the Modify Link dialog box. Other than the title, it is identical to the Add To Link Bar dialog box.

■ **Move Up or Move Down**   The links are displayed in the order in which they appear in the list. To rearrange the order, click on a link and click either Move Up or Move Down.

■ **Configure Additional Links**   To add the web site home page or the parent page to the custom link bar, check the Home Page check box or the Parent Page check box. Unlike the rest of the links in the custom link bar (which are the same no matter what page you place the link bar in), the parent page will change to show the parent page (if any exists for the current page).

■ **Change the Style**   If you change your mind about the style of the buttons, you can click on the Style tab and pick a different style.

10

Once you have created your first custom link bar, the Link Bar Properties dialog box appears immediately when you click the Finish button in step 4 (above). To create another new custom link bar, click the Create New button, type in the name of the link bar in the Create New Link Bar dialog box, and click OK. Then add links as described above.

To simply insert an existing link bar into a web page, pick the link bar from the Choose Existing drop-down list in the Link Bar Properties dialog box and click OK.

 *Want to place your custom link bar on every page in your web site? Piece of cake— just add a shared border to the pages in the web site and add the custom link bar to the shared border!*

Modify Custom Link Bar Properties

Once you have built a custom link bar and added it to a page, you aren't stuck with it. To modify the custom link bar, simply right-click on it and choose Link Bar Properties from the shortcut menu. This reopens the Link Bar Properties dialog box, where you can change any of the properties of the link bar, including changing the style, adding and removing links, rearranging the link order, and configuring additional links.

If you just want to quickly add another link to a custom link bar, all you have to do is click on the Add Link hyperlink at the right end (for horizontal link bars) or the bottom (for vertical link bars). Clicking on the Add Link hyperlink opens the Add To Link Bar dialog box, where you specify the additional link.

To delete a custom link bar from a page altogether, select the link bar and press the DELETE button.

Work with Custom Link Bars in Navigation View

Any custom link bars you build show up as separate structures in the Navigation Pane or the Navigation view, as shown in Figure 10-8. In this figure, you can see the hierarchical web site structure as well as custom link bars.

You can make the following modifications to the custom link bar in the Navigation Pane or the Navigation view:

- **Move a Page from the Web Site Structure to the Custom Link Bar**   You can remove a web page from the navigation structure (and thus from any navigation link bars you have created) and into a custom link bar. To do so, click and drag the web page from the navigation structure to the custom link bar. As you do, a shadowed line and rectangle indicate where the page will be located in the custom link bar when you release the mouse button.

- **Rearrange the Order of the Links in the Custom Link Bar**   You can rearrange the order of the links in a custom link bar. To do so, click and drag the link to its new position in the link bar. As you do, a shadowed line and rectangle indicate where the page will be located when you release the mouse button.

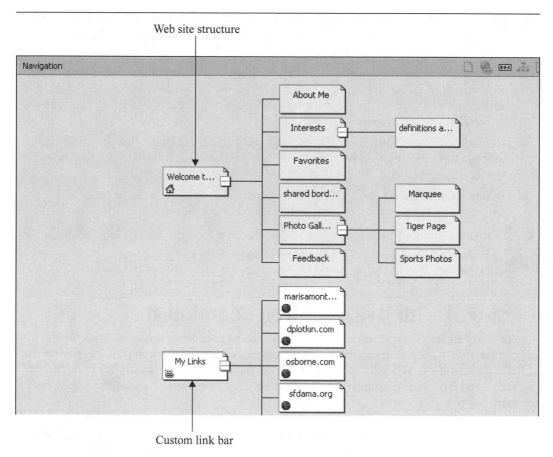

Web site structure

Custom link bar

FIGURE 10-8   The Navigation view displays the custom link bars as well as the web site structure.

■ **Add an Existing Page to the Custom Link Bar**   To add an existing web page to a custom link bar, right-click on the link bar name and choose Add Existing Page from the shortcut menu. This opens the Insert Hyperlink dialog box. From this dialog box, you can choose an existing page in the web site. You can also choose an address on the Internet, create a new document and hyperlink to it, and insert an e-mail address link.

■ **Remove a Link from the Custom Link Bar**   To remove a link from the custom link bar, click on the link and press the DELETE key or choose Delete from the shortcut menu.

■ **Rename a Link in the Custom Link Bar**   Renaming a link in the custom link bar changes the displayed text for the link anywhere it appears on a web page. To change the name of the link in the link bar, right-click on the link and choose Rename from the shortcut menu. Or, click on the link, pause, and then click again. Either way, the link name becomes editable and you can type in the new name.

- **Add a New Blank Page to a Custom Link Bar**   To create a new blank page and add it to a custom link bar all in one operation, right-click the link bar name and choose New | Page. A new blank web page is created and added to the custom link bar.

- **Create a New, Empty Link Bar**   To create a new, empty custom link bar, right-click in a blank area of the Navigation view and choose New | Custom Link Bar from the shortcut menu. You can then add links to the empty link bar using any of the techniques discussed previously.

- **Rename a Custom Link Bar**   To rename a custom link bar, right-click on the link bar top page (the topmost page when viewing the Navigation view in portrait mode) and choose Rename from the shortcut menu. Type the new name into this top page.

- **Delete a Custom Link Bar**   To delete a custom link bar, click on the top page and press the DELETE key or choose Delete from the shortcut menu.

 *While you can select a custom link bar and copy it (Edit | Copy or choose Copy from the shortcut menu), this doesn't seem to do anything useful—you can't paste the link bar into a page.*

Share Content with Dynamic Web Templates

Dynamic Web Templates provide another way to place the same content on multiple pages without having to physically place it on each page. If you update a Dynamic Web Template, all pages attached to that template will reflect the change. Since you can have as many Dynamic Web Templates—and their attached pages—as you want, they are more flexible than shared borders, since there can be only a single set of shared borders for the entire web site.

A Dynamic Web Template is broken up into two kinds of areas: *editable regions* and everything else. Once a web page has been attached to a Dynamic Web Template, the author of that page can add and edit content only within the bounds of the *editable region*. All other content that exists in the Dynamic Web Template is also present on the attached page, but the author of that page cannot modify that content. Figure 10-9 shows a page that has been attached to a Dynamic Web Template.

Build a Dynamic Web Template

To create a Dynamic Web Template, create a new web page or open an existing web page. Add the editable regions to the page by using the following steps:

1. Place the text cursor where you want the editable region.

2. Choose Format | Dynamic Web Template | Manage Editable Regions. This displays the Editable Regions dialog box:

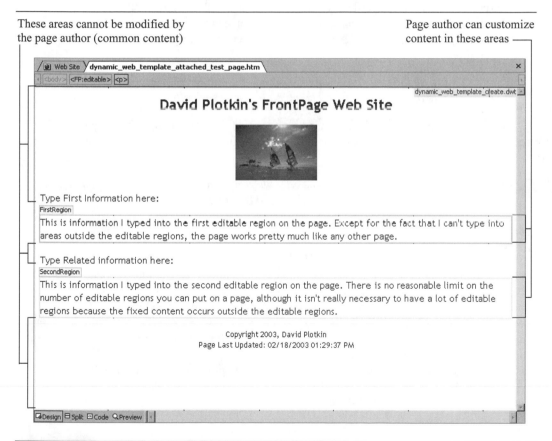

These areas cannot be modified by the page author (common content)

Page author can customize content in these areas

10

FIGURE 10-9   A page attached to a Dynamic Web Template limits where the author can make changes—and shows common content on all pages attached to the template.

If the web page has already been saved, FrontPage will prompt you to resave it as a Dynamic Web Template (.dwt) file.

3. Type in the name of the editable region and click the Add button. Once you click the Close button, the region you added is displayed with an orange border and the name of the region:

4. Save the Dynamic Web Template file.

There are several things to note about the editable region. First of all, it stretches completely across the screen. Unlike shared borders, you can't create an editable region that extends less than the full width. Next, once you place an editable region, you cannot click and drag it to another location. You can, however, move it up and down the screen by adding content above or below the editable region.

If you simply MUST have an editable region that doesn't stretch across the whole page, create a table and place the editable region in one of the cells.

Once you have the editable regions placed, you can add any other content to the page. This content will appear on any page attached to the template, but will not be modifiable by the author of the page.

You can also place content inside the editable region. Although this content can be changed by the author of the attached page, this content can provide a good starting point for creating the content of the attached page.

Attach a Web Page to a Dynamic Web Template

To make use of a Dynamic Web Template, you simply attach a web page to that template. To do so, open (or create) the web page, and choose Format | Dynamic Web Template | Attach Dynamic Web Template. Then choose the template to use from the Attach Dynamic Web Template dialog box (which is just a standard File Open dialog box). If the attached web page is empty, you are done. If the attached web page *does* have content, FrontPage provides the Choose Editable Regions For Content dialog box (shown in Figure 10-10).

This dialog box enables you to choose which editable region you want to place the content (shown as *(Body)* in the dialog box) into. To choose a different editable region, click the Modify button to display another version of the dialog box:

Pick the new region from the New Region drop-down list and click OK twice to close both dialog boxes and map the content to the editable region you prefer.

You can detach a page from a Dynamic Web Template by opening the page and choosing Format | Dynamic Web Template | Detach From Dynamic Web Template. The result is a page that contains all the content from the Dynamic Web Template as well as any content you added. You can now edit anything on the page, as it is not limited by the template.

You can also change the Dynamic Web Template to which a web page is attached. Choose Format | Dynamic Web Template | Attach Dynamic Web Template and pick the template from the list of files. You'll need to use the Choose Editable Regions For Content dialog box (see Figure 10-10) to map the existing editable regions to the editable regions in the new Dynamic Web Template.

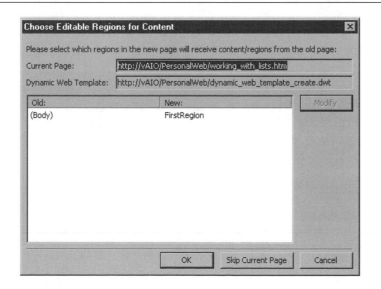

FIGURE 10-10   Anytime you need to map the editable regions from one page to another, you'll see the Choose Editable Regions For Content dialog box.

Modify a Dynamic Web Template

You can modify a Dynamic Web Template, adding and removing editable regions and any other content. Once you save these changes, FrontPage prompts you as to whether you want to update all the attached web pages. Just click Yes to update all the attached pages.

If you find that you need to manually update attached pages after changing a Dynamic Web Template (if, for example, you answered No when prompted to update attached pages), you have several ways to do that:

- ■ **Update an Open Page**   If the page you need to update is open, choose Format | Dynamic Web Template | Update Selected Page.

- ■ **Update All Pages Attached to the Selected Dynamic Web Template**   To update all pages attached to the selected Dynamic Web Template, choose Format | Dynamic Web Template | Update All Attached Pages.

- ■ **Update All Pages Attached to Any Dynamic Web Template**   If you modify several Dynamic Web Templates, you can update all pages attached to all the templates. To do so, choose Format | Dynamic Web Template | Update All Pages.

NOTE   *If the editable regions have changed, you'll need to use the Choose Editable Regions For Content dialog box (see Figure 10-10) to remap the editable regions from the existing web page to the new layout.*

Chapter 11

Collect Data with Forms

How to...

- Add forms with the Form Page Wizard
- Create a custom form
- Set up the form results destination
- Add and configure form fields
- Add a search form
- Build forms with the form templates: confirmation, feedback, guest book, and user registration

So far, you've learned quite a bit about building a web site. However, all the web pages you've learned to build and the capabilities you have learned to implement have one major limitation: the readers can look, but there is no mechanism for them to provide you with feedback or input. Forms change all that. If you add forms to your web site, your reader can send you information in a format you specify.

With FrontPage (and a web server running FrontPage server extensions), you can quickly build and customize forms and specify where you want the results to go—and you're done. No writing scripts, and no installing those scripts on a server.

What Are Forms?

A *form* is a special section of a web page (see Figure 11-1). A form can be a stand-alone web page, or it can be added to an existing page with other page elements. Within the form, you can place text and fields to collect data from the reader. Forms support many different kinds of fields—text boxes, drop-down lists, radio buttons, and so on. Later in this chapter you'll see how you can add and customize fields in a form and even apply validation rules to the data. A form must include at least one button (usually labeled "Submit") that sends the information to the web server. Most forms also include a button that clears the contents of the form, enabling the reader to start over.

As a web designer, you can use forms for many purposes. You can collect readers' opinions on your business or web site, provide a place for customer complaints or (hopefully!) praise, or enable a reader to subscribe to a newsletter. FrontPage even has a special form for searching the contents of your web site.

Since forms gather information from a reader that you usually want to keep, the form must have a way of forwarding the reader's input (the form's *results*) to you. FrontPage enables you to send form results to a text or HTML file that you can look at with a browser or download to your computer. If you send the results to a text file, you can format the results so they can be easily

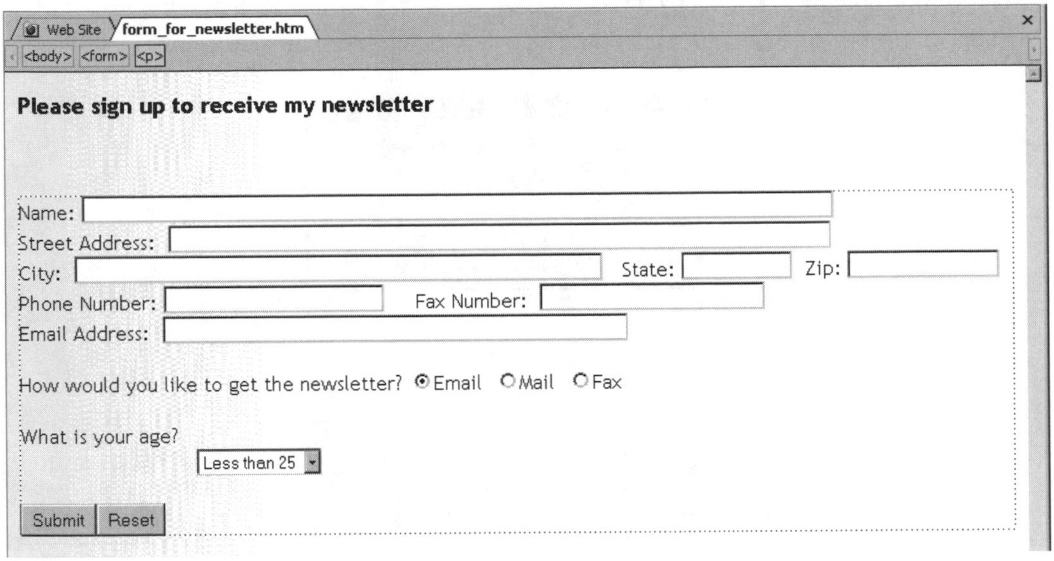

Please sign up to receive my newsletter

Name:
Street Address:
City: State: Zip:
Phone Number: Fax Number:
Email Address:

How would you like to get the newsletter? ⊙ Email ○ Mail ○ Fax

What is your age?
Less than 25

Submit | Reset

FIGURE 11-1   Use a form to gather input and return the input to you.

loaded into a spreadsheet or database. You can even have FrontPage send you an e-mail with the results.

> **NOTE**   *You can send the form results to a database for further analysis. For more information on this useful feature of FrontPage, see Chapter 19.*

FrontPage provides three different ways to create forms: the Form Page Wizard, customized forms, and form templates. Of course, once you finish using the Form Page Wizard or a form template, you can use the customizing tools to add fields, modify text, rearrange the form, and so forth.

Build a Form with the Form Page Wizard

FrontPage's Form Page Wizard enables you to create a form quickly and easily. It automates much of the grunt work involved in laying out a form and provides you with some pretty good formatting.

To start the Form Page Wizard, choose File | New to display the New Task Pane. Then click on More Page Templates to open the Page Templates dialog box. Select the Form Page Wizard and click OK. The first dialog box of the Form Page Wizard appears. Since no input is needed for the first dialog box, choose Next to proceed.

11

Add Questions to the Form

The next dialog box in the Form Page Wizard lets you add questions to your form.

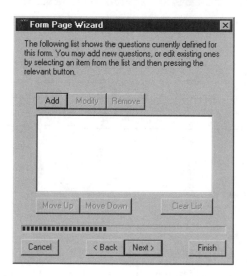

Each question you add requires you to specify various details about the question. Once you complete setting up the question, it will be listed in the text box below the Add button. At any time, you can select a question and either change it by clicking the Modify button or get rid of it by clicking the Remove button.

The questions appear on the finished form in the order in which they are listed in the Form Page Wizard. To change the order of the questions, click a question and click the Move Up or Move Down button.

To add a question, click the Add button. This displays a comprehensive scrolling list of questions you can add to your form. General question categories, such as Contact Information, Account Information, and Product Information, enable you to easily add a whole group of data elements to your form. Pick the question from the list and read the description in the Description field. If you wish, you can customize the text of the question by typing your text into the Edit The Prompt For This Question field. Click Next to move to the next Form Page Wizard dialog box.

Specify the Fields to Capture

The next dialog box you see lists the fields you might want to include as part of the question.

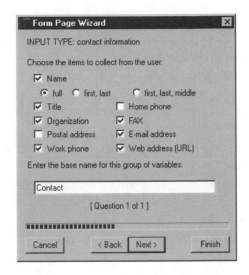

This list of fields is different for each question (that is, the list of fields for providing contact information is different from the list of fields for providing product information). Nevertheless, the format of the dialog box is the same: To add a field to the form, check the field's check box. For certain fields, you may also have options on how to display the requested information.

Click Next to return to the first dialog box, where you can continue adding questions. Once you are done adding questions in the first dialog box, click the Next button to proceed to the presentation options.

Add Your Own Questions

If none of the "canned" questions (such as providing personal data) meet your needs, the Form Page Wizard provides some very general questions you can customize. Once you pick one of these general questions, you can configure the question using different options. In addition to the options listed here, you must specify the text of the question and the name of the variable that stores the information.

NOTE *The variable name is used to reference the entered information in confirmation forms and results files (both discussed later in this chapter), and to provide the default names for database fields (see Chapter 19).*

To get at the general questions, scroll down the list of questions. Near the bottom, you find such options as:

■ **One of Several Options** This is a question that has a small number of possible answers. The reader can pick only one option. For this question, you specify the list of possible answers, and whether you want these answers presented as radio buttons, a drop-down menu, or a list.

■ **Any of Several Options** This is a question that has a small number of possible answers, and the reader can pick more than one of the options using check boxes. For this question, you specify the list of possible answers and whether you want these answers presented in multiple columns.

■ **Boolean** This is a question that can be answered yes/no or true/false. For this question, you specify whether you want the answers presented as yes/no radio buttons, true/false radio buttons, or a check box.

■ **Date** This question asks the user to provide a date. You can specify the format of the date entered.

■ **Time** This question asks the user to provide a time. You can specify the format of the time entered.

■ **Range** This question asks the user to rate something on a five-level scale. For this question, you can specify whether you want the scale to be numeric (1–5), bad to good (and three intermediate values), or disagree strongly to agree strongly (with three intermediate values). You also can choose whether to use the midrange value as the default value, and whether to use a drop-down menu instead of the default radio buttons.

■ **Number** This question asks the user to enter a number. You can set the maximum length allowed.

■ **String** This question asks the user to enter a text string. You can set the maximum length allowed.

■ **Paragraph** This question asks the user to enter one or more lines of text in a multiline text box.

Specify the Presentation Options

The next Form Page Wizard dialog box lets you specify how you want the data presented on the form.

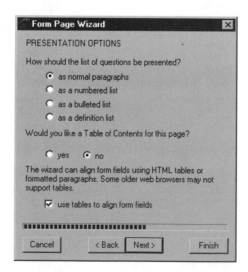

You can format the questions with the following options:

■ As normal paragraphs

■ As a numbered list

■ As a bulleted list

■ As a definition list

If your form is very long, you can choose to have FrontPage provide a table of contents. The table of contents appears at the top of the page. Clicking one of the questions jumps you right to that question on the page.

A recommended option is Use Tables To Align Form Fields. This makes sure that the fields line up and look ordered on the form. The table border is invisible, so the reader doesn't see the table. For more information about using tables, see Chapter 7.

Save the Results

The last Form Page Wizard dialog box lets you choose how the data entered in the form will be saved.

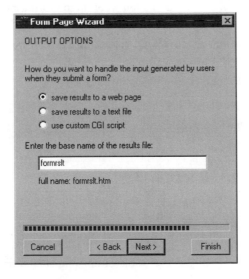

You have the following options:

■ **Save Results to a Web Page**   This option creates an HTML file in your web site. Each time a reader clicks on the Submit button at the bottom of the form, the set of paired values of the field name and the data (value) entered by the reader are saved to the web page. The web page file is given the name you specify in the Enter The Base Name Of The Results File field, appended with the appropriate extension (for example, .txt for a text file, .htm for a HTML file).

- **Save Results to a Text File**   This option creates a text file in your web site, and saves the data the same way as described in the previous bullet. A text file can be handy when you want to export the results to a database or a spreadsheet.
- **Use Custom CGI Script**   This option tells FrontPage that a CGI script (which you must write) is responsible for accepting the data and producing the results file.

Finish Up with the Form Page Wizard

Click Next, and then click Finish to create the new form (see Figure 11-2).

You need to do some customizing to the form before you save it. Here is what you need to change:

- The heading at the top of the page reads "New Page 1" (or something similar). You'll want to give the form page a more informative heading.
- Just below the heading is a line that reads "This is an explanation of the purpose of the form." Delete the text and replace with your explanation of what your form is for.
- The author name and copyright information are at the bottom of the page. You need to replace the placeholder text (for example, "Author information goes here") with your name and any copyright information you want on the form (including changing the default copyright year).
- Right-click the page and choose Page Properties from the shortcut menu. Change the page title to something meaningful.
- Finally, save the page and give it a meaningful filename.

Another oddity of pages generated by the Form Page Wizard is that FrontPage does *not* apply a theme to the form, although you can add one if you want. To do so, choose Format | Theme and choose the theme for the page.

View the Form Page Results

As people begin filling out your form and pressing the Submit button, you'll need to know where to go to look at the results. If you specified that the information should be saved as a web page, you'll see a new web page in your Folder List. You can open this page in a browser. If you specified that the information should be saved as a text file, you'll see the text file in your Folder List. You can view the text file with any application capable of opening such a file, such as Notepad or a word processor.

NOTE   *If you look for your results file (either a web page or a text file) immediately after creating your form, you won't see it. FrontPage creates the file automatically the first time someone fills out the form and submits the results.*

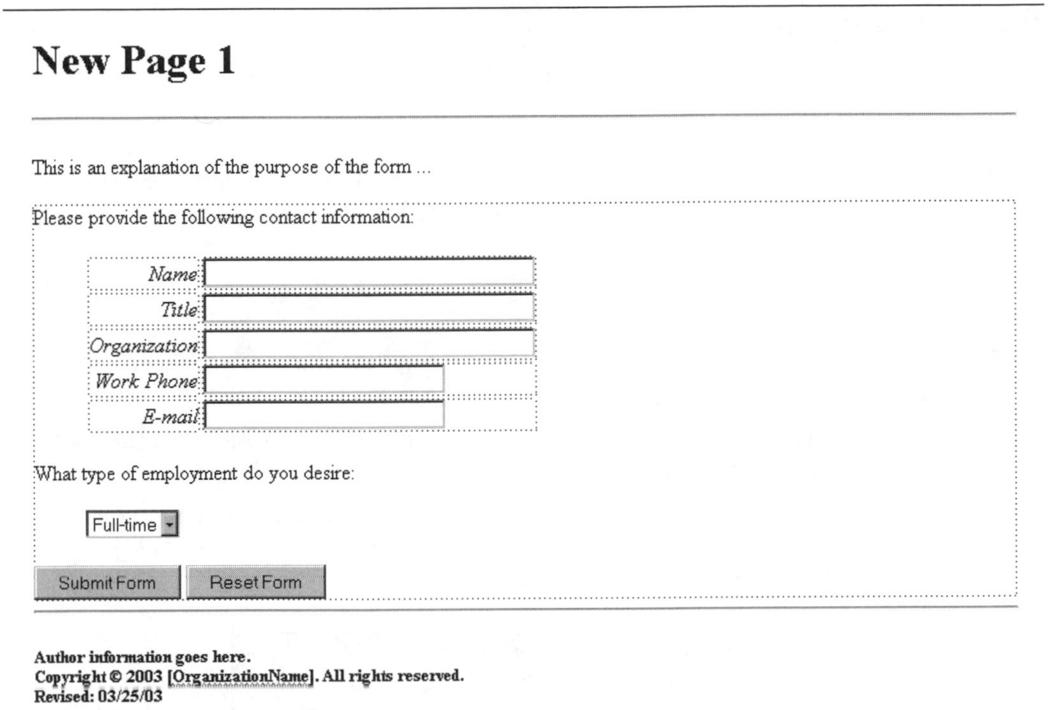

New Page 1

This is an explanation of the purpose of the form ...

Please provide the following contact information:

Name:	
Title:	
Organization:	
Work Phone:	
E-mail:	

What type of employment do you desire:

Full-time ▾

Submit Form	Reset Form

Author information goes here.
Copyright © 2003 [OrganizationName]. All rights reserved.
Revised: 03/25/03

FIGURE 11-2   You still need to customize some items on the "finished" form.

11

Build Custom Forms

The forms generated by the Form Page Wizard are pretty good, but they may not meet your needs, especially if you want to format your forms very differently from the options offered. You can customize a generated form using any of the techniques discussed in this section. However, you may just want to build a completely custom form.

NOTE   *If you inspect any form page, you'll see a dashed line surrounding the section containing the form. This dashed line identifies the form boundary. Insert any new fields* inside *this boundary. Inserting a form field outside the boundary actually creates a new form if you checked the Automatically Enclose Form Fields Within A Form check box in the General tab of the Page Options dialog box. Since form fields outside of a form are pretty useless, there is really no reason to clear this check box (it is checked by default).*

Create the Form

To create a custom form, use the following steps:

1. Open or create the page on which you want to place the form.

2. Choose Insert | Form | Form. FrontPage inserts the new form (with its dashed outline) into the page. The two default buttons (Submit and Reset) are also placed on the form:

3. To make room for your fields above the buttons, place the text cursor to the left of the buttons and press ENTER to give yourself some blank lines.

4. Enter any text and graphics using the standard editing tools discussed earlier in this book. Adding these elements to a form is just like building any other page.

5. To give the form a name, right-click anywhere in the form and choose Form Properties from the shortcut menu. Type the name for the form into the Form Name field near the bottom of the Form Properties dialog box.

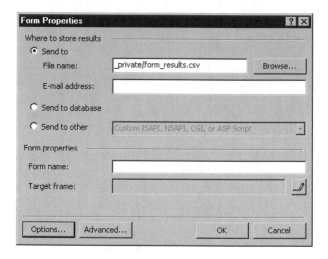

Save the Results

If you are not using the Form Page Wizard, you have a lot of options as to where the results go when someone submits the form. You can send the results to various types of text or HTML files, you can send the results in an e-mail, and you can choose which fields you want to see in the result set.

NOTE *You can also apply these customizations to the form created by the Form Page Wizard after the wizard finishes.*

To specify how the results get saved for a particular form, right-click in the form and choose Form Properties in the shortcut menu to open the Form Properties dialog box. In this dialog box you can set the name of the file where the results will go and the e-mail address to which the results will be sent. However, there are many more configuration options you can make to ensure that the results are handled just the way you want. To perform the rest of the configurations, click the Options button in the Form Properties dialog box. This opens the Saving Results dialog box (as shown in Figure 11-3).

Send Results to a File

The File Results tab (visible in Figure 11-3) lets you specify how to handle the results in a file. For a file, you can specify the following:

- **File Name**   If you specified a filename for the results file in the Form Properties dialog box, the filename will be visible in the File Name field. You can change the filename if you wish, or click the Browse button and pick an existing file.

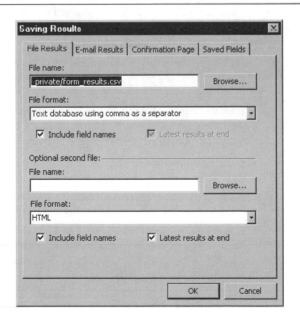

11

FIGURE 11-3   Use the many tabs in this dialog box to configure exactly how FrontPage should handle the form results.

- **File Format**   Use the File Format drop-down list to select the format of the result file. Table 11-1 details the available formats.

- **Include Field Names**   Check the Include Field Names check box to include the field names in the results file. If you leave out the field names, the results file will be smaller, but you may have a difficult time telling which data is which!

- **Latest Results at End**   Check the Latest Results At End check box to place the most recently submitted form results at the bottom of the file, rather than at the top (which is the default). This option is only available if you choose one of the XML or HTML formats. The text formats *always* place the latest results at the end, and you can't change that (this check box is checked and grayed out).

- **Specify a Second File**   You can specify all the above quantities for a second file. Using this option, you can (for example) send the results to both a text file and an HTML file.

Format	Format Description
XML	An XML-formatted page. An instance of an element called *Field* is created for each form field, using the *Name* attribute to identify the form field. The information submitted is between the *Field* element tags. The entire set of *Field* elements is contained within a *Record* element (see Figure 11-4).
HTML	Plain HTML text in a web page.
HTML definition list	HTML text formatted in a definition list. The "defined term" is the field name; nested below it (in the definition area) is the data entered by the user.
HTML bulleted list	HTML text formatted in a bulleted list. The content of each field (including the field name if you included it) is one bullet.
Formatted text within HTML	Standard formatted text, but inserted into a web page.
Formatted text	Standard formatted text in a text file. You can open and read such a file with Notepad or a word processor.
Text database using comma as a separator	All the data in one record is placed on a line (which may wrap) in the text file. The individual data elements are separated by commas.
Text database using tab as a separator	All the data in one record is placed on a line (which may wrap) in the text file. The individual data elements are separated by tabs.
Text database using space as a separator	All the data in one record is placed on a line (which may wrap) in the text file. The individual data elements are separated by spaces.

TABLE 11-1   The Available Formats for Form Results

```
 1 <?xml version="1.0" encoding="utf-8"?>
 2 <FormResults>
 3  <Record REMOTE_NAME="67.117.149.94" REMOTE_USER="STSBETA\dplotkin" HTTP_USER_AGENT="Mozilla/4.0 (compatible; MSIE 6.0; Windows 98; T312461; YComp 5.0.0
 4   <Field Name="MessageType">Complaint</Field>
 5   <Field Name="Subject">Web Site</Field>
 6   <Field Name="SubjectOther"></Field>
 7   <Field Name="Comments">The web site is not enabled for ASP, so the database stuff doesn&#39;t work!</Field>
 8   <Field Name="Username">David N Plotkin</Field>
 9   <Field Name="UserEmail">dplotkin@pacbell.net</Field>
10   <Field Name="UserTel">925-555-6655</Field>
11   <Field Name="UserFAX">925-555-9090</Field>
12   <Field Name="ContactRequested"></Field>
13  </Record>
14 </FormResults>
15
```

FIGURE 11-4   You can create XML output from a form.

Send Results to an E-Mail

Click the E-mail Results tab to specify the properties of a results e-mail.

Each time a reader submits the form, the results are gathered up into an e-mail by the FrontPage server and sent to an e-mail server for transmission.

For an e-mail, you can specify the following:

■ **E-mail Address**   Enter the e-mail address in the E-mail Address To Receive Results field. If you had previously entered an e-mail address in the Form Properties dialog box, it appears in this field.

- **E-mail Format** All the same format options detailed in Table 11-1 are available for composing an e-mail.

- **Include Field Names** Check the Include Field Names check box to include the field names in the results file.

- **Specify the Subject Line** Enter the subject for the e-mail in the Subject Line field. This is to help you figure out that this e-mail contains form results. If you want the subject line to contain the results from one of the form fields, check the Form Field Name check box and enter the name of the field into the Subject Line field.

- **Specify the Reply-To Line** If you want to specify the contents of the Reply-To line in the e-mail, type the contents into the Reply-To Line field. If you want the Reply-To line to contain the results from one of the form fields, check the Form Field Name check box, and enter the name of the field into the Reply-To Line field. Normally, you *do* want to collect the reader's e-mail address, and populate it automatically into the Reply-To line to save you the trouble of addressing a reply.

Display a Custom Confirmation Page

It is considered good manners to show the reader some sort of confirmation that their data has been received. By default, FrontPage provides a simple confirmation page that sums up all the data submitted. However, you can specify a different confirmation page if you wish. This confirmation form can be a standard web page that just acknowledges receipt of the data. As you will see later in this chapter, you can also build a specially formatted confirmation form using one of the general templates designed for this purpose.

To specify the URL of the confirmation web page (whether a regular web page or special confirmation form), use the Confirmation Page tab.

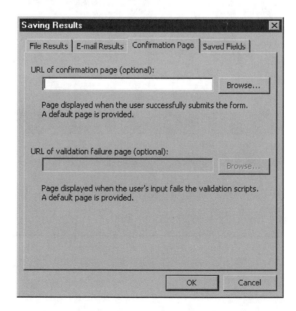

Enter the web page into the URL Of Confirmation Page field.

As you will also see later in this chapter, you can specify validation criteria for data someone enters into a form. For example, you can make a field required—the reader is not allowed to leave it blank. If you wish to provide a web page to tell a reader that the data they submitted is invalid, enter the URL for this web page into the URL Of Validation Failure Page field. This field is grayed out until at least one field in the form has validation criteria.

Specify the Saved Fields

You don't have to include all the fields on the form in the result set (although I can't think of a reason to ask the reader to provide the information unless you are going to save it!). To specify which fields to save in the result set, use the Saved Fields tab.

The Form Fields To Save text box initially lists all the fields on the form. You can select any of the fields and press BACKSPACE or DELETE to remove the field from the list. If you change your mind, you can bring back all the fields on the form by clicking the Save All button.

NOTE *In our example, we haven't added any fields to the form yet, so the list of form fields to save is empty with the exception of the Submit button (B1).*

In addition to the fields in which the reader enters data, you can also save some information about the reader and his or her computer. If you want to include the remote computer name, username, or browser type, check the appropriate check box. This information is gathered automatically (without the reader knowing it) when the reader submits the form results.

You can also set the display format of any date or time fields in the form results. To do so, choose the date format you want to use from the Date Format drop-down list and choose the time format you want to use from the Time Format drop-down list.

Specify Uploaded File Properties

If you add a File Upload field to your form (see "Add a File Upload Field," later in this chapter), you'll see an extra tab in the Saving Results dialog box: the File Upload tab.

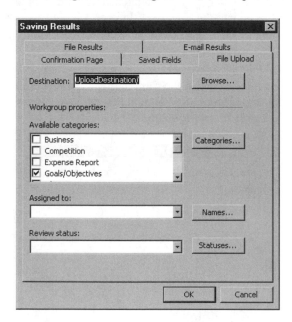

A File Upload field enables the reader to upload a file to the web site. Use the Destination field in the File Upload tab to specify the destination for the uploaded file. This is the folder within the web site where the uploaded files will be stored.

You can also specify a category for the uploaded files by checking one of the check boxes in the Available Categories list, or by using the Categories button to define a new category and then picking that category.

Although you can specify a category for the uploaded files and pick a value from both the Assigned To drop-down list and the Review Status drop-down list, these values are not assigned to the uploaded files. Further, the Assigned To drop-down list and Review Status drop-down list are empty the next time you open the dialog box.

Before you can upload files to the destination folder you selected, you'll need to configure that folder in a special way. To do so, right-click on the folder in the Folder List and choose Properties from the shortcut menu. This opens the Properties dialog box.

Clear the Allow Scripts To Be Run check box. This makes two additional check boxes available in the bottom section of the dialog box:

- Check the Allow Anonymous Upload To This Directory check box.
- If you wish to allow files in the directory to be overwritten by files of the same name, check the Allow Uploaded Files To Overwrite Existing Filenames check box.

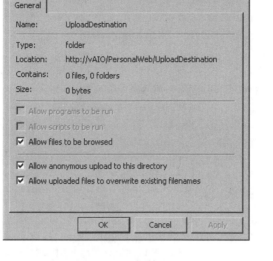

Send Results to a Discussion Form Handler

The Discussion Form Handler is designed to handle input from a discussion web site—a web site where people hold ongoing conversations, reading what others have said about a topic and replying. You can build a discussion web site using a FrontPage wizard. You may wish to direct the output from your custom form to a discussion web site. If you do, you must make some modifications to the form properties.

First, open the Form Properties dialog box, choose the Send To Other option, and select the Discussion Form Handler from the drop-down list. Click the Options button to open the Options For Discussion Form Handler dialog box with the Discussion tab displayed.

11

You can configure the following options:

- **Title** Set the name of the discussion group by entering it in the Title field. This title appears in all the articles in the discussion web site.

- **Directory** Use the Directory field to specify the directory in which FrontPage should store all the articles in the discussion web site. This directory must be hidden—which is why there is a leading underscore in the directory name.

- **Table of Contents** Use the Table Of Contents Layout section to customize how the table of contents will look. The table of contents is regenerated automatically each time someone submits an article. Use the Form Fields field to specify which fields appear for each article in the table of contents. Although Subject is the default, you can add other fields; just separate each field from the previous field with a space. Selecting a value (other than *none*) from the Date Format or Time Format drop-down lists displays the time and date the article was submitted. Checking the Remote Computer Name and User Name provides this information about the author of the article. You can check the Order Newest To Oldest check box to display the articles in that order. Finally, you can specify a page from which to get the background and colors for the table of contents page. Enter the name of the page to use into the Get Background And Colors From Page field.

The Article tab lets you customize how each article (posting) will look in the discussion web site.

You can include a web page to provide the header and a web page to provide the footer for each article. To do so, specify the URL of the web page in the URL Of Header To Include and the URL Of Footer To Include fields. You can include the time and date on which the article was submitted, and the format for the time and date by choosing them from the Date Format and Time Format drop-down lists. You can also include the Remote Computer Name and User Name of the author of the article by checking the appropriate check boxes.

Specify Hidden Fields

Sometimes it is helpful to include information that the reader did *not* enter in the form result set. This information could help you evaluate the results. An example of this sort of information is the version of the form the reader was using. To add your own information to the form so that it appears in the result set, you use *hidden fields*. For each hidden field, you specify two values: the field name and the value that goes with it. In our form-version example, the field name might be "Version" and the value that goes with it could be "1.0". This is called a *name/value pair*. The browser sends this information to the form result destination when the user submits the form.

To create and populate hidden fields, click the Advanced button in the Form Properties dialog box to open the Advanced Form Properties dialog box.

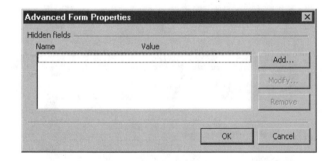

To create a hidden field and its value, click the Add button. In the resulting Name/Value Pair dialog box, enter the field name in the Name field and the associated value in the Value field. Then click OK to add the hidden field. At any time, you can select an existing pair and click Modify to change either the name or the value. You can also click Remove to remove the name/value pair from the list.

If you use the default confirmation form, the hidden fields will show on the confirmation form. If you don't want them to, build your own confirmation form!

Add Fields to a Form

To insert a field into a form, choose Insert | Form, and then pick the type of field you want to add from the submenu that appears. There are many types of fields, including a one-line text box, a check box, radio buttons, and a drop-down list.

You can select a field and change the alignment of the field on the form using the alignment tools in the Formatting toolbar. For example, you can center the field on the page by clicking the Center button in the Formatting toolbar.

Once you have added a field to a form, you can change its properties by right-clicking the field and choosing the Properties entry from the shortcut menu. This entry may be called Form Field Properties, Group Box Properties, or Advanced Button Properties, depending on the type of field. We'll discuss the specifics of the field properties for each type of field in the next few sections.

From the Properties dialog box you can also specify the field formatting for Font, Paragraph, Border, Numbering (for a numbered list or bullets), and Position (discussed in Chapter 14). To do so, click the Style button to open the Modify Style dialog box, and click on the Format button to display a list of formatting options:

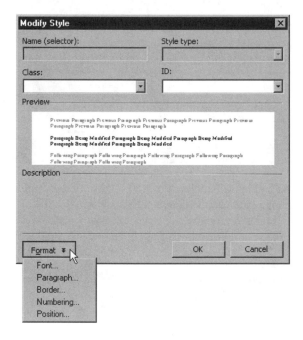

Make your choice from this list and then specify the formatting from the resulting dialog box.

For most fields, you can also specify validation criteria. To do so, click the Validate button in the field's Properties dialog box. We'll discuss the validation options for each type of field in the next few sections.

Add a One-Line Text Box

The one-line text box provides you with a field that is one line high and up to 999 characters long. It is useful (mostly) for short strings, such as a name, address, phone number, or e-mail address. When you choose a one-line text, the field appears in the form. You can change the length of the field (but not the height) by clicking the field and dragging the sizing handles.

To change the properties of the one-line text box, choose Form Field Properties from the shortcut menu and use the resulting Text Box Properties dialog box.

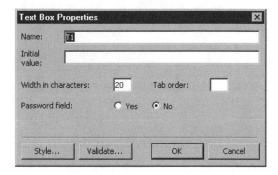

From the Text Box Properties dialog box, you can configure the field as follows:

■ **Change the Name**   The default name for the field is not very informative, so enter the name you want in the Name field.

■ **Specify the Initial Value**   If you want the field to start off containing a default value, enter that value in the Initial Value field.

■ **Specify the Field Width**   Enter the length of the field (as it appears on the form) in the Width In Characters field. This is *not* the maximum amount of information the field can hold, which is actually set in the Validation dialog box.

■ **Set the Tab Order**   The Tab Order field sets the order in which the cursor moves through the fields on the form when you press the TAB key. To remove the field from the tab order (so the cursor will *not* go into this field when you press the TAB key), enter –1 in the Tab Order field.

■ **Password Field**   Choose the Yes option if you want the text box to be a Password field. All this means is that anything the reader types in is masked with asterisks.

You can apply validation criteria to a one-line text box. Validating data enables you to reject data that doesn't meet your criteria. To establish validation criteria, click the Validate button to display the Text Box Validation dialog box.

The first step in setting up the validation criteria is to pick the type of data you expect from the Data Type drop-down list. Different options make different portions of the dialog box available. The options are

- **No Constraints**   This is the default. For this selection, you can establish the following criteria:
  - **The Display Name**   This is the name the reader sees in an error dialog box if the field name (as configured in the Form Field Properties dialog box) is different from the label text alongside the field as it appears on the form. The Display Name field is available only after you establish a constraint of some kind in the Validation dialog box.
  - **Whether the Field Is Mandatory**   If a value must be filled in, check the Required check box in the Data Length section.
  - **The Minimum and Maximum Length of the Data**   If you check the Required check box, you can specify the minimum (enter a value in the Min Length field) length of the data entered in the field. You can also enter the maximum (enter a value in the Max Length field) length of the data entered in the field regardless of whether the field is required or not.
  - **Valid Value Range**   If you want to establish a valid range of values, check the Field Must Be check box, and choose a comparison (such as Greater than or equal to, Less than, and so on) from the drop-down list. Use the Value field to specify the value to

compare the field contents to. You can also establish a second criterion by checking the And Must Be check box. Then pick the second comparison from the adjacent drop-down list and type the value to compare to into the Value field. By using both comparison options, you can establish both ends of a range of valid values.

- **Text**   Choose Text if you want to treat the field contents strictly as a string of characters. In addition to the validation options noted above, the options in the Text Format section enable you to establish whether to allow Letters, Digits, White Space, or Other special characters by checking one of these four check boxes. You can allow one or more of these items—checking none of the check boxes allows any characters at all. If you want to allow certain special characters, type them into the field adjacent to the Other check box, separated by commas.

- **Integer**   Choose Integer to allow only numbers without a decimal fraction. This choice grays out all the options in the Text Format section and makes the Grouping options available. Grouping indicates how numbers larger than 999 are displayed. For example, if you choose the Comma option, the number 1234 will be displayed as 1,234.

- **Number**   Choose Number to allow decimal numbers. This choice enables the same validation options as Integer, and adds the ability to specify whether you want the integer portion of the number separated from the fractional portion by a decimal point or a comma. Choose the appropriate Decimal option.

TIP   *Unless you resort to changing the Style (not recommended), any text label you place to the left of a text area is aligned with the bottom of the text area, which is not particularly attractive. To work around this limitation, place the label above the text area.*

11

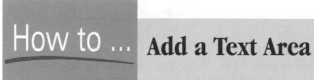

How to ... Add a Text Area

The Text Area field provides you with a field into which the reader can type multiple lines. It is most useful for such things as comments, complaints, and other blocks of text that won't fit easily on a single line. When you choose a text area, the field appears in the form. You can change the height and width of the field by clicking the field and dragging the sizing handles.

To change the properties of the text area, use the Text Area Properties dialog box. The properties are identical to a one-line text box, except that you can specify the number of lines.

The validation for a text area is identical to a one-line text box—it even uses the same dialog box (Text Box Validation).

Add a Check Box

Use a check box for a list of fields in which it would be reasonable to check one or more of the available options. For example, you might ask readers what types of computers they own (PC, Mac, WinCE, Palm Pilot, and so forth). You would provide a check box for each option, and the reader could check all that apply. To change the properties of a check box, choose Form Field Properties from the shortcut menu and use the resulting Check Box Properties dialog box.

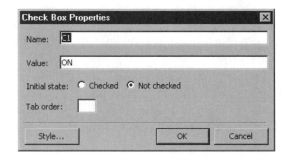

Name the check box field in the Name field, and set the value returned when the check box is checked in the Value field. The check box returns either the value in the Value field (check box is checked) or null (check box is cleared). You can also specify whether the check box should be initially checked or not by picking either the Checked option or the Not Checked option. Since a check box can only return two values, no validation is needed.

 *If you intend to add up the number of times a check box was checked on a form (for example, using a spreadsheet), set the checked value to 1.*

Add Option Buttons

Option buttons provide you with a way to capture data when the reader must provide one—and only one—value from a relatively short list of possible values. One of the buttons in the list is always selected, and picking a different button in the list deselects the initially chosen button. Option buttons are useful for determining such data as gender (one value from a short list), whether someone owns a car (yes or no), or their current marital status.

To change the properties of an option button, right-click the option button and choose Form Field Properties from the shortcut menu to open the Option Button Properties dialog box.

Set the group name for the option button in the Group Name field. All option buttons that work together must have the same group name. As with check boxes, enter the value returned by the option button when it is selected in the Value field. You can choose whether the initial state of the option button is Selected or Not Selected by selecting one of these options. However, only one option button in a group can be initially selected. Choosing another Option button to be initially selected deselects the first choice.

To validate an option button, use the Option Button Validation dialog box. For option buttons, you can only choose whether the data is required (check the Data Required check box). Making the data required for one option button in a group makes the data required for all the buttons in the group. In addition, making the data required enables the Display Name field. This field is where you can specify the text used to identify the option button in the error message that appears if you violate the data required requirement.

Add a Drop-Down Box

A drop-down box gives the reader another way to enter a choice—either a single choice from the list or multiple selections. You can use a drop-down box for the same sorts of things for which you use a check box (multiple selections) or radio buttons (a single selection).

When you insert a drop-down box on the form, it does not contain any data, and it is shown at a minimum size of about one character high and one character wide. Also, although sizing handles appear when you select the drop-down menu, you can only adjust the height (not the width) of the field by dragging it.

To set the properties of a drop-down box, choose Form Field Properties from the shortcut menu and use the resulting Drop-Down Box Properties dialog box.

11

Provide a name for the drop-down box in the Name field. The next thing you need to do is add values to the list. To do so, click the Add button to display the Add Choice dialog box.

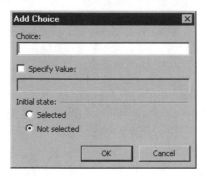

Use the following steps to configure a choice:

1. In the Choice field, type the entry that will appear in the drop-down menu.

2. If you want the form to return the value you specified in the Choice field, leave the Specify Value check box cleared. However, if you want the form to return a different value when the choice is selected, check the Specify Value check box and enter the value in the Specify Value field. You might want to do this if the text of the choice on the form is long and descriptive but you only need a shortened version to perform data analysis.

3. Choose whether this entry will be initially Selected or Not Selected by picking one of these options. Only one of the items in the list can be initially selected—if you choose another one to be initially selected, your first choice will be unselected.

Once you have specified your list of choices, you can work with the choices, as follows:

■ To modify one of the items in the list, select it and click the Modify button. This opens the Modify Choice dialog box, which is identical to the Add Choice dialog box.

■ To delete one of the choices, select the choice and click the Remove button. The choice is removed from the list.

■ To rearrange the items in the list, click an item and then click Move Up or Move Down.

You can set the height of the drop-down menu by typing a value in the Height field. You can also enable multiple selections by choosing Yes or No from the Allow Multiple Selections option. If allowed, the reader can make multiple selections using standard techniques for making multiple selections in Windows. The simplest way is to click the first item, then hold down the CTRL key and click other items you want. CTRL-clicking a selected item a second time deselects it.

When you only allow single selections and a height of one line, the drop-down menu looks like a classic drop-down list, with a down arrow on the right side. Clicking this arrow drops the list down so you can see its contents. However, if you allow multiple selections or a height greater than one line, the "drop-down menu" becomes a scrolling text list.

To validate the contents of a drop-down menu, you use the Drop-Down Box Validation dialog box.

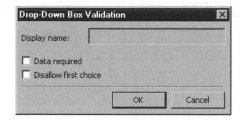

You can set the validation for a drop-down menu as follows:

- Check the Data Required check box to ensure that at least one item in the list is selected. If you check the Data Required check box, you can enter the Display Name (used to warn readers when they don't supply a value in a required field).

- If you specified that multiple selections are allowed, you can specify the limits on the number of items the reader can pick by typing values into the Minimum Items and/or Maximum Items fields. These two fields are missing from the validation dialog box if you don't allow multiple selections.

- If you don't want the reader to be able to pick the first item in the list, check the Disallow First Item check box. This enables you to make the first item an instruction, such as "Pick one item from the list." Clearly, you don't want to consider this item a valid choice!

Add a Push Button

A push-button field gives you a button on the form. There are three possible kinds of buttons: Normal, Submit, and Reset. The Submit and Reset buttons were mentioned earlier. The Submit type of button sends the form results to the designated destination, and each form must have at least one Submit type of button. The Reset type of button clears the form. A Normal type of button doesn't have any special functionality—it is just a button. You can, however, attach a hyperlink to a Normal type button, essentially providing a hyperlink on your form that looks like a button.

Although sizing handles appear when you click a push button, you cannot adjust the size of a push button by clicking and dragging a sizing handle. The size is set automatically by the label you place in the button.

11

You adjust the properties of a push button by right-clicking the button and choosing Form Field Properties from the shortcut menu to open the Push Button Properties dialog box.

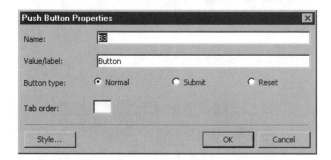

Other than the name and tab order, the only properties you can set for a push button are the label that appears on the button (type this into the Value/label field) and the type of button (pick one of the Button Type options).

Push buttons cannot be validated.

 *Just like any other graphic, you can attach a hyperlink to a push button by choosing Hyperlink from the button's shortcut menu, selecting the button and clicking the Hyperlink tool in the Standard toolbar, or choosing Insert | Hyperlink.*

Add an Advanced Button

Like a push button, an advanced button gives you a button on the form, and you can set the button type to Submit, Reset, or Normal. However, unlike a push button, you can set the width and height of an advanced button, and format the button.

When you first create an advanced button, the button text reads "Type Here." You can type in the button text and even press ENTER to split the name over multiple lines (the button automatically increases its height to contain the button text). To edit the button text, simply select it like any other text and edit it. You can also set the font, color, size, and effects by selecting the text and using the standard text formatting tools. Finally, you can select the button itself and set the text area background using the Highlight tool in the Formatting toolbar.

You can apply formatting to an advanced button from the options in the Format menu. However, if you select the advanced button and choose Format | Borders and Shading, the border and background color formatting is applied *not* to the button, but to the entire line of the form on which the button resides.

This is an Advanced Button

FrontPage uses a special hyperlink tag to display an advanced button: <button>. Since this is not a generally recognized tag, browsers earlier than Internet Explorer 5.0 and all versions of Netscape will not recognize the advanced button, and will fail to display it properly. For example, Netscape Navigator 4.7 will display only the button text. So, unless you can guarantee that all visitors to your site will have Internet Explorer 5.0 or later, don't use advanced buttons in your forms.

You can adjust the properties of an advanced button by choosing Advanced Button Properties from the shortcut menu to open the Advanced Button Properties dialog box.

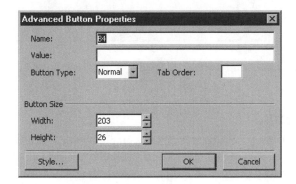

Like a push button, you can set the name, button type, and tab order for an advanced button. You can also specify a value in the Value field, although this value is not returned when the button is pushed (in fact, the Value field doesn't appear to do anything useful). Finally, you can specify the button size in pixels by specifying the width (in the Width spinner) and the height (in the Height spinner).

It is much easier to specify the button size by clicking on the edge of the advanced button so that the sizing handles are visible, and then clicking and dragging a handle.

Add a File Upload Field

A file upload field enables someone to specify a file to upload to the web site. The file is deposited in the web site folder you specified, as described earlier in this chapter ("Specify Uploaded File Properties"). When you add a file upload field to a form (see Figure 11-5), it consists of two parts:

Specify the file to upload here

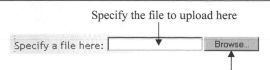

Click this button to open a dialog box where you can pick a file to upload

FIGURE 11-5   Use a file upload field to upload a file to the web site, where others can retrieve it.

a text box to specify the file to upload, and a Browse button that opens a Choose File dialog box where the reader can specify the file to upload.

To set the properties of a file upload field, choose Form Field Properties from the shortcut menu to open the File Upload Properties dialog box.

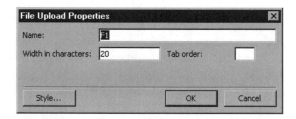

You can set the field name, initial value (the name of the file to upload), width (in characters), and tab order.

Add a Picture Field

A form picture field is actually nothing more than a graphic that has the same functionality as the Submit button. That is, clicking the picture field submits the form results. You can't configure anything about a picture field except the name. The confirmation page does tell you the picture coordinates (x and y) that the user clicked on, so you do have a record of that information.

To add a picture field, choose Insert | Form | Picture. Pick the graphic from the Picture dialog box, as discussed in Chapter 4. FrontPage inserts the graphic into the form. You can adjust the size and graphic properties of the picture using all the standard techniques. Choosing either Form Field Properties or Picture Properties from the field's shortcut menu opens the Picture Properties dialog box. This dialog box looks exactly the same as a standard Picture dialog box, except that it has one additional tab called Form Field, where you can name the field.

Add a Form Label

Although you can type text alongside a form field to give the reader an idea of what the field is used for, this text is not considered the field's "label" as defined by HTML standards. Defining a field's label doesn't provide much of an advantage except that the default field description used when flagging validation errors is the field's label (if it exists). By defining a field's label, you don't have to add a Display Name in the Form Field Validation dialog box.

To define a form's label, insert the field as usual and add some descriptive text alongside the field—just the way you would expect. Then select both the text and the form field, and choose Insert | Form | Label. The text appears with a dotted line around it (see Figure 11-6) to indicate that HTML now identifies the text as the field's label.

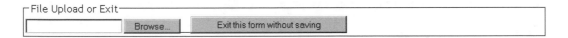

These dotted lines indicate that the text is the label for the adjacent field

FIGURE 11-6   A label for a field is displayed with a dotted line around it.

Add a Group Box

A group box is simply a graphical element you can use for visually grouping related form fields.

File Upload or Exit

Once you have added the group box to the form, you can change the label in the upper-left corner by selecting the text and editing it. You can format the text using all the text formatting tools. You can also resize the group box by selecting it and dragging the sizing handles.

To change the properties of the group box, choose Group Box Properties from the shortcut menu to open the Group Box Properties dialog box.

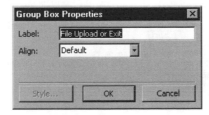

There are two fields you can set values for:

■ **Label**   Changing the label changes the label text of the group box. As mentioned earlier, you can also select the group box label text and edit it directly.

■ **Align**   Set the value in the Align drop-down list to Left, Center, or Right. This sets the alignment of the label text—*not* the alignment of any fields you add inside the group box. These fields are unaffected by the Align setting.

Of course, a group box is of little use unless you add fields to it. You can add fields inside a group box just like adding fields anywhere else on the form. Simply position the cursor inside the group box and choose a form field from the Insert | Form submenu. Or, drag existing fields inside the group box.

 *If you want to apply the same text formatting to group box label text and to any text contained in the group box, click the group box to get the sizing handles to appear. Then apply the text formatting.*

Add a Search Form

One of the handiest of FrontPage's extended features is the ability to add a search form. With a search form, the reader can enter words or phrases, and the form returns a list of all the web pages that contain those words or phrases. Since this list is actually a set of hyperlinks, the reader can just click one of the items in the list to jump right to that page (see Figure 11-7).

There are two ways to create a search form: create an entire search form page, or insert the search form component into an existing web page.

Add a Search Form Page

To create a search form page, choose File | New to open the New Task Pane. Click More Page Templates to open the Page Templates dialog box. Pick the Search Page icon and click OK. FrontPage creates a new search page (see Figure 11-8) that includes not only the operational elements for searching, but also a concise explanation of how to use the search facility.

Once you have your search page built, you can give it a title and save it just like any other page. You can also customize the properties of the search form component. To do so, right-click

---

Use the form below to search for documents in this web containing specific words or combinations of words. The text search engine will display a weighted list of matching documents, with better matches shown first. Each list item is a link to a matching document; if the document has a title it will be shown, otherwise only the document's file name is displayed. A brief explanation of the query language is available, along with examples.

Search for: hispanic

Start Search   Reset

Number of documents found: 9. Click on a document to view it, or submit another search.

Search Results

Document	Date	Size
Web Sites of Childrens Authors	1/31/2003 3:17:56 AM GMT	11,300
Sites for and about Hispanics	1/31/2003 3:17:56 AM GMT	4,051
Links	1/31/2003 3:15:24 AM GMT	2,317
Online Childrens Resources in Spanish	1/31/2003 3:15:24 AM GMT	5,899
Story Behind It	2/11/2003 8:44:34 PM GMT	12,046
About the author	1/31/2003 3:10:44 AM GMT	24,916
Results from Form 1 of Page guestbook.htm	1/31/2003 3:10:02 AM GMT	13,738
Guestbook	1/31/2003 3:15:24 AM GMT	15,634
Xmas Camel Story	12/1/2002 2:34:40 AM GMT	15,011

FIGURE 11-7   The results of a search are a set of clickable hyperlinks, making it very easy to go to a page of interest.

Click here to submit the search   Enter search term here (input field)

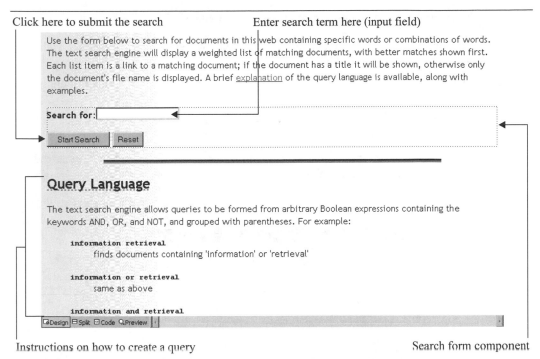

Instructions on how to create a query   Search form component

FIGURE 11-8   A search page includes the tools to perform a search, as well as instructions on how to do it.

in the component and choose Search Form Properties from the shortcut menu to open the Search Form Properties dialog box.

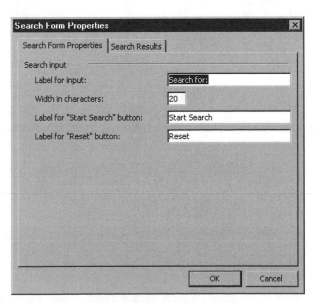

You can customize the search form using the following fields:

- **Label for Input** To change the label for the field into which you type your search criteria, enter the label into this field.
- **Width in Characters** To set the width of the Input field, type the number of characters into this field.
- **Label for "Start Search" Button** To change the label for the button you click to start the search, type the label into this field.
- **Label for "Clear" Button** To change the label for the button you click to clear the form, type the label into this field.

You can configure how you want the search results returned by clicking the Search Results tab.

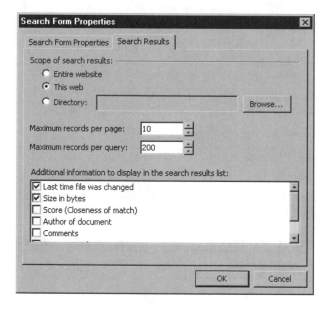

You can customize the search results as follows:

- **Scope of Search Results** Choose one of the options in this section to limit the scope of the search. The options are
  - **Entire Web Site** This option allows the search to proceed through (you guessed it!) the entire web site.
  - **This Web** This option limits the search to the current web site. The results are the same as for the previous option unless you are viewing the contents of a subweb (a web site contained within another web site). If you *are* viewing the contents of a subweb, the search is limited to the subweb and ignores pages in other subwebs and in the parent web site.

- **Directory** Choose this option to limit the search to a particular directory within the current web site. Select the directory by typing it into the field or clicking the Browse button and picking the directory from the resulting dialog box. This option is handy when your web site contains multiple discussion groups (as mentioned earlier in this chapter), each in its own folder.

- **Maximum Records per Page** To limit the number of records returned on each page of the search, set the limit in the Maximum Records Per Page spinner. If FrontPage finds more "hits" on your search term, it presents a button that enables you to view the next batch of pages that contain your search term.

- **Maximum Records per Query** To limit the number of records returned by the entire query, set the limit in the Maximum Records Per Query spinner.

- **Additional Information** FrontPage can provide information about each of the documents in the list of documents that meet your search criteria. Check the check box for each item of information you want included. The items are

  - **Last Time File Was Changed** The date and time that the file was last modified.

  - **Size in Bytes** The size of the file.

  - **Score (Closeness of Match)** A score that indicates how closely the found file matches your search criteria.

  - **Author of Document** The "author" of the document. This field is only populated for Microsoft Office documents (such as Word documents) contained in the web site. This field displays the contents of the Author field in the Summary tab of the document Properties dialog box.

  - **Comments** Any comments attached to the found page. As with Author, this field is only populated for Microsoft Office documents contained in the web site. It displays the contents of the Comments field in the Summary tab of the document Properties dialog box.

  - **Document Subject** Displays the contents of the Subject field in the Summary tab of a Microsoft Office document Properties dialog box.

  - **Matches** Displays the number of matches within a given document.

Add a Web Search Component

To add the Web Search component to an existing page, choose Insert | Web Component. Choose Web Search from the Component Type list on the left side of the Insert Web Component dialog box and Current Web from the list on the right side. Click Finish to open the Search Form Properties dialog box (as discussed in the previous section). Customize the properties of the component and click OK to add the Web Search component to the page. Only the component itself is added to the page—the explanations on how to create a query are *not* included when you add the Web Search component.

Build a Form Using the Forms Templates

FrontPage provides templates for many general-purpose forms. These forms include a confirmation form, a feedback form, and a guest book. With several of these forms, you still need to do some setup work, but using one of the templates minimizes the amount of work you need to do.

Add a Confirmation Form

As mentioned earlier, you can use the Form Properties dialog box to specify a custom web page that confirms the receipt of data submitted by someone on a form. This page is called a *confirmation form*. FrontPage provides a template for building a confirmation form that makes it relatively painless to build this page. Figure 11-9 shows a sample of what a confirmation page might look like.

The confirmation page in Figure 11-9 was automatically generated from the FrontPage confirmation form shown in Figure 11-10.

To add a confirmation form, choose File | New to display the New Task Pane. Click on More Page Templates, choose Confirmation Form from the Page Templates dialog box, and click OK.

 Realize that you don't have to build a confirmation form in order to achieve this functionality—FrontPage will provide a default confirmation form if you don't specify one. However, it is pretty ugly.

The key to creating a good confirmation form is to specify the names of the fields on the submitted form whose contents you want to appear on the confirmation page. These fields appear within square brackets. When the reader sees the confirmation page in a browser, the confirmation fields in the square brackets are replaced with the actual value the reader placed in that field.

Dear David Plotkin,

Here is the information you submitted:

First Time Request: Yes
How Delivered: Email
Age Range: 46-55
Email Address: dplotkin@pacbell.net

If any of this information is incorrect, please go back to the feedback form and change it. We thank you for taking the time to help us be a better company.

　　　Sincerely,

　　　Manager, Customer Services

You may return to the feedback form by using the *Back* button in your browser.

Revised: 02/11/03.

FIGURE 11-9　A good confirmation page should reflect the data submitted on the form.

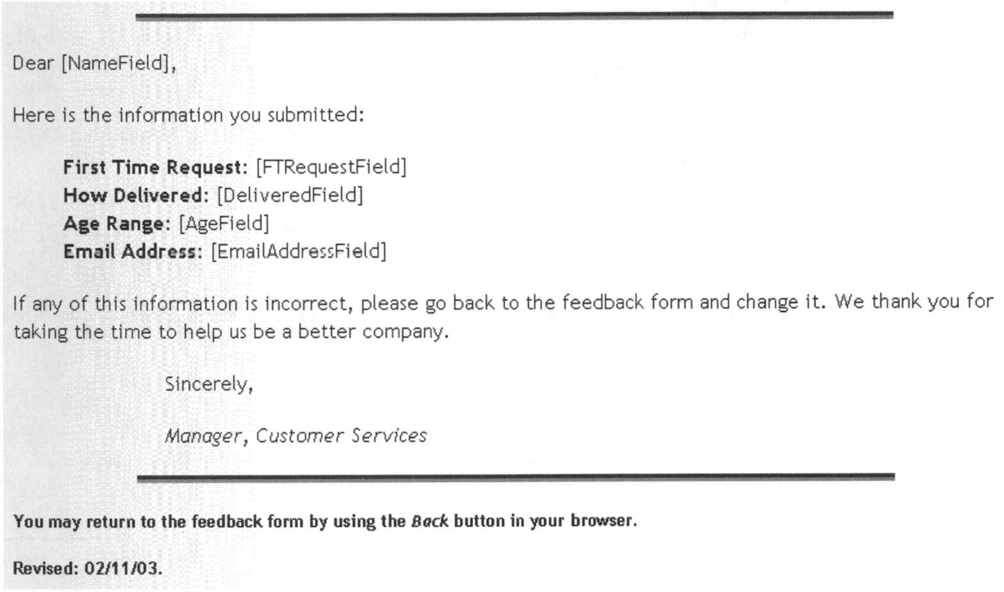

Dear [NameField],

Here is the information you submitted:

    First Time Request: [FTRequestField]
    How Delivered: [DeliveredField]
    Age Range: [AgeField]
    Email Address: [EmailAddressField]

If any of this information is incorrect, please go back to the feedback form and change it. We thank you for taking the time to help us be a better company.

       Sincerely,

       Manager, Customer Services

You may return to the feedback form by using the *Back* button in your browser.

Revised: 02/11/03.

FIGURE 11-10   Building a confirmation form is a fair amount of work, but you can customize exactly how you confirm the information you received.

The confirmation form generated by the template assumes that your form will have fields such as [username], [message type], [subject], and so on. If your original form does not include fields with these names, you must remove these references from the template-generated confirmation form. To change a field reference, you can either delete the field and add a field with the correct reference or change the existing field reference (both discussed shortly).

Normally, you won't want to be able to navigate to a confirmation page using hyperlinks, so don't add a confirmation page to the Navigation view. Or, if you do add it, deselect the Included In Navigation Bars option in the shortcut menu.

Modify the Confirmation Field Reference

To change an existing confirmation field reference, choose Confirmation Field Properties from the field's shortcut menu and change the name of the referenced field in the resulting dialog box.

Add a New Confirmation Field

To add a new field reference, you'll need to make a list of the field names on your submitted form. Switch to the confirmation form and choose Insert | Web Component to display the Insert Web Component dialog box. Choose Advanced Controls from the Component Type list on the left side of the dialog box, and select Confirmation Field from the list on the right side. Click Finish to display the Confirmation Field Properties dialog box, which has only a single field in it. Specify the name of the field from the submitted form to add to the confirmation form and click OK.

Add a Feedback Form

Feedback—about your web site, your organization, or just about anything else—can be valuable in finding out what works and what doesn't. FrontPage provides a template for a feedback form, which is just a normal form (see Figure 11-11 for a sample).

To add a feedback form, choose File | New to display the New Task Pane. Click on More Page Templates, choose Feedback Form from the Page Templates dialog box, and click OK.

Customize this form in any of the standard ways, including adding or removing fields, changing the text and graphics, applying validations to the fields (there aren't any by default), changing the values in the list, changing the type of file results, and attaching a confirmation form.

 *Remember to change the author and organization information at the bottom of the page. And change the copyright date (it reads 2001)!*

Build a Guest Book

The guest book is a form that enables people to make comments on a form, then displays a compilation of those comments on the same page as the form (see Figure 11-12).

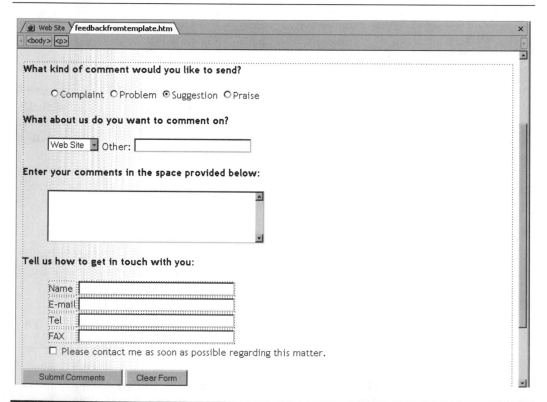

FIGURE 11-11 Use a feedback form to gather a reader's opinions.

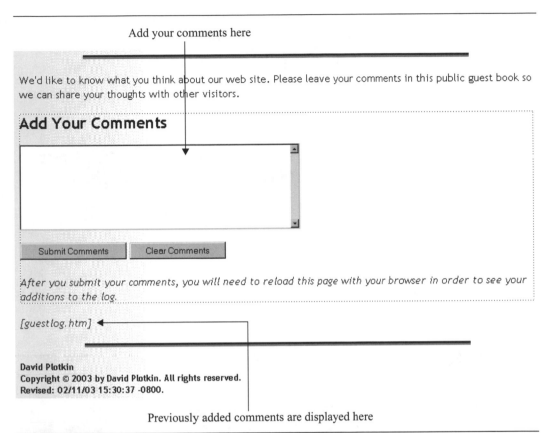

Add your comments here

We'd like to know what you think about our web site. Please leave your comments in this public guest book so we can share your thoughts with other visitors.

Add Your Comments

Submit Comments   Clear Comments

After you submit your comments, you will need to reload this page with your browser in order to see your additions to the log.

[guestlog.htm]

David Plotkin
Copyright © 2003 by David Plotkin. All rights reserved.
Revised: 02/11/03 15:30:37 -0800.

Previously added comments are displayed here

FIGURE 11-12   Compile public comments in a guest book.

The guest book "form" is actually a crafty combination of two FrontPage elements. The first element is a form into which you add your comments. These form results are saved into a HTML file in your web. The second element is a FrontPage component called an *include page* (see Chapter 13 for more information). Basically, the included web page—in this case, the form results HTML file—is embedded near the bottom of the guest book form. Thus, if you enter comments and press the Submit Comments button, these comments are written to the results HTML page. If you then refresh your browser, the results page updates and shows your comments—along with all the other comments that have been submitted. Pretty slick, eh?

To add a feedback form, choose File | New to display the New Task Pane. Click on More Page Templates, choose Guest Book from the Page Templates dialog box, and click OK. Once you have created the form, you can customize it just like any other form. You can even change the name of the file to which the results are sent—FrontPage will adjust the guest book page HTML to use the renamed results file. One thing you should *not* do is delete the filename for the results form or route only to an e-mail address. However, FrontPage will warn you if you make any changes like this that would invalidate the guest book form.

Chapter 12

Build a Frames Page

How to...

- Design frames pages
- Create and edit a frames page
- Use target frames
- Use FrontPage's frames templates
- Set up "no frames" support

Up to now, your web site design has only allowed you to display a single page at any one time. This constraint puts a significant burden on the web designer—you must provide navigation hyperlinks to other pages on every single page you build. Otherwise, a reader can get to a page and have no way to backtrack or move to another page except by using the built-in browser controls (the Back and Forward buttons). FrontPage eases this burden with shared borders and link bars, but the flexibility of these tools is somewhat limited. For example, you can't set the size of a shared border, and you must set up the web hierarchy using Navigation view in order to specify which navigational hyperlinks appear in the navigation bars.

What Are Frames?

With frames, you can place multiple web pages on the screen at the same time (see Figure 12-1) within a structure that you specify. This has the potential to make life much easier for someone visiting your site. For example, you can use one of the visible pages to display a list of hyperlinks to important sections of your site. When the reader clicks on a hyperlink, that page opens in another of the visible frame windows. The great advantage to frames is that you can keep your reader oriented as to where he or she is on your site. The links to other parts of the site (and to the home page) are always available. You can also use frames pages to display a constant header (with a company logo or name), footer, or both.

Here are the essential parts of a frame setup:

- **Frames Page** The frames page is the page that contains the other embedded pages. Each embedded page is contained within one frame of the frames page. The frames page is not visible to the reader, but it contains the frameset HTML tags that define the overall structure (size and number) of frames. In order to use frames, you will need to create a frames page.

TIP *If you want your whole site to be framed, you should make your home page a frames page.*

- **Frameset** *Frameset* is what FrontPage calls the collection of frames that appear together in the frames pages. The code within the FRAMESET tags (on the frames page) defines the layout of the frames page. The frameset is created automatically as you build the frames page.

FIGURE 12-1   With multiple pages available, the reader can click a link in one window and have that page appear in another window on the screen.

- **One or More Embedded Pages**   You need one initial page for each frame in the frames page. If you are using a simple content and main page layout (as shown in Figure 12-1), you need two embedded pages. If you use a more complex layout with additional frames, you need more embedded pages. Realize that the embedded pages themselves are just regular web pages. There is nothing special about the pages, and these pages can be displayed in a nonframe environment as well. The magic of frames is all contained in the definition of the frames page.

Frame Design Considerations

Designing frame-based pages can be a tricky business, and it is easy to create frames that are hard to use. The first thing you need to understand when designing a frame-based environment is the difference between static elements and dynamic elements. A static element is a page that does not change as the reader navigates the site. The static page remains visible no matter what the reader does—it can be scrolled, but it is always present in its frame. The contents frame (at the left side of the window) in Figure 12-1 is static. A dynamic element, on the other hand, changes according to the reader's input. For example, when the reader clicks on a hyperlink in the contents frame, the page displayed in the main window (to the right of the contents frame in Figure 12-1) changes. Thus, the main window is dynamic.

As you design your frames environment, keep the following in mind:

- Minimize your static elements, and make them as small as possible. In general, static elements provide navigation and a reminder of what site the reader is viewing, and the main information is provided in the dynamic windows—so make the dynamic windows as large as possible.

■ Don't use too many frames. The practical limit is about three, although you can get away with four if you keep three of them small. Adding too many frames to a page is confusing, and will force the reader to do too much scrolling in individual frames to see the information.

■ Don't use frames just because you can. They do crowd up the screen, so they should only be used if they provide value to your web site.

 The major drawback to frames is that it is difficult for a reader to bookmark one of the pages on your site. With frames, the only URL you can see is the URL of the frames page (which contains the other pages—one in each frame). Thus, if you add any framed page to your Favorites or Bookmark list and try to navigate back to that page, you return to the frames page, with its default contents visible.

Create a Frames Page

Before you create a frames page, you should decide whether the embedded pages you are going to associate with the frames page will be new pages (which you can create as you create the frames page) or existing pages. It is somewhat simpler to associate existing pages with a frames page because there are fewer steps involved in building and saving the frames page. If you want to embed existing pages, make sure you have built the pages before starting on the steps below.

Choose and Populate a Template

To create a new frames page, use the following steps:

1. Choose File | New to open the New Task Pane. Choose More Page Templates from the Task Pane to open the Page Templates dialog box, and click the Frames Pages tab, shown here.

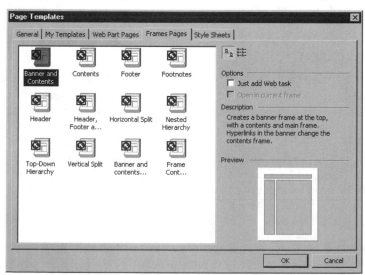

2. Click one of the templates and view the structure of the frames page that would result in the Preview section. When you have the layout you want, click OK to create the frames page (see Figure 12-2). The layout in this example places a navigational table of contents frame on the left side of the window, and the main window (which displays the page you choose from the hyperlinks in the left frame) on the right.

3. To embed an existing page in the right frame (or any other frame), click the Set Initial Page button. This opens the Insert Hyperlink dialog box. Use the Insert Hyperlink dialog box to specify the address of the initial page to show in the frame.

4. Once the page's URL has been entered into the Address field, click OK to place the page in the frame.

TIP   *You can click and drag an existing page from the Folder List into the frame.*

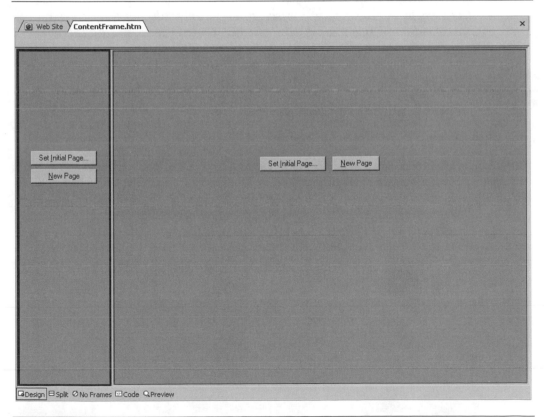

12

FIGURE 12-2   The new frames page shows you the structure, but not the contents, of the page.

You can now specify another existing page for the other frame. Alternatively, you can create a new page for the other frame. To create a new page, click the New Page button. This instantly creates a new, blank page in the frame. At this point, you can compose the page using any of FrontPage's tools. Remember to specify the page title from the Page Properties dialog box (choose Page Properties from the shortcut menu for the page).

One of the advantages to building the page within the frame structure is that you can see how the information on the page will be displayed. If you build the page normally (that is, not within the frame), you might find that the page doesn't work very well within the frame structure. One of the most common problems is that some of the information on the page is not visible because the frame is too small to show all the information you placed on the page.

Save the Frameset

Once you have your frames page set up the way you want, you need to save your work.

TIP   *Opening the Page Properties dialog box to change the page title of the frames page can be difficult. This is because right-clicking in the frames page does not bring up the page shortcut menu for the frames page—instead, it either displays the shortcut menu for a page in the individual frames (if you have assigned a page to the frame) or the Frame Properties shortcut menu (if you have not assigned a page). To easily access the shortcut menu for the frames page, click on a border between frames to highlight the outside of the frame page. Then choose File | Properties to open the Page Properties dialog box.*

The first time you save your work, FrontPage will prompt you to save the entire frameset—all the new pages you defined as well as the definition of the frames page. To save your work, use the following steps:

1. Choose File | Save. FrontPage opens the Save As dialog box. At the right side of the dialog box is a schematic of your frames page.

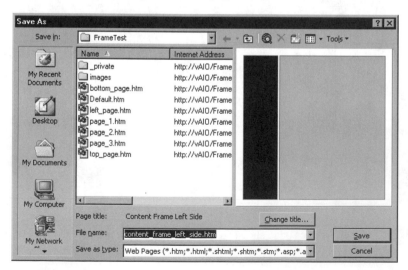

2. For each new page, FrontPage highlights the section of the frames page in which the new page is embedded. Enter the filename for that page in the File Name field and click Save.

3. FrontPage saves the file and prompts you for the next new page (returns to step 2).

4. After all the new pages have been saved, FrontPage prompts you for the filename of the frames page itself. You can tell that the frames page is being saved because of the heavy border around the whole page.

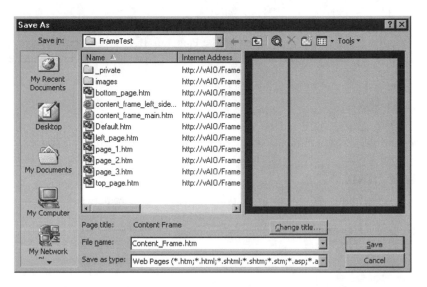

TIP *When viewing the list of pages on your web site, it can be confusing to remember where each page fits into a frameset. Thus, it is helpful to name the pages with some indication of where the page is normally displayed. For example, you can name the contents page that goes in the left frame as "leftmenu.htm" or the page that goes in the top frame as "banner.htm".*

12

5. If you have not already assigned a title to the frames page, click the Change Title button and specify a new page title in the Set Page Title dialog box. Click OK to return to the Save As dialog box.

6. Enter the filename for the frames page and click Save.

NOTE *If you make a change to a page in the frameset and want to save it right away, you can choose Frames | Save Page. This saves just the selected page. Using File | Save saves all the pages in the frameset, as well as any changes to the frames page itself (such as the frames' dimensions).*

Edit Pages in the Frameset

You can edit the pages visible within a frameset just as you would any other page. However, it can be quite awkward to work on a page if it is embedded within a small frame. To work around this, you can open the page normally from the Folder List and work on it in Design Page view. However, you must then save the page and open the frames page to see what the page will look like within the frame. And there is a better way! Use the following steps to edit a page embedded in a frame:

1. Open the frames page so that you can see the page you want to work on.

2. Right-click on the page and choose Open Page in New Window from the shortcut menu. The page opens as a full-size page.

3. Edit the page as you normally would and save the results (choose File | Save).

4. Switch to the frames page by clicking on the Page tab. If you like what you see, you are done. If not, click on the Page tab for the embedded page and make more changes.

Edit the Frameset

Once you've created a frames page and the associated frameset, you aren't stuck with your design. You can change the size of each frame, as well as add or remove frames from the frameset.

Adjust the Frame Size

To adjust the size of a frame, move the mouse pointer over the border between two frames. Click and drag the border to increase or reduce the size of the frame. Adjacent frames automatically adjust their size to compensate for the size change.

How to ... **Split a Frame**

You can split a frame into two frames. To do so, make sure the frame you want to split is selected. Then choose Frames | Split Frame. In the Split Frame dialog box, choose the option you want. Choose Split Into Columns to split the frame into vertical columns. Choose Split Into Rows to split the frame into horizontal rows. Choose OK to complete the split.

If you split the frame into columns, the leftmost column will contain the page originally associated with the frame you split. The rightmost column will display the standard buttons for associating a page with a frame: Set Initial Page and New Page. Use these buttons to associate a page with the new frame.

If you split the frame into rows, the uppermost row will contain the page originally associated with the frame you split. The lowest row will display the standard buttons for associating a page with a frame.

Delete a Frame

You can delete a frame if you decide you no longer need it. The page associated with the frame, if any, is *not* deleted. To delete a frame, make sure the frame you want to delete is selected. Then choose Frames | Delete Frames.

Rename the Frames Page

You may decide to change the filename of the frames page. A good reason to do so would be to use the frames page as the home page for your web site. In that case, you'll want to change the filename of the frames page to Default.htm or Index.htm. You change the filename of a frames page just like any other page. One way is to locate the frames page file in the Folder List, and choose Rename from the page's shortcut menu. Then type in the new name.

Create an Inline Frame

If you want to display the contents of one page in another, you can use an inline frame (you can also use an include page, described in Chapter 13). To create an inline frame, choose Insert | Inline Frame. An inline frame works much like a regular frame—you can specify the size of the frame, and you can either specify an existing initial page or create a new page "on the fly" using the standard frame buttons.

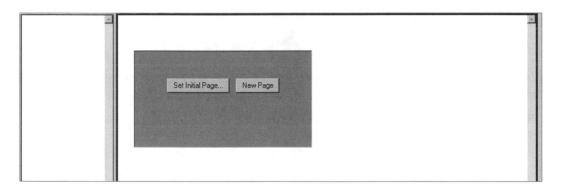

NOTE *You can quickly create a new page in an inline frame by choosing New Inline Frame Page from the inline frame shortcut menu.*

You can also specify the alignment of the frame, choosing from all the same choices (and with the same results) as you would with a graphic. Inline frames are quite versatile in that you can resize them either by clicking and dragging the sizing handles or by using the Properties dialog box.

Another advantage of inline frames is that they are easy to create—just place the text cursor where you want the frame and choose Insert | Inline Frame. To configure an inline

12

frame, choose Inline Frame Properties from the shortcut menu to display the Inline Frame Properties dialog box.

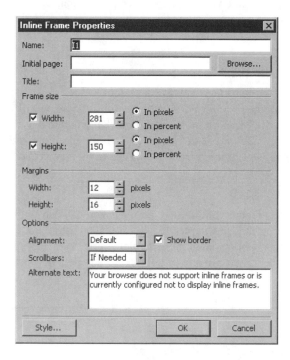

Besides the name (the significance of which is discussed in the next section), you can set the following properties:

- **Initial Page**   This is the page that will appear when the frame is first displayed. To choose this page from the dialog box, type in the address of the web page or click the Browse button and select the page from the Edit Hyperlink dialog box that appears. You can also choose the initial page by clicking the Set Initial Page button in the frame.

- **Frame Size**   Set the width or height by checking the Width check box or Height check box and setting the size in the appropriate spinner. Choose whether to specify the size in pixels or in percent by picking either the In Pixels options or the In Percent option.

- **Margins**   Set the width and height of the margins in pixels using the Width and Height spinners in the Margins section of the dialog box. These margins are the distances between the frame border and the page contained in the frame.

- **Alignment**   Set the alignment of the inline frame on the page using the Alignment drop-down list. As mentioned earlier, the alignment options work exactly the same way as the graphics alignment options. For example, aligning the frame to the left places it against the left border of the page.

- **Show Border**   If you want the border of the inline frame to be visible, check the Show Border check box. If you clear the check box, the borders of the frame are invisible in Preview and in a browser (the borders are always visible in Design Page mode).

- **Scrollbars**   Choose whether to show scroll bars from the Scrollbars drop-down list. The three options are If Needed (shows if the embedded page is larger than the frame), Never (scroll bars are never shown), and Always (scroll bars are always shown).

- **Alternate Text**   Not all browsers can display inline frames—this feature takes advantage of HTML 4.0. If the reader's browser can't display inline frames, the browser will display the text in the Alternate Text field instead.

Modify the Frame Properties

To modify the frame properties, right-click in the frame and choose Frame Properties from the shortcut menu. This opens the Frame Properties dialog box.

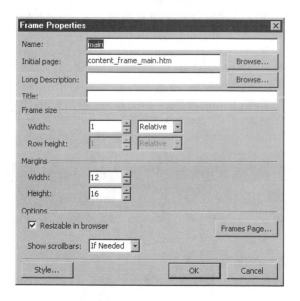

From the Frame Properties dialog box, you can configure the selected frame in the following ways:

- **Name**   Enter the frame's name in this field. This is *not* the name of the page; rather, it is the name of the frame, and it is used (as you'll see shortly) when specifying in which frame a hyperlinked page will open.

- **Initial Page**   Enter the filename of the page that will open in this frame initially—that is, when you first activate this frames page, the page that will be displayed in this frame. You can click the Browse button to pick a page from the Edit Hyperlink dialog box.

12

NOTE *You can also enter a title and long description for the Frame. These are helpful in providing information for some search engines.*

■ **Frame Size** Set the width and height using the appropriate spinners. The drop-down list alongside each quantity enables you to specify the width and height in Pixels, Percent (of the window), or Relative. Choose Pixels or Percent when you want a specific dimension (such as the width of the left column). Choose Relative when you want the frame to fill the rest of the window (examples of using Relative include the height of the left column, or both the width and height of the main window in Figure 12-1).

■ **Margins** Set the width and height of the frame margins in pixels. This invisible border is the distance between the frame border and the edge of the page that is embedded in the frame.

■ **Resizable in Browser** Check this check box to allow the reader to resize the frame in his or her browser by clicking and dragging on a frame border. Of course, this does not change anything about the page as it is stored on the server, and the next time this person views the page, it is displayed in its default dimensions. If this check box is *not* checked, the reader cannot resize the frame while viewing the page.

■ **Show scrollbars** Choose the option you want from the drop-down list. The default value of If Needed displays scroll bars in the frame if the content is either too wide or too long to be displayed all at once.

■ **Frames Page** Click this button to display the Frames tab of the Page Properties. In this tab, you can set the width of the borders using the Frame Spacing spinner. You can also show or hide the frame borders by checking or clearing the Show Borders check box.

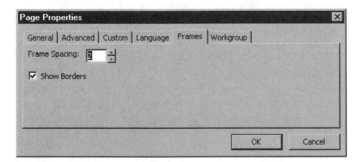

Understand Target Frames

One of the trickier aspects of setting up a frames page is specifying in which frame a hyperlinked page will open. For example, take a look at Figure 12-3. When you click a hyperlink in the banner frame across the top of the screen, the hyperlinked page should open in the contents frame that runs down the left side. When you click a hyperlink in the contents frame, the hyperlinked page should open in the main window. And when you click a hyperlink in the main window, the

Hyperlinks in this window should
open in the main frame

Hyperlinks in this window should
open in the contents frame

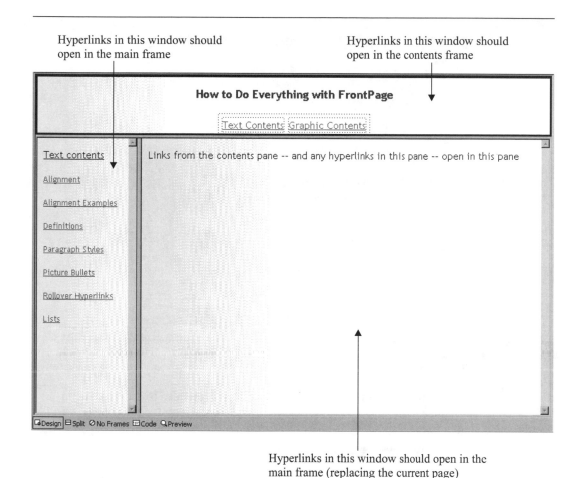

Hyperlinks in this window should open in the
main frame (replacing the current page)

FIGURE 12-3   You must control where a hyperlinked page opens in order to make frames
work the way you want.

hyperlinked page should open in the main window, replacing the current contents. But how do
you make all that happen?

Set the Page Default Target Frame

The name of the frame in which a hyperlinked page will appear is set by an attribute called a
target frame. You can set the target frame in one of two places. First of all, you can set the default
target frame for all hyperlinks on a page. To do so, open the Page Properties dialog box (see
Figure 12-4). In the General tab is a field called Default Target Frame. This field specifies the
name of the frame in which hyperlinks on that page will appear *if they are not overridden by the
hyperlink itself* (more on this in a moment).

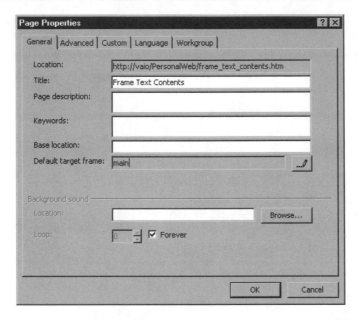

FIGURE 12-4 The Default Target Frame field specifies the name of the default frame for all hyperlinks on the page.

The contents of the Default Target Frame field are not directly editable. To set the value in this field, click the Change Target Frame button (the one with the pencil on it). This opens the Target Frame dialog box.

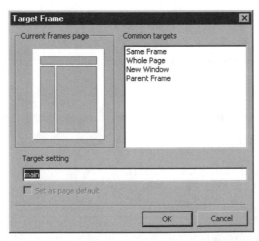

Although you can enter the name of the frame into the Target Setting field, it is much easier to simply click the frame in the graphic that you want to be the default target frame for the page. There are several additional options available to you in this dialog box, discussed in the next section. Click OK to choose the frame and close the Target Frame dialog box, then click OK again to close the Page Properties dialog box.

Direct Hyperlinks to Common Targets

In the Common Targets list in the Target Frame dialog box there are predefined targets that are understood by all browsers that can handle frames. Here is what they mean:

- **Same Frame**   Opens the hyperlinked page in the same frame window the current page uses. That is, the hyperlinked page replaces the current page in the same frame window. The other frames in the frameset are not affected.

- **Whole Page**   Closes the current frames window, and opens the hyperlinked page in the full browser window.

- **New Window**   Leaves the current frames window as it is and opens the hyperlinked page in a new instance of the browser.

- **Parent Frame**   This option only works for nested frames—that is, a frameset that exists in a page of another frameset. This option closes the current nested frameset and opens the hyperlinked page in the next higher frameset.

NOTE   *If you add an inline frame to a page, the list of common targets for hyperlinks on that page will include the inline frame (the name of the inline frame appears in the list).*

Define a Hyperlink Target Frame

You can also set the target frame for a hyperlink when you define the hyperlink itself. Any target frame you define in a hyperlink will override the default set for the page. Any hyperlink—text, graphics, buttons, or image maps—can have a target frame. To specify the target frame for a hyperlink, begin by defining the hyperlink in the usual way to get to the Insert Hyperlink dialog box. Alternatively, select an existing hyperlink and choose Hyperlink Properties from the shortcut menu to open the Edit Hyperlink dialog box. Then click the Target Frame button to open the Target Frame dialog box.

12

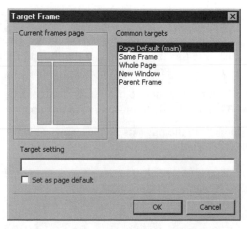

The Target Frame dialog box looks much like the one we saw previously, and you select a target frame the same way: click the frame in the graphic that you want as the target frame, or choose an item from the Common Targets list. However, there are two important differences in this version of the Target Frame dialog box. First of all, there is another choice in the Common Targets list: Page Default. You can pick the page's default target frame as the hyperlink's target frame by clicking the Page Default selection. The other difference is the Set As Page Default check box (which was grayed out before). Once you pick a target frame for this hyperlink, you can make that target frame the default for the whole page by checking this check box. Any hyperlinks that use the page default will now use the target frame you define here.

Create Template-Based Pages for a Frameset

We've already mentioned that you can add pages to a frameset using either the Set Initial Page button or the New Page button. However, if you choose the New Page button, FrontPage provides a blank web page for the frame. What if you want to create a new page for a frameset based on one of the many useful templates provided with FrontPage?

You can create pages based on a template and add the page to a frameset, provided that the frame (in the frames page) to which you want to add the new page does not currently have a page associated with it (that is, the frame still shows the Set Initial Page button). To create and add a new page to a frameset, use the following steps:

1. Open the frameset to which you want to add the newly created page.

2. Pick the frame in the frameset where the page will appear.

3. Choose File | New to open the New Task Pane. Click More Page Templates in the Task Pane to open the Page Templates dialog box.

4. In the Page Templates dialog box, click the tab containing the template you want to use. Pick a template, and be sure to check the Open In Current Frame check box. This check box is grayed out (unavailable) if the frameset has a page already associated with every frame.

5. Click OK to open the new page in the selected frame.

6. Right-click the page and choose Page Properties from the shortcut menu.

7. In the resulting Page Properties dialog box, click the Change Target Frame button (the one with the pencil on it). Use the Target Frame dialog box to set the default target frame for the page, and click OK to close the Target Frame dialog box.

8. Give the new page a title and any other configuration options you want in the Page Properties dialog box. Then click OK to close the Page Properties dialog box.

9. Make any changes you want to the page itself and then save your work. All hyperlinks on the new page will be directed to the specified target frame.

TIP *You can also simply create a page based on a template, and then specify that page as the Initial Page in the Frame Properties dialog box.*

Save a Custom Frameset as a Template

You can spend quite a bit of time building a frameset to get it just the way you want. If you think you might want to use the frameset again, you can save it as a template so it will appear on the Frames tab of the Page Templates dialog box. To save a frameset as a template, use the following steps:

1. Open the frameset in Page view.

2. Choose File | Save As to open the Save As dialog box. The overall frame is highlighted on the right side of the dialog box.

3. In the Save As Type list, choose FrontPage Template (*.tem). Supply the name of the template in the File Name field.

4. Click the Save button. FrontPage opens the Save As Template dialog box.

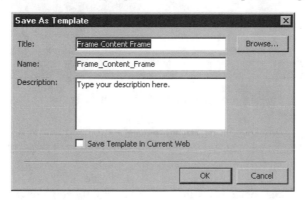

5. Enter the title of the template, the name, and a description. If you want the template saved only as part of the current web site (so it will only be available in the current web site), check the Save Template In Current Web check box.

6. Click OK to finish saving the template.

7. If any of the pages in the frameset use graphics, FrontPage provides the Save Embedded Files dialog box. This is because graphics associated with a template are saved in a different place than the graphics associated with a regular page in a web site.

8. Click OK to save the embedded files to the destination suggested by FrontPage and create the template.

The template will be available in the Frames tab of the New dialog box (which appears when you create a new web page). As you can see from Figure 12-5, you can now choose your new template by its title, see a preview of it, and read the description.

Set Up "No Frames" Support

Although it is getting rarer, there are still people who surf the Internet with browsers that don't support frames. You can provide a version of the frames page for non-frame-enabled browsers.

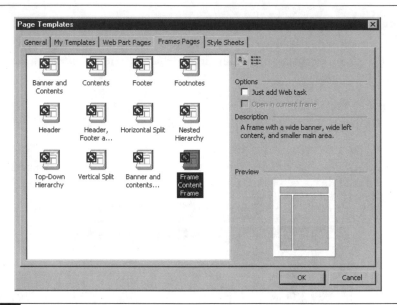

FIGURE 12-5 Pick your new template from the list of templates when you go to create a new web page.

To do so, open the frames page in Design Page view. At the bottom of the screen, you'll see a tab marked No Frames. Click it to view the No Frames page (see Figure 12-6).

This "page" is not a new page (you won't see it in the Folder List, for example). Instead, it is an alternate view of the frames page. By default, this page simply contains the text "This page uses frames, but your browser doesn't support them." However, you can customize this page just like any other page, including adding text and graphics, shared borders, navigation bars, and so on. Don't forget to save your work when you are done.

NOTE *If you made the home page of your web site a frames page, make sure that the "no frames" page includes information about the site. That is because most search engines will "see" only the "no frames" page when indexing your site, so it should be informative (in addition to presenting the "no frames" message).*

FIGURE 12-6 Use the No Frames version of a frames page to support non-frame-enabled browsers.

Part III

Advanced Web Tools

Chapter 13

Add Content with Components

How to...

- Understand web components
- Add various web components to the page

In this chapter we are going to cover some of the features that set FrontPage apart from other web site creation tools. Web components enable you to add sophisticated features to your pages without programming.

It is important to keep in mind that because of the sophistication of these features, they must be used with caution. For example, web components require a server-based web site to function—they won't run on a disk-based web. Furthermore, the server must have at least the FrontPage 2002 extensions installed.

 *A few of the items in the Insert | Web Component dialog box have been covered previously. These include the Confirmation Field, Search Form, Photo Gallery, Page Banner, and Link Bars.*

What Are Web Components?

Web components are where the real power of FrontPage starts to show. Web components (Microsoft called them webbots in earlier versions of FrontPage, and the HTML comments generated still reflect this heritage) automate certain processes that would otherwise have required you to write code in HTML or in a scripting language. When you add a web component to a web page, you are embedding some programming code in the web page. This code executes when certain events occur.

Place Web Components

In general, you add a web component to a web page by choosing Insert | Web Component, and choosing the component you want to add from the Insert Web Component dialog box. Most components require that you set some parameters that determine how the component operates—such as choosing the counter style for the hit counter. This might seem like a lot of work, but compared to what it would take to implement this web component using manual coding, FrontPage's web components make your web site construction work much easier.

Adding a Hit Counter

A hit counter counts the number of times a page has been viewed—the number of "hits" on the page. This can give you some idea how popular a page is.

Welcome to my Web site

This page has been viewed:

3 times

Hit counters are popular on the Web. Typical hit counters use some explanatory text, such as "This page has been viewed" and the date the hit counter started counting.

The hit counter works properly in version 3 browsers (both Netscape and Internet Explorer) and later.

To create a hit counter, use the following steps:

1. Choose Insert | Web Component and select Hit Counter from the Component Type list. The right side of the dialog box displays the various styles for hit counters.

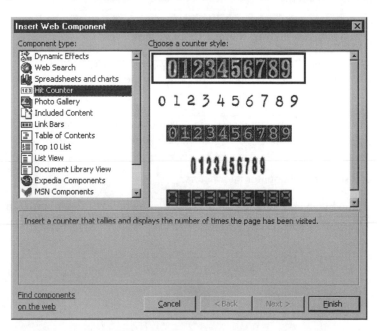

2. Select a style and click Finish to display the Hit Counter Properties dialog box.

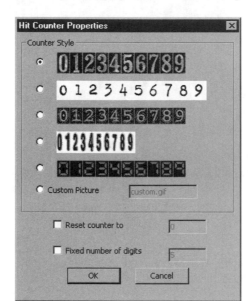

3. Select the style of the hit counter numbers by choosing one of the options in the Hit Counter Properties dialog box. If you choose the Custom Picture option, you must specify an image that includes all the numbers (0–9). The numbers *must* be evenly spaced. That is, all the rectangles that contain the numbers must be *exactly* the same size.

4. If you want to start the hit counter at a number other than 1, check the Reset Counter To check box and enter the starting number in the adjacent field.

You can also use the Reset Counter To check box to reset the counter to zero. You might want to do this when you first publish your page to the Internet, erasing the "hits" that resulted from testing the page.

5. If you always want the same number of digits (for example, you want to see 00007 instead of 7), check the Fixed Number Of Digits check box and fill in the number of digits in the adjacent field.

6. Click OK to save the hit counter parameters.

The position of the hit counter on the page is indicated by the set of numbers from the chosen style. To view the hit counter, switch to the Preview view or preview the page in a browser.

Create Interactive Buttons

Have you ever seen a button on a web site that seemed to know when the mouse pointer passed over it, or changed shape when you clicked on it? FrontPage enables you to build your own *interactive buttons*. To add an interactive button, place the cursor where you want to insert the button and choose Insert | Web Component. Select Dynamic Effects from the Component Type list and choose Interactive Button from the list on the right side of the dialog box. Click Finish to open the Interactive Buttons Properties dialog box.

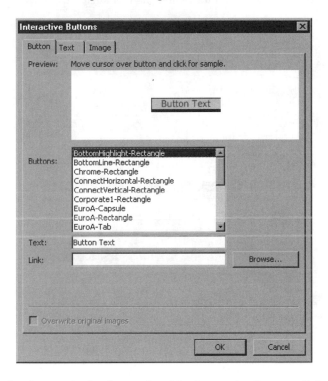

NOTE *As you make changes in the three tabs of the Interactive Buttons dialog box, you can move the mouse over the button in the Preview area and click to get an idea of what your button will look like.*

In the Button tab, configure the following fields:

- **Buttons**   Choose the style of button from this scrolling list. The styles control the effect that occurs when you hover the mouse over the button, as well as when you click the button.

13

■ **Text**   Type the text you want to appear on the button into this field. You can type more text than you can see in the Preview area—you'll have an opportunity to resize the button on the Image tab.

■ **Link**   To attach a hyperlink to the button, type it into the Link field or use the Browse button to open the Edit Hyperlink dialog box. From this dialog box you can also set the ScreenTip that explains what the button is for.

Click on the Text tab to set the size of the button and text attributes:

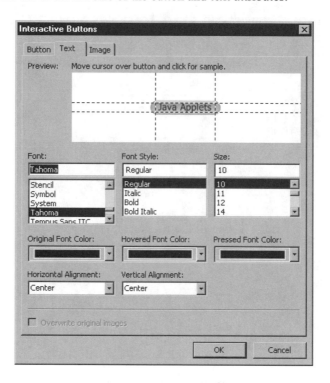

On the Text tab, you can set the Font, Font Style, and Size by selecting these quantities from the three scrolling lists. You can also choose separate font colors for the original image, the image that appears when the mouse is hovered over the button (Hovered Font Color), and the image that appears when you click on the button (Pressed Font Color). Finally, you can set the Horizontal and Vertical Alignments of the text on the button.

Click the Image tab to change image attributes.

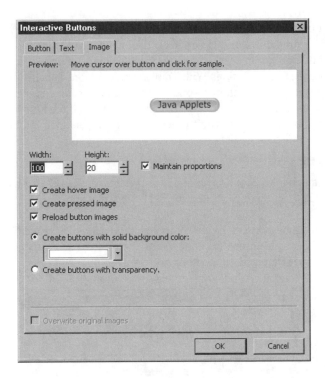

You can adjust the size of the button. This is especially necessary if the button isn't large enough to hold all the text you typed in on the Button tab. To change the button size, use the Width and Height spinners. If you check the Maintain Proportions check box, adjusting either dimension automatically adjusts the other dimension.

To choose how you want to handle the images associated with the button, check or clear the three check boxes:

- **Create Hover Image**   Checking this check box creates the "hover" version of the button. If you don't check this check box, moving the mouse over the button does *not* result in a visible change in the button.

- **Create Pressed Image**   Checking this check box creates the "pressed" version of the image. If you don't check this check box, clicking on the button does *not* result in a visible change in the button.

- **Preload Button Images**   If you choose to create the hover and pressed images, you should also allow the browser to preload the images for the button by checking this check box. Preloading the images does take a little longer, but if you don't preload the images, the browser will have to load them if the reader either hovers their mouse over the button or clicks the button.

13

You can create a button with a background color by picking it from the Create Buttons With Solid Background Color drop-down list. If you leave the background color set to automatic, the button will show a white background that can be noticeable against a dark-colored web page. Instead, you can choose the Create Buttons With Transparency option. This leaves the background transparent so that the web page can show through. This option is often less obtrusive.

Once you are done creating the button, save the page on which the button resides. The Save Embedded Files dialog box will prompt you to save the images generated by the button.

Place a Marquee

Marquees (the term is taken from Broadway and movie theatres) are boxes that have text scrolling through them. Marquees function only in Internet Explorer. They appear in Netscape Navigator, but do not scroll.

To insert a marquee, choose Insert | Web Component and select Dynamic Effects from the Component Type list. Choose Marquee from the list on the right side of the dialog box and click Finish to open the Marquee Properties dialog box.

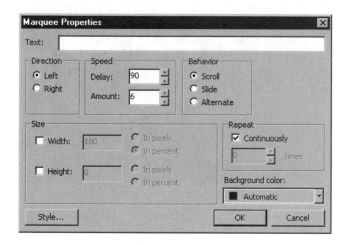

Configure the marquee as follows:

- **Text**   Place the text of the marquee in this field.
- **Direction**   Set the scroll direction by choosing the Left or Right option.
- **Delay**   Use the Delay spinner to set the delay. A large value causes the text to move in large increments; a small value causes the text to move more smoothly.
- **Amount**   Set the distance the text moves with each cycle. A large value causes the text to move quickly (with a somewhat jerky movement); a small value causes the text to travel slowly, covering a shorter distance each time it moves.
- **Behavior**   Set the scroll behavior of the text using the options. Scroll causes the text to scroll in from one side and scroll off the other side. Slide causes the text to scroll onto

the screen and stop. Alternate causes the text to scroll onto the screen, stop, disappear, and then scroll onto the screen again.

- ■ **Width**   You can set the width of the marquee by checking the Width check box, setting the width in the adjacent field, and choosing whether the width is to be measured In Pixels or In Percent. If you don't set the width, the marquee width will be the entire width of the window.

- ■ **Height**   You can set the height of the marquee by checking the Height check box, specifying the height in the adjacent field, and choosing whether the height is to be measured In Pixels or In Percent. If you don't set the height, the marquee height will be sufficient to hold the text with a small border. If you increase the text size, the marquee height will grow as well.

- ■ **Repeat**   By default, the marquee will scroll continuously. If you want to set a specific number of repeats, clear the Continuously check box and set the number of repetitions in the adjacent spinner.

- ■ **Background Color**   Set the background color of the marquee by clicking the drop-down list to display the standard color tool. The Automatic choice ensures that the marquee background is the same as the page.

You can adjust the font and paragraph properties of the marquee using the standard formatting tools. To do so, select the marquee (sizing handles appear) and apply the formatting you want. For example, you can align the marquee on the page by using the alignment buttons in the Formatting toolbar. Note that the text formatting applies to all the text in the marquee—you can't select just a portion of the marquee text. You can use the Font and Size drop-down lists in the Formatting toolbar, as well as the effects buttons (bold, italics, underline), the Text color tool, and the Font dialog box (choose Format | Font). You can also click the Style button in the Marquee Properties dialog box, then choose a formatting option from the Format button. In addition, you can click and drag a sizing handle to adjust the size of the marquee on the page.

13

TIP   *Want to use a graphic in the marquee? It's easy. Just choose Format | Borders And Shading, click the Shading tab, and specify a picture in the Background Picture field in the Patterns section. The chosen picture appears as a background to the marquee and the text scrolls over the picture. Make sure the background color is set to Automatic or you won't be able to see the picture. If the picture is too busy, you can center the marquee and decrease its width so that it appears in a section of the middle of the page. Change the background color of the marquee (in the Marquee Properties dialog box) to the same color as the page. That way, the marquee text scrolls across a solid color, but the background picture shows through at the edges of the marquee.*

Place an Include Page

One of the banes of the web site designer is information that must be present in many places throughout a web site. Examples might include your contact information or a set of graphics (such as a collection of logos). You can place such information on every page that needs it, but when the information changes, you must hunt down all its occurrences and change them. Of course, you've seen some tools—such as shared borders—that help this situation because they are the same on every page. But FrontPage offers another solution: Include Pages. The Include Page web component inserts the contents of one page into other pages (sometimes referred to as "parent" pages). By using the Include Page component, you only have to build the information content once, and then repeat it as many times as you need by using the Include Page component on other pages. The advantage to this approach is if the information changes (your logo or your e-mail address, for example), you only need to change the data in the included page. Each page that uses the Include Page component will change automatically when the included page changes.

To use the Include Page web component, choose Insert | Web Component and select Included Content from the Component Type list. Choose Page from the list on the right side of the dialog box and click Finish to open the Include Page Properties dialog box. All you need to do is specify the URL of the page to include. You can either type in the URL or use the Browse button to open the Current Web dialog box and choose the file from a list.

Place a Scheduled Picture

The Scheduled Picture component places a picture on a web page during a specified time period. If the time period has not yet arrived or has expired, an alternate picture is displayed (if one was specified) or nothing is displayed (if no alternate picture was specified). This component is especially useful when displaying graphics that are date-based. For example, a graphic related to Christmas or Valentine's Day would be a prime candidate for a scheduled picture.

To add a Scheduled Picture component to a page, Choose Insert | Web Component and select Included Content from the Component Type list. Choose Picture Based On Schedule from the list on the right side of the dialog box and click Finish to open the Scheduled Picture Properties dialog box.

In the dialog box, configure the Scheduled Picture using the following steps:

1. Use the During The Scheduled Time field to specify the image to display. You can either type in the URL of the image or click the Browse button to open the Picture dialog box and pick the image.

2. If you want an image to be displayed outside of the scheduled time, specify the image in the Before And After The Scheduled Time field. Once again, you can either type in the URL of the image or click the Browse button to pick the image. If you leave this field empty, no image is displayed outside of the specified time range when the reader views the page in a browser.

3. Specify the alternative text for the two pictures from the text fields in the Alternative Text section of the dialog box. Use the During The Scheduled Time field to provide alternative text for the scheduled picture, and use the Before And After The Scheduled Time field to provide alternative text for the picture that is displayed outside the scheduled time frame.

4. Use the fields in the Starting section to specify the beginning of the specified time.

5. Use the fields in the Ending section to specify the end of the specified time.

6. Click OK to finish defining the scheduled picture.

Save the page. As usual, if you picked an image that is not stored in the current web site, you'll see the Save Embedded File dialog box to give you an opportunity to save the image within the web site.

Although the image looks normal, the Scheduled Picture component does not behave like a regular image. You can select the image, but the Picture toolbar does not appear, so you don't have an opportunity to change the image. The shortcut menu for the image includes the item Scheduled Picture Properties, but it does not include Picture Properties, so you can't adjust the picture type, borders, or the other image properties. You can, however, adjust the alignment of the Scheduled Picture component using the alignment buttons in the Formatting toolbar. You can also assign a hyperlink to the Scheduled Picture component by choosing Hyperlink in the shortcut menu (or any of the other ways of inserting a hyperlink). However, you cannot assign hotspots to a Scheduled Picture component, so you cannot create an image map.

13

TIP

If you want to schedule a graphic that contains an image map, use the Scheduled Include Page component (see the next section for details). Add the graphic to the page you are going to include (and schedule) and modify the graphic to add hotspots and hyperlinks.

Place a Scheduled Include Page

A somewhat more versatile option than the Scheduled Picture component is the Scheduled Include Page. Like an Include Page, this component enables you to specify a page to be included in one or more parent pages. The difference is that you can schedule the included page—showing one page within the scheduled time, and a different page (or no page) outside the scheduled time.

To add a Scheduled Include Page component, choose Insert | Web Component and select Included Content from the Component Type list. Choose Page Based On Schedule from the list on the right side of the dialog box and click Finish to open the Scheduled Include Page Properties dialog box.

Scheduled Include Page Properties

Page to include

During the scheduled time:

[   ]   Browse...

Before and after the scheduled time (optional):

[   ]   Browse...

Starting: [2003 ▼] [Feb ▼] [05 ▼] [06:53:35 PM ▲▼]
           Wednesday, February 05, 2003

Ending: [2003 ▼] [Mar ▼] [07 ▼] [06:53:35 PM ▲▼]
          Friday, March 07, 2003

[OK]   [Cancel]

This dialog box enables you to fill in an HTML file (web page) for both During The Scheduled Time and Before And After The Scheduled Time. And, of course, you can specify the Starting and Ending date and times.

Once you've inserted the Scheduled Include Page, you can edit the properties by right-clicking on the area of the included page and choosing Scheduled Include Page Properties from the shortcut menu.

Place a Table of Contents

If you've got a complex site, you might wish to use the Table Of Contents component. This dynamic component creates a table of contents (see Figure 13-1) of the specified portion of your web site. The Table Of Contents component traces the hyperlinks from a specified web page. Thus, you can include all the pages that are linked from the home page or a subsection of your web. When readers view the table of contents, they can jump to any page by clicking the entry (hyperlink) for that page.

   *Since the Table Of Contents component uses the page titles as the text for the hyperlinks, make sure each page has a descriptive title.*

You can add a table of contents to your web site either by using the web component or by creating a table of contents page with one of the page templates provided by FrontPage.

   *The Table Of Contents component is not available if your web site is hosted on a server running Windows Server 2003 and SharePoint Team Services 2.0, as discussed in Chapter 8.*

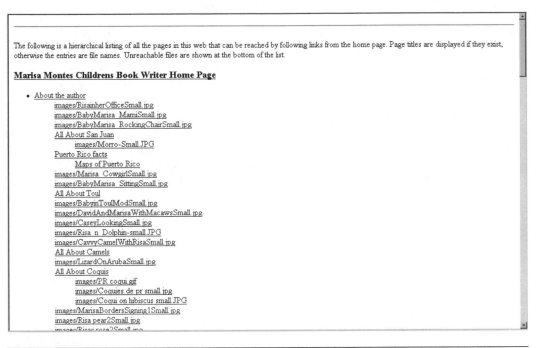

The following is a hierarchical listing of all the pages in this web that can be reached by following links from the home page. Page titles are displayed if they exist, otherwise the entries are file names. Unreachable files are shown at the bottom of the list.

Marisa Montes Childrens Book Writer Home Page

- About the author
  images/RisainherOfficeSmall.jpg
  images/BabyMarisa_MamiSmall.jpg
  images/BabyMarisa_RockingChairSmall.jpg
  All About San Juan
        images/Morro-Small.JPG
  Puerto Rico facts
        Maps of Puerto Rico
  images/Marisa_CowgirlSmall.jpg
  images/BabyMarisa_SittingSmall.jpg
  All About Toul
  images/BabyinToulModSmall.jpg
  images/DavidAndMarisaWithMacawsSmall.jpg
  images/CaseyLookingSmall.jpg
  images/Risa_n_Dolphin-small.JPG
  images/CavvyCamelWithRisaSmall.jpg
  All About Camels
  images/LizardOnArubaSmall.jpg
  All About Coquis
        images/PR_coqui.gif
        images/Coquies_de_pr_small.jpg
        images/Coqui_on_hibiscus_small.JPG
  images/MarisaBordersSigning1Small.jpg
  images/Risa_pear2Small.jpg
  images/Risas_rose2Small.jpg

FIGURE 13-1   A table of contents makes it easy to jump to any page on your site.

Add a Table of Contents Web Component for the Web Site

To add a Table Of Contents web component to a page, choose Insert | Web Component and select Table of Contents from the Component Type list. Choose For This Web Site from the list on the right side of the dialog box and click Finish to open the Table of Contents Properties dialog box.

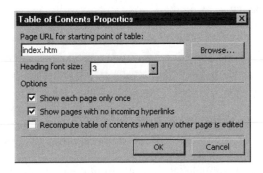

13

Configure the Table Of Contents web component as follows:

■ **Page URL for Starting Point of Table**   Specify the page from which the table of contents starts in this field. The web component follows all the hyperlinks from this page in constructing the entries in the table of contents. If you want all the linked pages in your site displayed in the table of contents, start from your home page. The starting page also determines which pages are displayed to the far left in the table of contents. Destination pages pointed to by hyperlinks on the starting page are indented one level in the table of contents.

■ **Heading Font Size**   Choose the heading size from the drop-down list. The heading is taken from the page title of the starting page. For example, if the starting page is the home page, the text of the heading will reflect the page title of your home page. The heading is a hyperlink to the starting page.

TIP   *Many web designers place their table of contents right on their home page, and make the home page the starting point. In this case, you probably don't want the heading hyperlink, which points to the starting page—a circular reference that does you no good. To suppress the heading, simply choose None from the Heading Font Size drop-down list.*

■ **Show Each Page Only Once**   Check this check box to keep a page that is the destination of many hyperlinks from appearing over and over in the table of contents. If you clear this check box, the page will be shown once for each hyperlink that points to it.

■ **Show Pages with No Incoming Hyperlinks**   Check this check box to show all pages on the site, including "orphan" pages that are not the destination of any hyperlink.

■ **Recompute Table of Contents When Any Other Page Is Edited**   Check this check box to automatically update the entries in the table of contents whenever you edit a page. This can take a while for a large site, so you'll probably want to leave this check box cleared. To manually update the table of contents at the end of an editing session, open the page that contains the Table Of Contents web component and resave it.

Once you've created your table of contents, you can't actually view it in FrontPage. In both Design and Preview Page views, you'll see three dummy entries, which you cannot edit. To view the table of contents, you must view it using a browser and accessing the page through a server (as in Figure 13-1, above). For a disk-based web site, you must publish the web site to the hosting service and view the page in a browser. For a server-based web site, you can view the page using the Preview In Browser function.

Add a Table of Contents Based on Page Category

If you've gone to the trouble of setting up categories for your pages (as described in Chapter 6), you can create a table of contents for pages in one or more of the categories. To do so, choose Insert | Web Component and select Table Of Contents from the Component Type list. Select Based On Page Category from the list on the right side of the dialog box and click Finish to open the Categories Properties dialog box.

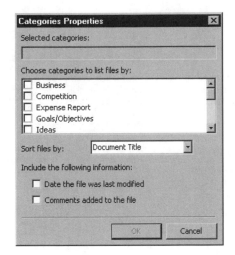

How to ... Create a Table of Contents Web Page

You may wish to simply create a separate page containing your table of contents, and link to the page from your home page using a link that might say "Site Table of Contents." You can certainly create an empty page and embed a Table Of Contents component in it, as discussed in the last section. However, you can also create a table of contents page using a FrontPage template. To do so, use the following steps:

1. Select File | New to open the New Page or Web Site Task Pane.

2. Choose Page Templates from the Task Pane, and select the Table Of Contents template from the General tab.

3. Click OK to create the page (see Figure 13-2).

The created table of contents page contains the Table Of Contents component, as well as comments explaining the page setup, author and copyright placeholders, and explanatory text. The default starting page is the home page. If you want to change this (or any of the other properties of the Table Of Contents component), right-click in the component and choose Table Of Contents Properties from the shortcut menu. This opens the Table Of Contents Properties dialog box, discussed previously.

> **NOTE**   *The default starting page is always Index.htm. This is fine if you are using a disk-based web site, but you'll need to change it (in the Table of Contents Property dialog box) to Default.htm if you are using a server-based web site.*

13

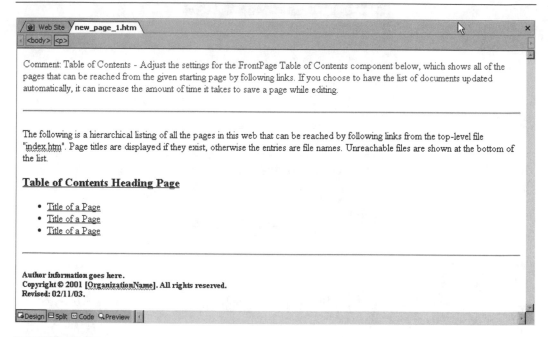

FIGURE 13-2   The table of contents page created by FrontPage instantly creates the page with no input necessary from you.

Check the categories you want to include in the table of contents, and use the Sort Files By field to choose whether to sort the files by Document Title or Date Last Modified. You can choose to include the date on which the file was last modified and the file comments in the table of contents by checking the appropriate check boxes.

As with the standard Table Of Contents web component discussed in the last section, you must preview the table of contents based on a category in a browser on a server-based web site.

Place a Substitution

The Substitution component adds a field to your web page that lets you show additional information to your visitors. When the page is displayed in the browser, the current contents of the specified field are displayed on the page. You can add two kinds of fields to the page using the Substitution component. The first type of field is a page configuration variable. These variables include page author, description, the person who last modified the page, and the page URL. To set the contents of the field that the substitution uses for the description, use the following steps:

1. In the Folder view or Folder List, right-click the page for which you want to add a description. Choose Properties from the shortcut menu to open the Properties dialog box for the page.

2. Click the Summary tab.

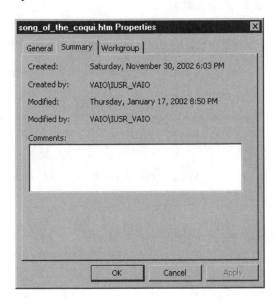

3. Enter the description for the page in the Comments field. This field is used for the description substitution.

The other type of field you can use in a Substitution component is used for web settings parameters. These are field/value pairs you can set yourself, which are then associated with the web site. A good reason to use a web settings parameter would be to inform visitors to your site when the site last had a major upgrade, or perhaps what version of the site they are now viewing. To create a web settings parameter, choose Tools | Web Settings, and click the Parameters tab. Then click Add to define the parameter. For more details on how to set up web settings parameters, see Chapter 15.

To add a Substitution component to a page, choose Insert | Web Component and select Included Content from the Component Type list on the left side of the Insert Web Component dialog box. Choose Substitution from the list on the right side. Click Finish to open the Substitution Properties dialog box.

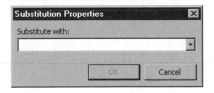

Pick the substitution you want to place on the page from the Substitute With drop-down list. The list includes any parameters you defined. Click OK and the component appears on the page.

13

Add Automatic Web Content

You've seen those nifty portal pages, such as My Yahoo, Excite, and MSN. Within limits, you can customize these pages to display news, weather, your horoscope, and even local TV listings. FrontPage enables you to place many of these same components on the pages of your FrontPage web site. You can even add a component to search the Internet for information, courtesy of MSN.

NOTE   *You must be connected to the Internet in order to insert and test these components. And, since some of the components use graphics that are loaded from the remote web site (such as MSN), the graphics will not be displayed if you view the page while you are not connected to the Internet.*

To add automatic web content components, choose Insert | Web Component and select one of the following types of components:

- **Expedia Components**   You can either link to a map or display a static map. If you choose to link to a map, you can specify the area you want to see a map of.

- **MSN Components**   The MSN components include searching the Web and getting stock quotes.

- **MSNBC Components**   The MSNBC component supplies a wide range of news headlines in various categories (Business, Living and Travel, News, Sports, Technology, and Weather). When a visitor to your site selects a particular headline, they can then read the entire story on the MSNBC web site.

Here is an example of placing the "Search the Web" component from MSN on your Web site:

Chapter 14

Use Positioning, Dynamic HTML, and XML

How to...

- Apply Dynamic HTML effects
- Create event-based DHTML scripts such as jump menus and pop-up messages
- Position elements on the page
- Set up a Data View and add the contents of an XML document to it
- Format the Data View and its contents
- Sort, group, and filter XML contents in a Data View

With the Dynamic HTML (DHTML) toolbar, you can use special commands to produce motion and special effects just by picking a few parameters. FrontPage also provides a way to interactively build Dynamic HTML *scripts*. These scripts respond to events—such as moving the mouse over a button. When the event occurs, the script executes. You can build some very useful scripts that were not possible before without writing your own code.

You can precisely locate items on a page using the positioning features of FrontPage, bypassing the inherent positioning limits of HTML.

Using *Data Views*, FrontPage enables you to add the contents of an XML document to a web page. You can change the layout, add and remove elements, and format the results using any of the text formatting tools. You can also filter, group, and sort your data—or let someone browsing your web site set up their own criteria. These abilities give you tremendous flexibility in how you display your XML data.

Work with Dynamic HTML Effects

One of the more recent developments has been the ability of web browsers to recognize and execute Dynamic HTML (DHTML). With DHTML, you can create all sorts of animations and special effects—even write games that run in a browser. Of course, you need to know how to write code to pull most of this off. However, as with so many other things, FrontPage makes some of the more common animations and effects available without writing any program code.

Understand Events

The effects produced by DHTML must be triggered by an *event*. That is, an event must occur that triggers the script to run and produce the desired effect. In effect, the DHTML-aware browser waits for one of these events to occur in connection with the text or graphic to which the DHTML effect is attached. The DHTML toolbar and the Behaviors Task Pane recognize two different lists of events. The events recognized by DHTML toolbar are

- **Click**   The reader clicked the text or graphic.
- **Double Click**   The reader double-clicked the text or graphic.

- **Mouse Over**   The reader moved the mouse over the text or graphic.
- **Page Load**   The reader's browser loaded the page (usually due to a hyperlink).

The Behaviors Task Pane recognizes these events, as well as many more, including events related to key presses (onkeydown, onkeypress, onkeyup) and more mouse events (ondblclick, onclick, onmousedown, onmousemove, onmouseout, onmouseover, and onmouseup). These events are referred to by their coding names and so are not as informative as the event names used by the DHTML toolbar, but in general they're not too hard to figure out. Because there are many more events to choose from, you have quite a bit of control over when your DHTML script runs.

Use the DHTML Toolbar

FrontPage provides the DHTML toolbar to add DHTML effects to a page. If the toolbar is not visible, choose View | Toolbars | DHTML Effects.

Build a DHTML Effect with the Toolbar

There are three basic steps in defining a DHTML effect. Depending on the effect chosen, a fourth step may also be necessary. The steps are

1. Add the text or graphic to which the DHTML effect will be attached to the page. Adding the text or graphic works just like adding any other text or image. There is nothing special about the text or graphic—yet.

2. Select the text or graphic and pick the event to which you want to attach the effect. A list of events is available from the leftmost drop-down list (On) in the DHTML toolbar.

3. Choose the effect you want to use. The list of available effects depends on the chosen event and whether you are attaching the effect to text or to a graphic. Table 14-1 shows the valid combinations of text/graphic, events, and effects. You choose the effect you want from the Apply drop-down list (second from left) in the DHTML toolbar.

4. If you chose an effect that requires additional information, you must specify this information. For example, if you specify that the text will fly off the screen, you must pick the direction. You choose the additional parameters from the rightmost drop-down list in the DHTML toolbar.

The DHTML effects available are as follows:

- **Fly out (available for text and graphics)**   The text or graphic flies off the page when the event occurs. You must set where the item leaves the page. Options include choices such as To Top Right, To Bottom Left, To Top, and so on.

14

Attached to Text or Graphic	Available Event	DHTML Effect
Text	Click	Fly out, Formatting
	Double Click	Fly out, Formatting
	Mouse Over	Formatting
	Page Load	Drop in by word, Elastic, Fly in, Hop, Spiral, Wave, Wipe, Zoom
Graphic	Click	Fly out, Swap picture
	Double Click	Fly out
	Mouse Over	Swap picture
	Page Load	Drop in by word, Elastic, Fly in, Hop, Spiral, Wave, Wipe, Zoom

TABLE 14-1   The Valid Combinations of Text/Graphics, Events, and Effects

- **Formatting (text only)**   The text changes format when the event occurs. There are two sets of parameters you can set: Choose Border and Choose Font. If you select Choose Border, FrontPage opens the Borders And Shading dialog box where you can set border, border color, background and foreground color, border style, and any other options in this dialog box. If you select Choose Font, FrontPage opens the Font dialog box, where you can set font, size, color, and effects.

- **Swap picture (graphic only)**   The currently visible picture changes to display another picture. Select Choose Picture in the DHTML toolbar to open the Picture dialog box and select the alternate picture.

- **Drop in by word, Elastic, Fly in, Hop, Spiral, Wave, Wipe, Zoom**   The set of effects available on page load are completely different than for the other events. These essentially consist of animation effects that automatically play when the page loads. Some of these options allow for additional parameters to be selected in the rightmost drop-down list. For example, Zoom has choices for Zoom In and Zoom Out, while Wipe has options that include Left To Right, Right To Left, and From Middle.

Did you know?

Swapping Pictures works in both directions? If you set up a DHTML event to swap pictures, clicking on the picture the first time changes the existing picture to a new one. Clicking on the new picture swaps it back to the original picture.

Edit the DHTML Effects

Once you've created DHTML effects, you can see where the effects are on the page by clicking the button at the far right end of the DHTML toolbar. This button is labeled Highlight Dynamic HTML Effects. When this button is pressed, FrontPage displays a blue bar on the page where the effects are in place.

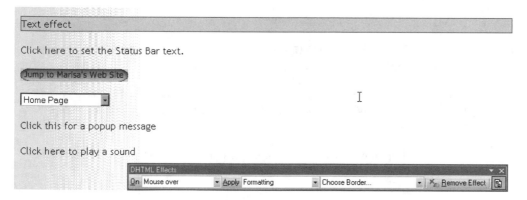

To edit the selected effect, click anywhere in the blue area. The DHTML toolbar will display the selected effect, and you can change it by making other selections from the toolbar.

NOTE

Some effects—such as Fly In—apply to an entire line, and the blue bar stretches across the entire page. Other effects—such as Swap Picture—apply only to the selected item. Another oddity is that if you apply a Fly In effect to a picture, you can't click the picture to edit the effect after you apply it. Instead, you must click alongside the picture in the blue bar.

To remove an effect, click in the blue bar for the effect you want to remove, and click the Remove Effect button in the DHTML toolbar.

Work With the Behaviors Task Pane

14

The Behaviors Task Pane gives you the ability to create many more DHTML effects and (as mentioned previously) attach those effects to many more messages.

The Task Pane shows a list of Events (such as *onmouseover*) and Actions (such as *Set Text of Status Bar*). Each time the event occurs, the action takes place. Thus, in this example, whenever the mouse moves over the target text or graphic (onmouseover), the text of the status bar is set. Most actions require additional information from you, such as the text to show in the status bar.

Create a DHTML Script

To create a DHTML script, use the following steps:

1. If you are going to attach the DHTML script to an item (text or graphic), highlight the text or select the graphic.

NOTE   *Some events don't require that you select an item first. For example, the onload event executes automatically when the page loads, so you don't need to select anything before choosing an action.*

2. Click the Insert drop-down list at the top of the Task Pane. This shows you a list of the various actions you can take.

3. Choose the action from the list. If additional information is required, FrontPage will display a dialog box (which varies depending on the selected action) to collect the information.

Did you
know?

You have to click on an item that has a DHTML script attached to it in order for the script to show up in the list in the Task Pane. For example, if you select some text and attach an onclick event/action to the text, you must click on the text to see the event/action pair in the Task Pane. This can make it difficult to find and edit actions that are attached to events not associated with an item (text or graphics)—such as an action attached to the onload event. You'll have to click around in the page until the event/action becomes visible.

4. Fill in the information required and click OK. The action and a default event appear in the list in the Task Pane.

5. To change the event, click the small down arrow alongside the event name and choose an event from the list.

6. If you wish, save the page and switch to Preview Page view and test the DHTML script.

The event list provided when you change events includes only valid events. The list of possible events in the drop-down list includes only events that are consistent with the selected action. In addition, the available events depend on whether or not you selected an item before creating the action.

To edit an event/action DHTML script, double-click on it in the Task Pane. This action reopens the dialog box for specifying the information for the event/action. You can also remove a script by right-clicking it and choosing Delete from the shortcut menu or clicking the Delete button in the top portion of the Task Pane.

NOTE   *You can attach multiple scripts (using different events) to a single item. To change the order that the scripts execute in, select the event/action you want to reorder, and use the up and down arrows just above the Actions list in the Task Pane.*

14

Build Useful DHTML Scripts

There is a long list of scripts (actions) you can create with DHTML using the Behaviors Task Pane. However, some of these scripts are more useful than others. Over the course of writing and updating this book, I have had many people e-mail me to ask me how to do many of the things that are now possible using DHTML scripts.

Create a Jump Menu

A *jump menu* appears on the screen as a drop-down list. When you choose an item from the list, the web page changes to the page attached to that item. To create a jump menu, use the following steps:

1. Click the Insert button and choose Jump Menu from the list. This opens the Jump Menu dialog box.

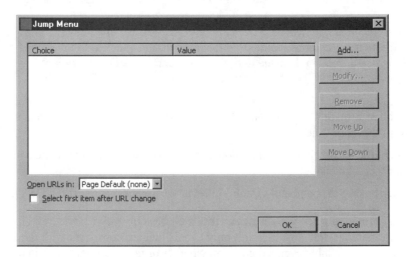

2. Click the Add button to open the Add Choice dialog box.

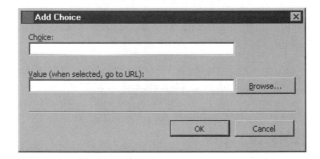

3. In the Choice field, type the text you want to see in the Jump Menu.

4. In the Value field, specify the URL of the web page that should open when the Jump Menu item is chosen.

5. Continue adding choices and values (steps 2 through 4) to build the Jump Menu.

6. Choose the destination browser window from the Open URLs In drop-down list. The choices in this list depend on whether you are using frames or not:

    ■ If you are not using frames, the choices include only Page Default (opens the new web page in the same browser window) and New Window.

    ■ If you are using frames, the choices include the Page Default and New Windows options, as well as a list of all available frames and common frame destinations (such as Same Frame, Parent Frame, and Whole Page).

7. Normally, if you click an item in a Jump Menu to switch web pages and then return to the web page with the Jump Menu, the Jump Menu will continue to display your last choice. If you would prefer that the Jump Menu always show you the first choice in the list, check the Select First Item After URL Change check box.

8. Click OK to create the Jump Menu. It looks just like a form drop-down box.

NOTE   *The Jump Menu dialog box enables you to modify an entry (click the Modify button), remove an entry (click the Remove button), and rearrange the order of the items in the menu (click the Move Up or Move Down buttons).*

Add a Popup Message

A popup message appears in a dialog box with the text you specify.

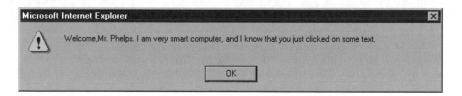

To create a popup message, click the Insert button and choose Popup Message to display the Popup Message dialog box. Simply type in the text and click OK. Don't forget to change the event if you need to.

Play a Sound

If you'd like a sound to accompany an action—such as clicking on a button—you can create a script to play a sound. To do so, click the Insert button and choose Play Sound to display the Play Sound dialog box. Specify the sound to play and click OK. Don't forget to change the event if you need to.

14

Swap An Image

You can create an action to swap an image when an event occurs. To do so, click the Insert button and choose Swap Image to display the Swap Images dialog box.

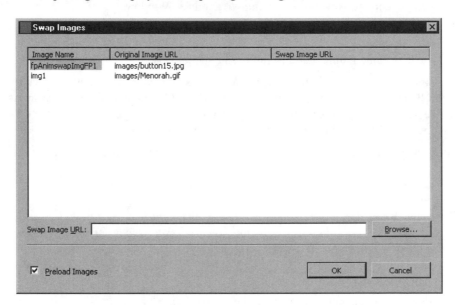

Select the image in the dialog box, and specify the image to swap it with in the Swap Image URL field. Note that all images on the page show up in dialog box list, so you'll have to choose the image you want to apply the swap action to.

To be able to click on the image and "swap back" to the original image, attach a Swap Image Restore to the image. When the event (such as ondblclick) occurs, the original image is restored.

Set the Text of the Status Bar

It can be very helpful to place text in the status bar (at the bottom of the screen). Thus, when you pass your mouse over a control or click on something, the status bar could provide help or a tip on how to use the control. To specify text for the status bar, click the Insert button and choose Set Text | Set Text of Status Bar to open the dialog box. Type in the text and click OK.

Change a Property

Each item on a web page has a set of properties. We discovered earlier (Chapter 3) that you can modify text properties, such as the font, borders, and shading. The Behaviors Task Pane enables you to change any of the item properties when an event occurs. For example, you can change the font, color, and borders of a text string when the mouse passes over the text. Using this facility, you can make the contents of your web pages highly interactive.

To change the properties of an item, select the item, click the Insert button, and choose Change Properties from the drop-down list to open the Change Property dialog box.

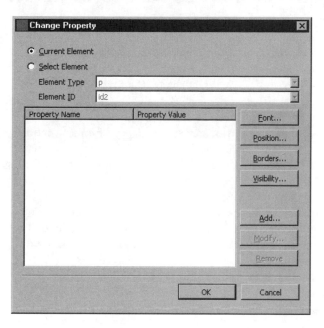

You don't have to select the item before choosing Change Properties, but it is easier that way. If you don't select an item, you'll need to click the Select Element option at the top of the dialog box. You can then choose the type of element (from the Element Type drop-down list) and the Element ID. To do this, you'll need to know the Element ID, which is not normally easily available.

From the Change Property dialog box, you can adjust the following properties:

- **Font**   Opens the Font dialog box, where you can adjust the font, style, size, color, effects, and character spacing.

- **Position**   Opens the Position dialog box, where you can adjust how text wraps around an image or a text string, as well as the location and size. Positioning is discussed later in this chapter.

- **Borders**   Opens the Borders and Shading dialog box, where you can adjust the type, style, color, and width of borders. You can also adjust the shading (background color, foreground color, and the background picture).

- **Visibility**   This simple dialog box enables you to set whether the item is visible or hidden.

14

How to ... Reset the Properties of an Item

Once you've used the Change Properties dialog box to modify the properties of an item when an event occurs, you might be wondering how you could change the properties back in response to a different event. For example, you might change the font, borders, and shading when the mouse passes over some text (onmouseover). But how do you get the properties to change back when the mouse is no longer over the text (onmouseout)?

As it turns out, it isn't enough to create another Change Property action (paired with the new event) with the font, borders, position, and so forth set to Automatic or Default. This does *not* change the properties back to the way they were. Instead, you must force the properties back to their original values—or as close as you can get. For example, if the text was originally black, you'll have to specify black as the text color in the Font dialog box. If you changed font typeface, you'll have to change that back as well. If you changed the color of the background (in the Shading tab of the Borders and Shading dialog box), you'll need to reset it to something close to the background color of the page—and you can't reset it to transparent. Finally, if you added a border, there is no way to turn the border off except by resetting the border color to page background color as well.

When you're done specifying the properties, they appear in the Change Property dialog box— click OK to finish up and apply the changes. Don't forget to change the event if you need to.

 *You can click on a property in the Change Property dialog box and modify (click the Modify button) or remove it (click the Remove button).*

Specify Position on the Page

As you've been building your own web pages, you may have noticed that getting text and graphics positioned exactly where you want them on the page can be quite a challenge. Extra spaces, tabs, and lines get ignored, making it difficult to get things where you want them. The problem is that the positioning tools in HTML are fairly coarse, and as a result web authors have evolved tricks over the years to try and compensate. Examples include using tables (and now FrontPage supplies layout tables) and single-pixel graphic files that are used as spacers on the page. FrontPage enables you to set up positioning with much more precision using the Positioning toolbar or the Position dialog box. FrontPage uses Cascading Style Sheets (CSS) to accomplish this.

Differences in Positioning on the Page

There are three kinds of positioning possible when you use CSS. Each behaves quite differently. The three kinds of positioning are None (or static), Absolute, and Relative.

Static HTML Positioning

This is the most limiting of the positioning options, but it will work with any browser. With static HTML positioning, you are limited in your options of where to place text or graphics. For example, you can place a graphic flush against the left or right margins, or you can center it. But you can't place it (for example) 1.5 inches from the left margin, unless you use a trick such as placing the graphic in a table cell and making sure that the empty cell against the left margin is 1.5 inches wide—which can be a trick in itself. You also can't just plunk down a block of text in the middle of a page.

Absolute Positioning

Absolute positioning gives you complete freedom over where you place a graphic or block of text. Once you set the positioning for the graphic or text to be absolute, you can specify exactly where on the page the item should appear. The item's positioning coordinates are specified by the top-left corner of the item and are measured from a fixed (absolute) point—the upper-left corner of the page. The position of the item is completely ignored by graphics or text that use static positioning—static graphics or text will flow over the absolute positioned item as if it wasn't there. This behavior is termed as not being "in the text stream," because text does not flow around the graphic or block of text.

To use absolute positioning, use the following steps:

1. Select the graphic or text block. Choose Format | Position to open the Position dialog box.

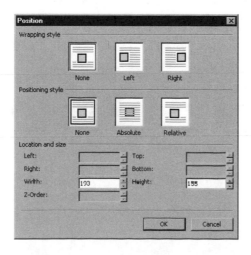

TIP
To apply absolute positioning to a paragraph (text block), simply click in the paragraph to place the text cursor within the paragraph. The positioning style applies to the entire paragraph—you can't apply it to just selected text.

   2. Choose Absolute from the Positioning Style section of the dialog box. You can use the Left and Top spinners to set the exact coordinates of the image or text block. The Width and Height spinners will already contain the dimensions of the image, although you adjust these if you wish.

   3. Click OK. The image or text appears on the page in the position you specified.

   You don't really need to specify the pixel coordinates in the dialog box. Instead, you can drag an absolute-positioned item to any position on the page. To do so, click the item to select it, and move the mouse pointer over the item until it becomes a four-headed arrow. Then click and drag the item to its destination.

NOTE
It can be difficult to get the mouse pointer to turn into a four-headed arrow when attempting to drag a text block. However, it will do so if you move the mouse pointer between two of the sizing handles on the perimeter of the text block.

   An alternative way to establish absolute positioning is to use the Positioning toolbar (see Figure 14-1). To open the Positioning toolbar, choose View | Toolbars | Positioning.
   To set an element's positioning to absolute, select the element and click the button at the left end of the toolbar (this has already been done in Figure 14-1). You can then enter the desired position in the Left and Top fields.

Tiger, Tiger, Burning Bright

The tiger is fierce beast -- the second-largest of the felines (smaller only than the lion). But it has been hunted here are few that are man-eaters, but these are rare, and are mostly the old or anything better tasting than a human being. The tigers roam Asia and the Indian sub-st nowhere else in the world, except for zoos. They are exclusively meat-eaters -- powerful front paws are awesomely efficient at scooping food into their jaws.

Bring Forward   Send Backward

FIGURE 14-1   Use the Positioning toolbar to specify the absolute-positioning parameters for an element on the page.

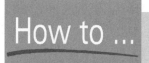
Position Multiple Elements

The freedom that absolute or relative positioning gives you in designing a web page is great, but what if you want to keep several elements together as you position them? To do so, make sure you select all the elements you want to move as a single item before specifying either absolute or relative positioning. All the selected items will move together, and maintain their spatial relationship on the page as you move them. To select multiple items, click on the first item, hold down the CTRL key, and click on the additional items.

NOTE *Take a close look at Figure 14-1. See how the text disappears behind the picture, rather than wrapping around it? That is because the graphic has been positioned absolutely, so the text stream ignores it!*

Relative Positioning

Relative positioning shares some of the traits of both absolute and static positioning. First of all, like static positioning, a relative-positioned item remains in the text stream, which means you can't place a relative positioned item on top of another item. And if you move a relative-positioned item (by dragging or typing in the coordinates), other items on the page (except for absolute-positioned items) move out of the way, just as they would with a static-positioned item. You also can't drag a relative-positioned item freely, the way you can an absolute-positioned item. But you can open the Position dialog box and enter a Left and Top quantity to locate the item anywhere you want.

Another difference between relative positioning and absolute positioning is how the coordinates are measured. With absolute positioning, the zero point (point from which the coordinates are measured) is always the upper-left corner of the page. However, with relative positioning, the coordinates are measured *relative* to the item's position if it were statically positioned. Thus, if you place an item on the page and switch its positioning to Relative, you'll see the starting Left and Top values are 0,0. If you enter 10 in each field, the item will move 10 pixels right and down from *where it would have been if it were statically positioned*. This behavior leads to an odd occurrence. If you have text flowing around a graphic and you use relative positioning to move the graphic, the text does *not* fill in the hole where the graphic was located.

NOTE *You cannot see the results of using relative positioning in the design Page view. You must switch to Preview Page view.*

Layer Items

With absolute positioning, you can stack multiple images on a page. As a result, you need a way to specify the stacking order. This order is called z-ordering or z-indexing (because the z axis in

14

algebra is the one that represents depth—while the x axis is width and the y axis is height). For example, say you wanted to stack three images: a table, a saucer, and a coffee cup. The table would be the lowest layer, the saucer would be the next layer, and the coffee cup would be the highest layer. To achieve this result, remember that the layers are specified relative to each other, with the highest number being the top layer. In our example, therefore, the table might be layer 0, the saucer would be layer 1, and the coffee cup would be layer 2. You could also skip layers to allow for adding more items in between the existing items later (for example, the table, saucer, and cup could be layers 1, 4, and 7). You can use negative layers, too. The table could be –5, the saucer could be –3, and the cup could be –1. It really doesn't matter, as long as you get the order right.

To set the z-order, you can use either the Position dialog box or the Positioning toolbar. In the Position dialog box, set the z-order in the Z-Order spinner. In the Positioning toolbar, set this quantity in the Z-Index field at the right end of the toolbar. You can also adjust the z-index of an object by selecting the object and clicking the Bring Forward button in the Positioning toolbar (second from the right) or the Send Backward button (far right).

Use XML In Your Web Site

We've already seen that you can generate XML from the output of a form (Chapter 11). The tagged elements (and their attributes) give "human readable" meaning to the data, which is contained between the elements. As people and companies turn to XML documents for storing and transmitting data, the ability to include XML documents in your web site becomes more important. FrontPage makes it possible to not only display the contents of an XML document, but to choose the style and formatting of the data. In addition, you can sort, group, and filter XML-based data just as you might with the contents of a database (see Chapters 19–21). Experienced programmers have been doing this for some time using Extensible Style Language (Transformation), or XSLT. As you format your XML data, FrontPage creates the necessary XSLT code in the background. Your data can then be displayed in any XML-compatible browser, which includes the latest versions of the major browsers.

You must have imported XML documents into your FrontPage web site to display them. FrontPage recognizes such documents by their .xml ending, so make sure your documents use this ending.

Create a Data View

The first step in displaying the contents of an XML document is to create a special place on a web page for displaying the data. This "special place" is called a *Data View*. To create a Data View, choose Data | Insert Data View to display the Data Source Catalog Task Pane (shown in Figure 14-2).

FIGURE 14-2   The Data Source Catalog Task Pane lists your XML documents so you can place them in a Data View.

This Task Pane lists all the data sources in your web site that you can place in a Data View—including any XML documents you have.

Add an XML Document to the Data View

To add an XML document to the web page, move the mouse over the document in the XML Files list and click on the down arrow to display the document's menu. Choose Show Data to display

14

the contents of a record in the Task Pane and switch to the Data View Details Task Pane (see Figure 14-3).

NOTE   *See "How To...View the Contents of Your XML Document in the Task Pane" for more details on viewing the data).*

Select the elements you want to use in the Task Pane. You can select multiple elements by clicking on the first element, holding down the CTRL key, and clicking on the rest of the elements. Choose the Insert Data View hyperlink in the Data View Details Task Pane to add the document to the Data View in the web page with the elements you selected. An example is visible in Figure 14-3.

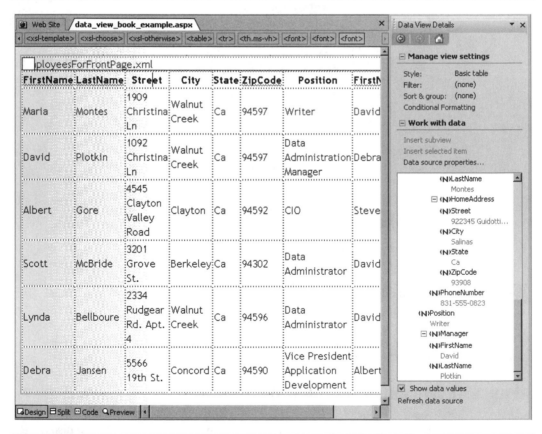

FIGURE 14-3   Your data is now in the web page, and you can make adjustments to it using the Data View Details Task Pane.

How to ... View the Contents of Your XML Document in the Task Pane

The Data View Details Task Pane shows the contents of the selected XML document data source in the XML Data section. You can expand an element that contains subelements by clicking the plus sign (+) alongside the element. For example, if you click the plus sign alongside the Employee element, you can see its subelements and any values for those subelements.

You can continue expanding any nested elements until you can see the actual data contained in the lowest-level elements. You'll need to do this anyway to gain access to the subelements so you can place them in the Data View.

14

The Task Pane only shows you one record (element) at a time. To move through the records, click the small arrowheads alongside any multiply occurring element (such as Employee in our example). If you only want to see the element names and *not* the data, clear the Show Data Values check box at the bottom of the Data View Details Task Pane.

Choose and Customize the Data View Style

There are a variety of basic styles you can use to display the contents of your XML document. The currently selected style is shown alongside the Style hyperlink in the Data View Details Task Pane. To change the style, click the Style hyperlink to display the View Styles dialog box.

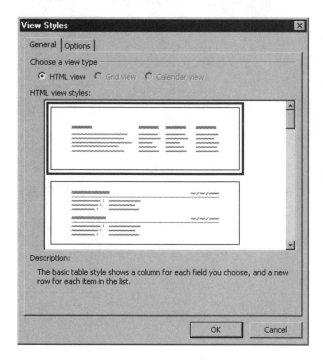

Choose a style from the list and read the description at the bottom of the dialog box. Then Click OK to choose that style.

You can also customize the style by clicking the Options tab in the View Styles dialog box.

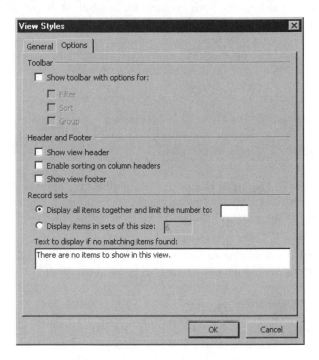

The options you can set are as follows:

■ **Show toolbars**   Check the Show Toolbar With Options For check box, then select the options you want from the list of check boxes below this item. The toolbar enables someone viewing the XML document in the Data View to apply their own filter on the records, or sort or group the records by the contents of any field. The toolbar is placed right on the page above the Data View.

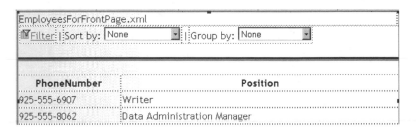

14

- **Add a Header or Footer** You can add an area above (header) or below (footer) the Data View that you can add descriptive content to. In addition, if the style you selected contains column headings (for example, the Basic Table style), you can enable viewers to sort the records on a column heading by checking the Enable Sorting On Column Headers check box. If you do check this check box, the column headers become hyperlinks. Clicking a column header sorts the records based on that column.

PhoneNumber	Position
925-555-6907	Writer
925-555-8062	Data Administration Manager

- **Limit the number of displayed records** You can limit the number of displayed records by choosing one of the two options in the Record Sets section of the dialog box. If you choose the Display Items In Sets Of This Size option, fill in the number of records you want to see at any time.
- **Set warning text when no records are found** Type the text you want displayed if no records match the specified filter in the text field near the bottom of the dialog box.

Modify the Data View Layout

While it is not strictly necessary to change the default layout of the Data View style, it can be very convenient to do so. For example, you can add columns to the Basic Table style or add rows to the Repeating Form style to hold additional data elements or make the layout more aesthetic.

To change the record layout of the Data View, you use the normal tools you've already learned. For example, if the Data View style includes a table (both the Basic Table style and the Repeating Form style do), you use the table tools to change the layout. Here is a repeating form style:

EmployeesForFrontPage.xml

PhoneNumber:	925-555-6907
Position:	Writer
PhoneNumber:	925-555-8062
Position:	Data Administration Manager
PhoneNumber:	925-555-0256
Position:	CIO
PhoneNumber:	925-555-0121
Position:	Data Administrator
PhoneNumber:	925-555-9223
Position:	Data Administrator
PhoneNumber:	925-555-8994
Position:	Vice President Application Development

To add rows to hold additional data, simply choose one of the records (Figure 14-4 shows six records) and use the table tools to add rows. Adding a row to one record automatically adds a row to all the other records, and splitting that row into cells—or adding content— is also reflected in all the other records.

Add Elements To the Data View

You can modify the displayed list of elements, adding or removing any elements available from the XML document. To add an element to the Data View, click that element in the Work With Data section of the Data View Detail Task Pane and drag that element into the Data View.

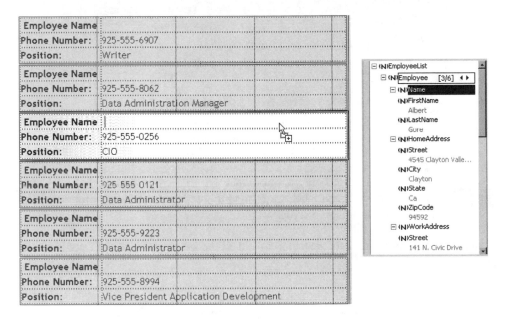

You can choose the element you want from any of the records in the Data Source Details Task Pane and drag it into any of the records visible in the Data View layout. The content of that element is populated from all the XML document records, and becomes visible in all the records in the Data View. In addition, you can drag and drop an element (such as Name) that contains

14

ployeesForFrontPage.xml				
Employee Name				
Phone Number:	925-555-6907			
Position:	Writer			
Employee Name				
Phone Number:	925-555-8062			
Position:	Data Administration Manager			
Employee Name				
Phone Number:	925-555-0256			
Position:	CIO			
Employee Name				
Phone Number:	925-555-0121			
Position:	Data Administrator			
Employee Name				
Phone Number:	925-555-9223			
Position:	Data Administrator			
Employee Name				
Phone Number:	925-555-8994			
Position:	Vice President Application Development			

FIGURE 14-4   A new row and a text label were added to just one record—but FrontPage added them to all the records.

subelements (such as FirstName and LastName) to add all the subelements to the Data View in one action.

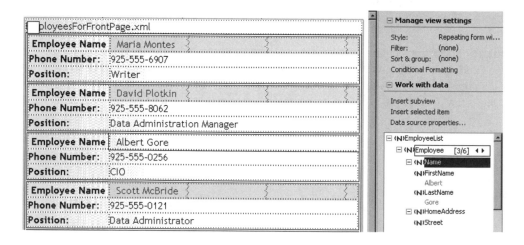

To delete an element from the Data View, click the element to highlight it and then press the DELETE *key. Deleting an element from one record in the Data View deletes it from all records.*

Format the Data View Elements

When you first add the contents of an element to the Data View, the format is the default for the page theme (or the default font if no theme is used on that page). However, you can apply text formatting (including style, font, size, effects, alignment, and color) to any element, using any of the text and paragraph formatting tools you learned to use earlier. Realize that once again, changing the text format of one instance of an element changes the text formatting for all instances. Thus, if you make phone number in one record bold, italics, and underlined, it appears that way in all records.

ployeesForFrontPage.xml	
Employee Name	Maria Montes
Phone Number:	*925-555-6907*
Position:	Writer
Employee Name	David Plotkin
Phone Number:	*925-555-8062*
Position:	Data Administration Manager
Employee Name	Albert Gore
Phone Number:	*925-555-0256*
Position:	CIO
Employee Name	Scott McBride
Phone Number:	*925-555-0121*
Position:	Data Administrator
Employee Name	Lynda Bellboure
Phone Number:	*925-555-9223*
Position:	Data Administrator

If you are XML-literate, you'll realize that this "change one changes them all" is because you are actually working with the XML document nodes.

Sort, Group, and Filter XML Records

The default order of the XML records in the Data View is the same order as in the XML document—and all the records are listed. However, you can change the sort order, group similar records together, and choose to display only certain records based on the contents of the elements.

14

Sort the XML Records

To sort the records in the Data View layout, click the Sort and Group hyperlink in the Data View Details Task Pane. This opens the Sort and Group dialog box.

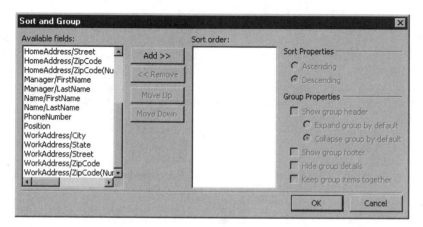

Choose the element(s) you want to sort on from the Available Fields list, and click the Add>> button to move the elements to the Sort Order list. You can choose to sort in either ascending or descending order by making the appropriate selection from the Sort Properties section of the dialog box.

Group the XML Records

If you sort the XML records (as discussed in the last section), you also have the option to group them using the Sort and Group dialog box. When you group records based on the contents of an element, you can display the records with a common header or footer (depending on the options you choose). You have the following options:

■ **Show Group Header** You can display the sort field(s) in a header above each group of records, as shown in Figure 14-5. If you do display a group header, you have the options to expand or collapse the group by default. Expanding the group by default simply shows the header and associated records. Collapsing the group by default displays only the group header (with its contents). To expand the group and view the records, click the plus sign (+) at the left end of the header. You can also collapse the group by clicking the minus sign (−) at the left end of the header.

When you add a group header, the header displays the name of the element as well as the element content. This is in addition *to that same element displayed in the record layout. Thus, you may want to remove the element from the record layout if you use group headers (or footers).*

■ **Show Group Footer** Displays the sort field(s) in a footer below each group of records.

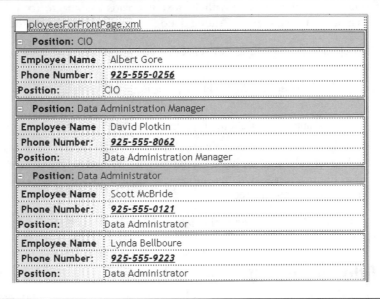

Adding a group header groups records with the same value of an element together.

- **Hide Group Details**   This option is available only when either the Show Group Header or the Show Group Footer check box is checked. If you check the Hide Group Details check box, only the header or footer is displayed in the Data View, and you cannot expand the header to show the details of the records.

- **Keep Group Items Together**   This option instructs FrontPage to avoid inserting a page break in the middle of a group of items if at all possible.

Filter the XML Records

You can display just the records you want to see by filtering them on the contents of an element. To establish filtering criteria, click the Filter hyperlink in the Data View Details Task Pane to open the Filter Criteria dialog box.

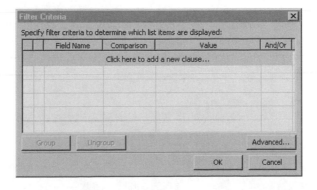

14

To create filtering criteria, click the line with the text that reads Click Here To Add A New Clause. This creates a new line in the Filter Criteria dialog box, where you can do the following:

- Choose the field name from a drop-down list that contains all the elements in the XML document.

- Select a comparison operator, such as Equals, Not Equal, Greater Than, Less Than, Contains, Not Contain, Begins With, and many others.

- Choose a value to compare the field to. Type the value you want into the Value column.

- Select an And/Or. If you want to combine multiple filter criteria, choose either And or Or from the And/Or column. Combining criteria with *And* means that all criteria must be true in order to return a record. Combining criteria with *Or* means that any of the criteria must be true in order to return a record.

Once you click OK, the filter is applied to the data and only those records matching the filter criteria are displayed.

Apply Conditional Formatting to an Element

You can specify the action to take when an element has a certain value—called *conditional formatting*. To apply conditional formatting to an element, right-click the element in a Data View and choose Conditional Formatting from the shortcut menu. Alternatively, you can select the field in the Data View and click the Conditional Formatting hyperlink in the Data View Details Task Pane. Either method opens the Conditional Formatting Task Pane (which is entirely empty at this point). Click the Create button to display a drop-down list of options. From the list, choose the action you want to take when the condition is met:

- **Show Content**   Show the element value in the Data View.
- **Hide Content**   Hide the element value in the Data View.
- **Apply Formatting**   Apply formatting to the element value in the Data View.

Once you make a selection from the list, the Condition Criteria dialog box appears, and you can fill it out exactly as described for the Filter Criteria dialog box (covered in the last section). You can choose the field name, comparison, and value, and you can join multiple condition criteria together with And and Or.

 If you chose the Apply Formatting option, once you set up the condition and click OK, FrontPage displays the Modify Style dialog box. Click on the Format button to choose options for formatting Font, Paragraph, Border, Numbering, and Position.

Chapter 15

Set Page Options and Web Settings

How to...

- Specify browser compatibility
- Choose web technology
- Add user-defined parameters to a web site
- Set the language options
- Set the navigation options

There are a lot of items you can configure about your web site using the Page Options dialog box and the Web Settings dialog box. Both of these are available from the Tools menu. Although the defaults work most of the time, you should at least be aware of the options available to configure how your web site will work.

Set Up the Page Options

To set up the page options, choose Tools | Page Options to display the Page Options dialog box. Most of the options don't require your attention, but there are a few that could prove useful.

Set Up Authoring Options

There are a lot of combinations of hardware and software on the Internet. Different browsers and different versions of browsers have different capabilities, and even the server software can affect which capabilities of a web site will be available. You may not be familiar with the subtle (and sometimes not so subtle) differences between the various browsers and server software, but FrontPage is. You can use the Authoring tab (see Figure 14-1) to tell FrontPage what browsers and server software you are designing for, and FrontPage will disable the unsupported features. For example, if you choose Netscape Navigator 3 and later as the browser you are designing for, then features such as VB Script (which is only understood by Internet Explorer) will be turned off. FrontPage won't allow you to embed VB (Visual Basic) scripts in your web.

Configure the Authoring tab as follows:

- **FrontPage and SharePoint Team Services Specific Technologies** Choose one of the options from the drop-down list to set which of these technologies are available on the web server where you are going to publish your web site. Alternatively, you can check or clear the individual check boxes (which automatically resets the drop-down list to Custom). Of course, you will need to gather this information from your WPP (web presence provider).

CAUTION *Clearing any of the technology check boxes will* not *cause FrontPage to warn you when you use a FrontPage component that requires these extensions. Instead, you will only get a warning when you publish the web site. At that time, you'll have to go back and remove any of the listed problem components from the web site—or at least not publish the pages containing the component.*

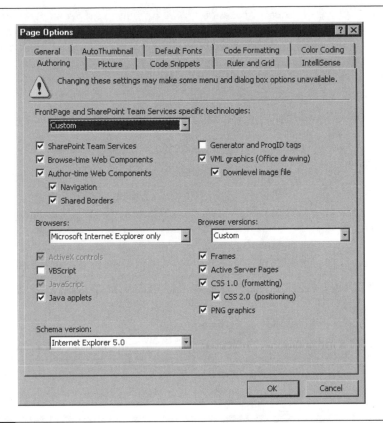

- **Browsers**   Select the browser(s) you want to design for from the drop-down list. Choices include such browsers as Netscape Navigator and Microsoft Internet Explorer. Although you can select only one choice from the list, one of the options enables you to select Netscape Navigator *and* Internet Explorer. In this case, the features that are supported by both will be available, and any features unsupported by either one will be turned off.

- **Browser Versions**   Select the version of the browser(s) you want to design for from the Browser Version drop-down list. You can choose to design for 3.0 browsers and later, 4.0 browsers and later, or 5.0 browsers and later. Alternatively, you can choose the combination of Internet Explorer version and Netscape Navigator version from the Schema Version drop-down list. Once you select the browser(s) and version, the check boxes just below the drop-down list reflect the capabilities of these choices. For example, if you select Netscape Navigator Only from the Browsers list and 4.0 browsers and later from the Browser Versions list, both the CSS 1.0 and CSS 2.0 check boxes are cleared.

15

NOTE

If you turn off any of the check boxes below the Browsers and Browser Versions drop-down lists (either by making choices from the drop-down lists or clearing the check boxes yourself), FrontPage will make that feature unavailable. For example, if you clear the Frames check box, the Frames tab disappears from the Page Templates dialog box. However, FrontPage does not *warn you about any existing web pages that already use this feature.*

CAUTION

The ActiveX Controls check box is grayed out and checked, meaning that ActiveX controls (see Chapter 16) are always available for use. However, Netscape Navigator does not work with ActiveX Controls, so if you are designing for Netscape Navigator, do not *use them.*

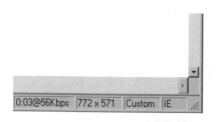

The selections you make on the Authoring tab are shown in the lower-right corner of the FrontPage working area.

The left-hand entry displays the current setting for the FrontPage and SharePoint Team Services specific technologies, while the right-hand entry displays the current setting for the Browsers/Browser Versions. You can quickly open the Authoring tab of the Page Options dialog box by double-clicking on either of the entries.

Once you establish what browsers you are designing for, you can check your web site to see if there are any problems. To do so, choose Tools | Browser Compatibility. This opens the Browser Compatibility dialog box, where you can select what pages to check (All Pages, Open Pages, Selected Pages, or Current Page). Simply click the Check button to run the check and display a listing of any errors.

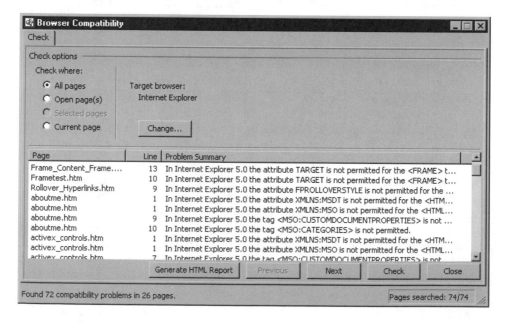

SharePoint Team Services (STS) is a special set of technologies that allows a group of people to work together on a web site, collaborating both on the building of the site and using the site to review Office documents, host discussion groups, and other group activities. The SharePoint Team Services component must be installed on the web server in order for these facilities to work.

TIP   *When you run the compatibility check, FrontPage opens the first page with a problem, changes to Split Page view, and highlights the section of code where the problem is.*

Set the Default Font

When you don't specify a font to use for text on a FrontPage web page, FrontPage needs to know what default font it should use. You set this quantity from the Default Font tab of the Page Options dialog box.

Page Options

| Authoring | Picture | Code Snippets | Ruler and Grid | IntelliSense |
| General | AutoThumbnail | Default Fonts | Code Formatting | Color Coding |

Select the font FrontPage should use for each language when no font is specified for text.

Language (character set):

Thai
Traditional Chinese (Big5)
Turkish
Unicode
Unicode (Big-Endian)
Unicode (UTF-8)
US/Western European
Vietnamese

Design View

Default proportional font: Times New Roman

Default fixed-width font: Courier New

Code View

Font: Courier New

Size: 9

OK   Cancel

15

Choose the character set you want to use from the Language list. Virtually all the readers of this book will want to use the US/Western European option. For the Design Page View, you need to specify a default proportional font and a default fixed-width font from the appropriate drop-down lists. A proportional font is a font in which each letter takes up a different amount of space. For example, the letter "i" takes up less room than the letter "W". A fixed-width font is a font in which each letter takes up the same amount of room. Unfortunately, both the Default Proportional Font drop-down list and the Default Fixed-Width Font drop-down list show *all* the fonts you have installed on your computer. For example, the Default Fixed-Width Font drop-down list displays options for Arial and Times New Roman, despite the fact that both of these are proportional fonts. Thus, it is up to you to know which type of font is which, and choose accordingly.

You must also choose a default font and size for the Code Page View from the drop-down lists in the Code View section of the dialog box. It is best to use a fixed-width font for code so that indented lines "line up" in the Code Page View.

A good choice for a default proportional font is either Times New Roman or Arial, both of which are proportional fonts and are available on virtually all computers. A good choice for a default fixed-width font is Courier New.

Specify the Web Site Settings

You can set configuration options for the web site as a whole. To do so, choose Tools | Web Settings to open the Web Settings dialog box.

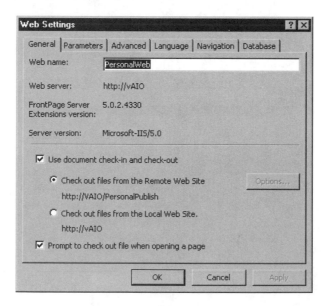

Change the Web Site Name

If you decide you don't like the name of your web site, you can change it. Simply type the new name into the Web Name field of the General tab.

Add Parameters

As mentioned in Chapter 13, you can specify parameters and place them in a web page using the Substitution component. To get these parameters to appear in the drop-down list from which you select the substitution items, you must add them to the web site. Each parameter consists of a parameter name and the value assigned to that parameter. Examples of parameters you might want to use include the version of the site or the last time a major update was done.

To add parameters to a web site, click the Parameters tab of the Web Setting dialog box, shown here (along with a few parameters I defined).

This tab displays a list of all the defined parameters, showing both the name and the value of the parameter.

To add a new parameter, click the Add button to open the Add Name And Value dialog box.

Type a name for the parameter into the Name field and the associated value into the Value field. Then click OK to add the parameter to the list of parameters. To change a name or value, select the parameter from the list and click Modify. To delete the parameter, select the parameter from the list and click Remove.

Set the Scripting Language

FrontPage has the capability of creating scripts to support its special features and components in either JavaScript or Visual Basic. To specify the default scripting language to use, switch to the Advanced tab of the Web Settings dialog box. Choose the scripting language from the Client drop-down list.

*Only Internet Explorer can execute Visual Basic scripts, so unless you want to lock out all the users of Netscape Navigator (*not *a good idea), choose JavaScript as the default. Both browsers can execute JavaScript scripts.*

Delete Temporary Files

If you create or open a web site on a server, FrontPage creates temporary files on your local hard drive that cache the information on the server. This makes it possible to open and work with files much more quickly because the files don't have to load from the server every time you access them. However, if many people are working on the web site at once, the temporary files can get out of synch with the web site on the server. Your first clue about this may be that your web management reports suddenly stop showing certain pages, or hyperlinks no longer work even though you didn't change either the hyperlink or the target of the hyperlink. If this happens, you need to synchronize your local temporary files with the latest information on the server. To do so, click the Delete Files button in the Temporary Files section of the Advanced tab. The next time you open the web site on the server, it will take longer because FrontPage has to reload all the information. However, the information should now be accurate.

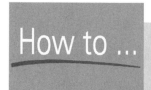 **Show Documents in Hidden Directories**

When viewing files in the Folder List, there are some folders and files you don't normally see. These include the folders that FrontPage uses for its own bookkeeping, such as the folders for themes and borders, and the folder (usually called "_private") that holds form results. These folders all have names that are prefaced by an underscore ("_"). It can be useful to view these folders on occasion. To do so, click the Advanced tab of the Web Settings dialog box, and check the Show Hidden Files And Folders check box.

Set the Navigation Options

If you have used navigation bars (see Chapter 10), you already know that you can't directly customize the text of the buttons that appear in the navigation bar. To change the text for buttons that refer to other pages in your web site, you must change the icon title for the page in Navigation view. But what about the text for the navigation buttons that enable you to move back and forward in the stream of pages you are viewing, as well as navigate up to the parent page and to the home page? To change the button text for these buttons, switch to the Navigation tab in the Web Settings dialog box.

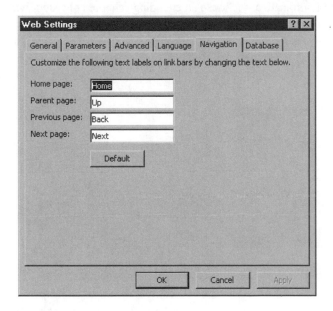

Enter the button text for the Home Page, Parent Page, Previous Page, and Next Page in the fields on this tab.

If you wish to return to FrontPage's default values, click the Default button.

Set the Server Message Language

15

FrontPage uses the server message language to determine which language to use to display messages from the FrontPage server extensions. These include edit error messages, as well as error messages displayed to the site visitor when an operation fails. Examples of these types of messages include the failure of a search to work or a form validation error. The server message language is also used when the FrontPage extensions generate web pages, such as the default form submission confirmation pages. To specify the server message language, click the Language tab of the Web Settings dialog box and choose the language from the Server Message Language drop-down list.

Set the Default Page Encoding

When FrontPage stores the information on a web page, it uses a feature called "encoding." The contents of the page are encoded using an encoding scheme, and it is important to choose the right one for the language. For example, if a web page is written in Chinese, it won't be saved properly if the encoding scheme is US/Western European (the default). To set the encoding scheme to use, click the Language tab of the Web Settings dialog box and choose the encoding scheme from the Default Page Encoding drop-down list.

FrontPage (and all the Office applications) are sensitive to the type of keyboard attached to the computer, and will automatically choose an encoding scheme consistent with the keyboard unless you check the Ignore The Keyboard When Deciding The Encoding Of New Page check box.

Chapter 16

Java Applets and ActiveX Controls

How to...

- Add Java applets to your site
- Configure Java applets
- Add ActiveX controls to your site

There is a lot you can do to add functionality to your web site with HTML and Dynamic HTML. In addition, you can add variety and some measure of interactivity to your Web pages using Java applets and ActiveX controls. Java applets are created using the Java programming language, while ActiveX controls are created using a variety of different programming languages—but the programming must conform to Microsoft's standards for creating these special controls. However, you don't have to be a programmer to use Java applets or ActiveX controls on your web pages. You can find a ready supply of prebuilt applets and controls on the Internet, and you can use them in your web site without any knowledge of how they were programmed. Both Java applets and ActiveX controls use sets of parameters (defined by the programmer), and as long as the documentation tells you what the parameters are and the valid values you can use for each, you can customize Java applets and ActiveX controls within the bounds set by the programmer.

Automate Your Web Site with Java Applets

A Java *applet* is a small application (which is why it is called an "applet") created in the Java programming language. An applet can be downloaded with a web page and executed by any browser that includes a Java virtual machine—basically, version 3 or greater of either Internet Explorer or Netscape Navigator. Although Java applets don't strictly need to be run from within a browser, that is their major use. Java is platform-independent—that is, as long as the browser is Java-aware, the applet (and thus the functionality of your web site) will run on a PC, Mac, Sun, or other computer. And, since the Java code executes locally on the reader's computer, it can be quite fast.

Some very interesting *Java applet construction sets* are beginning to appear on the market. These toolkits enable you to specify what you want the applet to do, and then generate the code for you (much like the Behaviors Task Pane). For example, there are several of these toolkits that construct banners. You can specify how large you want the banner to be, the background color, the text content, how fast and in what direction you want the text to scroll, and so on. Once you've got the banner looking the way you want it, you can generate your own Java applet. For some really good-quality toolkits of this type, check out www.coffeecup.com. This site includes downloadable demo versions of all their software.

Add a Java Applet to a Page

Once you have obtained the Java applets you want, you are ready to add them to your web page. To do so, use the following steps:

1. Copy the applet file and any support files into the same folder as the page to which you will be adding the applet. You'll recognize the applet file because it has an extension of .CLASS (or less frequently, .CLA). Many Java applets use graphics and small text files when they are running, so be sure to copy them all.

> **NOTE**   *When you download a Java applet, the download file (usually a zip file) will probably include the applet file, the support files, and any documentation on how to configure the applet.*

2. Choose Insert | Web Component and select Advanced Controls from the Insert Web Component dialog box. Choose Java Applet from the list on the right side of the dialog box. Click Finish to open the Java Applet Properties dialog box (see Figure 16-1).

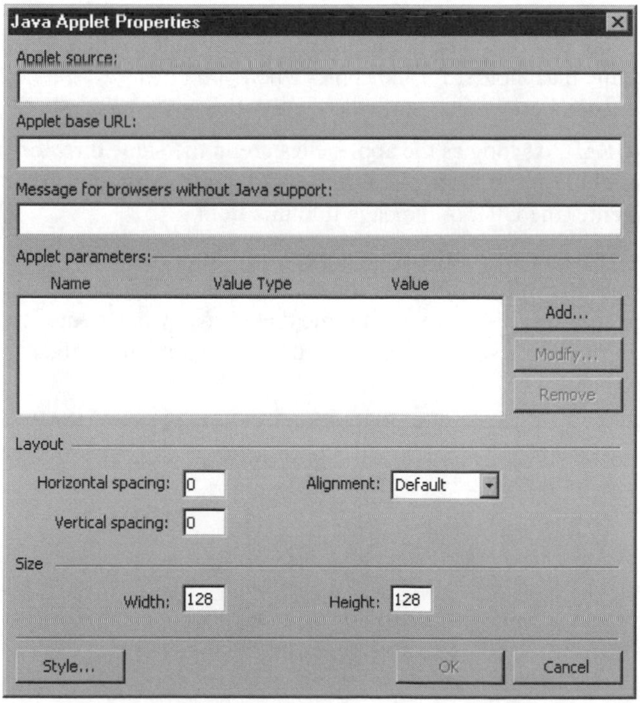

FIGURE 16-1   Specify the applet and set up its parameters using the Java Applet Properties dialog box.

16

3. Use the Java applet documentation to fill out the Java Applet Properties dialog box (step-by-step instructions for filling out this dialog box are included in the next section). At a minimum, you must enter the name of the .CLASS file into the Applet Source field.

4. Click OK to add the Java applet to your page. FrontPage places a placeholder on the page to show how large the applet will appear.

5. To see the Java applet in action, click on the Preview tab in Page view. After a few moments, the Java applet will start up and run. Figure 16-2 shows a clock (one of the most popular types of simple Java applets) running on the page.

JavaClock.class

If you want to see how the Java applet appears in the code, switch to the Code Page view and look over the code between the <applet> tags. Figure 16-3 shows how an applet with many parameters might look in the Code Page view.

Configure the Java Applet

You can control quite a bit about the applet with the Java Applet Properties dialog box (refer back to Figure 16-1). Configure the applet as follows:

■ **Applet source**   Enter the name of the Java applet file in this field. This is the .CLASS or .CLA file. Note that the name is case-sensitive. If you type the name in incorrectly, you'll still see the placeholder for the applet when you click OK, but nothing will appear on the page (except a gray rectangle) when you preview the page.

■ **Applet base URL**   As long as the applet files are in the same directory as the page, you can leave this field blank. If the applet is *not* stored in the same folder (not recommended), you'll have to enter the URL of the page into this field.

■ **Message for browsers without Java support**   Although it is rare for browsers to not support Java applets, you should enter the message that someone will see if their browser does not support Java. This is especially true these days, when people may turn off the Java support in their browsers to protect themselves against malicious applets.

FIGURE 16-2   Switch to the preview Page view to see the Java applet in action.

```
Web Site    java_applets.htm
 1 <html>
 2
 3 <head>
 4 <meta http-equiv="Content-Language" content="en-us">
 5 <meta http-equiv="Content-Type" content="text/html; charset=windows-1252">
 6 <title>Java Applets</title>
 7 <meta name="Microsoft Theme" content="network 011, default">
 8 </head>
 9
10 <body>
11
12 <h2 align="center"><font color="#0000FF">Java Applets</font></h2>
13 <p align="center">
14 <applet width="250" height="250" code="JavaClock.class">
15   <param name="sHandColor" value="green">
16   <param name="backcolor" value="lblue">
17   <param name="fontcolor" value="green">
18   <param name="fontsize" value="24">
19   <param name="hHandColor" value="blue">
20   <param name="mHandColor" value="blue">
21   <param name="typeface" value="Heritage">
22 </applet></p>
23 <p> </p>
24
25 </body>
26
```

FIGURE 16-3   Use the Code Page view to see how the applet looks in code.

- **Horizontal spacing**   Set the amount of spacing to the left and right of the applet.
- **Vertical spacing**   Set the amount of spacing above and below the applet.
- **Alignment**   This drop-down list lets you specify how the applet is displayed on the page. The Left, Right, and Center options specify the horizontal alignment. The rest of the options specify how text alongside the applet will be aligned. The values work identically to the alignment options for graphics, as detailed in Chapter 4.
- **Width/Height**   The documentation for the Java applet should provide you with the recommended width and height, and you can enter the quantities in these fields. You can also size the applet on the page by clicking on the applet placeholder to display the sizing handles. Drag the sizing handles to adjust the size.

The center section of the Java Applet Properties dialog box is used to specify parameters that affect how the applet looks and works. For example, the clock applet uses parameters to specify the typeface, size, and color of the font used to display the digital time, the color of the hands in the analog version, the background color, and many other quantities.

16

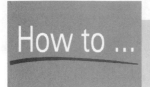

Duplicate a Java Applet on Many Different Pages

Want to duplicate a Java applet on many different pages, complete with all the parameters settings? Here's how:

1. Add and configure the applet on one page.

2. Switch to the Code Page view for that page and copy all the text between the <applet> tags.

3. Paste that text into the Code Page view of any other pages—voilà!

Just remember that all these pages must be in the same folder for this to work.

There is no standard set of parameters for Java applets—the programmer specifies the parameters. The documentation for the applet should tell you what parameters are available and what their valid values are.

To add a parameter to the Java Applet Properties dialog box, click the Add button to open the Set Attribute Value dialog.

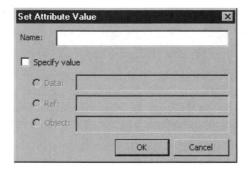

Enter the parameter name in the Name field, check the Specify Value check box, and enter the value in the Data, Ref, or Object fields (following the configuration instructions).

If the documentation simply specifies a value for an attribute, enter the value in the Data field.

NOTE   *Not all Java applets use parameters. Some just are what they are.*

To change the name or value assigned to a parameter, click the Modify button to reopen the Set Value Attribute dialog box. If you decide you don't need the parameter, select it and click Remove.

CAUTION   *Much has been written about the malicious use of Java applets. Although most applets are safe, there are a few twisted individuals who create Java applets that can potentially do damage to your machine. Obviously, you don't want to use such applets yourself, and you certainly don't want to post these applets on your web site. It is best to try out unknown Java applets on a test machine (if you have one), and only download Java applets from trusted web sites, such as those listed on the web site for this book (http://www.dplotkin.com).*

Automate Your Web with ActiveX Controls

An alternative to Java applets is ActiveX controls. Invented by Microsoft, ActiveX controls are similar to Java applets in that they typically (although not always) implement small, self-contained pieces of functionality. And like Java applets, they can be embedded in web pages and configured. They are often used to provide controls: sliders, media players, calendars, spreadsheets, progress bars, and so on. ActiveX controls can significantly extend the functionality of the browser, enabling you (if you are a proficient programmer) to customize Internet Explorer both in appearance and function. Unfortunately, however, ActiveX controls only work in Internet Explorer—Netscape Navigator users won't be able to take advantage of ActiveX controls.

ActiveX controls come in three flavors:

- Embedded ActiveX controls appear as rectangular windows in a web page. You may not be able to tell the difference between the control and a graphic—at least until you begin exploring the interactivity of the control, something you can't do with a plain graphic!

- A full-screen ActiveX control takes over the entire browser window and displays its own contents. With this type of control, the browser window can display information that is not supported by the browser.

- Hidden ActiveX controls are not visible, but add functionality to the browser that wouldn't otherwise be available.

16

Add ActiveX Controls to the Page

To add an ActiveX control to your web page, use the following steps:

1. Choose Insert | Web Component and select Advanced Controls from the Insert Web Component dialog box. Choose ActiveX Control from the list on the right side of the dialog box. Click Next to display a list of available ActiveX controls.

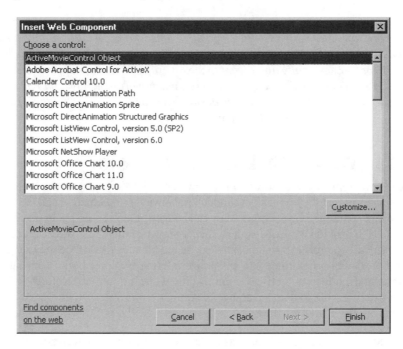

2. Click the ActiveX control you want to insert into the page and click Finish.

3. The ActiveX control appears on the page (see Figure 16-4). You can switch to preview Page view if you want, although many of the controls look the same in normal and preview Page views.

NOTE *Although there are quite a few ActiveX controls in the Insert Web Component dialog box, you actually have access to many more. To see a list of all the controls installed on your computer, click the Customize button in the Insert Web Component dialog box. A long list of controls appears in the Customize ActiveX Control List dialog box. Each has a check box next to it. Check the check box for the controls you want to see in the Insert Web Component dialog box, and clear the check box for the controls you don't want to see.*

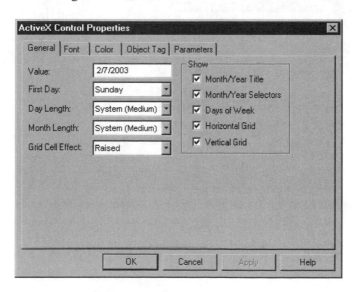

| FIGURE 16-4 | The calendar ActiveX control is one of the most popular—and a handy addition to many web pages. |

If you'd like to see how the ActiveX control is implemented in code, switch to the Code Page view (see Figure 16-5). The code for the ActiveX control is between the <object> tags.

Configure the ActiveX Control

To configure an ActiveX control, double-click on the control or choose ActiveX Control Properties from the shortcut menu. This opens the ActiveX Control Properties dialog box. It is very important to understand that the dialog box for each control is different—we'll cover the common aspects of the dialog box.

16

```
    Web Site  activex_controls.htm
   7 <!--[if gte mso 9]><xml>
   8 <mso:CustomDocumentProperties>
   9 <mso:Categories msdt:dt="string">Business;Goals/Objectives</mso:Categories>
  10 </mso:CustomDocumentProperties>
  11 </xml><![endif]-->
  12 <meta name="Microsoft Theme" content="network 011, default">
  13 </head>
  14
  15 <body>
  16
  17 <h2 align="center"><font color="#0000FF">ActiveX Controls</font></h2>
  18 <p align="center">
  19 <object classid="clsid:8E27C92B-1264-101C-8A2F-040224009C02" id="Calendar1">
  20     <param name="BackColor" value="-2147483633">
  21     <param name="Year" value="2003">
  22     <param name="Month" value="2">
  23     <param name="Day" value="7">
  24     <param name="DayLength" value="1">
  25     <param name="MonthLength" value="1">
  26     <param name="DayFontColor" value="0">
  27     <param name="FirstDay" value="7">
  28     <param name="GridCellEffect" value="1">
  29     <param name="GridFontColor" value="10485760">
  30     <param name="GridLinesColor" value="-2147483632">
  31     <param name="ShowDateSelectors" value="-1">
  32     <param name="ShowDays" value="-1">
  33     <param name="ShowHorizontalGrid" value="-1">
  34     <param name="ShowTitle" value="-1">
  35     <param name="ShowVerticalGrid" value="-1">
  36     <param name="TitleFontColor" value="10485760">
  37     <param name="ValueIsNull" value="0">
  38 </object>
  39 </p>
```

FIGURE 16-5   The code between the <object> tags belongs to the ActiveX control.

To set the values for the specialized tabs, such as the General tab, you'll have to have some documentation about the ActiveX control. Some of the controls are pretty self-explanatory, but others are something of a mystery. The good news is that many ActiveX controls have built-in help. For example, if you click the Help button on the calendar's ActiveX Control Properties dialog box, you'll get a list of the various parameters and what they mean, as well as guidance on how to set the options in the ActiveX Control Properties dialog box.

All ActiveX controls have at least the Object Tag tab and the Parameters tab, and these tabs are the same for all controls. The Object Tag tab is displayed in the following illustration.

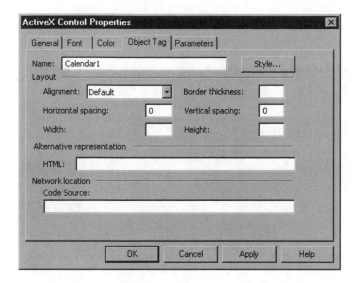

Configure the Object Tag tab as follows:

- **Name** Type a name for the control into this field. This name makes it easier to find the control in the HTML code later (you can just search for the name).

- **Alignment** This drop-down list lets you specify how the applet is displayed on the page. The Left, Right, and Center options in this list specify the horizontal alignment. The rest of the options specify how text alongside the control will be aligned. The values work identically to the alignment options for graphics, as detailed in Chapter 4.

- **Border thickness** The thickness of the border (in pixels) around the control. Leave this blank if you don't want a border displayed.

- **Horizontal spacing** Set the amount of spacing to the left and right of the applet.

- **Vertical spacing** Set the amount of spacing above and below the applet.

- **Width/Height** Enter the width and height into the appropriate fields. You can also size the control on the page by clicking on the control to display the sizing handles. Drag the sizing handles to adjust the size.

- **HTML** Enter the HTML code to display on the page if the browser doesn't support ActiveX controls or if the reader has turned off ActiveX support in his or her browser. For example, you could enter **<H1> Your Browser Does Not Support ActiveX </H1>**.

- **Code Source** If the code for the ActiveX control does not reside within your web site, you must provide the location where the code *is* located in this field.

16

The Parameters tab gives you an opportunity to modify how the ActiveX control behaves, somewhat similar to the parameters in Java applets.

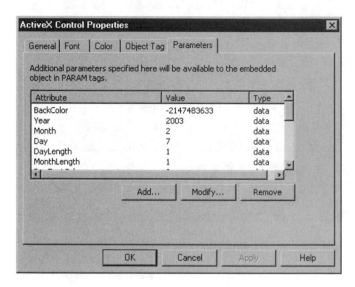

To add a parameter, click the Add button to open the Edit Object Parameter dialog box. You can type a new parameter into the Name field, but unlike Java, you can also pick an existing parameter from the drop-down Name list.

Enter a value in one of the fields in the Value area of the dialog box (Data, Page, or Object) by selecting one of the options and entering a value in the adjacent field. Click OK when you're done.

You can also modify the value of a parameter by selecting the parameter from the list and clicking the Modify button, which opens the Edit Object Parameter dialog box. This time, however, the parameter name and current value are prepopulated in the fields.

Finally, you can remove a parameter by choosing it from the list and clicking Remove.

Chapter 17

Manage Your Web Site with Tasks and Reports

How to...

- ■ Use the task list
- ■ Add a task manually
- ■ Add a task to build pages
- ■ Manage the tasks
- ■ Run reports
- ■ View and understand report results
- ■ Filter the report results
- ■ Quickly fix problem areas
- ■ Change the publishing status of your pages

When you first begin building a web site, you will probably focus on the mechanics of building the pages: typing in and formatting the text, adding the graphics, laying out the tables, specifying the hyperlinks, and making good use of forms and frames. But how do you manage the task of building and maintaining your web site? It seems like there are so many things to be done, and you may be constantly thinking of new ways to improve your site. Tasks can help with getting organized, reminding you of the things you need to take care of.

Another issue you may worry about is keeping track of everything on your site. Did you get all the hyperlinks right? Are any of the pages too slow to load? Reports can help you find problems with your site, and you can use reports to navigate right to the problem areas in your web site.

Keep Track of the Work with Tasks

When you are building a large web site with many pages, wouldn't it be helpful to be able to make a list of the pages you think you need—perhaps a few fixes that come to mind—and even jot down some long-term development plans (such as adding a search page)? FrontPage's Task view can help you get organized and stay organized as you build your web site.

What Are Tasks?

Think of the Task view as your "to do" list. You can list new tasks, mark tasks as in progress or completed, and prioritize the tasks. The Task view (see Figure 17-1) provides a consolidated view of tasks you have identified. Each of the tasks in the list is something you or someone on your team needs to take care of to finish the web site.

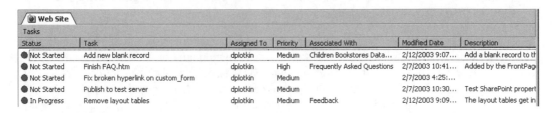

Status	Task	Assigned To	Priority	Associated With	Modified Date	Description
Not Started	Add new blank record	dplotkin	Medium	Children Bookstores Data...	2/12/2003 9:07...	Add a blank record to th
Not Started	Finish FAQ.htm	dplotkin	High	Frequently Asked Questions	2/7/2003 10:41...	Added by the FrontPage
Not Started	Fix broken hyperlink on custom_form	dplotkin	Medium		2/7/2003 4:25:...	
Not Started	Publish to test server	dplotkin	Medium		2/7/2003 10:30...	Test SharePoint propert
In Progress	Remove layout tables	dplotkin	Medium	Feedback	2/12/2003 9:09...	The layout tables get in

FIGURE 17-1   The Task view shows you everything you still need to get done. Isn't that jolly?

Add New Tasks

Before you can work with the tasks, you need to add them to the task list. There are quite a few ways to add tasks.

Add a Task Manually in Task View

To add a new task in Task view, right-click in a blank area of the Task view and choose Add Task from the shortcut menu, or choose Edit | Tasks | Add Task. Either way, the New Task dialog box appears (see Figure 17-2).

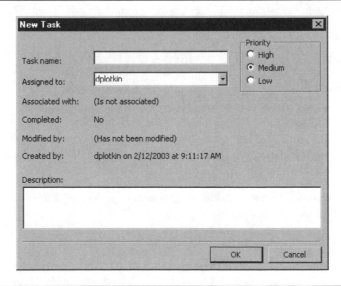

FIGURE 17-2   Specify the parameters of a new task in the New Task dialog box.

17

You can also create a new task from the Web Site Report view using Edit | Tasks | Add Task. Then configure the task as described below.

An important thing to notice in the New Task dialog box is that the Associated With field displays the value (Is Not Associated). This indicates that the manually created task is not associated with any page. As you'll see later, when a task is associated with a page, FrontPage provides a certain amount of automation to help you manage the task as you edit the page. However, this is not possible with tasks created in the Task view or Report view. These nonassociated tasks are appropriate for general web tasks, such as publishing the web site, changing the theme, adjusting the navigation bars, and so on. Configure the new task as follows:

- **Task name**   Enter a descriptive name for the task. This is the text that appears in the Task column of the Task view, so you should think carefully about the name you choose.

- **Assigned to**   Enter the name (or some other identifier, such as e-mail address) for the person responsible for completing this task. You can type the identifier into the field or click the down arrow and select from a drop-down list of previously assigned people. The contents of this field appear in the Assigned To column of the Task view.

- **Priority**   Set the task priority by selecting High, Medium, or Low. This quantity appears in the Priority column of the Task view.

- **Description**   Enter a description for the task. This text appears in the Description column of the Task view.

You cannot change the Associated, Completed, Modified By, or Created By fields. These are automatically filled in by FrontPage.

Click OK to create the task. The new task appears in the Task view, with a status of Not Started.

Add a Task in Page View

To create a new task in Page view, display the page to which you want to associate the task, then choose Edit | Tasks | Add Task to open the New Task dialog box. It looks just like the New Task dialog box displayed in Figure 17-2, except that now the task is associated with the open page. After filling out the New Task dialog box, click OK to create the task. To see the new task, switch to the Task view.

If you create a task without first displaying a page or selecting a file in the Folder List, the task will not be associated with any page.

Add a Task from the Folder List

If you can see the Folder List, you can quickly create a task associated with any page in the list. To do so, select the page and choose Edit | Tasks | Add Task to open the New Task dialog box. Fill in the New Task dialog box as described previously, and click OK to create a task associated with the selected page.

You can drag and drop a page from the Folder List into the Web Site Task view, creating a task associated with that page.

Add a Task in Other Web Site Views

In Web Site Folders view, you can select a page from the list and add a task associated with that page by choosing Edit | Tasks | Add Task to open the New Task dialog box. Configure the task and click OK to create it.

In Web Site Remote Web Site view (see Chapter 18), you can select a page from the list of pages in the local web site and add a task associated with that page, again by using Edit | Tasks | Add Task.

You can add a new task from the Web Site Navigation view or Web Site Hyperlink view. Either of these views displays icons for pages in the main window of the screen. To add a task associated with a page, click the page and then select Edit | Tasks | Add Task to open the New Task dialog box. Configure the task and click OK to create.

If you choose Edit | Tasks | Add Task without first selecting a page, the created task will not be associated with any page.

Create a Task When You Create a Page

FrontPage makes it easy to create a task when you create a page. By using this feature, you can come back and build the page later. This makes an excellent planning tool—just specify a page you need, create a task to build the page later, and repeat the process until you have all the pages queued up to build. Using this technique, you don't have to stop your planning process to actually build the pages.

To create a task as you create a page, use the following steps:

1. Choose File | New to display the New Task Pane. Click More Page Templates to display the Page Template dialog box.

2. Pick the template you want to use from the Page Templates dialog box.

3. Check the Just Add Web Task check box.

4. Choose OK. FrontPage opens the Save As dialog box.

5. Type the filename for the page into the File Name field.

6. Click the Change Title button to change the page title. Type the title into the Set Page Title dialog box and click OK.

7. Click Save to create the page and a task to remind you to finish the page later. The task is titled "Finish *FileName*" where *FileName* is the name you gave the page. You can rename the task in the Task view if you wish, as detailed in the next section.

17

 *If you cancel the new page from the Save As dialog (by clicking the Cancel button), the new task is still created, but it is associated with an unknown page. You'll need to delete the task as detailed in the next section.*

Delete a Task

If you need to remove a task from the Task view, select the task and either press the DELETE key or select Edit | Delete. Confirm that you want the task deleted by clicking Yes in the Confirm Delete dialog box, and the task disappears.

Manually Adjust Task Properties

From the Task view, you can manage your tasks manually, changing the status of the task as well as its properties. You can double-click the task or choose Edit Task from the shortcut menu to open the Task Details dialog box, which looks just like the New Task dialog box (see Figure 17-2). This dialog box works identically to the New Task dialog box, except that if the task is associated with a page, the dialog box has one additional button, Start Task. Clicking the button opens the page associated with the task in Page view. From the Edit Task dialog box, you can also adjust the task name, the person it is assigned to (use the Assigned To drop-down list), the priority, and the description.

NOTE *You cannot change the contents of either the Associated With column or the Modified Date column. FrontPage sets these automatically.*

Each task has a shortcut menu, accessed by right-clicking the task, from which you make selections to manage the task. The shortcut menu contains the following elements:

- **Edit Task**   This opens the Task Details dialog box.
- **Start Task**   This option is available only if the task is associated with a page. Selecting this option opens the page in Design Page view. You can also choose Edit | Tasks | Start Task.
- **Mark Complete**   This changes the status of the task from either Not Started or In Progress to Completed. By default, once a task has been completed, it will appear in the task list only until you refresh the list of tasks (choose View | Refresh). Upon refreshing the list, all completed tasks disappear. You can also choose Edit | Tasks | Mark Complete.
- **Delete Task**   This deletes the task from the Task view.

TIP *If you want to see all the tasks for this web site, including completed tasks, choose Edit | Tasks | Show History. This toggle displays the completed tasks in the list. Select this option again to turn it off.*

Perform Tasks

If a task is associated with a web page, you can "start the task" by clicking the Start Task button in the Task Details dialog box. Alternatively, you can start it by right-clicking the task to display the shortcut menu and selecting Start Task, or by selecting Start Task from the Edit | Tasks menu. Starting the task opens the associated page in the Design Page view. Once the page is open, you can customize the page any way you want using any of FrontPage's tools. When you save the page, FrontPage will query you (see Figure 17-3) about whether you want the task marked as completed. If you do, click Yes. When you return to the Task view, you will find that the task status has changed to Completed. If you click No, the task status will change to In Progress. You can reopen the page from the Task view and make additional changes, and upon saving the page FrontPage will once again query you about whether to mark the task as completed.

NOTE   *FrontPage will only query you to mark the task as completed if you open the page from the Task view by starting the task. If you open the page any other way, FrontPage won't prompt you about the task.*

Check Your Site with Web Site Reports

FrontPage provides a series of reports that will help you manage your web site and find (and fix) problems. By using these reports religiously, you can avoid web no-nos such as broken hyperlinks, pages that take too long to load, and pages containing outdated information.

Access the Reports

To begin working with reports, click the Reports button in the Web Site view. If this is the first time you've used the Reports tool, the Site Summary report appears (see Figure 17-4). You can also view this report by choosing it from the Report toolbar or selecting View | Reports | Site Summary.

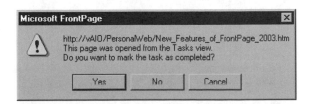

FIGURE 17-3   If you want, FrontPage will mark the task as completed when you save a page.

17

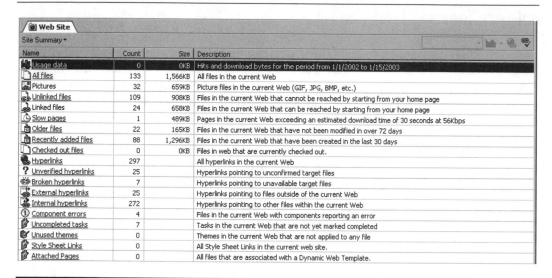

Name	Count	Size	Description
Usage data	0	0KB	Hits and download bytes for the period from 1/1/2002 to 1/15/2003
All files	133	1,566KB	All files in the current Web
Pictures	32	659KB	Picture files in the current Web (GIF, JPG, BMP, etc.)
Unlinked files	109	908KB	Files in the current Web that cannot be reached by starting from your home page
Linked files	24	658KB	Files in the current Web that can be reached by starting from your home page
Slow pages	1	489KB	Pages in the current Web exceeding an estimated download time of 30 seconds at 56Kbps
Older files	22	165KB	Files in the current Web that have not been modified in over 72 days
Recently added files	88	1,296KB	Files in the current Web that have been created in the last 30 days
Checked out files	0	0KB	Files in web that are currently checked out.
Hyperlinks	297		All hyperlinks in the current Web
Unverified hyperlinks	25		Hyperlinks pointing to unconfirmed target files
Broken hyperlinks	7		Hyperlinks pointing to unavailable target files
External hyperlinks	25		Hyperlinks pointing to files outside of the current Web
Internal hyperlinks	272		Hyperlinks pointing to other files within the current Web
Component errors	4		Files in the current Web with components reporting an error
Uncompleted tasks	7		Tasks in the current Web that are not yet marked completed
Unused themes	0		Themes in the current Web that are not applied to any file
Style Sheet Links	0		All Style Sheet Links in the current web site.
Attached Pages	0		All files that are associated with a Dynamic Web Template.

FIGURE 17-4 The Site Summary report shows you the results of the various FrontPage reports at a glance.

You can run any of the FrontPage reports (including a few that *don't* appear in the Site Summary report) from the drop-down list in the Web Site Reports title bar or from the submenu that appears when you choose View | Reports.

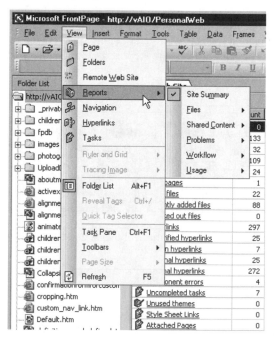

Set the Report Parameters

If you take a quick look at the Site Summary report, you'll see some reports that list pages that load slowly, or that have been added recently, or are considered old. You can configure the reports to specify the parameters used by these reports. To do so, choose Tools | Options to open the Options dialog box. Then click the Reports View.

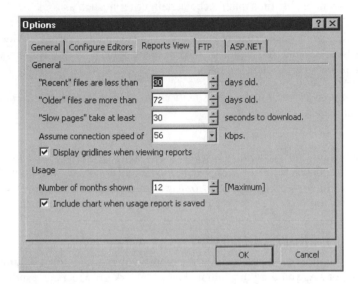

Set the parameters for the reports as follows:

- **"Recent" files are less than**   Choose what you consider recent files. Files that were added to the site more recently than the number of days you specified are considered recent and are included in the Recently Added Files list.

- **"Older" files are older than**   Choose what you consider old files. Files that were added to the site more than the specified number of days ago are included in the Older Files list.

- **"Slow pages" take at least**   Choose what you consider to be the length of time it takes a slow page to download.

- **Assume connection speed of**   Choose the speed of the Internet connection you want to use when calculating slow pages. Common speeds between 28.8 Kbps and 1,500 Kbps are available in the drop-down list, and 56 is usually a good value to use.

- **Display gridlines when viewing reports**   If you want to see the grid in the Reports view, check this check box.

- **Usage data**   FrontPage has a whole collection of usage reports, including page hits (monthly, weekly, daily), visiting users, referring domains, and many others. To set the number of months of data included in the usage reports, use the Number Of Months

17

Shown spinner. If you want a chart created that graphically displays the data (available for some of the usage reports), check the Include Chart When Usage Report Is Saved check box.

Work with Files in the Report View

Many of the reports available list files that meet a certain criteria, such as files that load slowly or recently added files. You can work directly with the files in the reports by right-clicking on a file and choosing an option from the shortcut menu. Most of the available options are identical to those in the Folder List, covered in Chapter 1. The one extra option is Copy Report, which copies the entire contents of the report to the clipboard.

To correct a problem on a web page, simply choose Open from the shortcut menu to open the page so you can edit it.

If you want to save the contents of a report, use Copy Report from the shortcut menu to place the report on the clipboard. Then, open Excel and paste the report into Excel. Each of the cells in the original report (intersection of columns and rows) is pasted into a cell in Excel, and you even get the column headings (in bold, no less!).

Rearrange the Report Columns

If you don't care for the order of the columns in the report, you can click on a column header and drag it to a new position. As you drag the column header, a dark gray rectangle indicates where the column will be positioned when you release the mouse button.

Filter the Report Results

The reports that FrontPage provides all follow a common format—rows of information with columns (and headings) that tell you what the information means. You can see a sample in Figure 17-5. However, many of the reports can be overwhelming, providing too much information to easily work with. For example, even a moderate-size web site can contain hundreds of files, so finding a particular file—or a specific set of files—in the All Files report can be difficult. Further, a single report displays both broken hyperlinks and unknown hyperlinks. What do you do if you only want to see the broken ones?

Name	Title	Modified Date	Created Date	Size	Type	Total Hits	In Folder
Background...	images/Backgroundtransp...	3/2/2001 10:37 PM	3/2/2001 10:35 PM	4KB	gif	0	images
j0234657.gif	images/j0234657.gif	3/2/2001 10:35 PM	3/2/2001 10:35 PM	4KB	gif	0	images
cropped_ti...	images/cropped_tiger.gif	3/2/2001 10:28 PM	3/2/2001 5:47 PM	5KB	gif	0	images
Menorah.gif	images/Menorah.gif	3/2/2001 10:05 PM	3/2/2001 10:05 PM	5KB	gif	0	images
cloud.gif	images/cloud.gif	3/2/2001 9:56 PM	3/2/2001 9:56 PM	3KB	gif	0	images
j0332364.gif	images/j0332364.gif	3/2/2001 5:47 PM	3/2/2001 5:47 PM	7KB	gif	0	images
2040212.JPG	images/2040212.JPG	3/2/2001 5:26 PM	3/2/2001 5:26 PM	13KB	JPG	0	images
2250942.JPG	images/2250942.JPG	3/2/2001 5:26 PM	3/2/2001 5:26 PM	16KB	JPG	0	images
2250012.JPG	images/2250012.JPG	3/2/2001 5:26 PM	3/2/2001 5:26 PM	12KB	JPG	0	images
3000942.JPG	images/3000942.JPG	3/2/2001 5:26 PM	3/2/2001 5:26 PM	10KB	JPG	0	images
3390982.JPG	images/3390982.JPG	3/2/2001 5:19 PM	3/2/2001 5:19 PM	8KB	JPG	0	images
CLASS3A1...	images/CLASS3A1.GIF	3/1/2001 8:17 PM	3/1/2001 8:17 PM	2KB	GIF	0	images
feedback.txt	_private/feedback.txt	3/1/2001 7:28 PM	3/1/2001 7:28 PM	0KB	txt	0	_private
mycat.jpg	images/mycat.jpg	3/1/2001 7:28 PM	3/1/2001 7:28 PM	18KB	jpg	0	images
mount.gif	photogallery/photo26003/...	3/1/2001 7:28 PM	3/1/2001 7:28 PM	4KB	gif	0	photogallery/ph
parrot1.jpg	photogallery/photo26003/...	3/1/2001 7:28 PM	3/1/2001 7:28 PM	15KB	jpg	0	photogallery/ph
mycat.jpg	photogallery/photo26003/...	3/1/2001 7:28 PM	3/1/2001 7:28 PM	18KB	jpg	0	photogallery/ph
mount.gif	images/mount.gif	3/1/2001 7:28 PM	3/1/2001 7:28 PM	4KB	gif	0	images
parrot1.jpg	images/parrot1.jpg	3/1/2001 7:28 PM	3/1/2001 7:28 PM	15KB	jpg	0	images
3390982.JPG	photogallery/photo26003/...	3/1/2001 7:28 PM	3/2/2001 5:19 PM	3KB	JPG	0	photogallery/ph
real_x.htm	photogallery/photo26003/...	3/1/2001 7:28 PM	3/1/2001 7:28 PM	2KB	htm	0	photogallery/ph
JavaClock....	JavaClock.class	2/4/2001 8:43 AM	2/7/2003 9:03 AM	9KB	class	0	

FIGURE 17-5   The Older File reports, all neatly arranged in rows and columns.

Fortunately, FrontPage provides a way to filter the reports so you can choose what you want to see. At the top of each column is the column heading, and alongside each heading is a small down arrow (see Figure 17-6). Clicking on the down arrow exposes a list of potential filters.

The list of filters looks like this drop-down list — Click here to expose a list of filters for this column

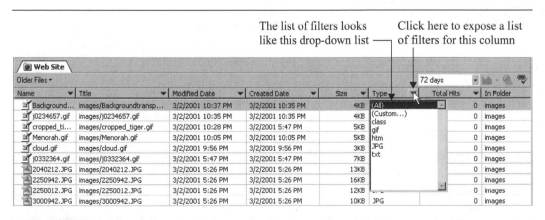

FIGURE 17-6   Filters available for each column help you narrow down the amount of information you see.

17

The entries in the filter drop-down list include the following items:

- **(All)**   Click this entry to remove any filters you have set and view all the records in the report.

- **A list of all unique values**   Most of the list consists of all unique values for the items in the report. For example, the filter for Type in any of the file reports lists all the types of files (CLASS, GIF, HTM, JPG, and so forth). The Status column in the Broken Hyperlinks report displays the values Broken and Unknown. If you choose a value from the list, only items that meet the selected criteria (files of the specified type, or only broken hyperlinks, for example) will be displayed in the report.

- **(Custom...)**   Choosing this entry enables you to create your own custom filter, as described below.

The real power of filters is the Custom AutoFilter, accessed by choosing (Custom...) from any of the filter drop-down lists. When you do, the Custom AutoFilter dialog box appears.

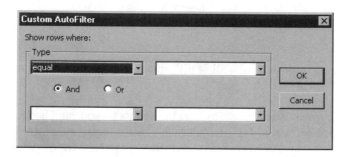

To specify the filter criteria, use the following steps:

1. Choose the comparison function from the top-left drop-down list. The list includes Equal, Not Equal, Is Greater Than, Is Less Than, Begins With, Does Not Begin With, Ends With, Does Not End With, Contains, and Does Not Contain.

2. Specify the value to which the value in the column will be compared in the top-right drop-down list. You can either choose from the list of unique existing values or type in a value for comparison. You cannot, however, use wildcards such as "*" to match any string the way you can with many other filtering tools.

NOTE   *If any of the records in the report have a blank in the filtered column, the values (Blanks) and (NonBlanks) appear at the end of the list, making it easy to pick these values if you wish.*

3. If you wish to add a second criteria (comparison function and value) for the column, enter it in the bottom two drop-down lists. Choosing the And option means that only records that meet *both* criteria will be displayed. Choosing the Or option means that records that meet *either* criteria will be displayed.

4. Click OK to engage the filter and view the results.

NOTE *You can specify a filter on multiple columns if you wish. For example, you can choose to view only broken hyperlinks (set in the Status column) for page titles greater than "B". Only files that meet both criteria will be visible. For example, if the page* Breaking News *has broken hyperlinks, it will display because it meets both criteria. However, even if the page* After the Meet *has broken hyperlinks, you won't see it in the report because the page title is not greater than "B".*

Understand the Site Summary Report

The Site Summary report gives you a quick idea of any problems with your site. For example, if the Site Summary report lists a few broken hyperlinks, you'll want to check those on the more detailed report. To run any of the available detailed reports whose summaries appear in the Site Summary report, click the name of the report you want to run (the name is shown in blue underline) in the Site Summary report. The entries in the Site Summary report that do *not* have their own detail reports are

- **Pictures**   A summary of the files in the web site that are image files. These files are listed among the files in the All Files report.

- **Linked files**   This line lists a summary of all the files in the web site that can be reached via hyperlinks. This is the counterpart of the Unlinked Files report, which does have a detailed report.

- **Hyperlinks, Unverified hyperlinks, External hyperlinks, Internal hyperlinks, Broken hyperlinks**   All of these entries in the Site Summary report take you to the Hyperlinks report. From the Hyperlinks report, you can inspect and fix any broken or unverified hyperlinks. You can also filter the report to show you just the type of hyperlinks you want to see.

- **Uncompleted tasks**   Clicking this summary switches you to the Task view.

- **Unused themes**   If you changed your mind about using a theme while you were building your site, your web site will still contain the now-unused files for that theme. These files can take up a fair amount of space. To get rid of the unused theme files, click the Unused Theme entry in the Site Summary report. FrontPage will confirm that you want to eliminate the unused files (and recalculate the hyperlinks in the process). Confirm that you want to do this by clicking Yes, and the files will be removed.

The Site Summary report contains the following columns:

- **Name**   The name of the report being summarized.

- **Count**   The number of records that meet the report criteria. For the Older Files report, for example, the Count column contains the number of old files on the web site.

17

- ■ **Size**   For reports that return multiple files, this is the total size (in KB) of all the included files. Of course, many reports don't have files associated with them. These include the various hyperlink reports, unfinished tasks, and component errors.

- ■ **Description**   A description of what the summary report measures.

After you have made changes, such as repairing broken hyperlinks or removing unused theme files, you can refresh the Site Summary report by pressing F5 or selecting View | Refresh.

Details of the Files Reports

The Files reports include the All Files, Recently Added Files, Recently Changed Files, and Older Files.

All Files Report

The All Files report (see Figure 17-7) provides a listing of the major files in your web site. This is useful if you want a complete picture of all the files that make up your web site.

You can change the contents of the Name, Title, and Comments columns. To do so, click in the column for the file you want to modify to make the column editable. Type in the new contents for that column.

The All Files report includes many columns. Most of them are obvious, but a couple need further explanation:

- ■ **Title**   The title of the file. If the file is not a page (for example, a graphic, a Java applet, and so on), this is just the filename with the full path.

- ■ **Type**   The type of file. For example, page files are type HTM, while most graphics are either GIF or JPG.

- ■ **Total Hits**   The number of times this file has been viewed by visitors to your site. The contents of this column are only valid if you are collecting usage data (see "Details of the Usage Reports," later in this chapter).

You can open the files listed in the All Files report. To do so, double-click a file. The file opens in the editor associated with that file type. For example, HTM files normally open in the FrontPage editor.

Recently Added Files

The Recently Added Files report shows you a list of files that have been added to the site, well, recently (the default is files that have been added in the last 30 days). This is especially useful if more than one person is working on the site. Using this report, you can keep track of what is new on the site. To modify a page, double-click it in the report to open the page in Page view.

You can adjust what FrontPage considers a "recently added file" either from the Reports View tab in the Options dialog box (covered previously) or from the Reports title bar. When viewing

Name	Title	In Folder	Size	Type	Modified Date	Modified By	Tot
swf13.swf	images/swf13.swf	images	13KB	swf	2/10/2003 12:48 PM	VAIO\dplotkin	
swf08.swf	images/swf08.swf	images	24KB	swf	2/10/2003 12:48 PM	VAIO\dplotkin	
swf07.swf	images/swf07.swf	images	10KB	swf	2/10/2003 12:48 PM	VAIO\dplotkin	
swf06.swf	images/swf06.swf	images	16KB	swf	2/10/2003 12:48 PM	VAIO\dplotkin	
swf05.swf	images/swf05.swf	images	9KB	swf	2/10/2003 12:48 PM	VAIO\dplotkin	
swf03.swf	images/swf03.swf	images	9KB	swf	2/10/2003 12:48 PM	VAIO\dplotkin	
swf00.swf	images/swf00.swf	images	24KB	swf	2/10/2003 12:48 PM	VAIO\dplotkin	
parrot1.jpg	images/parrot1.jpg	images	15KB	jpg	3/1/2001 7:28 PM	IUSR_VAIO	
mycat.jpg	images/mycat.jpg	images	18KB	jpg	3/1/2001 7:28 PM	IUSR_VAIO	
MsoPnl_sh_...	images/MsoPnl_sh_r_71A....	images	2KB	jpg	2/11/2003 9:54 AM	VAIO\dplotkin	
MsoPnl_sh_...	images/MsoPnl_sh_b_71B...	images	2KB	jpg	2/11/2003 9:54 AM	VAIO\dplotkin	
MsoPnl_Cnr...	images/MsoPnl_Cnr_tr_61...	images	1KB	gif	2/11/2003 9:49 AM	VAIO\dplotkin	
MsoPnl_Cnr...	images/MsoPnl_Cnr_tl_61...	images	1KB	gif	2/11/2003 9:49 AM	VAIO\dplotkin	
MsoPnl_Cnr...	images/MsoPnl_Cnr_br_6...	images	1KB	gif	2/11/2003 9:49 AM	VAIO\dplotkin	
MsoPnl_Cnr...	images/MsoPnl_Cnr_bl_61...	images	1KB	gif	2/11/2003 9:49 AM	VAIO\dplotkin	
mount.gif	images/mount.gif	images	4KB	gif	3/1/2001 7:28 PM	IUSR_VAIO	
Menorah.gif	images/Menorah.gif	images	5KB	gif	3/2/2001 10:05 PM	IUSR_VAIO	
LASER.WAV	images/LASER.WAV	images	2KB	WAV	2/6/2003 11:44 AM	VAIO\IUSR_VAIO	
j0332364.gif	images/j0332364.gif	images	7KB	gif	3/2/2001 5:47 PM	IUSR_VAIO	
j0234657.gif	images/j0234657.gif	images	4KB	gif	3/2/2001 10:35 PM	IUSR_VAIO	
cropped_ti...	images/cropped_tiger.gif	images	5KB	gif	3/2/2001 10:28 PM	IUSR_VAIO	
cloud.gif	images/cloud.gif	images	3KB	gif	3/2/2001 9:56 PM	IUSR_VAIO	
CLASS3A1....	images/CLASS3A1.GIF	images	2KB	GIF	3/1/2001 8:17 PM	IUSR_VAIO	
button21.jpg	images/button21.jpg	images	2KB	jpg	2/11/2003 8:47 PM	VAIO\dplotkin	
button20.jpg	images/button20.jpg	images	2KB	jpg	2/11/2003 8:47 PM	VAIO\dplotkin	
button1F.jpg	images/button1F.jpg	images	2KB	jpg	2/11/2003 8:47 PM	VAIO\dplotkin	
button15.jpg	images/button15.jpg	images	3KB	jpg	2/4/2003 9:25 PM	VAIO\IUSR_VAIO	
button14.jpg	images/button14.jpg	images	3KB	jpg	2/4/2003 9:24 PM	VAIO\IUSR_VAIO	
button13.jpg	images/button13.jpg	images	4KB	jpg	2/4/2003 9:24 PM	VAIO\IUSR_VAIO	
Brothers4x...	images/Brothers4x6.jpg	images	485KB	jpg	2/10/2003 10:15 AM	VAIO\IUSR_VAIO	
Background...	images/Backgroundtransp...	images	4KB	gif	3/2/2001 10:37 PM	IUSR_VAIO	

FIGURE 17-7   The All Files report lists all the files in your web site.

the Recently Added Files report, a drop-down list appears at the right end of the Reports title bar. Click this drop-down list and select how recently the file must have been added for it to show up in the report.

The columns in the Recently Added Files report are identical to the All Files report, except that the Modified Date is replaced by the Created Date, and the Comments column is missing. As with the All Files report, you can select a file in the report and click the name or title to modify it.

Recently Changed Files

The Recently Changed Files report shows you a list of (can you guess!) recently changed files. Using this report, you can keep track of what pages have been modified.

You can adjust what FrontPage considers a "recently changed file" either from the Reports View tab in the Options dialog box (covered previously) or from the drop-down list in the Reports title bar.

17

The columns in the Recently Changed Files report are identical to the Recently Added Files report. As with the All Files report, you can select a file in the report and click the name or title to modify it.

Older Files

The Older Files report shows you a list of files that are older than a certain date. The default value is files that are older than 72 days. Use this list to keep an eye on files that might be getting outdated.

You can adjust what FrontPage considers an "older file" either from the Reports View tab in the Options dialog box (covered previously) or from the drop-down list in the Reports title bar.

The columns in the Older Files report are identical to the Recently Changed report, except that this report displays both the Created Date and the Modified Date. As with the All Files report, you can select a file in the report and click the name or title to modify it.

Details of the Problems Reports

Problems reports include Unlinked Files, Slow Pages, Hyperlinks, and Component Errors.

Unlinked Files

The Unlinked Files report lists any page file in your web site that cannot be reached by starting from your home page. This is either because the link is missing (you forgot to create it) or the link that was supposed to point to the page is broken. Another reason is that you decided you didn't need the page any longer and deleted the links, but neglected to delete the page. The Unlinked Files report also lists any graphic elements that are not used in the web site. You may wish to get rid of these elements to save space. You can remove a file directly from the Unlinked Files report. To do so, select the file and choose Delete from the shortcut menu.

Slow Pages

The Slow Pages report lets you know which pages will take a long time to load into a reader's browser. This report injects a dose of reality into your web design, because many web creators forget that most people will be viewing their pages over a dial-up modem connection. If the page takes too long to load, the reader might well give up and go elsewhere. To modify the page, double-click it in the report to open the page in Design Page view.

TIP   *You can see the estimated load time for a page as you are working on the page. The load time is near the right end of the status bar along with the assumed connection speed. To change the assumed connection speed used for calculating download time, right-click the connection speed and choose the connection speed from the shortcut menu.*

The normal cause of a slow page download is one or more large graphics. You can reduce the size of graphics (and improve the page download speed) by shrinking the size of the graphic, reducing the number of colors, or using a thumbnail so the reader can decide by viewing the thumbnail whether to view the full graphic. To adjust the size or number of colors in a graphic, you will need to use a graphic tool. For more information on using the Auto Thumbnail feature, see Chapter 9.

It is considered good web etiquette to note that a page has a long download time on hyperlinks that point to that page. That way, at least the reader will be warned that they have to be patient!

You can adjust what FrontPage considers a slow page either from the Reports View tab in the Options dialog box (covered previously) or from the drop-down list in the Reports title bar.

The columns in the Slow Pages report are identical to the All Files report, except that the Slow Pages report is missing the Comments column and has an additional column (Download Time) that states the download time in seconds. As with the All Files report, you can select a file in the report and click the name or title to modify it.

Hyperlinks

The Hyperlinks report shows the status of hyperlinks in the web site. If you click on Hyperlinks in the Site Summary report, all hyperlinks in the site are displayed. The other "Hyperlink" entries in the Site Summary report (Broken Hyperlinks, Unverified Hyperlinks, External Hyperlinks, and Internal Hyperlinks) show various subsets of the hyperlinks. The most useful reports can be reached by clicking on either the Broken Hyperlink or Unverified Hyperlinks entries. These reports show both broken hyperlinks—hyperlinks with known invalid destinations—and unverified hyperlinks (see Figure 17-8).

Status	Hyperlink	In Page	Page Title	Link Type	Modified By
Broken	feedbackfromtemplate.htm	feedbackfromtemplate.htm	FeedbackFromTemplate	Form Action	VAIO\dplotkin
Broken	form_custom_form.htm	form_custom_form.htm	Custom Form	Form Action	VAIO\dplotkin
Broken	form_custom_form_build.htm	form_custom_form_build....	Form Custom Form Build	Form Action	VAIO\dplotkin
Broken	form_for_newsletter.htm	form_for_newsletter.htm	Form for Newsletter	Form Action	VAIO\dplotkin
Broken	guest_book.htm	guest_book.htm	Guest Book	Form Action	VAIO\dplotkin
Broken	index.htm	table_of_contents.htm	Table of Contents	Web Componen...	VAIO\dplotkin
Unknown	/help.gif	working_with_lists.htm	Working with Lists	Image	VAIO\dplotkin
Unknown	/help.gif	working_with_lists.htm	Working with Lists	Image	VAIO\dplotkin
Unknown	/help.gif	working_with_lists.htm	Working with Lists	Image	VAIO\dplotkin
Unknown	/help.gif	working_with_lists.htm	Working with Lists	Image	VAIO\dplotkin
Unknown	http://active.macromedia.com/flash...	shockwave_flash.htm	Shockwave Flash	Code	VAIO\dplotkin
Unknown	http://go.msn.com/AG/E/0.asp	web_content.htm	Web Content	Image	VAIO\dplotkin
Unknown	http://moneycentral.msn.com/home...	interest.htm	Interests		VAIO\dplotkin
Unknown	http://search.msn.com/advanced.asp	web_content.htm	Web Content		VAIO\dplotkin
Unknown	http://search.msn.com/results.asp	web_content.htm	Web Content	Form Action	VAIO\dplotkin
Unknown	http://www.carpoint.com/	interest.htm	Interests		VAIO\dplotkin
Unknown	http://www.dplotkin.com	links_page.htm	Links Page	Navigation	VAIO\dplotkin
Unknown	http://www.dplotkin.com	custom_nav_link.htm	Custom Nav Link	Navigation	VAIO\dplotkin

FIGURE 17-8   Check out broken hyperlinks as well as unverified hyperlinks with the Hyperlinks report.

Broken hyperlinks (shown with a status of Broken in the report) are a major pain to someone browsing your web site. There is very little more frustrating than searching for a particular piece of information, only to be stymied by a broken hyperlink. In addition, broken hyperlinks make the webmaster (that would be you!) look silly. Thus, the Hyperlinks report is one of the most important you'll use in managing your web site.

You can repair broken hyperlinks right from the Hyperlinks report. For details, see "Repair Broken Hyperlinks" later in this chapter.

As mentioned earlier, the Hyperlinks report also shows you unverified hyperlinks—hyperlinks that may or may not be broken. These are shown with a status of Unknown in the Broken Hyperlinks report. Details on how to repair or verify unverified hyperlinks are discussed in "Verify Hyperlinks," later in this chapter.

The columns in the Hyperlinks report are

- **Status**   The status of the hyperlink. It is either Broken, Unknown, or OK.

If none of your hyperlinks are of a certain status, that status won't be available from the Status filter. For example, if none of your hyperlinks are Unknown, the value Unknown won't be in the Status list.

- **Hyperlink**   The destination of the hyperlink.
- **In Page**   The filename of the page in which the hyperlink is located.
- **Page Title**   The page title of the page in which the hyperlink is located.
- **Link Type**   The purpose of the hyperlink, such as navigation or form action.
- **Modified By**   The person who last modified the page in which the hyperlink is located.

None of the columns in the report are directly modifiable.

Component Errors

As discussed earlier, components add quite a bit of functionality and interactivity to your web site. However, because components may need other support files, something can go wrong with a component. The Component Errors report lists any components that are not functioning properly. To edit the page on which the component is located, double-click the entry to open the page in Design Page view. The details of the error are displayed in the Errors column. If you want to read the full text in the Errors column, you can right-click the entry and choose Properties from the shortcut menu. This opens the Properties dialog box, showing the Errors tab, where you can easily read the entire error message.

As with the All Files report, you can select a file in the report and click the name or title to modify it.

Repair Broken Hyperlinks

You can repair broken hyperlinks right from the Broken Hyperlinks report. To do so, use the following steps:

1. Either double-click a broken hyperlink entry or choose Edit Hyperlink from the shortcut menu to open the Edit Hyperlink dialog box.

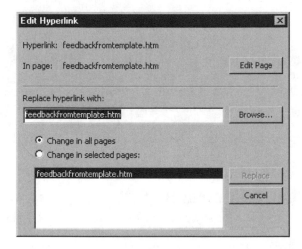

2. Enter the correct hyperlink destination in the Replace Hyperlink With field (this may take some research!). You can click the Browse button to open the Select Hyperlink dialog box and choose the hyperlink destination from your web site or the Internet.

3. Select the option to decide how you want to apply the correction: Change In All Pages or Change In Selected Pages.

4. If you select Change In Selected Pages, select the pages to which you want to apply the change.

5. Click the Replace button to make the hyperlink replacement.

You can also click the Edit Page button to open the page containing the broken hyperlink in Page view. You can then manually edit the hyperlink properties to fix the broken hyperlink.

The Broken Hyperlinks report also enables you to jump directly to the page containing the broken hyperlink, where you can edit the hyperlink to correct the destination. Simply right-click the broken hyperlink entry in the report and choose Edit Page from the shortcut menu.

You can add a task to go back and fix the broken hyperlink later. Choose Edit | Tasks | Add Task to open the New Task dialog box, which you saw earlier in this chapter. Unfortunately, FrontPage does not associate a task created in this way with the page containing the broken hyperlink.

17

How to ... Verify Hyperlinks

The Broken Hyperlinks report also displays unverified hyperlinks—hyperlinks that may or may not be broken. Typically, these are links outside your web site that FrontPage has not verified actually exist. The shortcut menu for unverified hyperlinks (which have a status of Unknown in the report) include many of the same choices as broken hyperlinks: Edit Hyperlink, Edit Page, and Add Task. These options work the same as for broken hyperlinks. However, unverified hyperlinks have an additional option: Verify Hyperlink. If you select this option (and are connected to the Internet), FrontPage will notify you that it is verifying the link. If it fails to find the destination you specified, the link status becomes Broken. However, if it does find the link you specified, the link status becomes OK. You can verify all hyperlinks in the web site by clicking on the Verifys Hyperlink in the Current Web button at the far right end of the Hyperlinks report title bar.

Details of the Shared Content Reports

The Shared Content reports present the shared content for each of the web pages in the web site. The reports are

- **Dynamic Web Templates**   Displays the Dynamic Web Template (if any) attached to the web page.
- **Shared Borders**   This report shows which of the shared borders a particular web page uses (for example, Left, Top, Bottom).
- **Style Sheet Links**   This report documents whether a web page is linked to a Cascading Style Sheet. These style sheets give you very fine control over the formatting of the web page.
- **Themes**   Lists the theme attached to a web page, and whether theme options (Vivid Colors, Active Graphics, and Background Picture) are used on that page (see Figure 17-9).

Details of the Workflow Reports

FrontPage includes several other reports that will help you manage the web development process. These reports include the Review Status, Assigned To, Categories, and Publish Status reports.

Review Status

The Review Status report (see Figure 17-10) gives you an overview of all the files in your web site and their review status.

Name	Title	Theme	Vivid Col...	Active G...	Backg...	In Folder
aboutme.htm	About Me	Network (default)	No	Yes	Yes	
activex_controls.htm	ActiveX Controls	Network (default)	No	Yes	Yes	
alignment.htm	Alignment	Network (default)	No	Yes	Yes	
alignment_examples.htm	Alignment Examples	Network (default)	No	Yes	Yes	
children_bookstores_database...	Children Bookstores Data...	Network (default)	No	Yes	Yes	
children_bookstores_database...	Children Bookstores Data...	Network (default)	No	Yes	Yes	
children_bookstores_database...	Children Bookstores Data...	Network (default)	No	Yes	Yes	
Collapsible_lists.htm	Working with Lists	Network (default)	No	Yes	Yes	
confirm.asp	Bookstores -- Confirm					childrenbookstor
confirmationformforcustomfor...	ConfirmationFormForCust...	Network (default)	No	Yes	Yes	
cropping.htm	Cropping	Network (default)	No	Yes	Yes	
custom_nav_link.htm	Custom Nav Link	Network (default)	No	Yes	Yes	
database_editor.asp	Bookstores -- Home					childrenbookstor
Default.htm	Welcome to my Web site	Network (default)	No	Yes	Yes	
definitions_and_defined_terms...	definitions and defined ter...	Blank	No	Yes	Yes	
delete.asp	Bookstores -- Delete					childrenbookstor
detail.asp	Bookstores -- Home					childrenbookstor
dhtml.htm	DHTML	Network (default)	No	Yes	Yes	
edit.asp	Bookstores -- Edit					childrenbookstor

FIGURE 17-9 The Themes report gives you a summary of which themes are used on which web pages.

Name	Title	Review Sta...	Assigned To	Review Date	Reviewed By	Expiration Da
aboutme.htm	About Me	Pending Review	dplotkin	2/12/2003 11:02 AM	VAIO\dplotkin	
activex_controls.htm	ActiveX Controls	Pending Review	dplotkin	2/12/2003 11:00 AM	VAIO\dplotkin	
alignment.htm	Alignment	Approved	dplotkin	2/12/2003 11:00 AM	VAIO\dplotkin	
alignment_examples.htm	Alignment Examples	Approved	dplotkin	2/12/2003 11:00 AM	VAIO\dplotkin	
Collapsible_lists.htm	Working with Lists	Pending Review	dplotkin	2/12/2003 11:00 AM	VAIO\dplotkin	
confirmationformforcus...	ConfirmationFormForCust...	Approved	dplotkin	2/12/2003 11:00 AM	VAIO\dplotkin	
cropping.htm	Cropping	Denied	dplotkin	2/12/2000 11:00 AM	VAIO\dplotkin	
custom_nav_link.htm	Custom Nav Link	Pending Review	dplotkin	2/12/2003 11:00 AM	VAIO\dplotkin	
Default.htm	Welcome to my Web site	Approved	dplotkin	2/12/2003 11:00 AM	VAIO\dplotkin	
definitions_and_define...	definitions and defined ter...	Approved	dplotkin	2/12/2003 11:01 AM	VAIO\dplotkin	
dhtml.htm	DHTML	Approved	dplotkin	2/12/2003 11:01 AM	VAIO\dplotkin	
FAQ.htm	Frequently Asked Questions	Pending Review	dplotkin	2/12/2003 11:01 AM	VAIO\dplotkin	
favorite.htm	Favorites	Approved	dplotkin	2/12/2003 11:01 AM	VAIO\dplotkin	
feedback.htm	Feedback	Pending Review	dplotkin	2/12/2003 11:01 AM	VAIO\dplotkin	
feedbackfromtemplate....	FeedbackFromTemplate	Pending Review	dplotkin	2/12/2003 11:01 AM	VAIO\dplotkin	
form_custom_form.htm	Custom Form	Approved	dplotkin	2/12/2003 11:01 AM	VAIO\dplotkin	
form_custom_form_buil...	Form Custom Form Build	Pending Review	dplotkin	2/12/2003 11:01 AM	VAIO\dplotkin	
form_for_newsletter.htm	Form for Newsletter	Approved	dplotkin	2/12/2003 11:01 AM	VAIO\dplotkin	

FIGURE 17-10 Use the Review Status report to manage the status of the pages in your web site.

17

Typically, you don't care about the review status of anything except web pages. To quickly filter the report results so that you see only web pages, click on the small down arrow in the Type column and choose htm from the list.

The columns in this report include general file properties (Name, Title, In Folder, Type) as well as the same fields you can specify in the Workgroup tab of the Page Properties dialog box:

- **Review Status** The current review status. To change the review status, click the contents of this column and choose a value from the drop-down list or type in another review status.

- **Assigned To** The person who is responsible for this page. To change the assignee, click the contents of this column and choose a value from the drop-down list or type in another assignee.

- **Review Date** The date on which the review status was last changed. Try it—go to the Review Status column and choose or add a new value. The review date changes to today's date. This column is not directly editable.

- **Reviewed By** The identifier for the person who last changed the review status. This column is not directly editable.

- **Expiration Date** The date on which the file expires. To change the expiration date, click on the drop-down list and choose None (removes any expiration date), Expired (sets the value in the column to Expired), or Custom. If you choose Custom, FrontPage opens the Date and Time dialog box where you can enter the date and time on which the file expires. Once you select a date and time, FrontPage evaluates the date/time and enters either Expired (the date and time specified has past) or the date and time you entered (the date and time is still in the future).

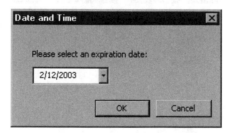

To choose the expiration date from a calendar, click the down arrow in the Date and Time dialog box and use the Calendar tool to pick a date.

To edit a page in Design Page view, double-click the file's entry in the report.

Assigned To

The Assigned To report displays who is responsible for developing a particular web page. In addition to the standard file properties, the columns in the Assigned To report are

- **Assigned To**   The person who is responsible for this page. To change the assignee, click the contents of this column and choose a value from the drop-down list or type in another assignee.

- **Assign Date**   The date on which a person was assigned responsibility for the page. This is the last date a value was entered or changed in the Assigned To column. This column is not directly editable.

- **Assigned By**   The identifier for the person who last changed the assignment. This column is not directly editable.

To edit a page in Page view, double-click the file's entry in the report.

Categories

The Categories report lists all the categories that have been assigned to a page in the Categories column. You can't directly edit the contents of the Categories column. Instead, choose Properties from the shortcut menu and choose the Workgroup tab in the Properties dialog box. As discussed earlier in this book, check off the categories you want to assign to the page. These categories then appear in the Categories column of the Categories report.

NOTE   *You can filter the list on a single category by choosing the category from the drop-down list in the Reports toolbar. If you* do *filter this way, FrontPage ignores any filter you apply in the Category column.*

To edit a page in Page view, double-click the file's entry in the report. As with the All Files report, you can select a file in the report and click the name or title to modify it.

Publish Status

The Publish Status report (see Figure 17-11) displays every file in your web site and whether the file is slated to be published the next time you publish your site. This report is how you control which pages get published. If the file's status is Publish, the page will be sent to the host server the next time you publish your web site. If the file's status is Don't Publish, the page will not be sent to the host server when you publish your web site. To edit any page listed in the report in Page view, double-click the file.

In addition to the standard file properties, the columns in the report are

- **Publish**   The publishing status. To change the status, click the column and select a value (Publish or Don't Publish) from the drop-down list.

- **Review Status**   The current review status. To change the review status, click the contents of this column and choose a value from the drop-down list or type in another review status.

Name		Title		Publish		Modified Date		Review Status		Size		Type	
Default.htm.cnt		_private/Default.htm.cnt		Don't Publish		2/11/2003 8:39 PM				1KB		cnt	
dhtml.htm		DHTML		Publish		2/12/2003 11:03 AM		Approved		6KB		htm	
real.htm		This is the page		Publish		2/11/2003 12:13 PM				5KB		htm	
real_p.htm		This is the page		Publish		2/11/2003 12:13 PM				5KB		htm	
favorite.htm		Favorites		Publish		2/12/2003 11:03 AM		Approved		13KB		htm	
search_page_from_tem...		Search Page from Template		Publish		2/11/2003 12:13 PM				4KB		htm	
alignment_examples.htm		Alignment Examples		Publish		2/12/2003 11:03 AM		Approved		2KB		htm	
New_Features_of_Front...		New Features of FrontPa...		Publish		2/12/2003 9:19 AM				1KB		htm	

FIGURE 17-11   The Publish Status report is where you control whether to publish a page or not.

Checkout Status

If you have set up your web site to allow people to check web pages in and out (to prevent multiple people from changing the same page at the same time), you can use the Checkout Status report to check on this status for all the files in your web site. The report simply lists the files (and their properties) as well as a column for the Checkout status.

Details of the Usage Reports

The Usage reports help you analyze what pages on your site are most (and least) popular, as well as summarizing information about the people who visited your site. There are three major categories of reports included in the Usage reports: Time-Based Summaries, Page Hits, and General Information Counts.

> **NOTE**   *The usage information has to be collected by the server that hosts your web site. The server must be configured by your web presence provider (WPP) to provide usage information. You can also test some usage information using a local server-based web site. However, information such as top referrer, top referring domain, and so forth can only be collected on a remote server. Also, if usage information is not being collected, all the usage reports will all be blank.*

Time-Based Summary Reports

The time-based summary reports include the Usage Summary, Monthly Summary, Weekly Summary, and Daily Summary reports.

The Usage Summary (see Figure 17-12) lists summary data items, such as the total visits to the site, top referring web site, most popular web browser, and other general information. Clicking on one of the hyperlinked items (such as Total Visits) takes you to a Monthly Summary report.

The Monthly Usage Summary report summarizes information by month for the following columns:

■   **Month**   The month for which the summary information is provided. You can set the number of lines in the report (one for each month) by using the Reports View tab of the

Options dialog box (choose Tools | Options). Select the number of months from the Number Of Months Shown spinner.

- **Visits** The number of unique visits to your web site during that month.
- **Hits** The number of unique page hits for that month.
- **Total Hits** The total number of page hits for the month.
- **Download Size** The total amount of information downloaded from your site. This amount is only populated if you make files available for download on your site.

The Weekly Summary report summarizes information by week. It is similar to the Monthly Summary report, except that each line in the report represents one week, with the date range for that week being shown in the Week column. The Weekly Summary report does not show the download size; instead, it has a new column entitled Percentage Of Hits, which calculates and displays the percentage of the total hits on the site that occurred during that week.

The Daily Summary report summarizes information by day. It is identical to the Weekly Summary report, except that each line in the report represents one day, with the date being shown in the Day column.

Page Hits Reports

There are three Page Hits reports: Monthly Page Hits, Weekly Page Hits, and Daily Page Hits. Each of the reports displays columns for Name (filename), Title (page title), In Folder (the folder containing the file), and Total Hits (hits on that page for the time period).

The Monthly Page Hits report (see Figure 17-13) lists one column for each month from the current month back. The default is to go back one year, but you can change the number of months from the Reports View tab of the Options dialog box (choose Tools | Options). The

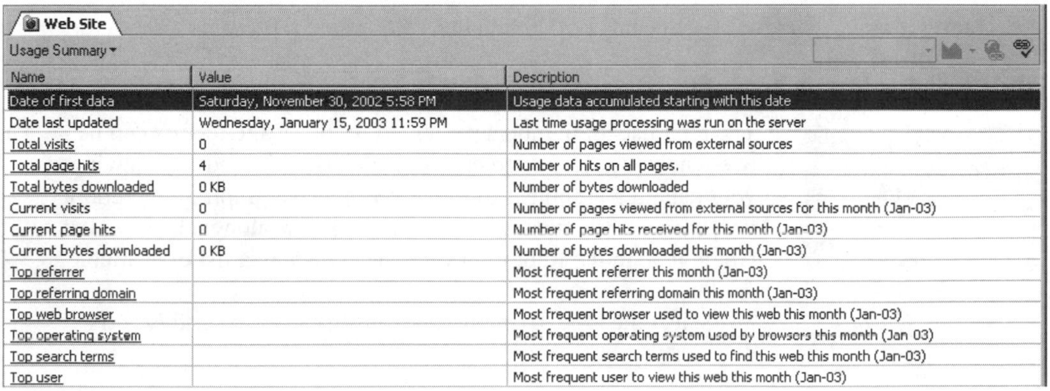

Name	Value	Description
Date of first data	Saturday, November 30, 2002 5:58 PM	Usage data accumulated starting with this date
Date last updated	Wednesday, January 15, 2003 11:59 PM	Last time usage processing was run on the server
Total visits	0	Number of pages viewed from external sources
Total page hits	4	Number of hits on all pages.
Total bytes downloaded	0 KB	Number of bytes downloaded
Current visits	0	Number of pages viewed from external sources for this month (Jan-03)
Current page hits	0	Number of page hits received for this month (Jan-03)
Current bytes downloaded	0 KB	Number of bytes downloaded this month (Jan-03)
Top referrer		Most frequent referrer this month (Jan-03)
Top referring domain		Most frequent referring domain this month (Jan-03)
Top web browser		Most frequent browser used to view this web this month (Jan-03)
Top operating system		Most frequent operating system used by browsers this month (Jan-03)
Top search terms		Most frequent search terms used to find this web this month (Jan-03)
Top user		Most frequent user to view this web this month (Jan-03)

FIGURE 17-12 The Usage Summary report gives you a quick summary of your web site statistics.

Name	Title	Type	In Folder	Total Hits	Jan-03	Dec-02	Nov-02
a_circle_of_time.htm	A Circle of Time	htm		0	0	0	
a_circle_of_time_excerpts.htm	A Circle of Time Excerpts	htm		0	0	0	
A_Circle_of_time_reviews.htm	Circle of Time Reviews	htm		0	0	0	
about.htm	About the author	htm		0	0	0	
abuelita_zapatona.htm	Abuelita Zapatona: Grann...	htm		0	0	0	
alexander_giraffe.htm	Alexander Giraffe	htm		0	0	0	
all_about_camels.htm	All About Camels	htm		0	0	0	
all_about_cardinals.htm	All About Cardinals	htm		0	0	0	
all_about_coquis.htm	All About Coquis	htm		0	0	0	
all_about_san_juan.htm	All About San Juan	htm		0	0	0	
all_about_toul.htm	All About Toul	htm		0	0	0	
ALLLIBS.HTM	Document Libraries	HTM	_layouts	0			
animal_band.htm	Animal Band	htm		0	0	0	
books.htm	Books	htm		0	0	0	

FIGURE 17-13. Check out the number of hits on a page during each month using the Monthly Page Hits report.

Weekly Page Hits report lists one column for each week for the past month. The Daily Page Hits report lists one column for each day for the past week.

General Information Count Reports

The General Information Count reports provide counts for Visiting Users, Operating Systems, Browsers, Referring Domains, Referring URLs, and Search Strings. Each of these counts is provided in a different report, but except for the first column (which details what is being counted), all the reports display the same information:

- **Count** The number of times a particular value of Visiting User, Operating System, and so forth occurs for the given time period.
- **Percentage** The overall percentage of the total that this value represents.

Graphing the Usage Reports

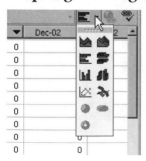

The long lists of numbers presented in the Usage reports can be overwhelming. It is often easier to understand trends by viewing your data in a graphical format. To produce a graph of the report you are currently viewing, click on the arrow alongside the small Graph icon in the Reporting title bar to display a list of available graphs.

Select the type of graph you want from the list and FrontPage displays the graph for you.

Chapter 18

Publish Your Web Site

How to...

- Publish your FrontPage web site to a remote host server
- Publish Pages from the remote to the local web site
- Synchronize your local and remote web sites
- Publish your FrontPage web site using FTP

The time has finally come—your carefully crafted web site is done. Now you have to publish your web site to your WPP's server.

Publish Your Web Site to a WPP Host Server

Once you get an account on a host server, you need to publish your site. "Publishing" consists of transmitting the web site files over the Internet to the host server. FrontPage makes this relatively simple, especially if the host server has the FrontPage server extensions installed. To publish your site, you need to know three things:

- The URL (destination on the Internet) for publishing
- Your username on the host server
- Your password

Once you sign up for web hosting services, the web presence provider should supply all three of these items to you. The URL is usually in the format of http://www.servername.net/username/ or something similar. Just make sure you write down all three of these important items or you won't be able to publish your web site!

Publishing to a Server with FrontPage Server Extensions

To publish your web site to a host server that supports the FrontPage server extensions, you have a lot of options, including publishing from your local site to the remote site, moving files from the remote site back to your local site, and even synchronizing the two sites. You accomplish all this from the Remote Web Site view (see Figure 18-1).

Filter the files you can see

Open the Remote Web Site Properties

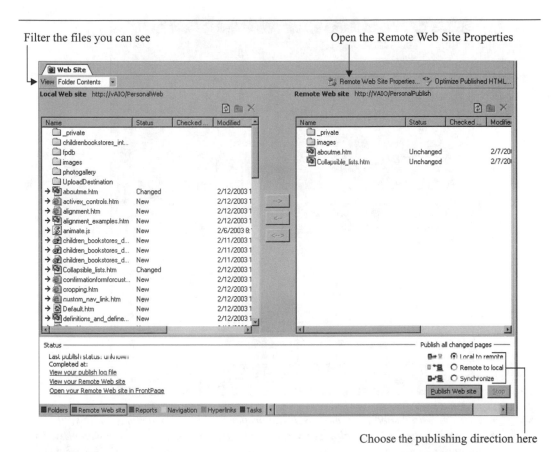

Choose the publishing direction here

FIGURE 18-1   The Remote Web Site view is where you select what (and in which direction) you want to publish your files.

Specify the Remote Web Site Properties

Switch to the Web Site view and click the Remote Web Site button at the bottom of the view. This displays the Remote Web Site view. If you have not established the Remote Web Site Properties, FrontPage will display the Remote Web Site Properties dialog box.

18

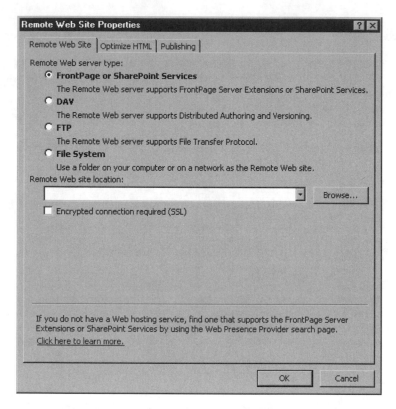

NOTE *Once you've established the remote web site properties, FrontPage stores these settings and does not redisplay the dialog box when you switch to Remote Web Site web view. To redisplay the Remote Web Site Properties dialog box so you can change the properties, click the Remote Web Site Properties button in the upper-right corner of the Remote Web Site view.*

Fill in the Remote Web Site tab of the Remote Web Site Properties dialog box using the following steps:

1. Select the FrontPage Or SharePoint Team Services option.

2. Type the publishing destination (supplied by your web presence provider) into the Remote Web Site Location field. Type the full URL, including the http://.

3. If your host requires a secure connection, check the Secure Connection Required (SSL) check box.

If you wish to configure the publishing options, click the Publishing tab in the Remote Web Site Properties dialog box.

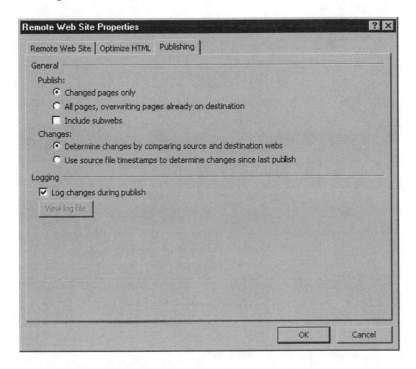

From this tab, you can set the following options:

- **Publish Changed Pages Only**   Choose this option if you want to publish just the pages that have changed on the web site. Otherwise, choose Publish All Pages, Overwriting Pages Already On Destination.

- **Include Subwebs**   If you want to publish any subwebs in your web site, check the Include Subwebs check box.

- **Determine changes between source and target**   If you choose to publish only the files that have changed, you need to specify how FrontPage is going to figure out *which* files have changed. If you want FrontPage to compare the files between the source (your PC) and the destination (your hosted web site), choose Determine Changes By Comparing Source And Destination Webs. If you would rather use the file timestamps, choose Use Source File Timestamps To Determine Changes Since Last Publish.

- **Log the publishing changes**   If you want to keep track of exactly what was published, check the Log Changes During Publish check box.

18

If you don't understand HTML and want to optimize the site HTML (which removes the explanatory comments you don't use anyway), click the Optimize HTML tab in the Remote Web Site Properties dialog box.

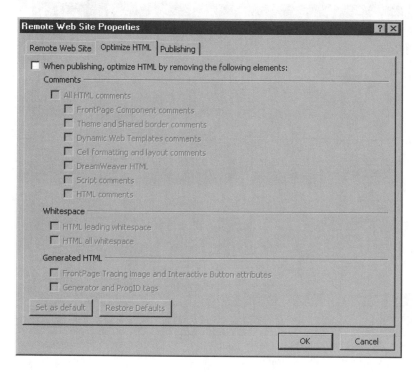

This tab enables you to remove unnecessary HTML components, such as various types of comments and how to handle white space (blanks and tabs) in the HTML.

When you're done specifying the Remote Web Site properties, click OK to close the dialog box.

Publish Your Web Site

Once you are done setting up the remote web site properties, you are ready to use the tools in the Remote Web Site view to publish your site. The basic steps are simple: choose a publishing direction from the options in the lower-right corner, and click the Publish Web Site button. The publishing directions are

- **Local to Remote** This is the standard way of publishing your pages. It publishes the changed or new pages from your local site to the remote web server.

- **Remote to Local** This choice brings the files from the remote site to your local site. This is handy for importing a remote web site so you can work on it locally.

- **Synchronize** This choice synchronizes the files between the remote and local web sites. Files that exist on one site but not the other are copied to the site on which they don't exist. FrontPage examines files that exist on both sites and copies the newer version to the site containing the older version of the file.

If the remote web site is secured from unauthorized changes (the normal case), you'll be prompted for your userid and password when you click the Publish button (or try to drag and drop a file for the first time during a session). Make sure you have your userid and password handy!

The Remote Web Site view provides a lot of information about the status of your web pages, and how they will be published. To the left of each file is an area that shows which direction the file will be published in, as well as the publishing status. The information in this area is

- **Blank**   This file will not be published because it is not necessary (the file is the same on both the local and remote web sites).
- **Right arrow**   The file will be published from the local to the remote web site.
- **Left arrow**   The file will be published from the remote to the local web site.
- **Red Circle with an X**   This file is set to "Don't Publish" status. To set this status from the Remote Web Site view, right-click on the file and choose Don't Publish from the shortcut menu. Selecting Don't Publish again turns off the Don't Publish status.

The status column shows you how the files in the local web site compare to the files in the remote web site. The values in this column are

- **New**   This page has never been published.
- **Changed**   This page was previously published, but has been changed since the last time you published the web site.
- **Unchanged**   The page was previously published, and has not been changed.
- **Conflict**   This value indicates that the file on your local machine is not only different from the file on the remote server, but the remote file is more up to date. Thus, publishing the local file will overwrite a more recent file and may not be a good idea. This condition occurs for files that are updated on the remote server, such as the guest book or form results files. In this case, it is best to use drag and drop (see below) to copy the file from the remote server to your local machine.

Once you've published your web site, you can view it in a browser by clicking the View Your Remote Web Site link in the bottom-left corner of the Remote Web Site view. You can also directly open the published web site in FrontPage (using the hyperlink in the lower-left corner), making it easy to modify files directly on the remote web site.

Opening the remote web site is a quick way to make repairs to the site. For example, if someone leaves an inappropriate comment in your guest book, you can quickly open the remote web page containing those comments, edit them, and resave them to the remote web site.

Publish Individual Files

You can publish individual files either from the local site to the remote site or from the remote site to the local site. To begin this process, select the files in either the local web site or the remote web site. Then do one of the following:

- **Click one of the arrows**   There are three arrow buttons in the section between the local web site and remote web site. Click one of the arrows to publish the file in the indicated direction, or click the two-headed arrow to synchronize the files between the two web sites.

- **Use the shortcut menu**   Choose Publish Selected Files from the shortcut menu to publish the files. Choose Synchronize Selected Files to synchronize the files between the two web sites.

- **Drag and Drop the Files**   Click on the files you want to publish and drag the files to the other web site. For example, select files in the local web site and drag them to the remote web site.

NOTE   *If you want to work with files that are inside a folder (such as images), double-click on the folder in the Publish Remote Web Site view to display the contents of the folder.*

You can work with individual files by right-clicking on the file and making a selection from the shortcut menu. You can rename a file by choosing Rename, and Delete a file by choosing Delete.

TIP   *You can also delete a file by selecting it and clicking on the small X near the upper-right corner of either the left or right windows in the Publish Web dialog box.*

Filter the Remote Web Site View

The View drop-down list in the upper-right corner of the Remote Web Site view enables you to filter the files you can see in both the local web site and the remote web site. The options in the drop-down list are

- **Folder Contents**   Displays all files and folders.
- **Files to Publish**   Lists the files due to be published the next time you publish your web site. For example, files that have a status of Unchanged on both the local and remote web sites will not show up in this list.
- **Files not to Publish**   List the files that are set to Not Published status.
- **Files in Conflict**   Lists the files that have a status of Conflict.

Publish to an FTP Server

If (and only if) the server to which you are publishing does not have the FrontPage server extensions installed, you can use File Transfer Protocol (FTP) to publish your web site. Of course, none of the advanced features of FrontPage will work (more about this a little later in the chapter), but a basic web site can be published without the extensions. Since most of the free hosting services on the Internet do *not* have FrontPage extensions, you may be stuck with such a service if you can't afford to pay for web hosting.

> **TIP** *Many Internet service providers (ISPs) provide their members with free space that can be used to host a small web site. This feature is often not publicized (I wonder why?). For example, as of this writing, America Online, MSN, Yahoo, Excite, and CompuServe provide such space.*

Publishing to an FTP server is not very different from publishing to a FrontPage server. To do so, use the following steps:

1. Switch to the Remote Web Site view and open the Remote Web Site Properties dialog box. This will either happen automatically (the first time you publish a site) or you can click the Remote Web Site Properties button.

2. Choose the FTP option in the Remote Web Site Properties dialog box.

3. Fill in the Remote Web Site Location, which should begin with ftp://.

4. If necessary, fill in the FTP directory and check Use Passive FTP (your web presence provider will let you know if these are necessary).

5. Set the options in the Publishing tab as discussed earlier in this chapter.

6. Click OK to return to the Remote Web Site view.

7. Set the publishing direction (usually Local To Remote) and click the Publish button. If you are not connected to the Internet, just click Connect when FrontPage prompts you. When prompted, supply your userid and password.

8. FrontPage begins publishing your web site. Once the publishing process has completed, you can click View Your Remote Web Site link to view the site.

> **NOTE** *If your site uses any features or components of FrontPage that won't work without the FrontPage Server extensions, you will be warned when you try to publish your web site. You really should remove these components before publishing the web site. Otherwise, you'll get strange results. For example, if you try to use a search form, the only result you'll get is a page that tells you that FrontPage extensions are not installed. Guess how I know that?*

18

Part IV

Database Integration and Advanced Formatting

Chapter 19

Route Form Results to a Database

How to...

- Store form results in a database table
- Specify the columns into which field data is placed
- Create a new database for your form results
- Verify that the database connection is working

Earlier in this book we discussed how to build forms and how to place the results from the form into a text or HTML file. There is a lot you can do with these results, but there are also some significant limits.

Why Use a Database?

Once you start to get a significant number of results (say, several hundred or a thousand), keeping form results in a text or HTML file gets unwieldy. It is very hard to analyze the results, looking for trends and statistics. However, a database is *designed* to handle a large volume of data. In addition, most databases have tools available to enable you to run reports, archive old data, find or replace all records that contain specified information, and in general, "mine" your data for valuable information. Thus, if you anticipate that a form will generate a lot of data that could prove of value, you may well be better off routing the form results to a database.

Another very good reason to route form results to a database is if you need a database application to process those results. For example, if you take orders on your web site, you are likely to want to create an order form and send the results to your orders database. Sending the information to a text or HTML file would be counterproductive in this instance.

Store Data in a Table

As you may be aware, a database consists of one or more *tables*. The results from a form are stored in a single table, which FrontPage will create for you if you wish. Each row in the table contains a single set of form results. That is, each time someone submits the form, a new row is created in the table to contain those results. Each field on the form corresponds to a column in the table. The table columns do not have to have the same name as the form fields, but it is less confusing if they do. For example, if you build a form with fields called Last_Name and First_Name, the data submitted will normally go into columns called Last_Name and First_Name in the table. Table 19-1 shows a sample of what a database table might look like after three form submissions. The top row displays the column names.

ID	Last_Name	First_Name	Occupation
1	Jones	Sam	Data Administrator
2	Smith	Mary	Police Officer
3	Greenlee	Sarah	Hotelier

TABLE 19-1 Sample Database Results from Three Form Submissions

NOTE *The first column in this table illustrates a common database requirement: the need for a column that uniquely identifies each row in the database. While this unique identifier can be a collection of multiple columns, it is more typical to use a unique and meaningless number. If you allow FrontPage to create your database table for you, the default behavior is to automatically create the unique identifier column and populate this column with a unique number when the form is submitted. You do not need a field on your form for this column. However, if you already assign a unique identifier to the person submitting the form results (such as a customer ID), you can have the person fill in that value on the form and use that column as the unique identifier. To override FrontPage's unique ID behavior, choose Tool | Page Options. In the General tab of the Page Options dialog box, clear the Assign Unique IDs To New Tables check box.*

Basics of Database Connections

In order to send form results to a database, you must establish a connection between FrontPage and the target database. At its simplest level, you can instruct FrontPage to create a connection to an Access database using point and click (and we'll show you how shortly). In fact, FrontPage can build an Access database and the connection to the database all in one step. However, database connections are completely separate from the database itself—you can connect to a database using more than one database connection, and you can reuse a database connection to connect to the database from multiple forms. If you aren't using an Access database running on your local machine, however, database connections can become considerably more complex. The type of database connection you create will depend not only on the database you are trying to connect to, but where that database is located. There are four possibilities for database connections:

- Access database running on your local machine (and published to the web server along with your FrontPage web site)
- Any other database (such as FoxPro, Paradox, dBase, Approach, and so on) running on your local machine (and published to the web server along with your FrontPage web site)
- A database running on a web host server
- A database running on a network server

Each of these possibilities requires that you perform a different set of tasks to set up the connection to the database. And, in most cases, you will need special information provided by a network administrator, database administrator (DBA), or web host administrator to set up the connection.

NOTE   *This book is limited to using a local Access database (that is published to the web server with the web site). In addition, using databases in this manner is limited to web servers running FrontPage Server Extensions along with SharePoint Team Services 1. If your web provider is running SharePoint Team Services version 2 on a Windows 2003 Server, Access databases will not work.*

Connections on the Web Server

The web server to which you publish forms that use database-based results must be configured properly. At a minimum, the server must have the FrontPage server extensions installed, as well as the Microsoft Data Access components. If you are testing a server-based web site on your local machine, installing the Office Web Server on IIS running in Windows 2000 or XP provides all the functionality you need.

NOTE   *ASP is a technology for dynamically generating web pages from the contents of a database—or populating a database from the contents of a web page. Support for ASP is built into IIS, so you can test routing form results to a database using server-based web sites on your own PC if you are using IIS 5.0 or later.*

Save Form Results to a New Access Database

The quickest and easiest way to save form results to a database is to use an Access database that resides within your web site. You don't need to do anything special to set this up, and FrontPage will even create the database you need. Of course, to view and manipulate the contents of the database you do need a copy of Access, but given that Access is inexpensive and easy to use (at least, in comparison with the other databases available), using Access isn't a bad choice.

To route the results of a form to a new Access database, use the following steps:

1. Create the form from which you want to route the results to a database. You can use any techniques you want, including the Form Page Wizard or one of the form templates, or you can build the form from scratch. Save the page (File | Save) and give the page a name that ends with the extension .asp.

NOTE   *The ending .asp (which stands for active server page) is necessary for the form to correctly route the results of the form to the database. If you don't use the .asp ending at this point, FrontPage will warn you that the form won't work when you later save the form after inserting the database information.*

2. Right-click in the form and choose Form Properties from the shortcut menu. This opens the Form Properties dialog box. Choose the Send To Database option. Don't click OK yet.

3. Click the Options button to open the Options For Saving Results To Database dialog box.

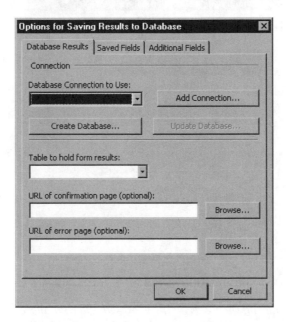

4. Click the Create Database button. FrontPage creates an Access database with the same name as the form whose results are being saved to the database, and places the Access database file into the fpdb directory. Once this operation is complete, FrontPage confirms the creation of the database.

NOTE   *If the form page contains more than a single form element, FrontPage will create multiple Access databases. Each Access database is named for the form, but contains a sequential number at the end of the database name. For example, if you have an HTML page entitled Interest_Form that contains three form elements, the Access databases will be named Interest_Form1.mdb, Interest_Form2.mdb, and Interest_Form3.mdb. Each Access database contains a single table called Results.*

5. If you wish, you can specify a confirmation page and error page, just as with any other form. Use the URL Of Confirmation Page field and the URL Of Error Page field to do so.

6. The new Access database contains only a single table, called Results. In addition, FrontPage creates a database connection (displayed in the Database Connection To Use drop-down list) and connects FrontPage to the new database through that connection.

19

7. Click the Saved Fields tab to see how the form fields are associated with the database columns.

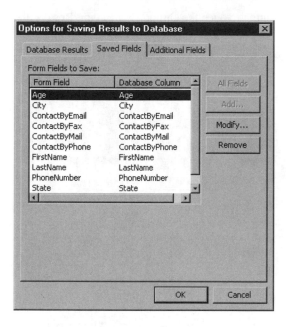

SHORTCUT *To quickly associate all the fields on the form with their database columns, make sure you are on the Database Results tab and click the Update Database button. This is especially handy if you rename some of the fields on the form.*

8. Click OK to return to the Form Properties dialog box. Click OK again to finish creating the database and associating the form results with it.

9. Choose File | Save to save the form. If you did not use the .asp extension earlier when naming the form, FrontPage saves the form but warns you that it won't work unless you rename it to use the .asp extension. Click OK to get past this warning.

10. If FrontPage warned you about the form name (previous step), rename the form by right-clicking it in the Folder List and choosing Rename from the shortcut menu. Change the extension to .asp and press ENTER. FrontPage will warn you that the file may become unusable, but click Yes to complete the rename.

To test the form, you must be using a server-based web site and open it in a browser—just previewing the page generates an error when you try to submit the form. However, if you open the page in a browser (and are using a server-based web site), you can fill in the information and submit the results to the database by clicking the Submit button. To actually view the submitted data, double-click the Access database to open it in Access—provided you have Access installed on your computer. Once the database is open, double-click the Results table in the Access main dialog box to open the table in Browse mode (see Figure 19-1).

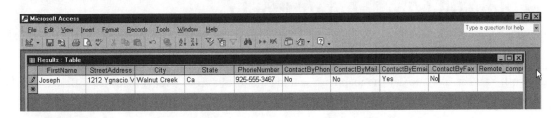

FIGURE 19-1   Use Microsoft Access to view the contents of the Results table.

CAUTION   *If you have Access, you can change the structure of the table, including changing the table name, column names, and even data types. However, if you do, FrontPage won't be able to route the form results to the database correctly. You'll need to manually associate form fields with the renamed table and columns (as discussed shortly). So, unless you really know what you are doing, resist the temptation to change the Results table structure in Access.*

Send Results to a Different Table

You aren't stuck just using the one automatically generated table in a database to store your form results. For example, you might wish to create an Access database that contains multiple tables, one for each set of form results. This could be handy if you use many forms and just want to download one Access database file from the web site that contains all the form results. Or, you might have an existing Access database that you imported into your web site (as detailed later in this chapter). Assuming that you know enough about Access to create tables, you can direct the results of a form to any table in the database.

To select an existing table in a database to store the form results, use the following steps:

1. Open the web page (.asp) that contains the form. Right-click the form portion of the web page and choose Form Properties from the shortcut menu. Click the Options button to open the Options For Saving Results To Database dialog box.

2. Click the Table To Hold Form Results drop-down list. The drop-down list contains a list of all the tables in the database.

3. Assuming that the alternate table contains columns with the same name as the form fields, simply click OK in the Options dialog box and the Form Properties dialog box to route the results to a different table.

NOTE   *If the database columns are named differently than the form fields, you'll have to manually associate the fields with the columns, as detailed in the next section.*

Change the Field-To-Column Mapping

You have complete control over how the fields on a form are mapped to database columns. You can break the link between a field and a column (handy if you need to delete a form field), or manually establish a link between a field and a column (handy if you need to add another field to the form). You can also modify the mapping, sending the results from a form field to a different database column than the one to which it is currently mapped.

NOTE   *Although you will normally be working with the Saved Fields tab in the Options For Saving Results To Database dialog box, everything in this section that applies to the Saved Fields tab also works for the Additional Fields tab. The Additional Fields tab contains the field mappings for the Browser Type, Remote Computer Name, Timestamp, and Username.*

Delete a Form Field

If you decide you no longer need a form field, you can delete the field from the form. However, this action does *not* remove the mapping from the (now nonexistent) field to the database column. To remove the mapping, open the Form Properties dialog box and click the Options button to open the Options For Saving Results To Database dialog box. Click the Saved Fields tab, and select the deleted form field and its associated database column. Click the Remove button to remove it from the list.

NOTE   *Deleting the mapping between a form field and a database column does not remove the column from the database table. The column remains, but it will always be empty.*

Add a Form Field

If you decide to add a field to a form, it will not be associated with a database column initially. You can correct this situation in one of two ways: add the column to a table manually and associate the column with the field, or let FrontPage add the column for you (as detailed in the following How to...). Obviously, letting FrontPage add the column for you is easier, but this only works for databases under your control, such as an Access database within your own web site.

Add and Delete Form Field Mappings

If you simply want to break the connection between a form field and a database column, you can click the Remove button in the Saved Fields tab of the Options For Saving Results To Database dialog box. The field remains on the form, but its results no longer go to any database column. You might want to do this prior to remapping a different field to this same column. You can only modify the field mapping to point to a column that is *not* currently associated with a form field. Thus, you might need to break an existing connection first.

NOTE *If you remove the field and its database column and click OK, the next time you open the Options For Saving Results To Database dialog box, the form field will be redisplayed in the Form Field list—but it won't be associated with any database column.*

Once you have removed a field from the Saved Fields tab, both the Add button and All Fields button become available. Clicking the All Fields button redisplays any removed form fields, but they are no longer associated with a database column. This makes it easy to choose the unassociated form field, and then click Modify to associate the form field with another database column.

If you choose the Add button, the Add Field dialog box appears (see Figure 19-2). The top portion of the dialog box displays all form fields that are unassociated with a database column. The Database Column To Save To drop-down list contains a list of all the database columns that are currently unassociated with a form field.

To associate a form field with a database column, select the field from the Form Field To Add list, and choose the database column to associate it with from the Database Column To Save To drop-down list. Then click OK. When you click Modify, a simple dialog box opens that displays the selected form field and a drop-down list that includes the currently associated database column (if any) and any unassociated database columns. Simply choose a database column from the drop-down list and click OK to modify the association.

How to ... Add a Column to a Local Access Database

Adding a column for the new form field to a local Access database couldn't be simpler. Use the following steps:

1. Add the field to the form, making sure to give it a descriptive name. To change the name of the form field, right-click it and choose Form Field Properties from the shortcut menu. Then fill in the name in the Properties dialog box and click OK.

2. Save the form. You must do this or step 4 won't work properly.

3. Right-click the form portion of the web page and choose Form Properties from the shortcut menu. Click the Options button to open the Options For Saving Results To Database dialog box.

4. Click the Update Database button. FrontPage automatically adds the new column to the database. Click OK twice to complete the operation.

The next time someone submits the form, this new column will contain the contents of the new field. Older records, of course, will have no data in the new field.

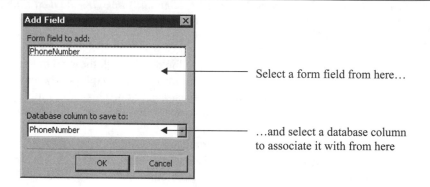

Select a form field from here...

...and select a database column
to associate it with from here

FIGURE 19-2   Use the Add Field dialog box to associate a currently unmapped form field
to a currently unmapped database column.

Connect to a Database

If you are not going to use the automatic database connection created by FrontPage, you will
need to define your own database connection. To open the dialog box you'll need, you do one
of two things. Your first option is to choose Tools | Web Settings and click the Database tab.
Alternatively, you can right-click a form and choose Form Properties from the shortcut menu.
Once the Form Properties dialog box opens, click the Options button and then click the Add
Connection button. Either way, the Database tab of the Web Settings dialog box is displayed:

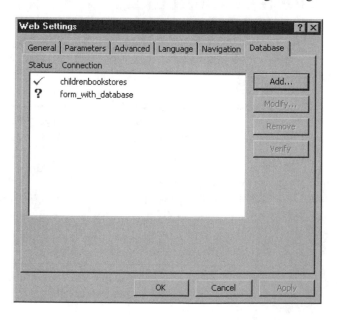

Click the Add button to open the New Database Connection dialog box.

The first step in defining a new database connection is to type the identifying name into the Name field. Next, you'll need to pick the type of database connection to create by selecting one of the options in the Type Of Connection section. The four types of connection are

- **File or folder in current Web**   Use this option to identify a file or a folder that actually contains the database. For example, an Access database is contained in a file with an .mdb extension.

- **System data source on web server**   This option enables you to select a system data source connected to a database on the web server. The system data source will probably have to be set up for you by a database administrator with the authority to do so. It is unlikely you'll have the permissions to create the system data source yourself.

- **Network connection to database server**   This option lets you specify a particular database on a server and connect to that database. A database administrator is likely to have to set up the necessary permissions in order for you to connect to the database, as well as supplied the variety of values you will need in order to connect to the network database.

- **Custom definition**   This option simply allows you to select a file to use to specify how to connect to a database. The file must have been created by someone who is knowledgeable about the specifics of connecting to the database, and who can supply you with the values you'll need to configure the connection (such as the connection string).

Once you select the type of connection you want, follow the instructions for the type of connection you selected.

19

Create a Connection to a File or Folder in the Current Web

To create a connection to a file or folder in the current web, click the Browse button to open the Database Files In Current Web dialog box.

Select the type of database file or folder you want from the Files Of Type drop-down list. This list contains a list of all the drivers for the local database you have installed. Select the file or folder from the large central area of the dialog box, or type it into the URL field and click OK to close the dialog box.

If you need to specify any additional parameters in order to connect to the database (you don't normally need to for local databases), click the Advanced button in the New Database Connection dialog box to open the Advanced Connection Properties dialog.

Fill in any necessary information in the following fields:

- **Username**   If you need to supply a username to access the database, supply the value in this field. This should be a username with permission to write data to the database, as capturing the results from a form requires writing those results into the database.

- **Password**   If the username requires a password, enter it in this field.

- **Connection**   In the Timeouts section, fill in the number of seconds you want FrontPage to wait before timing out when attempting to establish a connection with the database. Filling in a low value may cause the connection to fail even if a connection was available (but slow). Filling in a high value may cause you to wait (and wait) for a connection that is simply not available. The default of 15 seconds is a reasonable compromise, although you may have to tune this number for your database—especially if that database is located on a network server.

- **Command**   In the Timeouts section, fill in the number of seconds you want FrontPage to wait before timing out when attempting to execute a command (such as writing a record) to the database.

- **Other parameters**   If the database connection requires any special name/value parameter pairs, click the Add button to open the Add Parameter dialog box. Fill in the Name and Value, and click OK to add the parameters.

Modify or Remove a Database Connection

Once you have built one or more database connections, you can modify the connection by selecting it in the Database tab of the Web Settings dialog box and clicking the Modify button. This reopens the Database Connection Properties dialog box so you can modify any of the parameters or change any of the information in the Advanced Connection Properties dialog box.

If you no longer need a connection, you can select that connection and click Remove to discard it.

Verify a Database Connection

If you have built a database connection but not tested it, a question mark will appear in the Status column next to the connection name in the Database tab of the Web Settings dialog box (choose Tools | Web Settings).

To make sure the database connection is working properly, select the connection and click the Verify button. If FrontPage is able to successfully verify the database connection, the question mark in the Status column will change to a check mark. If FrontPage cannot successfully verify the connection, you can modify the connection to get it working by clicking the Modify button.

Import an Access Database into Your Web Site

If you are knowledgeable about databases, you may have already constructed and populated the Access database you want to use with your web site. If so, you'll need to import the database into your web site before using it to capture data from forms (as explained in this chapter) or to display data in a form (as explained in the next chapter). FrontPage makes it easy to import an Access database, and even offers to build the database connection automatically.

To import an Access database, use the following steps:

1. Choose File | Import to open the Import dialog box.

2. Click Add File to open the Add File To Import List dialog box, and pick the database you want to import.

3. Click Open to return to the Import dialog box with the database added to the list of files to import.

4. Click OK. FrontPage displays the Add Database Connection dialog box.

5. Fill in the name of the database connection in the Name field and click Yes. FrontPage imports the database and creates the database connection for accessing the database.

Present Database Contents Using the Database Results Wizard

How to...

- Do the preparatory work to use a database
- Specify the data to display
- Set up filtering and sort order
- Provide an interactive search form
- Format the returned records
- View the results in a browser

If the information you want to display in your web pages is fairly static, creating the web pages by typing in text and adding graphics works fine. However, there are times when building such static pages is not appropriate. This is especially true if the information changes fairly frequently or if there is a lot of information people might want to search through. Examples of such data might include

- Available products your company sells. Not only might the actual products themselves change, but their current availability can vary from one moment to the next.
- Membership list for your organization.
- Computer applications by category. This list is especially volatile if you include shareware, as shareware programs arrive and disappear more frequently than commercial software.
- Results from sports competitions, where people might wish to search by race, competitor name, or team.

TIP *Anytime your information consists of a long list, it is a prime candidate for the techniques discussed in this chapter.*

Typically, you might consider keeping this kind of information in a database application, making it easy to add new information and modify existing information. If you do use a database, you can display the contents of the database in a dynamic web page, and even include an embedded search form to help readers find specific information. For example, if you categorize the products you sell, you could allow readers to type in a category of product they are interested in, and just display that category in a table on the web page.

Another excellent candidate for inclusion in a database (and subsequent display on a dynamic web page) is information that people who visit your site can update themselves, such as membership information and preferences. First, you create a search form in which a reader inputs their username and password so you can find their record. By capturing the data the reader enters directly into the database (using the techniques discussed in Chapter 19), the information is not only updated, but the reader can see the new information (taken from the database) on the screen immediately.

FrontPage's Database Results Wizard makes it fairly straightforward to build a web page that takes its source data from a database. Although the Database Results Wizard is more complex than other wizards, it still reduces to manageable proportions the complexity of what was previously an extraordinarily difficult task.

Perform Initial Setup

There are a few things you'll need before beginning work on a web page to display the contents of a database. First of all, you'll need the database itself. You have all the same options for source databases that were discussed in Chapter 19: a local file in your web site, a database running on the web server, or a database running on a network server. Unlike routing form results to a database, however, you do *not* have the opportunity to create a new database while setting up the web page. You must have the database designed and built prior to building the web page.

You will also need a connection to the database. Setting up the connection works exactly as described in Chapter 19, and you *do* have the opportunity to define a new connection while building the web page. Just be sure you have all the necessary setup work done ahead of time, including installing any necessary ODBC or native database drivers and obtaining permissions from the database administrator (if necessary).

Finally, you'll need the structure of the database, called the *schema*. This includes the names of tables, the names of the columns in those tables, and their data types (for example, numeric, character, date, and so on). You will also need to understand the purpose of each column so you can make an informed decision as to what information is stored there.

Configure the Database Results Wizard

To display the contents of a database on a web page, you need to create the web page and then run the Database Results Wizard. The Database Results Wizard places a *Database region* on the page. This Database region is a table or list that contains the specified columns from the database. When you publish the page to a web server running FrontPage extensions, the contents of the table is populated with data from the database. If you built a server-based web site using Microsoft IIS 5.0 or later, you can also preview the page in a browser to see the database results.

Create the Initial Web Page

The first step is to create the web page. Choose File | New to open the New Task Pane, choose More Page Templates from the Task Pane, and select the Normal Page template from the Page Templates dialog box. When the new page appears, right-click and select Page Properties from the shortcut menu, then fill in the title. Choose File | Save and enter the name you want in the File Name field. It is very important to use the .asp ending, as you are creating a dynamic web page.

NOTE *If you don't name the file using an .asp ending, FrontPage will complain when you save the page after running the Database Results Wizard. You'll need to rename the page at that point if you want the page to operate correctly.*

20

After you have created the web page, run the Database Results Wizard by choosing Insert |
Database | Results to open the first panel of the Database Results Wizard.

Specify the Data to Display

The first panel of the Database Results Wizard lets you select the database connection for the
database that contains the data for the web page.

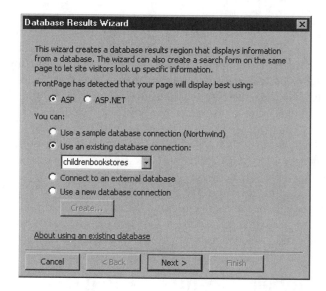

You have four options for the database connection. First, you can use the sample Northwind
database that comes with Access (provided you installed it) by selecting the Use A Sample
Database Connection option. You can choose an existing database connection by selecting the
Use An Existing Database Connection option and selecting the connection from the drop-down
list. You can choose an external database (such as an Oracle database on a network) by choosing
Connect To An External Database. Finally, you can define a new database connection (as
discussed in Chapter 19) by choosing the Use A New Database Connection option and clicking
the Create button.

This book only discusses how to use an existing database connection.

When you are done selecting the database connection, click Next to continue.

The second panel of the Database Results Wizard lets you either select a record source or create a custom SQL query.

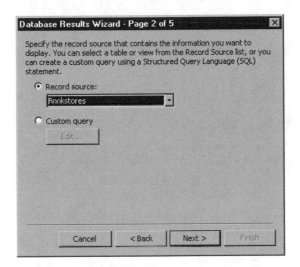

Choose a Record Source

To choose a record source, click the Record Source option and choose the source from the drop-down list. This list contains all the tables in the target database, as well as any views that exist. A *view* is a logical grouping of physical data with filters and sorting applied—Access queries are actually views. Thus, if the source is an Access database, the drop-down list contains any queries (displayed with the word VIEW after the query name).

> NOTE   *Although the Database Results Wizard enables you to select fields and establish selection criteria and sort order, if you are familiar with Access (and are using an Access database as your source) or your database's View facility, you may want to consider building the view using your database and then just using it as your record source in FrontPage. For example, an Access query (and most other database View facilities) enables you to join multiple tables (connected by foreign keys), include the columns you want, establish filtering and sorting criteria, group by the value in a column, and add calculated results. Not only is this considerably more power than is provided by the Database Results Wizard, but if you frequently change the sort or filtering criteria, you can just adjust the criteria in the database View facility and you won't have to modify the database results properties on the web page.*

When you are done selecting a record source, click Next to move to the next step.

Create a Custom Query

You can create a custom query by choosing the Custom Query option in the second panel of the Database Results Wizard and clicking the Edit button to open the Custom Query dialog box.

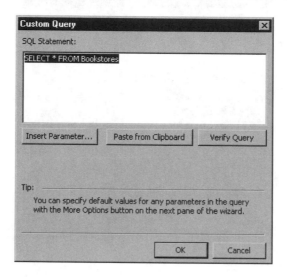

The Custom Query dialog box enables you to enter a SQL query that returns results from the database. You can (if you know what you are doing) create a complex query that returns exactly what you want from the database. To build the SQL query, simply type it into the Custom Query dialog box. To check the syntax of the query, click the Verify Query button. If all is well, FrontPage will confirm the correctness of the query. If there is an error, FrontPage will report that as well. The initial error message doesn't contain much information, but if you click the Details button, you'll get a lot more information.

If you want to write your query in another tool (such as a SQL editor), you can copy it from that tool and paste it into the Custom Query dialog box by clicking the Paste From Clipboard button.

As we will discuss in more detail later, you can set up a search form into which the reader can enter values for information they are looking for. For example, if you were querying a database of bookstores, you could create a search form field called QueryState, and if the reader was looking only for California bookstores, he or she could type **Ca** into this field. If you are creating a custom query, you will want to add a WHERE clause to the SQL to select those records where a particular column matches the value in the search form field. To do this, create the WHERE clause in the Custom Query dialog box and click the Insert Parameter button. This opens the Insert Form Field Parameter dialog box.

Type the name of the search form field into the Insert Form Field Parameter dialog box and click OK. This inserts the search form field name (surrounded by double colons) into the Custom Query dialog box, which might then look like this:

```
Select * from Bookstores where StateAbbrev = ::QueryState::;
```

When the query is submitted to the database, the contents of the search form field (input by the reader on the search form) are used to replace the reference to the search form field (::QueryState:: in this example). This gives you considerable power—including using "like" matching and enabling the reader to use wildcards (which are not supported by the Database Result Wizard's normal search form).

When you are done creating the custom query, click OK to return to the Database Results Wizard, and click Next to go to the next step.

Select the Columns to Display

You can choose the columns to include in the Database Results region from the third panel of the Database Results Wizard.

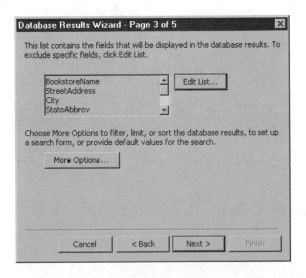

Click the Edit List button to open the Displayed Fields dialog box.

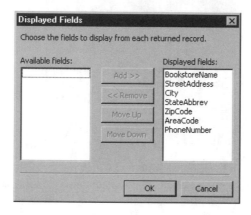

The Available Fields list shows all the fields in the record source that are *not* included in the Database region of the web page. The Displayed Fields list shows all the columns in the record source that are included. To remove a field from the Displayed Fields list, select the field and click the Remove button. To add a field from the Available Fields list, select the field and click the Add button.

The columns displayed in the Database region on the web page are arranged in the order in which they appear in the Displayed Fields list. To change the order of the fields, click a field and use the Move Up or Move Down button.

If you want to establish filtering criteria, set up a search form for returning results from the database, or specify sort order, click the More Options button to open the More Options dialog box (see Figure 20-1).

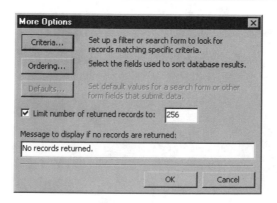

FIGURE 20-1   More options include sorting and filtering.

Establish Filtering Criteria

To establish filtering criteria, click the Criteria button to open the Criteria dialog box.

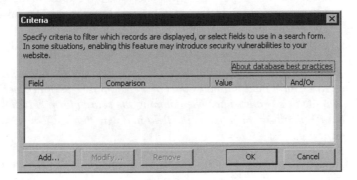

The Criteria dialog box displays any criteria you have specified to filter the records returned from the database. For example, if you only wanted to see bookstores where the State was "Ca," you would specify that condition in the Criteria dialog box.

To add criteria, click the Add button to open the Add Criteria dialog box.

Specify the criteria using the following fields:

- **Field Name**   Use the drop-down list to specify the name of the field whose contents you will be inspecting for a value matching your specification. The list contains every column in the table or view—the field does *not* have to be one of those displayed in the Database region of the page.

- **Comparison**   Choose the operation you want to use to compare the field name to the value. Options include Equals, Not Equals, Less Than, Not Less Than, Greater Than, Not Greater Than, Is Null, and Is Not Null. For the comparisons Is Null and Is Not Null, the Value field is not available.

- **Value**   Type in the value to which you want to compare the field name. You can also type in a character string (such as QueryState) that names a search field.

- **Use this search form field**   If you check this check box, the value in the Value field will be used as the name for a field on a search form. Later in the Database Results Wizard, you will be offered the opportunity to have the wizard construct the search form. The form will automatically contain any field you specify as part of the filter criteria.

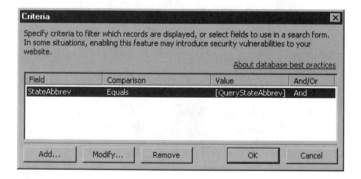

NOTE   *The search form field name must begin with a letter and cannot use spaces. This is because the search form field is used as part of a custom ASP script (which you never see). If you violate these constraints when naming the search form field, FrontPage will warn you, but it will allow you to name the field in a way that will cause an error later when the script executes.*

- **And/Or**   Choose either And or Or to connect the current criteria to the next criteria (if any). If you connect two criteria together with an And, *both* must be true before the record is returned in the Database Results region. If you connect two criteria together with an Or, if either condition is true the record will be returned in the Database region.

If you check the Use This Search Form Field check box to use the value in the Value field as a form field name, the criteria displays the Value quantity in square brackets, indicating that it is a search form field.

You can delete a criterion by selecting it and clicking the Remove button. To change the criterion, select it and click the Modify button. When you are done creating criterion, click OK to return to the More Options dialog box.

Specify the Record Sort Order

To specify the order in which returned records will be displayed, click the Ordering button to open the Ordering dialog box.

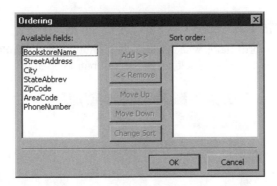

The Available Fields list displays all the available fields on which you can sort. To sort on a field, select it and click the Add button to move the field to the Sort Order list. To remove a field from the Sort Order list, click it and select Remove. If you choose more than one field to sort on, you can change the order of the fields in the Sort Order list using the Move Up and Move Down buttons. The order is important, because the records are sorted first on the topmost field. Any records that have the same value for the topmost field are then sorted by the second field, and so on.

TIP   *Strictly speaking, the sort field does not have to be one that is displayed on the page, but readers will be confused about how order was established if you sort on a nondisplayed field.*

By default, any fields you add to the Sort Order list are sorted in ascending order—the lowest value first, then the next higher value, and so on. If you wish to change the type of sort (from ascending to descending or from descending to ascending), select the field and click the Change Sort button. The yellow rectangle alongside the sort field changes to indicate whether the sort order is ascending (pointing up) or descending (pointing down). The Ordering dialog box might look like the following if you built a two-level sort (ascending on both columns):

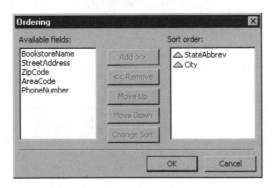

Establish Defaults for Search Form Fields

If you specified any search form fields when establishing criteria, the Default button in the More Options dialog box becomes available. Clicking the Default button opens the Defaults dialog box.

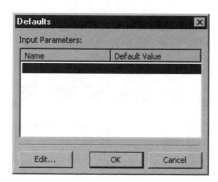

You can use the Defaults dialog box to establish default values for any of the fields on the search form. That is, if the reader does not enter any value in the field, the value submitted to the database during the query will be the default value. This is handy if you know that a search form field will normally be populated with a particular value.

To specify a default value, select the search form field from the Defaults dialog box and click the Edit button to open the Default Value dialog box.

Fill in the value and click OK. Once you are done with the Defaults dialog box, click OK to return to the More Options dialog box.

Database columns have data types (for example, character, date, number, and so on). If you specify a default value that does not match the data type of the database column, the search will return no records—and, depending on the database, may also return an error. This behavior will also occur if the reader inputs a value to the search field that does not match the data type, so you may want to add instructions to the search form about what data type the search form field (and thus the database) is expecting.

Limit the Number of Returned Records

Databases can be really huge, and an injudicious search could return a lot of records. This could take quite a while over a dial-up line. Because of this, you can set the maximum number of records that a database search will return to the web page. To do so, check the Limit Number Of Returned Records To check box, and enter the number in the adjacent field.

If you do decide to limit the number of records, be sure to add a note to the web page telling the reader what the maximum number of records allowed has been limited to. Otherwise, readers may think they have retrieved all the records matching their criteria (and indeed, they may want to see them all), which could be misleading.

Specify the No Records Message

A highly selective query might return no records, so it is best to specify a message telling readers that no records matched their query. Type this message into the Message To Display If No Records Are Returned field.

> **TIP** *The default message (No records matched your query) is uninformative because it doesn't tell the reader what to do next. You should change the message to give readers an idea of what to try next if they don't get any records. Perhaps a better message would be "No records were returned. Try removing one or more conditions from your query."*

Once you have finished specifying the items in the More Options dialog box, click OK to close it and return to the Database Results Wizard. Then click Next to move to the next panel.

Select the Results Format

The next step is to select how you want the database results presented. There are three options: as a table, as a list, or as a drop-down list.

Return Results as a Table

The most common method of presenting the results from a database query is as a table. Choosing Table–One Record Per Row from the drop-down list in the Database Results Wizard gives you the following version of the fourth panel:

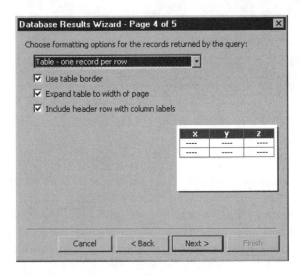

You have the following options:

- **Use table border**   Checking this check box displays the table boundary and cell outlines as a solid grid. Leaving this check box cleared makes the borders invisible in a browser or in Preview mode.

■ **Expand table to width of page**   Checking this check box expands the table to fill the page width. You may not want to do this if the data returned is very small, but normally you will want to check this option.

■ **Include header row with column labels**   Checking this check box adds a row at the top of the table. This extra row contains the column names. Since column names from databases can often be quite cryptic, you may want to edit the header row after the Database Results Wizard finishes.

Return Results As a List

If you select List–One Field Per Item from the drop-down list, you get the following version of the fourth panel of the Database Results Wizard:

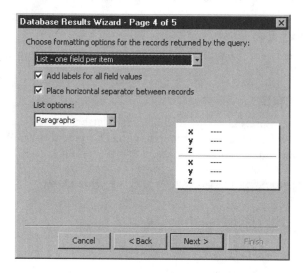

This option presents the data as a list, with one field on each line. The following options are available:

■ **Add labels for all field values**   Since a plain list of values is pretty confusing, you'll probably want to check this check box to ensure that each field has a label. The label is just the database column name (which can be cryptic), but it's better than nothing, and you can customize the label on the web page once the Database Results Wizard finishes.

■ **Place horizontal separator between records**   Checking this check box places a horizontal break between the set of items that make up each record. This gives you a visual cue where one record ends and another begins.

■ **List options**   Select the list formatting from this drop-down list. Options include standard paragraphs, bulleted list, numbered list, definition list, text fields, and even a table.

Return Results as a Drop-Down List

Choosing Drop-Down List–One Record Per Item gives you the following version of the fourth panel of the Database Results Wizard:

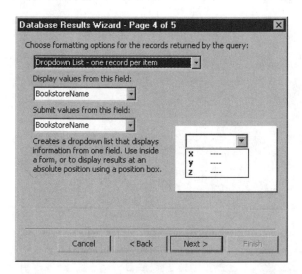

This option is especially useful if you want to populate a drop-down list in a form from the contents of a database. However, since each item in the list is one record in the database, you have to be careful about how you populate the database table. If the table includes multiple records with the same value, those values will show up multiple times in the drop-down list (unless, of course, you built your own SQL query and used `Select Distinct`).

To specify how the drop-down list will behave, you must specify two quantities: the field from which the drop-down list gets its values, and the field that contains the value you want to submit using the form. The reason is that frequently you will have two fields in your database: one that contains a code (such as "F") and one that contains a description (such as "Girls"). The person filling out the form will need to see the description in the drop-down list, but you may wish to submit (and store) the code instead. Thus, you would select the field containing the description to use for the Display Values From This Field drop-down list and the field containing the code to use for the Submit Values From This Field.

Of course, you can set both fields to the same value—in which case the reader will see the same field you are submitting and storing.

Finish with the Database Results Wizard

The last panel of the Database Results Wizard lets you set grouping options and automatically create the search form right on the same page with the Database Results region:

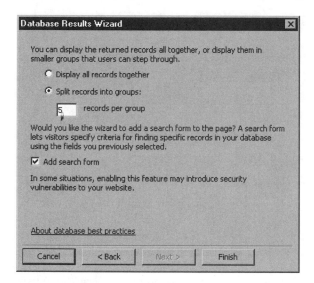

Group Your Records

There are two options available for visually grouping your records in the Database region of the web page. Display All Records Together does just that—all the records are returned in the table, with no breaks between records. This works fine if you don't expect a lot of records to be returned. The other option—Split Records Into Groups—enables you to enter the number of records to display at once in the table or list (see Figure 20-2). To move to the next group of records or the previous group of records, use the navigation buttons at the bottom of the Database region. This option is handy if you expect many records to be returned.

You can use the Split Records Into Groups setting to break records across printed pages.

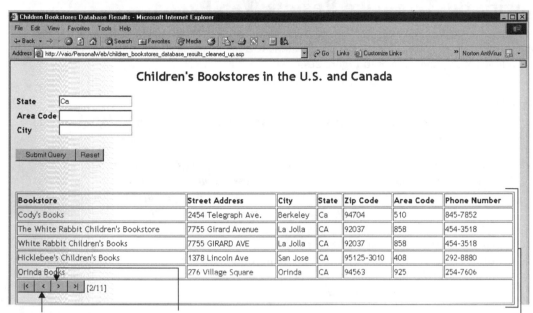

Return previous set of records   Return next set of records   Records returned from the database

FIGURE 20-2   Grouping records in the Database region can make them easier to read and to print out.

 Grouping records is not available if you chose the option to return the database records in a drop-down list.

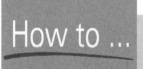

How to ... Create the Search Form Automatically

One of the most powerful options available in FrontPage 2003 is the ability to return selected records from the database using a search form. If you created filter criteria earlier (using the Criteria dialog box) that use search form fields, the Add Search Form check box is enabled. Checking this check box instructs the Database Results Wizard to create the search form above the Database Results region on the web page. The search form will automatically include all search fields you specified as part of the criteria.

Work with the Database Results Web Page

To finish creating the database results web page, click the Finish button on the last panel of the Database Results Wizard. This inserts the Database region and the search form (if you specified one) into the web page, similar to Figure 20-3.

Modify the Layout

The default layout that results from running the Database Results Wizard isn't bad, but it can be improved to make it easier to use.

CAUTION *Do not change the column names enclosed in << >>! These refer to the data source columns in the database, and if you change these column names, no data will be returned for that column. Also, depending on the database, you may get an error when you try to retrieve data. Note, though, that if you change the structure of the record source (say, by using your database tool to change the column name), you will need to reflect that change in the column names on the page. The easiest way to do that is to right-click the column name, choose Database Column Value Properties from the shortcut menu, and choose the new column name to display from the Column To Display drop-down list in the Database Column Value dialog box.*

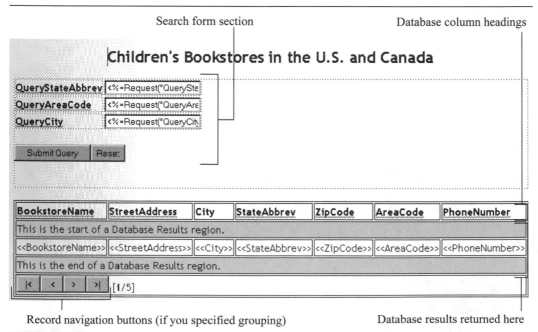

FIGURE 20-3 The "finished" database results web page, ready for customization and use

Here are some areas to focus on:

- **Table headings**   If you returned your results as a table, the column headings are the database column names. These can be cryptic and hard to read, so consider replacing them with more descriptive headings.

It is a proven fact that database results are used more frequently and to better effect when the reader understands what the data means. Add a hyperlink to each column heading that jumps to another page where the meaning of that column is explained in great detail. Experienced users can ignore the link, but new users can easily find out what the data means.

- **List field names**   If you returned your results as a list, the list field names are the database column names. As with table headings, consider replacing them with more descriptive names.

- **Search form instructions**   You'll notice that the search form contains no instructions on how to use it. You'll probably want to add instructions telling the reader how to enter the data they are searching for. In addition, if you added multiple fields, you'll want to explain how the fields are connected (with an And or an Or) and what that means for the returned database results.

- **Search form field names**   Spaces are not allowed in the search form field names, and the default label for the field is the field name. You'll probably want to change the label to make it easier to read.

- **Search form field valid values**   Often, only a certain set of valid values are allowed for a particular field. For example, the StateAbbrev field used in this example allows only valid abbreviations for states. However, if readers do not know which values are valid, they may keep trying values that return no records, which is very frustrating. And if there are a lot of possible values, the chances that the reader will type in an invalid value are much greater. It *is* possible to convert the search form field to a drop-down list (as discussed later in this chapter), but it is pretty complicated and even requires that you write a simple custom query (which I'll show you how to do). Instead, you may want to figure out a way to inform the reader which values are valid. One way is to add a note to the form. Another way (which works better if there are a lot of valid values) is to add a hyperlink alongside the search form field, perhaps labeled Valid Values. The reader can click the hyperlink to navigate to another page where the valid values are detailed, along with their meanings.

View the Results

To view the database web page in action, you'll have to publish the page and open it in a browser. Either publish the page to your web hosting service and open it on the Internet or, if you created the web as a server-based web site in IIS, simply display the page and choose File | Preview In Browser. It may take a moment or two for the page to open, since the database results must be retrieved and formatted. Eventually, however, you should see the database results on your web page (see Figure 20-4).

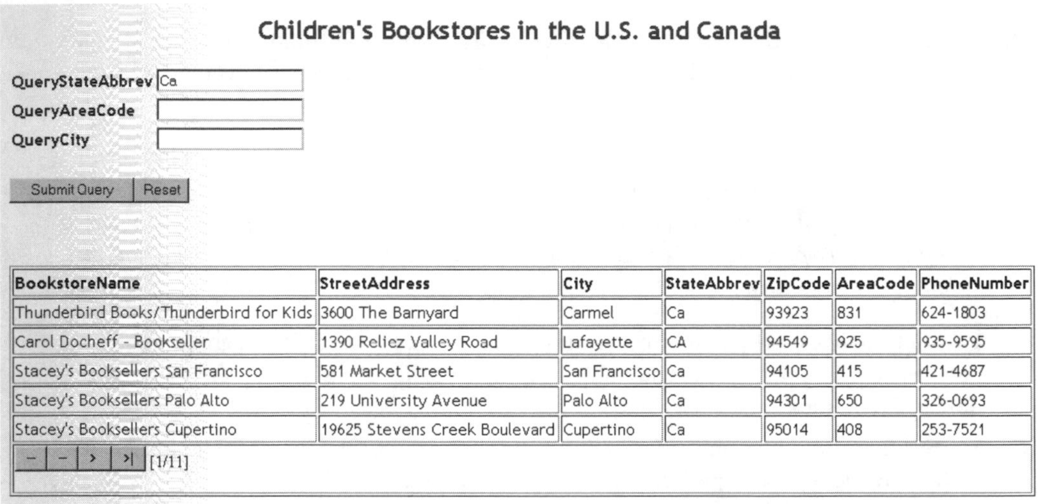

Children's Bookstores in the U.S. and Canada

QueryStateAbbrev [Ca]

QueryAreaCode [   ]

QueryCity [   ]

[Submit Query] [Reset]

BookstoreName	StreetAddress	City	StateAbbrev	ZipCode	AreaCode	PhoneNumber
Thunderbird Books/Thunderbird for Kids	3600 The Barnyard	Carmel	Ca	93923	831	624-1803
Carol Docheff - Bookseller	1390 Reliez Valley Road	Lafayette	CA	94549	925	935-9595
Stacey's Booksellers San Francisco	581 Market Street	San Francisco	Ca	94105	415	421-4687
Stacey's Booksellers Palo Alto	219 University Avenue	Palo Alto	Ca	94301	650	326-0693
Stacey's Booksellers Cupertino	19625 Stevens Creek Boulevard	Cupertino	Ca	95014	408	253-7521

[-] [-] [>] [>|] [1/11]

FIGURE 20-4   The database results are returned in a browser running on a web server.

NOTE   *If you take a look at the HTML version of the web page, you'll notice that unless you created a custom query, the automatically generated SQL query that retrieves data from the database actually retrieves* everything *(Select * from...), then filters out the columns you don't want. This method of retrieving records can seriously affect performance, especially if you have one or more nondisplayed fields that contain large amounts of data (such as a long description field). If you are noticing poor performance, this may be the reason. Unfortunately, the only way to fix this is to create a custom query that obtains just the needed data from the database.*

Advanced Techniques for Finding Database Records

As mentioned earlier, when FrontPage creates a search form, the fields in the form are simply text fields into which you must type the value you want to search for. If the values are fairly complicated, such as the names of bookstores, the probability is relatively high that the reader will type in a value that doesn't exist in the database. For example, one of the bookstores is called Woozles. But if you accidentally typed it in as Woozels, no records will be returned by a search—probably leaving the reader wondering what happened.

Ideally, what you'd like to do is pick a value from a list of valid values, presented in a drop-down list. To do that, though, you'll have to do more work. First, build a standard form that includes a Database Results component and a search form, as described earlier in this chapter. Make sure that you include (in the Criteria under the More Options button) criteria based on all the fields you are going to want to search on. In the next example, we have built a standard Database Results component with a search form that includes City (QueryCity), StateAbbrev (QueryStateAbbrev), and the Area Code (QueryAreaCode)—and cleaned up the field names.

Children's Bookstores in the U.S. and Canada

State	<%=Request("QuerySte
Area Code	<%=Request("QueryAre
City	<%=Request("QueryCit

Submit Query   Reset

Bookstore	Street Address	City	State	Zip Code	Area Code	Phone Number
This is the start of a Database Results region.						
<<BookstoreName>>	<<StreetAddress>>	<<City>>	<<StateAbbrev>>	<<ZipCode>>	<<AreaCode>>	<<PhoneNumber>>
This is the end of a Database Results region.						
|< < > >| [1/5]					

At this point, the form looks just like what we discussed previously.

> **NOTE**   *We are going to delete the search fields in the search form. Before doing so, make a record of what the search form field was called. For example, our search form field for the state was called QueryStateAbbrev. You are going to need this field name later.*

The next step is to select and delete the search fields in the search form. This causes the table cell containing the search field to shrink, but don't worry about that.

To replace each search field with a drop-down list, use the following steps for each search field (the example below will illustrate this for the StateAbbrev field, labeled State on the form):

1. Click in the table cell where you want to insert the drop-down list. Choose Insert | Database | Results to open the Database Results Wizard dialog box.

2. In step 1, choose the Use An Existing Database Connection option and select the same database connection you used to build the form originally. Then click Next to continue.

3. In step 2 of the Database Results Wizard, choose the Custom Query option and click the Edit button to open the Custom Query dialog box.

4. Type in the SQL query that returns a list of all the unique values in the database for the column you want to search on. The syntax is

```
SELECT Distinct(ColumnName) FROM DatabaseName
```

20

For example, if you wanted to search on the StateAbbrev column in the Bookstores table, you would type in the following SQL query:

```
SELECT Distinct(StateAbbrev) FROM Bookstores
```

5. Make sure you typed everything correctly (and selected a valid column name and database name) by clicking the Verify Query button. If the query verifies OK, proceed to the next step by clicking OK in the Custom Query dialog box and then clicking Next in the Database Results Wizard. Otherwise, correct the query.

6. Step 3 of the Database Results Wizard should display the single field you named in the custom query—click Next to continue.

7. In step 4 of the Database Results Wizard, click on the drop-down list at the top of the dialog box and select Drop-Down List–One Record Per Item. Both of the other two drop-down lists should display the name of the column you used in the custom query.

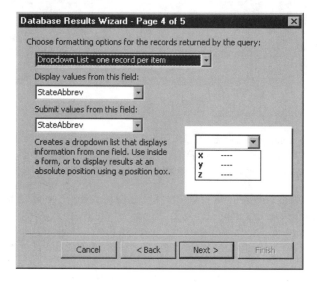

8. Click Next to advance to step 5, then click Finish to close the Database Results Wizard dialog box.

9. If necessary, rename the drop-down list form field that appears in the new Database Results area. This form field name *must* match the original name of the field you deleted just prior to starting these steps to insert the drop-down list. To rename the form field, right-click on it, choose Form Field Properties from the shortcut menu, and type the new name into the Name field. Then click OK.

Did you forget to record the name of the Search Form field before you deleted it? You can figure out what the name should be by reopening the Database Results Wizard for the table that returns the results. To do so, right-click on the start of the Database Results region in the table, and choose Database Results Properties from the shortcut menu. Click OK to get past the warning, and step through the Database Result Wizard till you reach step 3. Click the More Options button, and click the Criteria button. This displays the search criteria, and the field names you need are in the Value column. Once you know what the search form fields should be called, cancel out of all the dialog boxes.

If you now look at the search form, you can see that the Database Results component you just built is embedded in the search form. Repeat the above procedure for all drop-down lists you want in your search form.

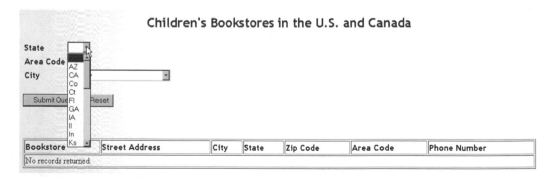

If your web site is server-based, preview it in a browser to see the result. Click on the search form field drop-down list to see a list of the distinct values in that column in the database (the result of the custom query you built).

When you make a selection from the drop-down list, the field returns the value you just selected, making it available to the search form. When you click the Submit Query button in the search form, the search is carried out in the database, returning the records that match your query. And since you are absolutely, positively guaranteed that the value you picked exists in the database, you won't get any search results that contain no records.

NOTE

Of course, if you use multiple search fields, and combine them with And clauses, you may still get empty search results. For example, you can pick QueryStateAbbrev of Ca, QueryCity of Seattle, and QueryAreaCode of 201. These are all valid values in the database, but because this combination *of records doesn't include any records (Seattle is not in California, and area code 201 is in New Jersey), the* combination *of the three criteria won't return any records.*

Chapter 21

Build a Database Web Site Using the Database Interface Wizard Template

How to…

■ Create a new web site with the Database Wizard

■ Create a new database or use an existing database with the Database Wizard

■ Use the Results page

■ Use the Submission page

■ Work with the Database Editor forms

■ Protect your database with a login

Although FrontPage makes it easier than it has ever been to send form results to a database (see Chapter 19) and display the contents of a database in a form (see Chapter 20), it is still quite a bit of work to set all this up—after all, it took us two entire chapters to understand how to add this functionality to a web site. The Database Interface Wizard is a web site template that automates much of the process of creating a database-driven web site. This powerful tool asks you a set of questions and then constructs forms for collecting new records, and viewing existing records. In addition, you can instruct the Database Interface Wizard template to create the forms (collectively called the "Database Editor") that enable you to update existing records, delete records, and view a single record from a list. You can even have the Database Interface Wizard template create a login screen to control who has access to your data.

Create a New Site with the Database Interface Wizard

To create a new site with the Database Interface Wizard, use the following steps:

1. Choose File | New to open the New Task Pane. Click More Web Site Templates in the Task Pane to open the Web Site Templates dialog box.

2. Fill in the location of the web site in the Specify The Location Of The New Web field. Make sure to specify a server-based web site if you want to be able to preview and test the database in a browser on your local machine.

3. Choose the Database Interface Wizard from the list of available templates and click OK.

> TIP
> *You can use the Database Interface Wizard template to implement a database within an existing web site. To do so, first create a web site as usual, and use the techniques discussed in Chapter 19 to create a connection to a database. In the Web Site Templates dialog box, check the Add To Current Web check box. This procedure enables the option to choose an existing database connection in the next step of the Database Interface Wizard.*

4. From the next panel of the Database Interface Wizard (see Figure 21-1), choose how you want to connect to the database. Your options are the same as those discussed in Chapter 20 (Specify the Data to Display*)*: Create a new Access database within your web, Use an Existing Database Connection, Connect To An External Database (Oracle or SQL), and Use A Sample Database Connection (Northwind).

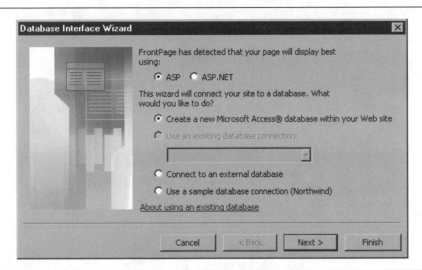

FIGURE 21-1   Choose your connection to a database from this version of the Database Interface Wizard dialog box. Since this is new web site, you can't use an existing Access database.

Exactly what happens next depends on the option you selected above. We'll cover the options related to Access databases in the next two sections.

Create a New Access Database Within Your Web Site

If you select the option to create a new Access database within your web site and click Next, the next panel of the Database Interface Wizard requests the name of the database connection.

Enter the name and click Next to proceed. The next panel of the wizard enables you to define the columns in the Results table of the database.

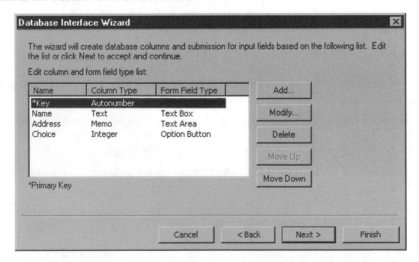

 *The table is always called "Results"—you do not get an opportunity to rename it.*

There are few default columns provided. Each column has a Name, Column Type, and Form Field Type (defined below).

To add a new column to the database table, click the Add button. This opens a new version of the Database Interface Wizard:

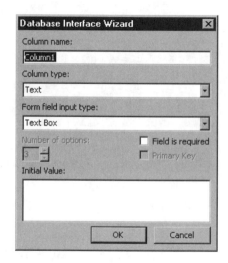

Here you can define the following items:

- **Column Name**   The name of the column in the table.
- **Column Type**   The Column Type defines what kind of data the database will expect in the column (text, integer, float, double, date, and so forth). Select the column type from the drop-down list.
- **Form Field Input Type**   The Form Field Type defines what kind of form field will be available for data input (text box, drop-down box, option button, or text area). Pick the form field input type from the drop-down list. If the column type doesn't allow input (such as the Autonumber type in Access), there are no options available in this drop-down list.
- **Number of options**   This field is only available if you picked a form field input type of option button or Drop-Down Box because FrontPage needs to know how many option buttons to place on the form or how many entries will be available in the drop-down box.
- **Field is Required**   Check the Field is Required check box if the field is not allowed to be left blank.

- **Initial Value**   If you want the field to be populated with a default value each time a new record is created, enter that value in the Initial Value field. The user can override this value if they wish. Make sure that the initial value matches the column type (integer, date, and so forth) or you'll get an error when you create a new record.

- **Primary Key**   If the column is the primary key (identifies the row uniquely), check the Primary Key check box. Since there can be only a single primary key in a table, the Primary Key check box is not available if any other column has already been identified as the primary key.

NOTE *To remove an existing primary key, click the column in the Database Interface Wizard dialog box and click the Modify button. In the resulting dialog box, clear the Primary Key check box.*

You can also modify any of the columns by selecting the column and clicking the Modify button. Or, if you don't need a column, you can select it and click Delete to remove it altogether.

Once you have finished defining the database table columns, click Next to proceed. FrontPage takes a moment to create the database and connect to it. When prompted, click Next to proceed.

The next panel in the Database Interface Wizard enables you to pick the table (only one is available: Results) and specify the folder where the forms will be created. You can specify a location by typing in a new folder path or clicking the Browse button to pick an existing folder.

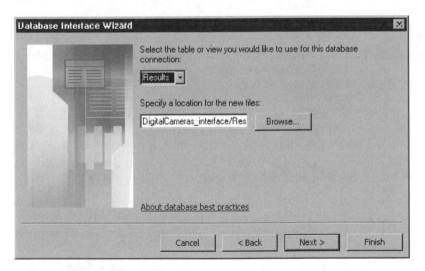

Click Next to proceed.

From here, the rest of the Database Interface Wizard proceeds as described in the "Specify the Forms to Build" section later in this chapter.

Use an Existing Database Connection

If you've chosen to add the results of the Database Interface Wizard to an existing web site, and that web site already has at least one existing database connection, you can choose the database connection to use from the Use An Existing Database Connection drop-down list (visible in Figure 21-1). Click Next to continue.

NOTE *If you chose Use A Sample Database Connection (Northwind), the steps you follow are identical to those outlined in this section. FrontPage simply adds the Northwind database to the current web site before moving on to the steps below.*

The next panel of the Database Interface Wizard enables you to pick which table or view in the database you want to use as your data source, as well as the folder where you want the Database Interface Wizard forms to be built.

Select the table or view from the drop-down list in the dialog box and click Next to continue. The next panel displays a list of columns, their column type, and the form field type, as described in the previous section. However, because you are using an existing database, you cannot add or delete columns, and selecting a column and clicking Modify enables you to change only the Form Field Input Type—everything else is grayed out and unavailable.

Once you have made any adjustments to the Form Field Input Type (and returned to the main Database Interface Wizard dialog box), click Next to continue. From here on, follow the procedure discussed in the following "Specify the Forms to Build" section.

Specify the Forms to Build

The next panel of the Database Interface Wizard (see Figure 21-2) enables you to pick which forms you want the wizard to build automatically. You can check one, two, or all three of the check boxes. Here is what they mean:

- **Results Page** Provides a form with a Database Results region (as detailed in Chapter 20). The form presents the contents of the database and includes a hyperlink to the Submission form (if you create a Submission form). The default layout of this form is relatively ugly and groups records in sets of five. However, you can use the techniques detailed in Chapter 20 to customize the Database Results region on the form.

- **Submission Form** Provides a form that routes the submitted contents into the database, as described in Chapter 19. You can customize this form (and will probably want to, at least to make the field labels more friendly). This form includes a hyperlink to the Results page, if you created a Results page.

- **Database Editor** Provides a set of forms you can use to update existing records, add new records, view individual records, and even delete records from the database. If you wish, you can even protect the Database Editor screens with a login ID and password.

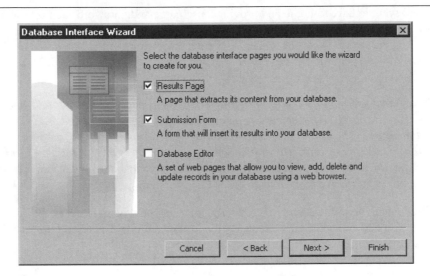

Database Interface Wizard

FIGURE 21-2   Select the forms you want the wizard to build from this dialog box.

If you chose to include the Database Editor, the next panel in the Database Interface Wizard offers you the option of setting up a username and password to protect your Database Editor.

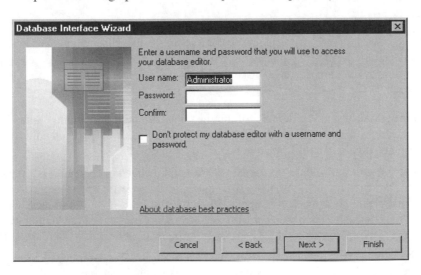

If you *don't* want to have to log in and provide a username and password each time you (or anyone else) use the Database Editor screens, check the Don't Protect My Database Editor With A Username And Password check box. Otherwise, enter a username in the Username field, and type the password twice: once in the Password field and once in the Confirm field. Then click Next to continue.

NOTE *If you set up username and password protection as described in the previous paragraph, FrontPage displays a login screen each time someone tries to access one of the Database Editor screens. The user will need to know both the username and password in order to gain access to the screens. This protection does not apply to the Submission form—so don't provide a Submission form if you don't want anyone entering new records without having to supply a username and password.*

In the final panel, the Database Interface Wizard informs you where the forms you requested will be placed. You had an opportunity to specify this while using the Database Interface Wizard. Click Finish to create the forms.

Understand the Database Interface Wizard Results

Once you turn the wizard loose, FrontPage gets busy and creates the forms you requested. This section assumes you instructed FrontPage to create them all, and discusses each one in turn. A certain amount of customization is also a good idea, and this section describes how to do that as well.

The Results Page

The Results page (see Figure 21-3) displays the contents of the database in a table. The data is displayed in a Database Results component, as described in Chapter 20.

You can customize the Results page to make it easier to view. Some of the things you'll probably want to change are

- **Column Headings** The default column headings are just the column names in the database table. These tend to be cryptic and difficult to read. Select each column heading and replace it with more informative text.

- **Adjust the number of listed records** By default, the Database region lists the records in groups of five. For any reasonably sized database, this doesn't provide enough records. To adjust the number of records, right-click in the Database Results and pick Database Results Properties to open the Database Results Wizard, described in Chapter 20. Step through the wizard to step 5, where you can set the number of records in a group or suppress grouping altogether.

- **Add a search form** The Results form (and its associated Database Results component) does not include a search form to locate records that meet a certain criteria. This can make it absurdly difficult to find what you are looking for. To fix this situation, right-click in the Database Results and pick Database Results Properties to open the Database Results Wizard. Step through the wizard until you reach step 3, and click the More Options

Results Page   Results Page | Submission Form | Database Editor

Key	CameraModelName	ManufacturerName	MegaPixelCount	BuiltInFlash	MemoryCardType
This is the start of a Database Results region.					
<<Key>>	<<CameraModelName>>	<<ManufacturerName>>	<<MegaPixelCount>>	<<BuiltInFlash>>	<<MemoryCardType>>
This is the end of a Database Results region.					

|< < > >| [1/5]

FIGURE 21-3   FrontPage uses a Database Results component to display the contents of a database table.

button to open the More Options dialog box. Click the Criteria button and establish the criteria for finding records, as described in Chapter 20. Don't forget to check the Add Search Form check box (it is actually checked by default).

■ **Sort the results**   Unless you really want to see the contents of the database in whatever order they were entered, you'll need to establish a sort order. Once again, right-click in the Database Results and pick Database Results Properties to open the Database Results Wizard. Step through the wizard until you reach step 3, and click the More Options button to open the More Options dialog box. Click the Ordering button and establish the sort order you want, as described in Chapter 20.

The Submission Form

The Submission form enables you to do one thing: enter new records into the database. It is simply a form that sends its results to a database, as described in Chapter 19.

Submission Form   Results Page | Submission Form | Database Editor

CameraModelName

ManufacturerName

MegaPixelCount
0.0

BuiltInFlash
☑ BuiltInFlash

MemoryCardType
Compact Flash Type 1

OK   Reset

Once again, you are probably going to want to customize the form in the following ways:

- **Field names** The default field names are just the column names in the database table. These tend to be cryptic and difficult to read. Select each field name and replace it with more informative text.

- **Option buttons** If you are using option buttons, the labels for the buttons are something like "Option 1", "Option 2", and so on. The only exception to this is if you choose a Boolean data type for the column—then the labels are "True" and "False". Select each option button label and change it to make it more descriptive of what values are being placed in the database. The default value inserted into the database when an option button is selected is also "Option 1", "Option 2", and so forth, except for Boolean, in which case the values are 0 (false) and 1 (true). To set your own values, you'll need to right-click on each option button field, choose Form Field Properties from the shortcut menu, and change the value in the Value field.

- **Drop-down boxes** If you are using drop-down boxes, the Database Interface Wizard uses "Option 0", "Option 1", and so on as the values in the list (and also as the values to place in the database). The only exception to this is if you chose a Boolean data type for the column—then the values are "True" and "False". To specify your own values, right-click on the drop-down box, choose Form Field Properties from the shortcut menu, and change the entry. To change the entry, select it in the Drop-Down Box Properties dialog box, click Modify, and change the values in the Choice field and the Specify Value field.

CAUTION *If you are in the habit of using spaces when you name columns in your database, you'll have to stop using spaces, and remove any spaces in existing column names (and table names, too). This is because the Database Interface Wizard writes a set of custom scripts for updating the database, and these scripts won't work if the table name, column name, or form field name (group name for an option button) contain a space. The default that the Database Interface Wizard uses for group names or field names is the column name—which includes any spaces. FrontPage does not warn you of the errors—the first time you'll find out about them is when you try to use the forms in a browser.*

The Home Page

If you choose to create a new web site using the Database Interface Wizard, it provides a simple Home page (Default.htm) with links to the Results page, Submission form, and the Database Editor.

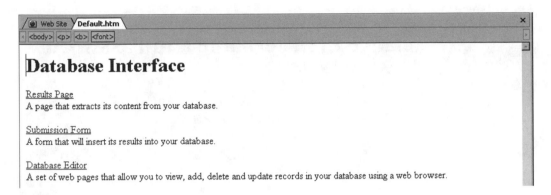

NOTE *The Database Interface Wizard does not create the home page (with the three hyperlinks) if you add the Database Interface Wizard forms to an existing web site, so you'll have to build this page yourself.*

The Database Editor

If you decided to include the Database Editor forms, the Database Interface Wizard creates a whole series of forms for you, including the Log In form (provided you asked for one), the Database Editor form, the new record (Submission) form, and an edit form for changing existing records.

The Login Form

The Database Editor Login form provides a place for someone to enter a username and password.

Once they click the Login button, FrontPage checks them against the values you specified when you built the form. If they match, the user is allowed access to the database editor. If not, the user is given another opportunity to enter the correct values.

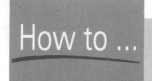 **Change the Username and Password**

If you want to change the username and password assigned to the database editor, it is pretty easy. Double-click on the file login.asa in the Folder List to open the file.

```
1 <%
2 ' Username and password for the digitalcameras.Results Database Editor
3 ' are set here:
4
5 Username="dplotkin"
6 Password="Marisa"
7 %>
8
9
```

Change the entries for username and password in the login.asa file and save the results (File | Save).

When setting up your web site, you don't need to provide a link to the login screen (login.asp). Instead, you can provide a link directly to the Database Editor form (database_editor.asp), and FrontPage will display the login screen automatically.

The Database Editor Form

The Database Editor form (see Figure 21-4) is the heart of Database Editor. From this form, you can get to any of the other Database Editor forms (except the Login form). Thus, the Database Editor form is the form that your application should provide a link to in order to edit the database contents.

Previewing the Database Editor form in a browser (see Figure 21-5) clearly shows how the form functions.

The Database Editor form is actually a frameset consisting of a top frame and a bottom frame. The top frame displays the list.asp page, which itself contains a Database Results component. This component is used to display a list of database records. As described in Chapter 19, you can customize the component if you wish. The bottom frame displays the detail.asp page, which also contains a Database Results component. This component displays all the fields in a single record.

Here is what you can do with the Database Editor form:

■ **View a single record**   In the top frame, scroll through the listed records (using the provided buttons). When you find a record you want to view in the bottom frame, click on the hyperlink in the first column of the list (the primary key of the record). This displays the detail for the record in the bottom frame.

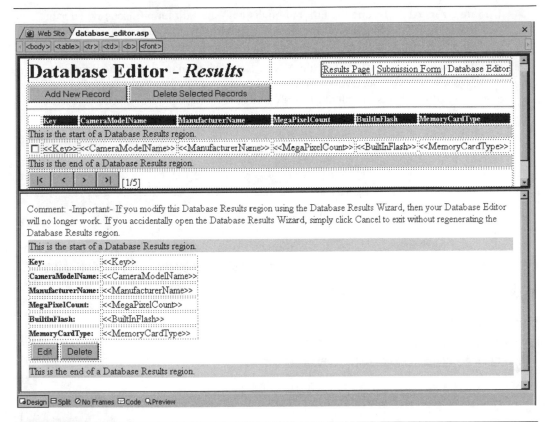

FIGURE 21-4   Link to the Database Editor form to allow readers to modify the database contents.

TIP   *View the properties of the hyperlink (right-click on the hyperlink and choose Hyperlink Properties from the shortcut menu). You'll discover that the hyperlink is accessing the database to recover the record where the primary key matches the value of the selected record in the list in the top frame. In order for this to work, you* must *structure your database records to use a single-column primary key.*

■ **Delete selected records**   To delete one or more records, check the check box alongside the records you want to delete. Then click the Delete Selected Records button. After confirming, the records are removed from the database. You can only select visible records. That is, if you check off a record, use the Forward button to scroll to the next set of records, then scroll back, you'll find that the original record is no longer checked.

■ **Delete a single record**   Once you are viewing a single record in the bottom frame, you can click the Delete button to remove that record. After confirming, the single record is removed from the database.

■ **Update a record** Clicking the Edit button displays the Edit form (discussed later in this chapter) with the data from the selected record displayed. You can change any of the data in a record and click OK to update the database record.

■ **Create a new record** Click the Add A New Record button to display the Submission form, from which you can create a new record, and click OK to add the record to the database. Although this form looks exactly like the Submission form discussed earlier, it is *not* the same web page, so if you have added a Submission form *and* the Database Editor form set, you'll have to customize both versions of the Submission form. Thus, if you are going to have the Database Interface Wizard create the Database Editor form set, you may wish to forgo creating the Submission form.

Click here to select this record for deletion | Click here to view the detail of the selected record in the bottom frame | Click here to delete any records you have checked off | Click here to open the Submission form | Top frame

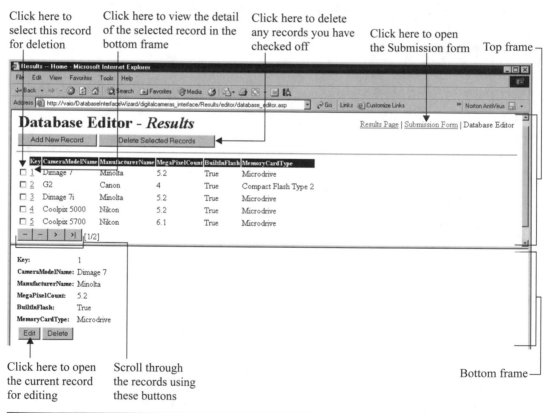

Click here to open the current record for editing | Scroll through the records using these buttons | Bottom frame

FIGURE 21-5 Need to modify the contents of a database from a browser? No problem...

The Edit Form

You can update a database record using the Edit form (edit.asp).

When you click the Edit button in the Database Editor form, the Edit form opens, displaying the selected record in the bottom frame. All the fields are present *except* the primary key; thus you can't use this form to add a new record (you use the Submission form for that). What makes the Edit form unique is that it displays the contents of the record in the form, ready for you to edit. When you click OK, the updated contents are written back to the database.

As you should recall, you had the option to represent fields from the database as text boxes, text areas, drop-down boxes, or option buttons. As mentioned earlier, if you choose to use drop-down boxes or option buttons, you have a fair amount of customization to do in order to set up the correct values to be written to the database and add meaningful labels. There is another, even more significant disadvantage to using drop-down boxes and option buttons: When a record is retrieved from the database, any text box or text area fields display the contents of that column in the database. However, drop-down boxes and option buttons *do not*. A drop-down box or option button always shows the default value. You can change the value and click OK to save the result. *But if you don't reset the value in a drop-down box or an option button to the correct value for that record, the default value is what gets written back to the database.* This is a serious problem, and one that should make you think hard before using drop-down boxes or option buttons in an Edit form (it's not a problem in a new record, where you have to set all the values anyway).

For example, take a look at the screen in Figure 21-6.

Note how the first record in the top frame shows that this camera uses a Microdrive for the MemoryCardType. However, the Edit record (visible in the bottom frame) shows a value of Compact Flash Type 1 in the MemoryCardType drop-down box because that is the first item in the list. If you click OK at this point, the record will be written back to the database as Compact Flash Type 1.

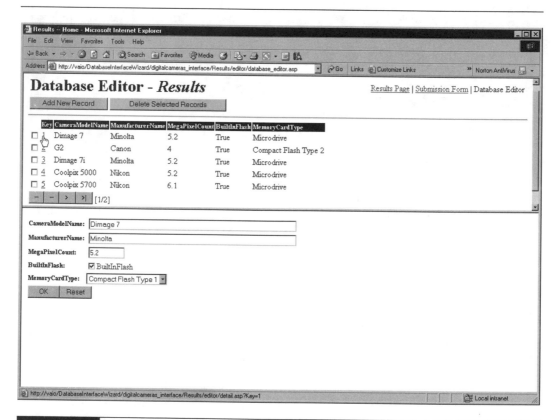

FIGURE 21-6   The detail record (top) and the editable record (bottom) don't match!

Index

X

INTERNATIONAL CONTACT INFORMATION

AUSTRALIA
McGraw-Hill Book Company
Australia Pty. Ltd.
TEL +61-2-9900-1800
FAX +61-2-9878-8881
http://www.mcgraw-hill.com.au
books-it_sydney@mcgraw-hill.com

CANADA
McGraw-Hill Ryerson Ltd.
TEL +905-430-5000
FAX +905-430-5020
http://www.mcgraw-hill.ca

**GREECE, MIDDLE EAST, & AFRICA
(Excluding South Africa)**
McGraw-Hill Hellas
TEL +30-210-6560-990
TEL +30-210-6560-993
TEL +30-210-6560-994
FAX +30-210-6545-525

MEXICO (Also serving Latin America)
McGraw-Hill Interamericana Editores
S.A. de C.V.
TEL +525-1500-5108
FAX +525-117-1589
http://www.mcgraw-hill.com.mx
carlos_ruiz@mcgraw-hill.com

SINGAPORE (Serving Asia)
McGraw-Hill Book Company
TEL +65-6863-1580
FAX +65-6862-3354
http://www.mcgraw-hill.com.sg
mghasia@mcgraw-hill.com

SOUTH AFRICA
McGraw-Hill South Africa
TEL +27-11-622-7512
FAX +27-11-622-9045
robyn_swanepoel@mcgraw-hill.com

SPAIN
McGraw-Hill/
Interamericana de España, S.A.U.
TEL +34-91-180-3000
FAX +34-91-372-8513
http://www.mcgraw-hill.es
professional@mcgraw-hill.es

**UNITED KINGDOM, NORTHERN,
EASTERN, & CENTRAL EUROPE**
McGraw-Hill Education Europe
TEL +44-1-628-502500
FAX +44-1-628-770224
http://www.mcgraw-hill.co.uk
emea_queries@mcgraw-hill.com

ALL OTHER INQUIRIES Contact:
McGraw-Hill/Osborne
TEL +1-510-420-7700
FAX +1-510-420-7703
http://www.osborne.com
omg_international@mcgraw-hill.com

Microsoft
Office 2003
Answers for Everyone

Make the most of the entire Office system with help from these other books from Osborne